# Created Equal

# Created Equal

*How the Bible Broke with Ancient*
*Political Thought*

JOSHUA A. BERMAN

OXFORD
UNIVERSITY PRESS

2008

# OXFORD
UNIVERSITY PRESS

Oxford University Press, Inc., publishes works that further
Oxford University's objective of excellence
in research, scholarship, and education.

Oxford   New York
Auckland   Cape Town   Dar es Salaam   Hong Kong   Karachi
Kuala Lumpur   Madrid   Melbourne   Mexico City   Nairobi
New Delhi   Shanghai   Taipei   Toronto

With offices in
Argentina   Austria   Brazil   Chile   Czech Republic   France   Greece
Guatemala   Hungary   Italy   Japan   Poland   Portugal   Singapore
South Korea   Switzerland   Thailand   Turkey   Ukraine   Vietnam

Copyright © 2008 by Oxford University Press, Inc.

Published by Oxford University Press, Inc.
198 Madison Avenue, New York, New York 10016

www.oup.com

Berman, Joshua.
Created equal : how the Bible broke with ancient political thought / Joshua A. Berman.
    p.   cm.
Includes bibliographical references and index.
ISBN 978-0-19-537470-4
    1. Equality—Biblical teaching.   2. Bible. O.T. Pentateuch—Criticism, interpretation,
etc.   3. Jews—Politics and government—To 70 A.D.   4. Jews—Social conditions.   I. Title.
BS1199.E72B47 2008
221.8'32—dc22
2008008000

9 8 7 6 5 4 3 2 1

Printed in the United States of America
on acid-free paper

*To*
*Edward L. Greenstein*
mentor, friend
עשה לך רב
וקנה לך חבר

# Acknowledgments

Throughout the course of this work, I have found myself overwhelmed by feelings of gratitude on a regular—in fact, weekly—basis. This happens on Saturday evenings, at the conclusion of the Sabbath, as I recite the *havdalah* service, surrounded by family. These thoughts well up within me as I pronounce the blessing for the creation of fire, over the soft glow of a large candle of many wicks. The origins of this rite are found in a rabbinic parallel to the myth of Prometheus and the origins of fire. The Talmud (*b. Pesaḥim* 54b) says that there were two things God withheld and did not create during the six days of Creation: fire and the mule. At the conclusion of the Sabbath, God brought Adam two stones of flint, endowed him with understanding, and enabled him to create fire. And He brought him a horse and a donkey, and endowed him with the wisdom to crossbreed them, and create a mule. Put differently, at the conclusion of the Sabbath of Creation, human creativity itself was brought into the world, and Adam became empowered as a partner in the act of creation, bringing into the world that which God had not created in the previous six days.

Reciting the blessing over the fire that commemorates Adam's first creative act overwhelms me with gratitude, as I look forward to a week of my own creative work. Just as Adam created out of that which he had been given, so, too, I feel keenly aware of the fact that my own creative work is but a function of what I have been given, the exposure that I have had to those who have taught me, to great sources of wisdom, both rabbinic and academic, and particularly to the continuous erudition of colleagues and scholars near and far. It is a pleasure at the conclusion of this work to publicly share those debts of thanks.

As I explain in the introduction, this book draws connections between subjects and texts in biblical studies that are normally studied in isolation. The inspiration to explore these connections came from a work titled *Radical Then Radical Now* by the British chief rabbi Sir Jonathan Sacks. He has been very generous with his time in my visits to his residence in London over the years, and I am greatly indebted to him for his mentorship.

This study was undertaken while I was an associate fellow at the Shalem Center in Jerusalem, during the 2004–5 and 2005–6 academic years. The generous material support the Center offered was matched by the stimulation I received while there from many scholars in many disciplines. Often I would attend a lecture or a seminar, quite convinced that the subject matter was interesting in its own right but unrelated to my work as a biblicist, only to discover that the more one understands about the human condition—particularly through the social sciences—the more one is equipped to understand the Bible. My thanks to Yoram Hazony and Dan Polisar for creating the Center and for affording me the opportunity to be a part of its work, and for their careful critiques of my writing. My thanks also to Meirav Jones and the editorial board of *Hebraic Political Studies*, published by the Center, for their permission to reproduce in chapter 2 here material that originally appeared as Joshua Berman, "Constitution, Class and the Book of Deuteronomy," *Hebraic Political Studies* 1:5 (2006): 523–48.

Many colleagues at Bar-Ilan University, where I lecture in Bible, were gracious with their time and talents. These include Amnon Altman, Aaron Demsky, Adam Ferziger, Rimon Kasher, and Lisa Maurice. Generous material support for this volume was received from the Dr. Naim Dangoor Interdisciplinary Program of Universal Monotheism at Bar-Ilan University.

One of the lessons I learned while writing this book is to seek out the elder statesmen of the profession. Jerusalem is blessed with a number of biblicists in this category, and I have been the fortunate recipient of generous amounts of time and a lifetime of insight from Baruch Levine and from Shalom Paul. May they both be blessed with many more years of inspired and productive work.

Many scholars from around the globe have been good enough to critique my writing in spite of heavy workloads: Benjamin Balint, Daniel Doneson, Tamara Cohn-Eskenazi, Norman Gottwald, Steven Grosby, David Hazony, Bernard Levinson, Marshal Huebner, Win Robins, Asaf Sagiv, and Joshua Weinstein.

As I discuss in the introduction, in many ways this book goes against some of the accepted wisdoms of the field of biblical studies. Courage to pursue the unbeaten path was warmly provided by Yossi Klein Halevi and John Gager. Material support in this vein was graciously offered by Lawrence Collamore, a true friend.

This book is dedicated to Professor Edward L. Greenstein. Ed was my doctoral thesis advisor, but he has continued to be a mentor in my academic activity ever since, and is now also a colleague in the Bible Department of Bar-Ilan University. Ed took my love for the biblical text and showed me how to garner additional insight into Scripture by seeing it in the context of the ancient Near East. More important, he has shown me what it means to be dedicated to one's students, and I can only pray that I shall be there for my students as he has been there for me.

In the period from submission to publication I have had the privilege to work with Cynthia Read, Meechal Hoffman, and Brian Desmond. To them and the entire team at Oxford University Press, I express my thanks for their patience and guidance.

As a youngster, I used to receive a "once-over" from my father, George Berman, as we departed for the walk to synagogue on Saturday mornings. This usually resulted in a slight yanking of my tie to a more central position, or pulling up my suit jacket so that it would rest more squarely on my shoulders. The point was that I should look as presentable as I could before I headed out the door. Dad has continued this tradition even in my adulthood by scrupulously checking over the manuscript before final submission, as it were, before *it* headed out the door.

Filled with gratitude to all those who have assisted me in the work of my creativity, I conclude with the prayer of thanks that the talmudic sage R. Nehuniah b. HaKanah used to recite on the conclusion of his study: "I thank thee, Almighty, that you have determined that my lot should be with those who dwell in the house of study."

Joshua A. Berman
Bet Shemesh, Israel

# Contents

# List of Abbreviations

AB      Anchor Bible

*ABD*    *Anchor Bible Dictionary*. Ed. D. N. Freedman. 6 vols. New York: Doubleday, 1992.

*ANET*   *Ancient Near Eastern Texts Relating to the Old Testament*. Ed. James B. Pritchard. 1950. Princeton: Princeton University Press, 1969.

ASOR    American Schools of Social Research

*CANE*   *Civilizations of the Ancient Near East*. Ed. Jack M. Sasson et al. 4 vols. Peabody: Hendrickson, 1995.

*CBQ*    *Catholic Biblical Quarterly*

*COS*    *The Context of Scripture*. Edited by W. W. Hallo. 3 vols. Leiden: Brill, 1997–.

*CTH*    Emmanuel Laroche. *Catalogue des textes Hittites*. Paris: Klincksieck, 1971.

FRLANT  Forschungen zur Religion und Literatur des Alten und Neuen Testaments

*HAR*    *Hebrew Annual Review*

*HUCA*   *Hebrew Union College Annual*

*JBL*    *Journal of Biblical Literature*

*JNES*   *Journal of Near Eastern Studies*

*JSOT*   *Journal for the Study of the Old Testament*

JSOTSup  *Journal for the Study of the Old Testament*: Supplement Series

| | |
|---|---|
| *NIDOTTE* | *New International Dictionary of Old Testament Theology and Exegesis.* Edited by Willem A. VanGemeren. 5 vols. Grand Rapids: Zondervan, 1997. |
| *RA* | *Revue d'assyriologie et d'archéologie orientale* |
| *VT* | *Vetus Testamentum* |
| VTS | *Vetus Testamentum* Supplements |
| *ZAW* | *Zeitschrift für die alttestamentliche Wissenschaft* |

# Created Equal

# Introduction

This book proposes to read the Bible in a novel way—as a document of political and social theory.

Machiavelli, Hobbes, Locke, and the American founding fathers all sought within the Bible inspiration for their various political theories, mining it to substantiate political teachings.[1] Liberation theology is one movement that continues to invoke the Bible in the service of a political platform to this day. My purpose in this book, however, is not to harness the biblical text to any contemporary political agenda. Rather, I wish to go back to the beginning and to seek out political teachings in the Bible in the context of its own world—the social and political world of the ancient Near East.

While ancient Greece is often considered the cradle of modern political thought, the patrimony of modern political thought rests no less squarely in the texts of the Bible, particularly the Pentateuch. In seeking out its political teachings—even if no longer fully applicable today—we do so as one who returns and searches for the most cherished memories in the home of one's birth. In looking today for the landmarks by which we find our own bearings, there is purpose and meaning in seeking to uncover the lost systems of coordinates by which past thinkers navigated. Indeed, our ancestors stand at a great distance from us. Yet we may think of the history of ideas, not as a straight line across all of time, but as a winding procession. It is likely that our circumstances may bring us into proximity with similar situations encountered in an earlier age. Examining this idea may open us up to new possible answers to the central questions of today, and at least lead us to question what is permanent and what is mutable in the fundamentals of our social and political thought. As Shakespeare noted, "What is past is prologue."[2]

This book traces the varied way a wide body of biblical texts, primarily in the Pentateuch, sought to appropriate existing concepts, laws, and institutions that were de rigueur within the social and political landscape of the ancient Near East in an effort to articulate the fundamentals of a new and more egalitarian order. The new order articulated in these texts stands in contrast to a primary socioeconomic structure prevalent at many junctures throughout the history of the ancient Near East: the divide between the *dominant tribute-imposing class* and *the dominated tribute-bearing class*.[3] For my purposes, a *class* is a group that forms around the extraction, production, transformation, distribution exchange, and consumption of economic surplus.[4] These two groups, the exploiters and the exploited, are opposite sides of the same coin. The dominant tribute-imposing class consists, in short, of the political elite. The term is used broadly and could refer to native or foreign rulers alike. This class includes not only the nobility but all who benefited by association with it: administrators, military and religious retainers, merchants, and landowners who directly or indirectly benefited from state power. What all of these have in common is that they all participated in the extraction of produce, or surplus, from the dominated tribute-bearing class: agrarian and pastoral producers, slaves, unskilled workers, all who do not draw surplus from other workers but whose station in the culture dictates that their own surplus is to be taken by members of the elite class and its subsections. Their production was drawn as surplus in the form of taxation, slave labor, rent, or debt service.[5] This model was true for major as well as lesser states of the ancient Near East, with variations on the general form.

Identifying clear and explicit class distinctions in the ancient Near East is tricky. The Code of Hammurabi and the Laws of Eshnunna dating from the early second millennium B.C.E. are structured around a tripartite division of classes, but many other ancient Near Eastern documents fail to indicate such a clear and explicit division of society according to class.[6] Even defining the borderline between slave and nonslave labor has been daunting, as we have evidence of individuals going in and out of slavery, and of individuals who themselves are labeled "slaves" and at the same time emerge as the controllers of the labor of others.[7] But the dichotomy between those who produced tribute and those who consumed it is an essentially valid one.

This is not to say that ancient Near Eastern states were unadulterated "oriental despotisms." The total domination of a society through the concentration of statist power was a momentary achievement.[8] More often, the dominion took the form of a tacit social contract between the exploiter and the exploited. In return for demanding taxation and the conscription of labor, states and their rulers had to make good on their claims to protect their subjects' general welfare by maintaining irrigation systems, adjudicating legal disputes, putting down insurrection, and, of course, protecting the populace from military invasion.[9]

While this social dichotomy between those who extracted and benefited from tribute and those who produced and bore the burden of tribute certainly characterized ancient megastates, the dichotomy could also be true of polities of more modest size. This is important to note, because the advent of Israel in Canaan comes during a period when megastates were in decline. From the middle of the second millennium B.C.E., the megaempires of the ancient Near East underwent a breakdown, and smaller states arose, such as Israel, Edom, and Moab.[10] In periods where the concentration of power in large states waned, tighter systems of city-state control emerged. This was so, for example, in Canaan during the latter part of the second millennium B.C.E. By means of land grants in return for service, local potentates would build up economic, social, and political dependencies.[11] Even in the absence of the large state apparatus, base communities participated in the schematized system of tributary economies and political hierarchies.[12]

In the books of the Pentateuch we find a blueprint for a social and religious order that is more egalitarian in nature, eschewing the social stratification dividing the dominant tribute-imposing class and the dominated tribute-bearing class. To sharpen the claim, a definition of terms is in order. By *social stratification* I mean the permanent and institutionalized power given to particular classes to control the economic, military, and political resources of society.[13] I take an *egalitarian* society to be one in which the hierarchy of permanent and institutionalized stratification is dissipated.

To concretize these definitions, we may locate them in terms of our own western tradition. One of the defining features of the European revolutions of the eighteenth and nineteenth centuries was the rejection of the privileges of rank and of the political power traditionally granted the nobility, resulting in the delegitimation of entrenched caste, feudal, and slave systems. It is important to stress that even in the wake of these revolutions, inequality could and did persist. But inequality was no longer the function of hereditary rules of closure. Rather it was deemed the justifiable outcome of competition among persons of differing abilities.[14]

Greece and Rome knew their respective reformers. Yet neither in the writings of Solon, the political reformer of Athens in the sixth century B.C.E., nor in those of Lycurgus, the legendary seventh-century lawgiver of Sparta, nor in the two-hundred-year political struggle between plebeians and patricians known as the Conflict of the Orders of Rome do we find a struggle to do away with class distinctions. Nor do we find this articulated as a desideratum by any of the ancient authors in their ideal systems, including those of Aristotle, Plato, and Polybius.[15] "From the hour of their birth," Aristotle wrote, "some are marked out for subjection, others for rule."[16] It was assumed that some would be rich and that many, many more would be poor. Not simply because that's the way things were but because that was the way things were actually supposed to be. To be sure, Plato and Aristotle called for justice; lower classes should not be wantonly persecuted. But in the Greek context, justice required, as Aristotle opined, that equals be treated as equals and unequals as unequals.[17] The Greeks and Romans possessed an overwhelming belief in the harmony of various classes (Greek *homonoia*, Latin *concordia*). For the medieval mindset, too, an ordered society was one in which each socioeconomic class performed its tasks for the common good.[18] The distinctions of class were deemed to be an essential factor of social function. For political theorists from classical times through the Italian Renaissance, it was assumed that independence could not be achieved by those who did not already possess it.[19]

The entrenchment of social stratification was likewise endemic to the empires and lands of the ancient Near East. Indeed, Egyptian and Mesopotamian rulers (among others) claimed to perform acts of benevolence for the downtrodden, and their cultures produced exhortatory texts calling on individuals to do the same, especially in Egypt.[20] Yet, as in Greece, nowhere in the ancient Near East is there articulated the ideal of a society without class divisions founded on the control of economic, military, and political power.

To be sure, the Pentateuch manifestly speaks of multiple classes of individuals within the Israelite polity, an order that may not be termed egalitarian in the full sense of the word. The Pentateuch speaks of those with entitlements and privileges, such as the king, priests, and Levites. But the control of economic and political resources enjoyed by these groups is greatly attenuated in contrast to the surrounding cultures of the ancient Near East. At the bottom of the social ladder, the Pentateuch codifies the laws of servitude. Here, too, the Pentateuch reworked existing norms concerning debt-servitude in an effort to blunt the distinction between the servant and the freeman. In primary fashion, however, I will demonstrate that among the free members of the Israelite polity who were neither priests nor Levites, the Pentateuch eschews the divide between a class of tribute imposers, which controls economic and political power, and an even larger class of tribute bearers. In its place, the Pentateuch articulates a new social, political, and religious order, the first to be founded on egalitarian ideals and the notion of a society whose core is a single, uniformly empowered, homogeneous class.

While I take the books of the Pentateuch to be among the clearest statements of this new order, I invoke other scriptural texts as well that, to my mind, also express this voice, or tradition. Of course, in highlighting the texts that do so, I shall also have occasion to indicate the texts that do not share in this voice. There will be no attempt here to claim a monolithic view—"*the* biblical view"—of this or of that. The Bible speaks with many voices across many centuries. My objective here is to tune in to a certain egalitarian voice that reverberates across the tradition, particularly within the books of the Pentateuch.

Like any scholarly work, this one is predicated on a series of methodological assumptions, and I would like to make mine clear at the outset. The first is that this is a book that seeks to identify a strand of social and political thought within what is commonly termed *biblical religion* and not *Israelite religion*. By *Israelite religion*, I mean the actual practice of religion in Iron Age Israel (from the eleventh to sixth centuries B.C.E.), its varieties, and its evolution over time.[21] Much scholarship has attempted to retrace the evolution of the religion of ancient Israel. While Julius Wellhausen, for example, is known for his division of the Pentateuch into its composite sources, his primary interest in his magnum opus *Prolegomena to the Religion of Israel* was not the history of the text of the Pentateuch but a history of Israelite religion. Such an endeavor often seeks to get at the reality of religious life in Israel beyond or behind what the written text says. Such an endeavor is a legitimate line of inquiry, but it is not mine. I take it as a given at the outset that many of the texts I will be analyzing do not accurately reflect the social, religious, and political reality lived by the majority of ancient Israelites at any juncture of their history. These texts, in practice, may reflect the customs, beliefs, and norms of mere individuals, schools, or specific segments of the society. Judging from the censures of the prophets, it is doubtful that Israel often lived up to the calling the sacred texts outlined for it. By *biblical religion* I mean the vision—idealized, at times—of the concepts and institutional blueprint for Israelite society that one may derive from a reading of the texts.[22]

The ideas and institutions I will be highlighting and assessing were not created by the Bible ex nihilo. The Bible assumes as its sine qua non the social, political, and religious milieu of the ancient Near East. To appreciate ideologies and institutions contained in the Bible, however, it is insufficient merely to note that they are predicated on preexisting parallel phenomena elsewhere. Rather, attention must also be paid to the way these parallel phenomena contrast. One must investigate the phenomena against the wider literary and cultural environment, in an effort to gauge the degree to which the issue at hand within the Bible reflects that environment or, rather, stands in distinction and displays elements of innovation.[23]

The issue of the dating of the biblical texts, particularly the materials found in the Pentateuch, is perhaps the most vexing of all issues in biblical scholarship. I wish, therefore, to clarify my operating assumptions in this work in advance. The source-critical method of biblical analysis has a long history and is still dominant in many scholarly circles. This approach involves a mining of the received biblical text in an effort to discover its prehistory: its composite parts, or documents; the historical and social setting of their composition; the textual evolution of various passages, and the attendant explanations why they evolved as they did. This approach implies a primary interest in discovering the social and religious history of the people of Israel. The text is viewed as merely a means for uncovering that social and religious history by identifying and laying bare individual textual stages as the witnesses to specific periods of history and the history of religion. Indeed, the final form of the text is regarded as an arbitrary, and ultimately misleading, veil that has to be removed in order to lay bare what really counts: access to the real persons and events that created the original documents and their oral predecessors.

In this study, I examine the text of the Pentateuch in its received form, at the conclusion of the editorial and redaction processes, with little attention to what its prehistory may have been. The shape of these texts, as they have come to us, suggests that the Pentateuch was intended to be read as a whole and in order.[24] In so doing, I place a premium on the way the present form of the text functions as an integrated whole. I take it as axiomatic that when we divorce parts from their wider whole, when we examine words, phrases, and rhetorical tools without reference to the larger meaning of the work, we are doomed to read the biblical text out of its communicative context. This does not, however, imply that a seamless, harmonious reading of either its narrative or its legal portions is readily available. My reading strategy seeks to identify the inconsistencies and discrepancies between various legal sections, and I will refer to the diachronic studies of these passages in the notes. But mainly, hopefully without failing to give difference its due, I will seek to point out the way we may see in the disparate passages overarching motifs and ideas that point to the social and programmatic agenda I outlined earlier.

A sustained focus on the final form of the text, while telling us little of how the text came to be, does carry a particular methodological advantage. Diachronic analyses—those that concern the range and content of the documents, their dates of origin and relative chronology, and the processes through which they evolved textually—are all matters of great dispute. One witnesses within biblical scholarship today an ever-burgeoning array of methodologies and theories to address these issues, yet with precious few assumptions of yore discarded along the way.[25] Part of this, no doubt, is a welcome openness to a multiplicity of approaches as we come to appreciate the variety of human perception and experience. Yet this refusal to shed anything along the way, one suspects, is reflective of methodological weakness. As the late British economist Joan Robinson is reported to have said, "In a subject where there is no agreed procedure for knocking out errors, doctrines have a long life."[26] The synchronic approach I adopt here seeks to engage a text that—for all its unevenness—is a given, relatively fixed, and concrete entity. The conclusions about meaning and interpretation that I reach may well be subject to dispute. But the general parameters of the text itself that I examine will not be.

As indicated earlier, I seek to analyze these texts and highlight their egalitarian program in light of the geopolitical domain of the ancient Near East. The political and socioeconomic experiences of the cultures of this region will serve as a comparative resource through which we may adduce the implications of the texts under study. In most cases, it will be clear that the ancient Near Eastern parallels that I bring to bear predate the biblical materials, and I will be able to explore the way the biblical texts reflect a reworking of the older material within a new social and theological agenda.

The book's opening chapter presents the argument that drives the rest of the book. I claim that the rejection of hierarchy is rooted in a major theological shift. Social and political hierarchy in the ancient Near East received metaphysical legitimation, as the heavenly order was construed as paralleling the terrestrial one. In this scheme, the common person emerges as a servant, the lowest rung in the hierarchy, as is evidenced in Mesopotamian creation epics, and echoed elsewhere as well. The theology of covenant in the Pentateuch rejects this. In light of parallels with Late Bronze Age (fifteenth to thirteenth centuries B.C.E.) suzerainty treaties, the covenant narratives implicitly suggest that the whole of Israel—not its king, not his retinue, not the priests— bears the status of a subordinate king entered into treaty with a sovereign king, God. While much of this material has been extant in the scholarship for some fifty years, I reexamine the material in new light, and from two directions. The first borrows observations from the field of anthropology concerning the role and display of honor between superiors and subordinates that offers new insight into the suzerain-vassal paradigm for the relationship between God and Israel. The second is a revisiting of the Hittite treaties whose form and language are paralleled in the covenantal material in the Pentateuch. I conclude from this study that not only does Israel as a collective whole attain the status of a subordinate king but that indeed, hierarchy is eschewed as every man in Israel becomes endowed with this status as well. This theology is the underpinning of a set of social and political policies that I explore in chapters 2 through 5.

In chapter 2, I examine the way Deuteronomy offers an egalitarian political prescription for the shape of Israelite society and its leadership regime. Within its pentateuchal framing, Deuteronomy, the last of the five books, consists of an address by Moses, at the end of the wilderness sojourn, that seeks to introduce new governing institutions and to refashion features of the wilderness regime that had led until that point in preparation for a new social and political order that will emerge after his demise. The program is egalitarian, in that it attenuates, in the first place, the institutional power of the monarchy as construed in the ancient Near East in the following realms: the military, the cult, the judiciary, the economy, and the harem. The program further establishes a set of checks and balances that curb the power of the various seats of authority: the king, the priesthood, the judiciary, and the prophet. While Deuteronomy seeks to cast Israel as a community without caste distinctions founded on economic or political terms, the priests and Levites do maintain a distinct status, the parameters and meaning of which I discuss. Finally, I claim that Deuteronomy's egalitarian program for the regime is reflected in its rejection of the institutions and language of tribal patriarchy that are very evident in the other pentateuchal texts in favor of collective, national identity. Whereas earlier studies that have examined Deuteronomy's plan for the regime have focused on chapters 16–18, I maintain that one must read all of Deuteronomy as an integrated whole in order to perceive the full intricacy of its blueprint for a society in the land of Israel. In particular, I attend to the role played in this regard by the so-called narrative frames of the book—chapters 1–4 and chapters 27–30. While previous studies have noted that Deuteronomy seems to adopt a form of checks and balances, I locate the statement it makes in this regard within the history of political thought on the subject. Scanning theories from Roman jurists through Montesquieu, I conclude that the kernel of a theory of checks and balances that one may adduce from a reading of Deuteronomy is suggestive of formulations we do not encounter again until the writings of the American founding fathers.

An egalitarian order, however, cannot limit itself to an articulation of the common person's relationship to God and to the political order. As noted, *class* may be defined as the formation of groups around the extraction, production, transformation, distribution, exchange, and consumption of economic surplus. A program for an egalitarian order, therefore, must address the distribution of capital. In the capitalist world that we inhabit, social relations become embedded in the economic system. Yet in premodern societies, including the ancient Near East, the dynamic was reversed: The economic order was merely a function of the social order in which it was contained. Having laid out the theological underpinnings of the social order, and how it gains expression in the structure of the regime, in chapter 3 I examine stipulations concerning land tenure, taxation, lending, ownership rights, debt easement, and poverty relief. To be sure, the various legal corpora found in the Pentateuch concerning nearly all of these issues reveal inner tension and discord. Yet we may see that in many instances, concepts and institutions that originated in statist and feudal orders elsewhere in the ancient Near East are recast in these legal corpora in accordance with a new communal agenda. I will maintain that where the greatest reworking has been done, we may see that it has been carried out with the aim of ensuring that a broad swath of the citizenry remains landed and economically secure. What emerges is the western tradition's first prescription for an economic order that seeks to minimize extreme advantage and the distinctions of class based on wealth.

In chapter 4, I turn to the role technology may have played in advancing this egalitarian platform. We understand today that the social impact of a technology of communication such as the internet or the printing press is very much a function of the social institutions and prevailing ideologies of a given culture. The printing press ushered in enormous change precisely in cultures that were open to the empowerment of the individual, now engendered by the spread of literacy. The adoption of the technology of the alphabetic script and its use in creating texts in ancient Israel was a result of a dynamic relationship between technology on the one hand and a distinct theological and social mind frame on the other that is unafraid of educating the masses. In Mesopotamia and Egypt, by contrast, texts were produced, read, memorized, and transmitted by a scribal elite and were composed in scripts that were inherently difficult to master—hieroglyphics and cuneiform. Literacy in ancient Israel was probably always the purview of professional scribes. But passages in Deuteronomy, Exodus, and the prophetic writings of the eighth and seventh centuries suggest that such texts should be produced for the masses, read to them, remembered by them, and transmitted by them. The new, popular role for texts as vehicles for the communication of ideas whereby a fully literate minority facilitates the production of texts for popular consumption is associated with the use of an alphabetic script to produce these texts. The role of the printing press in the flourishing of sixteenth-century western Europe sheds light on the way the Bible sought to optimize the new technology of the alphabetic script in the southern Levant in an unprecedented way: by utilizing the communicative power of the alphabetic text and its potential for wide circulation. Whereas in Mesopotamia and in Egypt writing was turned inward as a guarded source of power, in Israel it was turned outward and reflected the

Bible's egalitarian impulse. The dissemination of such texts to the masses through writing and reading accords with other biblical emphases—the domestication of national religion, the shift from a cult of objects to a cult of words and ideas, and the rise of a national vernacular literature. An examination of the role and status of writing within Greek thought generally—and the thought of Plato in particular—highlights the special status accorded writing within biblical thought.

Scholars of the rise of the novel in eighteenth-century England have noted that the evolution of the genre of the novel in place of the drama or the epic poem reflected Enlightenment thinking about nature, the individual, and class. The novel emerged as a vehicle for the development of new literary techniques that both reflected and in turn further spurred these humanist impulses. This development serves as a heuristic prism for chapter 5, in which I demonstrate how biblical narrative adapted and advanced modes of storytelling in the ancient Near East to better convey its egalitarian agenda. This occurs on the level of content: the Pentateuch's stories place the entire nation at center stage—as opposed to some divinely elected monarch—in a way not evinced anywhere else in the ancient Near East. But biblical narrative also advances the egalitarian agenda in a more subtle way—through the rhetorical tools it employs, the mechanics of storytelling. Even as covenant addresses the entire nation, it essentially challenges each member of the polity to strive for moral and spiritual excellence. The Pentateuch's stories—much like its sermons and law codes—essentially address each member of the polity. The poetics employed by biblical narrative place a premium on complex characterization and on highlighting the dilemmas and trials its protagonists face. From the story of the Garden of Eden through the challenges of leadership faced by Moses, biblical narrative emerges as an educational tool well suited to instructing the members of the polity, as each of them faces the challenges of jealousy, temptation, rising above self-interest, heeding God's word. To demonstrate how biblical narrative technique reflects and serves a covenant theology, I compare the biblical account of the rescue of Moses after his birth (Exod 2:1–10) with the legend of the rescue of Sargon of Akkad as an infant. The two accounts are strikingly similar, yet it is precisely on the score of characterization and highlighting the moral choices faced that the Bible's refinement of rhetorical tools emerges.

In the conclusion, I locate the ideas developed in these pages on the map of notions of equality in the history of western thought. My purpose here is to adumbrate what may be considered lines for future comparative study. I do so with three distinct periods in mind: Greek notions of equality; early Christian notions of equality; and modern notions of equality, spawned by the great political theorists of the seventeenth and eighteenth centuries. For each system, I probe two primary questions: What is the basis for claiming that such equality exists? What is the commodity that gets equalized between putatively equal persons? The conclusions, I maintain, may well be able to contribute to our thinking about the relation of the rights we possess to the duties that are incumbent on us. The conclusions can elucidate our notions of the rights of individuals as opposed to the rights of groups, the relationship between different groups in political theory, and the very origins of rights themselves.

Those familiar with the literature that attempts to study the Hebrew Bible from the perspective of the social sciences generally, and political theory more specifically, will have noted strong lines of convergence between the program I have set out here and that set out over a lifetime in the writings of Norman Gottwald. Reflecting on all those whose scholarship has informed this study, I may honestly say that I do not know if this project would have been possible without the benefit of his scholarship, specifically with regard to chapters 2 and 3. Agreeing with him in many substantive matters, I have tried to bring the discussion further in two areas. The underlying aim of Gottwald's work is the attempt to reconstruct the social and political history of ancient Israel. Where Gottwald has sought the social and political history that lies behind the text, I have focused on the ways the text itself may function as an integrated whole. In many instances, I have taken ideas that originate in his work and returned to the text in a close reading, to show how they animate such a reading and are in turn buttressed by the nuances such a reading strategy produces. Moreover, I have located parallel material from the ancient Near East, so that ideological points of departure delineated within the biblical text may stand out in bolder relief.

As I lay out what I take to be the egalitarian voice within biblical tradition, with emphasis on the Pentateuch, I do so with a keen awareness that the picture I paint of a biblical polity that rejects class distinction on the basis of the control of economic and political power pertains primarily to Israelite men, and not necessarily to Israelite women. At some junctures, as in the collective address of the entire polity (the second person plural "you"), it may be that men and women are addressed in equal fashion. Yet it is at least as clear that the blueprint the Pentateuch lays out takes for granted women's subordination to men, excluding them from participation in many areas, including the judiciary, the cult, the military, and land ownership, to name just a few. For this reason, I have adopted the somewhat anachronistic term "common man" in my discussion of the egalitarian voice within biblical tradition. The Oxford English Dictionary says that "*man* as thus used primarily denotes the male sex, though by implication also referring to women." I find that the phrase "common man" communicates this ambiguity nicely—at once suggesting something that is universal to all persons, all members of the polity, while at the same time expressing a patriarchal, androcentric focus that is endemic to the thinking of the entire ancient Near East, and the Bible within it.[27]

It is also clear that a fuller study of the Pentateuch's sketch of the Israelite polity would need to attend to the institutionalized role and status of the resident alien (gēr) and the foreigner (nōkri).[28] My work, therefore, can be only a start—an attempt to show how a core Israelite citizenry of free persons was envisioned in an ancient Near Eastern milieu in which stratification between those who imposed tribute and those who bore tribute was the norm.

In closing, I am also aware that this is a book of ambitious scope. The topics that any of these chapters takes up have already been the subject of numerous monograph-length treatments, and it is inevitable that I have slighted developments in many of these fields or otherwise ignored facets that a longer treatment would allow, nay, necessitate. This perhaps is inevitable in a book that seeks to synthesize material, often arcane, as it reaches out to an audience beyond specialists in the field of biblical studies or comparative ancient Near Eastern studies.

At the same time, this book seeks to advance the state of scholarship. I have mentioned the contributions I believe each chapter makes s to the current scholarship. It may very well be, however, that the book's greatest contribution is in the very process of the synthesis. In an age where access to primary sources is almost unlimited and the secondary literature to any subject continues to grow exponentially, we witness in the academy a tendency to compose books on narrow subjects. Only books of narrow focus can truly exhaust the literature on a given subject. But if our collective output consists only of books of narrow focus, our scholarship will be impoverished. The classification systems of the modern academic library will list "kingship," "land redemption," and "literacy" as distinct topics. Yet social and political phenomena have never been lived and experienced in isolation from one another, and within the biblical text these topics emerge as they were naturally experienced, hence naturally construed and envisioned—as parts of an integrated whole. The wholeness of human experience mandates a book that seeks the interrelationship of these phenomena. One may attempt to listen closely to the cellist in a symphony. But, ultimately, the whole is greater than the sum of its parts, and the symphony is greater than the endeavor of listening to each of its players in isolation. It has been my aim in this work to listen to a chorus of voices harmonizing around a common melody.

# I

# Egalitarian Theology

*The Commoner's Upgrade from King's Servant
to Servant King*

As we embark on exploration of social and political thought in the ancient Near East and in the Bible, we must check at the door some of our assumptions as modern readers and thinkers concerning the relationship between affairs of religion and affairs of state. In the ancient Near East and in the Bible as well, it is impossible to disentangle social and political thought from religious thought and ideals.

The attempt to treat things social and political as distinct from things religious is a thoroughly modern notion. It derives from the fact that the development of political thought in early modern Europe was largely a conscious effort to leave behind the theologically laden political systems, dominated by the medieval Church, of the period following the general disintegration engendered by the barbarian invasions. In the view of the medieval church, the purpose of the republic was to serve as a vehicle of the salvation of the individual, and with this rationale, the Church imposed theocracy in its rule over empires, monarchies, and city-states. It was hostility toward this theocracy that ultimately gave rise in Italy to the first secular culture in Europe, in the writings of figures such as Dante, who were the first to challenge the political power of the papacy. Machiavelli sought to articulate a new political order as a response to what he saw around him: the tenuous political structure of the Florentine city-state, weakened by the domination of the Church. Machiavelli was the first European political thinker who rejected the Church's position whereby the religious good was superior to the political good. Instead, he conceived of the purpose of the political order, not in terms of the spiritual salvation of man, but rather in terms of the protection of the physical welfare of the masses under its jurisdiction. The decoupling of the engine of religion from the train of politics was furthered in the writings of Hobbes, who witnessed firsthand the English Civil War, which was as much religiously as politically driven. Protestantism had taught the dogma that each individual is "holy" and can lay claim to "having grace" and has to obey his or her own "inspiration." Yet through his own experience of the English Civil War, Hobbes saw that these religious notions led to political arrogance and disrespect for one's neighbor. He reasoned that the quarrels of men concerning the definition of the noblest religious virtues had, in the end, brought about the war of all against all. It was with reference to this war of all against all that Hobbes penned his famous statement in chapter 13 of his *Leviathan* that human life in the state of nature is "solitary, poore, nasty, brutish and short."[1] For both Machiavelli and Hobbes, the political order had to be rid of any higher goal other than protecting the welfare of the individuals within its jurisdiction. These men articulated their ideas from a view of human nature as lacking any positive qualities that might give human lives, and the political order in which they function, a larger metaphysical purpose. Their ideas were a sharp departure from those of the Scholastic thinkers who preceded them in the medieval period, for whom the political order served a higher end, the service of the Catholic Church.[2]

To understand social and political thought in the ancient Near East, including Israel, we must bear in mind that within the lands of Europe and the Near East from antiquity until the Renaissance, social and political orders were constructed and construed as serving some higher cosmic order and not merely the protection of individuals. In later chapters, I will trace how voices in the Hebrew Bible, particularly in the Pentateuch, sought to depart from the notion of a society founded on the basis of stratification and hierarchy, in the political, social, and economic, realms. But at the core, these shifts and transformations are rooted in theology, and it is with theology we must begin—by understanding the metaphysical rationales that legitimated social hierarchy in the cultures of the ancient Near East, and the theological revolution evidenced in the Bible that ushers in an entirely new socioreligious mindset.

To examine the cosmic role assigned to the structure of the social order within the cultures of the ancient Near East and Israel, I shall use a particular litmus test. This test is based on observations Peter Berger makes in his seminal work on the sociology of religion, *The Sacred Canopy.*[3]

Imagine, Berger says, that you are the highly conscious founder of a new social order (whom he calls, serendipitously for our purposes, "a combination of Moses and Machiavelli"). You wish to ensure the strength and endurance of the new order, so you employ all the classic methods of totalitarian domination: you imprison or otherwise remove all opposition. You bring into your control the reins of the economy and of communication. You establish mechanisms for the transfer or inheritance of leadership. Nonetheless, Berger says, your regime will require metaphysical legitimation in the eyes of the public. It is imperative that the controlled public perceives the artificial, constructed, and therefore tenuous nature of your regime as rooted in a metaphysical rationale for its existence.

Enter religion. Your imposed institutional order will receive immeasurable legitimation if the masses under your control believe that it is rooted in ultimate reality of an unchanging truth—that its significance is located in a cosmic and sacred frame of reference. When the masses comply with and participate in the constructed social and political order, they will see themselves as acting in accord with the fundamental order of the universe.

A simple way to implement this strategy would be to declare, and educate for, the notion that your rule is legitimate because you are an agent of the gods; indeed, you were chosen by them to lead. Yet, as Berger notes, ancient cultures went a quantum step further in the way they harnessed earthly rule to metaphysical meaning: the political institutions in the earthly realm, they maintained, were merely an analogue to a parallel institution in the heavenly realm. The institutional order "down below" manifested the divine order of the cosmos "up above" in the relationship of microcosm to macrocosm, within what Paul Ricoeur termed "the logic of correspondences."[4]

In the explorations that follow, I shall employ Berger's hermeneutic of suspicion—the critique of certain views by exposing their real motives—in which religion is taken to be merely a self-interested distortion that masks the human construction and exercise of power.[5] I will draw from the existing literature and demonstrate how the logic of correspondences between the earthly realm and the heavenly realm was articulated in representative cultures of the ancient Near East. At each juncture, I will further demonstrate how the stratification of society derived metaphysical legitimation and, in the process, dictated a low cosmic value for the common man, hence a low position of power for the vast majority of society's members.

From there, I shall turn to the Bible. Here, I will claim that one indeed finds constructions of power, particularly within the notion of a covenant with the Davidic line, that are open to the same hermeneutic of suspicion.[6] Alongside these, however, we find many texts, particularly in the Pentateuch, in which the pattern is broken. The metaphors adopted from the experiences of day-to-day affairs to conceptualize the encounter between God and man do little, if anything, to buttress the earthly power structure. Moreover, they serve to attenuate the hierarchical stratification of society in a fashion unmatched in the other thought systems of the ancient Near East. In particular, I seek to expand the existing discussion of these issues by reassessing the role that Late Bronze (fifteenth to thirteenth centuries B.C.E.) Hittite treaties can play in illuminating our understanding of the theological and political term *covenant*.

## Hierarchy and the Logic of Correspondences: The Cases of Mesopotamia and of Ugarit

To demonstrate how social stratification was legitimated through the logic of correspondences in the ancient Near East, I turn to two representative cultures. Mesopotamia and Ugarit both display this dynamic, each through its own distinct terms and metaphors.

In the fourth millennium B.C.E., Mesopotamian culture had its origins in small, tightly knit villages. There was little social differentiation, and the head of one's village could well be a relative. Over time, wars became an increasing threat, and shelter could be found only in collective security agreements between villages, particularly within the person of the king, who would stand at the helm of the unity of these new collectives. With the emergence of territorial states that began to incorporate larger areas and a wider range of people, a tendency emerged to organize stronger, centralized political structures. Rulers would no longer be petty princes whom one saw on a regular basis but would now be exalted above many persons from many areas and would rule over them with unprecedented power at their command. The scale of political greatness was now measured in different terms. This process culminated with the rise of Sargon, the king of Akkad in around 2300 B.C.E., who achieved hegemony over a vast region, a hegemony that was later revived—following a period of decline—by the great Hammurabi around 1800 B.C.E.[7]

It was at this time that the political structure associated with the exalted sovereign emerged as the central metaphor of Mesopotamian civilization and was mirrored in its conception of the heavenly realms. Within the earthly realm, the king presided over a vast hierarchy, a pyramid of lesser authorities. And so it was in the supernal realm. The realm of the gods had a king as well—Enlil. But while Enlil stood as an uncontested ruler, this hardly meant that he stood alone. The elaborate pantheon of Mesopotamian gods corresponded to the range of lesser authorities who served under earthly kings like Sargon and Hammurabi. When we think of the polytheistic tendencies of ancient cultures, we often assume that they stem from a primitive inability to see the big picture, the unity of the natural order. But in Mesopotamian religion of the third millennium onward, the rejection of monotheism as we conceive of it today was based in their conception not solely of nature but also of the polity, according to the logic of correspondences. Enlil, like his earthly counterparts, ruled by delegating responsibilities to lesser dignitaries and functionaries. He presided, like his earthly counterpart, over a large assembly. Like the earthly king, he resided in a palace with his wives, children, and extended "house."[8]

The analogue between earthly and heavenly king, however, was not only of title and role but also of nature, character, and disposition. Enlil the king god completely resembled his human counterpart in the most human of terms. The gods were considered to be corporeal beings. Like earthly men, they had needs; they ate, they drank, and they wore clothes. They desired (and struggled to achieve) a carefree existence and enjoyed large banquets in their honor. Like kings in their palaces, gods needed palaces, or what we would call temples, where they, too, could reside in splendor, in separation from the masses, with subjects caring for them and seeking their gracious assistance in a host of earthly matters. Thus, much like servants of the royal palace, temple servants prepared meals for the gods, arranged their clothes, and kept the divine quarters neat.[9]

The metaphysical legitimation accorded to the social hierarchy and the relatively lowly status of the common man in Mesopotamia are well illustrated in the cosmogony of Atrahasis—a Mesopotamian epic that tells how humans became created. The oldest fragments we have of Atrahasis are dated to the seventeenth century B.C.E., the reign of the fourth monarch after Hammurabi, and the tale is believed to be not much older.[10]

The story opens with an account of the hierarchy of the gods. The upper class, or Annunaki, are served by the lower class, or Igigi, who engage in all manner of menial labor in the service of their lords, the Annunaki. The Igigi gods' primary task is the excavation of the system of rivers and canals that irrigate the fields and that are vital for the Mesopotamian economy. They carried out "hard work, night and day," the epic says, as they "groaned and blamed each other" and "grumbled over the masses of excavated soil." Finally, after 3,600 years of this, they engage in what may be the first mass job walkout described in the history of literature. At this point, one of the worker gods instigates a decisive course of action: he proposes that a posse surround the house of the Igigi gods' taskmaster, Enlil, counselor to the higher gods, and drag him out of his house. The more things change, the more they stay the same: what labor demonstration is complete without the proverbial tire burning?

The disgruntled lower gods assemble their tools and spades and set them afire. The posse of embittered laborer gods reaches Enlil's house and surrounds it. A lynching is in the offing. Enlil's personal servant, Nusku, makes gallant efforts to save the day:

> And they listened to the clamor of [the Igigi gods].
> Nusku woke [his] lord,
> He got [him] out of bed,
> "My lord, [your] house is surrounded,
> "Battle has run right up [to your gate].
> "Enlil, your house is surrounded,
> "Battle has [ru]n right up to your gate!"
> Enlil had [ ]...to his dwelling.
> Enlil made ready to speak
> And said to the vizier Nusku,
> "Nusku, bar your gate,
> "Get your weapons and stand before me."
> Nusku barred his gate,
> Got his weapons and stood before Enlil.
> Nusku made ready to speak,
> And said to the warrior Enlil,
> "My lord, your face is (gone pale as) tamarisk.
> "Your own offspring [i.e. the Igigi gods]! Why did you fear?
> "My lord, your face is (gone pale as) tamarisk.
> "Your own offspring [i.e. the Igigi gods]! Why did you fear?
> "Send that they bring Anu down [here],
> "And that they bring Enki be[fore yo]u."[11]

Stalling for time, Nusku arranges for the two sage gods, Anu and Enki, to arrive for consultation. A meeting of the upper-class Annunaki is hastily convened, and it is decided that the best strategy is to identify the strike leaders and to liquidate them. Agents of the Annunaki are sent out to the crowd seeking to learn the identities of the strike leaders. The union spirit of the workers quickly becomes manifest, as they cover for their instigators:

> "Every [one of us gods has declared] war;
> "We have set [ ] in the excavation.
> "[Excessive] drudgery [has killed us],
> "Our forced labor was heavy, [the misery too much]!
> "Now every [one of us gods]
> "Has resolved on [a reckoning?] with Enlil."[12]

The Annunaki reconvene, and the god Enki/Ea prevails, with a recognition of the problem and a proposition for a solution:

> Ea made ready to speak,
> And said to the gods [his brethren],
> "What calumny do we lay to their charge?
> "Their forced labor was heavy, [their misery too much]!
> "Every day [ ]
> "The outcry [was loud, we could hear the clamor].
> "[Belet-ili, the midwife], is present.
> "Let her then create a hum[an, a man]
> "Let him bear the yoke [ ],
> "Let him bear the yoke [ ]!
> "[Let man assume the drud]gery of god."[13]

A deliberation then ensues concerning just how to go about fashioning this new being, a human. He must be closer to the gods than are animals, and thus a god is sacrificed, and his flesh and blood are mixed with clay. The first human is displayed to the other gods for their approval, after which mass production of the new biotechnology commences, so that a corps of new workers will be able to relieve the lower-class Igigi gods of their former drudgery.

The tale is a virtual celebration of social hierarchy. From the beginning of time, the gods have already been divided along social lines. The rebellion of the lower gods simply serves as an occasion to bring humans onto the scene in order to occupy the lowest rung on the ladder. The purpose of humankind is to serve as a toiling servant of the gods, carrying out the most menial, backbreaking tasks on their behalf.[14] While the myth speaks of humanity's existential purpose vis-à-vis the gods, it is clear that the relationship depicted is merely a reflection of the earthly social hierarchy. The raison d'être of the common man is to serve the king, to offer him his constant labor, all to allow the king and his house to rule in comfort and splendor. The divide between the dominant tribute-imposing class, and the dominated tribute-bearing class is granted religious sanction.

Jean Bottéro, a prominent Assyriologist, has noted that there is strong resemblance between the accounts of the creation of man in Genesis 2 and in Atrahasis. According to Genesis 2:6, man is fashioned out of dirt, and infused by God with "the spirit of life." Bottéro also rightly points out that it is here that the similarity ends. In Atrahasis, man is created to engage in backbreaking work on behalf of the gods. In Genesis 2, man is created to till the ground—but ultimately for his own nourishment and pleasure.[15]

Bottéro sought to compare the creation of man in Atrahasis and in Genesis 2 citing the common topos of man being created through a fusion of physical and metaphysical elements. But if we look to compare not the question of how but why man was created, an even sharper contrast emerges between the creation of man in Atrahasis and in Genesis 1 (1:26–29):

> And God said: Let us make man in our own image, after our
> likeness: and let them have dominion over the fish of the sea, and
> over the fowl of the air, and over the cattle, and over all the earth, and
> over every creeping thing that creepeth upon the earth. . . . And God
> blessed them, and God said unto them, Be fruitful, and multiply,
> and replenish the earth, and subdue it: and have dominion over the
> fish of the sea, and over the fowl of the air, and over every living
> thing that moveth upon the earth. And God said, Behold I have
> given you every herb bearing seed, which is upon the face of all the
> earth, and every tree, in which is the fruit of a tree yielding seed; to
> you it shall be for food.

In Atrahasis, man is created in order to be a servant; in Genesis, all men are created to have dominion.[16] There is no inkling in Genesis 1 that either man or the created world around him was created in order to provide for God in any way; rather, the world is created for man to have dominion of it, as expressed in Psalm 8:5–6:

> For thou hast made him a little lower than the angels,
> and hast crowned him with glory and honor.
> Thou madest him to have dominion over the works of thy hands;
> thou hast put all things under his feet.

Few phrases in the Bible have stirred as much interest as has the phrase of Genesis 1:26, "Let us make man in our image." The dominant understanding of the phrase today stems from seeing it within the context of Psalm 8:5–6: to be created in the likeness of God means to share in His glory, to share in His dominion of the world.[17]

For the Mesopotamian imagination, the assignment to man of the role of merely a toiling servant of the gods was not without difficulty. For if in fact man had been created to do the gods' bidding, why would the gods, who control all, introduce illness and famine in the world? What could possess the gods to inflict misery and death on those whose only purpose was to serve them? The Atrahasis epic attends to this very point, in a way that further underscores the low metaphysical standing of the common man. Continuing, the story enumerates how Enlil, the king of the gods, becomes disenchanted with the human race:

> [The land had grown wide], the people had increased,
> The [land] was bellowing [like a bull].
> The god was disturbed with [their uproar].
> [Enlil heard] their clamor
> [He said to] the great gods,
> "The clamor of mankind [has become burdensome to me],
> "I am losing sleep [to their uproar]."[18]

The din of an overpopulated earth is apparently disturbing the divine serenity, making napping difficult. Enlil then concocts various methods of extermination to control human population growth, so that there will be less noise to disturb his sleep. When an epidemic doesn't do the trick, he sends illness. When that doesn't work, he sends drought, which results in a famine. And when that doesn't work, he ultimately sends the flood.[19] In between the accounts of each attempted liquidation, the myth repeats the refrain about how humanity's numbers continue to swell, continuing to disturb Enlil's sleep. Following the dubious success of the flood, the gods seek a way to reap the benefits of man's labors while yet restricting his reproduction and agree on three measures. First, henceforth some women would be created infertile. Second, a new female demon would be created and charged with introducing stillbirth and infant mortality into the world. Finally, the gods will now demand the establishment of a caste of priestesses who, by sacral necessity, will not be allowed to be impregnated except by the king.[20] To summarize, the picture that emerges of the common man in Mesopotamian thought is an undignified one indeed. Created in order to serve and support the gods, man suffers various afflictions at their hands, is decimated by the flood, and all for the sole reason that his presence disturbs their sleep. After the flood, Enlil demands a reorganization of the human race. The tablet containing this section is damaged, but what appears to follow is a classification of the populace by marital status, and the author seems to conclude his work with a description of the social structure of his time, further lending mythic support to the social stratification of the day.[21]

The conclusion to the flood narrative in Genesis could not stand in greater polemical tension with the one just described with regard to the metaphysical standing of the common man. If the Atrahasis epic sees human reproduction as distressful in the eyes of God, in Genesis the tables are turned completely. The Genesis flood narrative ends with a most ringing affirmation of human reproduction and a most stinging condemnation of the taking of human life. On disembarking from the ark, Noah receives a blessing (Gen 9:1–6):

> God blessed Noah and his sons, and said to them, "Be fruitful and multiply, and fill the earth. The fear and dread of you shall be upon all the beasts of the earth and upon all the birds of the sky—everything with which the earth is astir—and upon all the fish of the sea; they are given into your hand.... For your life-blood I will require a reckoning: of every beast will I require it; of man, too, I will require a reckoning for human life, of every man for that of his fellow man! Whoever sheds the blood of man, by man shall his blood be shed; for in the image of God was man created."[22]

The flood was indeed a punishment for the iniquities of man. But it was a punishment for the iniquities of a single generation. The metaphysical standing of man in future generations will remain unchanged: man, created in the image of God, has been created in order to have dominion of the earth. Far from seeking to limit the reproduction of man, God seeks to promote it.

As noted, the metaphysical legitimation of social hierarchy is evident in the ancient culture of Ugarit as well as Mesopotamia. The kingdom of Ugarit—modern-day Ras Shamra—was located on the Syrian coast, 100 miles north of present-day Beirut. The site, first uncovered by a peasant plowing the land in 1928, has given us particularly good documentation of the kingdom that stood there from roughly 1450 B.C.E. until its destruction sometime around 1200 B.C.E. This kingdom paled in size relative to the kingdoms of Mesopotamia: the entire realm encompassed only some 1,200 square miles, roughly a 20-mile by 60-mile stretch of coast. Yet for the purpose of comparing and contrasting biblical culture, the myths and rituals described in the texts of Ugarit are unsurpassed in importance, as Ugarit is the most proximate culture to that of biblical Israel—both in period and in location—from which substantial records remain.

The logic of correspondences applies equally to the legitimation of social hierarchy in Ugarit and that in Mesopotamia. As in Mesopotamia, the pantheon paralleled the sociopolitical hierarchy and reflected its bureaucratic structure.[23] Yet in Ugarit, the conception of the pantheon had a distinctly local color. In Ugarit, the highest level of association was the family—the clan. Because of its relatively modest size, society in Ugarit was structured as a hierarchy of nested households, one within another: nuclear families within a multitiered clan structure. Typically, the structure of the patriarchal household was headed by the oldest male relative, the patriarch, who presided over multiple nuclear families headed by his sons and other male relatives. At the bottom of this social hierarchy were workers and slaves who served the members of higher rank within the order. It was the task of the patriarch to mediate interactions and conflict within the household and to negotiate relations between his household and other households in the society. His ultimate task was to ensure the welfare of the household and to guarantee its perpetuation, its holdings, and its good name.[24] He was the judge and the chief warrior. As one scholar has noted, in Ugarit, personal names abound that bear the form *bn/bt* (son/daughter of) + proper name. Often, this is the only identifier of an individual, which suggests that membership in a household was the key element of identification within Ugaritic society.[25] Two of the most significant literary works bequeathed to us by Ugaritic culture, the Epic of King Keret and the Epic of Aqhat, both center on the efforts of childless royal deities to ensure the birth of an heir.

The patriarch was not only the sovereign monarch but also the ultimate father. It is important to stress that in Ugarit, kinship and kingship go hand in hand, that is, to be king over all is to be father over all as well. The genealogical metaphor of "father" found both at the apex of the political structure and the pantheon, represents social and political markers of authority and dependence.[26] As in Mesopotamia—where earthly ruler and the chief diety were both considered kings of empires—the power of the central metaphor to legitimate the earthly polity does not imply a reign of tyranny.[27] In Ugarit despotism and benevolence naturally coexisted. On the one hand, the patriarch king had the right to dominate all individuals, goods, and services under his mastery. Yet in return for filial loyalty came the expectation that he would treat the members of his household with benevolence. The staying power of the construct of the patrimonial household rose from the intrahousehold loyalty that was at its core.[28]

We possess no Ugaritic cosmogony on a par with Atrahasis that describes the creation of man and the origins of his metaphysical standing. Yet as in Mesopotamia, the language and conceptual structure of the earthly polity of Ugarit was mirrored in the language and concepts used to describe the heavenly polity as well. What emerges is a well-attested hierarchy. Broadly speaking, the Ugaritic pantheon exhibited a four-level structure. The highest ranking god, El, is depicted as an aging patriarch, and his divine wife, the goddess Athirat (also known as Asherah, especially in Hebrew), was conceived as the *rbt*, the lady, or matriarch, of the divine household. Together they represented the authoritative deities. As the king-patriarch, El presided over the whole pantheon and, indeed, over humanity. The second level of the pantheon, the active deities, included the divine royal children, the seventy sons of Athirat. As in the earthly realm, these sons inhabited their own respective houses, and they are often depicted in conflict with one another.[29] The third level of the pantheon, of which we know relatively little, seems to have consisted of godly "craftsmen" who served the deities of the upper two realms. The fourth and lowest level of the pantheon consisted of "the divine workers (or servitors)," the *ins 'ilm*, or "men of the gods." This group included maidservants, messengers, and gate-keepers, who paralleled the servants of the earthly king in his palace.[30]

## An Alternative Model: King as Demigod in Egypt

In addition to the logic of correspondences, we discover a second strategy through which the metaphysical legitimation of earthly power and hierarchy was augmented in the cultures of the ancient Near East. Instead of articulating a series of correspondences between earthly and heavenly leaders, we find evidence of some belief systems that took an even bolder step: the king himself was considered a demigod. Nowhere was this more evident than in Egypt. The king in ancient Egypt was considered to be both the living son and the immediate divine reincarnation of his predecessor.[31] There is much debate as to the precise nature of the king's divinity, but for our purposes we may adopt a relatively minimalist position, namely, that the king was the visible image of a god and assumed a divine role on earth.[32] Only the king had access to the world of the gods, and indeed he is a ubiquitous figure in scenes of worship inscribed on temple walls. Like the cult image of the gods, the king was steadfastly hidden from the view of his subjects. When he entered the public arena, however, he was surrounded by signs of power and protection and represented for the public the presence of the gods. His decrees were considered "the utterances of god himself," his actions "not the work of men."[33]

A vast state apparatus developed around the figure of the king in Egypt, who had ultimate authority over every aspect of life. These administrative structures revolved around the treasury, the collection of agricultural produce, its storage and redistribution. These structures also governed mining, quarrying, the building of military installations, granaries, temples and the development and maintenance of a vast military and police force; and centralized control over the provinces. All of this mandated enormous resources of craftsmen and workers, arranged within a social hierarchy.[34] The gods formed the highest level and humanity, in general, the lowest. Within humanity, the administrative and title-holding elite commanded an ideologically legitimated supremacy over the rest of society.[35]

Within the Mesopotamian, Ugaritic, and Egyptian conceptions I have discussed so far, it is not the common man who is the central focus of the gods but the king. In Mesopotamia, portents of evil, for example an eclipse or an earthquake, mandated human action to placate the gods, but the action mandated was solely that of the king. Only he recited prayers, offered sacrifices, or shaved his body in obeisance. Nothing was required of the people at large. It was not the people the Mesopotamian gods held accountable but their king.[36] In Egypt, this was expressed even in graphic terms: the symbolic representation of the community from the earliest dynasties is simply the figure of the king.[37]

In these cultures, persons who made up the dominated tribute-bearing class were thought of as servants, at the lowest rung of the metaphysical hierarchy. The gods were interested in humans to the extent that a baron or feudal lord would have interest in ensuring the well-being of the minions running his estate and supplying its needs.[38] Servants, no doubt, play a vital role in any monarchical order, but it is an instrumental role. From an existential perspective, it is a decidedly diminished and undignified role. The key player in each of these cosmic narratives was the king, and to a lesser degree the varying hierarchies that surrounded him.

## The Hermeneutics of Suspicion and the Davidic Dynasty

To be sure, the same hermeneutic of suspicion might well be applied to the institution of monarchy as it appears in some biblical passages, for example, the covenant heralding the establishment of the Davidic dynasty in 2 Samuel 7. Yet even when we examine those passages that grant the greatest legitimation to Davidic rule, some fundamental differences may be seen within the mechanism of legitimation at play. In Psalm 2, perhaps the most promonarchal of the so-called royal psalms, we note that from a phenomenological perspective, the identification between the deity and the monarch is not nearly as strong as that made elsewhere in the ancient Near East. The claim here of affinity or identification between the deity and the monarch is a relatively modest one: the king is legitimate because he has been chosen by God. The concluding phrase of the psalm, in which God says, "You are My son, I have fathered you this day" (v. 7), does not imply deification of the king. The phrase "You are my son" is a legal term found in the Code of Hammurabi, implying adoption. "I have fathered you *this day*" perhaps implies the adoption of the king by God at the king's coronation. The king is not the "visible image of a god," as in Egypt. Nor does his rule mimetically resemble that of the king of kings in the "logic of correspondences" to nearly the same extent as in Ugarit and Mesopotamia.

While biblical passages such as Isaiah 6 envision God as a king on a throne, which implicitly strengthens the institution of kingship, by and large, the logic of correspondences between the earthly and heavenly polities that appears to have been so prevalent in Mesopotamia is absent in biblical thought. The account of the anointment of Saul in 1 Samuel 8–10, whereby a king is chosen because the people ask for one, may be the only account in the annals of ancient Near Eastern historiography that depicts the historical beginnings of the institution of kingship in nonetiological and noncosmic terms. Indeed, the king in many biblical passages—and especially in the Pentateuch—was not deemed to be a necessary bond between God and the people. This dissociation of a people from its leader in relation to the divine is found nowhere else in the ancient Near East.[39]

As elsewhere in the ancient Near East, the social order within the Pentateuch is etiologically rooted in the sanction of cosmic narrative. Yet the Pentateuch, eschewing the logic of correspondences, seeks to ground an egalitarian order within a completely new set of metaphysical coordinates. It does so by adapting a concept from the political lexicon of the ancient Near East for theological purposes: the concept of *covenant*.

## The Suzerainty Treaty as a Metaphor for the Relationship between God and Israel

The term *covenant* is much used—and, I would add, abused—in discussions of biblical theology. As the *Oxford English Dictionary* points out at the beginning of its entry, the word is no longer in ordinary use in English except when colored by legal or theological associations. Put differently, as moderns, we have no points of reference in our day-to-day affairs through which to even begin to understand the full implications of this term, other than to say that, apparently, a covenant is broadly similar to a pact, treaty, contract, or agreement.

Political theorists with an interest in Scripture have tried to marshal the biblical term "covenant" for contemporary applications. But these more often than not have only clouded our understanding of the biblical concept of covenant. Later understandings of the word *covenant* or, worse, anachronistic political theories are imposed on the term and then read back into the biblical text. Daniel J. Elazar's *Covenant and Polity in Biblical Israel* is a good example. Seeking to mine the term for its contemporary implications, Elazar—following Max Weber—investigated it in terms of what it does as a bonding agent among members of the Israelite community; yet the covenant in the Bible is between

God and Israel, and any definition that is not built around this relationship must necessarily miss the point.[40] Moreover, Elazar discovers "covenant" at every turn—even in the account of creation—and he attempts to show how the principle of covenant underlies every major story in the Bible. Yet, by invoking the principle of "covenant" in so many different instances, Elazar makes a precise definition of the term difficult to attain. A more recent work, *The Jewish Political Tradition*, a major compendium of sources and commentaries edited by Michael Walzer, Menachem Lorberbaum, and Noam J. Zohar, likewise avoids any attempt to engage covenant on its own terms within its biblical and ancient Near Eastern contexts. Instead, the relevant chapter assesses the covenant narratives in the Bible in light of modern consent theory.

In the ensuing discussion, I will examine the biblical concept of covenant between God and Israel within its ancient Near Eastern setting. Expanding on the work of earlier scholars, I maintain that it is in covenant, properly conceived, that we may discern a radically new understanding of the cosmic role of the common man within the thought systems of the ancient Near East, one that constituted the basis of an egalitarian social order.

As scholars began to note more than fifty years ago, the pact between God and Israel displays many common elements with what are known in biblical studies as ancient Near Eastern suzerainty treaties. The suzerain, according to the *Oxford English Dictionary,* is "a sovereign having supremacy over another state which possesses its own ruler or government but cannot act as an independent power." It is important to stress that in certain circumstances, the vassal state of the ancient Near East retained its autonomy and territorial hegemony and, as we shall see, occupied a place that retained more independence, and perhaps dignity, than is suggested by the term "vassal." For the purposes of clarity, therefore, I shall refer to "the suzerain" simply as "the sovereign" and to the vassal as "the subordinate."

The Bible articulates the relationship between God and Israel as one between a great king and a lesser king engaged in just such a treaty. To understand the extent to which this is really the case, and the theological import deriving from this fact, it is essential to understand the forms of such international treaties and their role within the political life of the ancient Near East. Letters of correspondence among kings attest to the fact that treaties between states abounded in all ages of the period. Yet we possess actual treaty texts in significant number from only two eras: the Hittite kingdom of Anatolia during the Late Bronze Age (roughly the fifteenth to thirteenth centuries B.C.E.) and the Neo-Assyrian empire of the eighth and seventh centuries B.C.E.[41] There are significant differences both in terms of form, tone, and content between these two corpora. A vast scholarship has emerged over the last fifty

years that seeks to compare these two bodies of literature with biblical covenant passages, and a vigorous debate as to whether various covenantal passages
in the Bible more closely resemble the Hittite or the Neo-Assyrian materials.
There is a consensus today that the fullest illumination of the biblical texts in
question may be drawn by invoking both bodies of treaty literature.[42]

For the purposes of elucidating the meaning of covenant, I will focus primarily, though not exclusively, on the numerous parallels that may be drawn
from some eighteen Hittite treaties, as these form the closer parallels to the
covenant between God and Israel in the Pentateuch.[43]

I should like to say a word or two about my methodological considerations
in comparing these treaties and several biblical covenant passages. The first
concerns what we mean by the standard "form" of a treaty. Under the influence of the great German scholar Hermann Gunkel, many scholars in the
early twentieth century sought out the standard forms of various biblical and
ancient Near Eastern literary genres. Thus, a psalm of lament, say, or a prophetic call narrative in which a prophet received his first revelation and mission, could be identified on the basis of a set of core elements that it was supposed to possess. In this light, some scholars sought to identify the standard
form of the Hittite suzerainty treaty, on the basis of the various treaty texts
that were known at the time. The effort, however, reflected an error of concep-
tualization: no standard, set, invariable, "form" of the treaty ever existed.
Today we may say that it is possible to adduce from these materials a spectrum
of rhetorical tendencies, and a clustering around recurrent themes, patterns,
and commonalities.[44] But no single treaty text in our possession is a "pure"
example. The reason for this is that the Hittites drew from a large template of
elements that were then tailored to suit the needs of the particular circumstances surrounding the relationship between the sovereign Hittite king and
the foreign subordinate king. The variation in elements employed might reflect the past relations between the two sides or the geopolitical climate of the
day. Thus, what makes these treaties a distinct group is not the invariable invocation of a set form.[45] Rather, what they have in common is a flexible form,
such that recognizable commonalities across a spectrum could be employed to
serve the needs of the given circumstance—the particular relationship between the treaty partners and the particular matter at hand.

The second methodological concern I wish to address up front concerns
the notion of literary and conceptual borrowing across cultures. Although the
Hittite kingdom of Anatolia was not contiguous with the land of Israel, it is possible that an original common tradition of treaty formulation, and conceptions
about relationships within treaties, developed in parallel yet distinctive fashions in various locales in the region.[46] The development that occurs in a given

locale partly elaborates shared concepts, and partly introduces distinctive ones. Similar circumstances and needs in different locales within the same region may give rise to similar forms of what was originally a common inheritance.[47] Therefore, when comparing the Hittite treaties with the covenantal passages of the Pentateuch, it is inappropriate to validate only perfect matches between the structure of a biblical passage and that of some supposedly "standard form" of Hittite treaty. As noted, the Hittite treaties have a flexible form, and draw from a template of commonalities. The biblical covenant passages, in like fashion, may well have been drawn from a broad template of commonalities, and varied the employment of formal elements as dictated by the theological agenda of the passage.[48]

I will delineate the elements typically found in the Hittite suzerainty treaty, and demonstrate how the various pentateuchal accounts of the Sinai covenant adopt and rework these elements, but generally hew to this pattern.[49] While some scholars propose a more elaborate scheme of parallels, I shall focus here on five: (1) the historical prologue; (2) the stipulations enjoined on the subordinate; (3) the deposit of the treaty within the Temple; (4) the calling of witnesses to the treaty; and (5) the issuance of blessings for adherence to the treaty and of curses on its breach.

## Historical Prologue

Almost universally, the Late Bronze Age suzerainty treaty opened with a historical prologue in which the events that led up to the establishment of the treaty are delineated. This section, often very long, is designed to show the basis on which the subordinate king has submitted to the subjugation of the sovereign. It is critical here to note the variety of circumstances we encounter in these prologues. Of the Hittite suzerainty treaties known to us, only a single one documents a situation whereby the subordinate king was forcibly subjugated by the sovereign.[50] Instead, these treaties document the subordinate king entering into subordination to the sovereign through a consensual arrangement. These treaties fall into two broad categories. In one, the subordinate king is installed by the suzerain as the ruler of territories that have already come into his domain, and the treaty outlines the terms of the subordinate's rule in deference to the Hittite king. In the second, which may be termed self-subjugation treaties, autonomous rulers approach the Hittite king and request his patronage or deliverance in exchange for their fealty as subordinates.[51] A single underlying principle determines the argument of these historical prologues: moral and legal obligation on the part of the subordinate in return for the favor bestowed on him by the sovereign.[52] Universally in these treaties, we find that the Hittite king acts first on behalf of the subordinate and is then later repaid through the fealty the subordinate owes according to the terms of the suzerainty treaty. The nature of the favor bestowed varies in the self-subjugation treaties. In the prologue of one treaty, we find an account of how the subordinate, the king of Ugarit, begged the Hittite king to save him from rival kingdoms, offering in return his gratitude and loyalty in the expression of a treaty of subordination.[53] In another treaty, the Hittite king lists his gracious deeds on behalf of the subordinate land of Mitanni, and includes among them a claim to have delivered that land from famine.[54] In some of the treaties, it emerges that the sovereign gave his sister to the subordinate in order to cement the amicable relationship of gratitude through royal marriage.[55]

We cannot know the historical veracity of the events depicted in these prologues, and one could argue that they are subject to deep suspicion, as these are texts produced by the Hittite court and in service of it. Yet even if this is true, the discourse itself is telling of the political ethos. Apparently the Hittite kings of the fifteenth to thirteenth centuries B.C.E. felt that their claims to suzerainty could be deemed legitimate only if power was exercised on a moral or legal basis. Put differently, the moral and legal obligation of fealty on the subordinate's part was the basis on which a sovereign could lay claim to suzerainty, and only when the subordinate had submitted to the terms of the treaty of his own volition. It is worth repeating that beyond the actual stipulations enjoined on the subordinate, the historical prologue emerges as the most ubiquitous element common to the various Hittite suzerainty treaties. Their use of history as a source to chronicle the beneficence of the sovereign as a basis for gratitude and loyalty on the part of the subordinate is nearly unique to this corpora of ancient Near Eastern treaty texts. The dominant concept that underlies the Late Bronze Hittite treaties and, indeed, sets them apart from eighth- and seventh-century Neo-Assyrian ones is that they nearly universally underscore the loyalty due to the sovereign on account of the beneficence he has already bestowed on the subordinate.[56]

This brings us to the parallel Sinai narratives. The fact that the Sinai covenant of Exodus is preceded by the exodus narrative represents, broadly speaking, a use of history to document the beneficence of the sovereign toward the subordinate that is similar to that found in the Hittite suzerainty treaties. It is more instructive, however, to observe that the historical prologues of the Hittite political treaties typically begin with the formula "The words of [name of the Hittite king]," followed by a delineation of the favor bestowed on the subordinate that has resulted in his present expression of gratitude through subordination. The Decalogue itself also reveals such an introduction. Before the delineation of the laws themselves, we find the following introduction

(Exod 20:1–2): "God spoke all these words, saying: 'I the Lord am your God who brought you out of the land of Egypt, the house of bondage.'" Notice the moral or legal basis on which God enjoins the children of Israel. He identifies himself not as the God who created heaven and earth but as the God who bestowed a great favor on the "kingdom" of Israel, and is thus deserving of their subordinate loyalty. Note that the phrase "I the Lord am your God who brought you out of the land of Egypt, the house of bondage" is surely tautological, after 19 chapters of exodus and delivery that clearly delineate that this is so. At this juncture in time, however, God is entering into "treaty" with the Israelites, and hence the formal need within the written contract for the grace of the sovereign to be documented.[57]

As noted, the self-subjugation treaties usually indicate that the relationship between the two kings is initiated by the subordinate king, appealing to the sovereign king for assistance. This pattern appears in the narrative of the early chapters of Exodus. The process of divine salvation begins only after the Children of Israel cry out (Exod 2:23). Scripture then notes that God indeed hears their cry (2:24–25), a detail God repeatedly underscores as he tells Moses of his intention to deliver them from bondage (3:7, 9).

## Stipulations Enjoined on the Subordinate

Following the historical prologue, the Hittite suzerainty treaties typically enumerate the stipulations imposed on the subordinate by the sovereign that were to be the expressions of his loyalty. These would commonly revolve around security arrangements: delineation of borders, repressing acts of sedition, capture and extradition of escaped fugitives, and the like. What is particularly important about these stipulations is the terminology they employ, and how these terms are carried over into the Sinai narratives as paradigms for the relationship between God and Israel. In the first place, many of the treaties restrict the political activity of the subordinate king. He may enter alliance only with the sovereign. One Hittite treaty warns the vassal of punishment: "if you [do not seek] the well being [of Hatti and] the hand of [the Great King of Hatti], but (rather) you seek the well-being of another ... thereby you will break the oath."[58]

Such clauses add new dimensions to readily familiar biblical passages. The opening stipulation of the Decalogue, "You shall have no other gods beside Me," is readily understood by a contemporary reader from an epistemological perspective: the Lord God who took the Children of Israel out of Egypt is the only true god, and hence the need to underscore the falsehood of placing stock in any other god. Yet the command takes on a different light when seen in the context of ancient Near Eastern treaty formulations. God is the sovereign, Israel the subordinate. To revere another god is to violate a relationship; it is to express implicit ingratitude in light of the favor and grace bestowed on Israel the subordinate by God the sovereign, as laid down in the "historical prologue" of the Decalogue, indeed, as laid out in the entire narrative of the book of Exodus to that point.[59] For the subordinate king to establish treaties or other ties with another power would be tantamount to treason.[60]

The demand for exclusive fealty underlies the phrase in the Decalogue that pronounces God to be a "jealous god" (Exod 20:5).[61] With the exception of the short-lived Aten revolution in Egypt, no other Near Eastern religion had posited the notion of a god who demanded exclusive loyalty.[62]

The terminology of the treaties and of the dynamics that governed the relationship between the partners is especially illuminative of several biblical passages. What does it mean to "love God," as Deuteronomy mandates (Deut 6:5; 11:13)? Medieval thinkers such as Maimonides understood that one was required to yearn for God even as a man yearns for a woman who is beyond his attainability.[63] The term "love" (root '-h-b), however, plays an important role in the language of ancient Near Eastern political treaties. To love, in the political terms of the ancient Near East, is to demonstrate loyalty. In the El Amarna letters (fourteenth century B.C.E.), the King of Byblos (in Phoenicia, present-day Lebanon) writes to the Pharaoh about the rebellion in his own city: "Behold the city! Half of it loves the sons of 'Abd-Asir-ta [who fostered the rebellion]; half of it (loves) my lord."[64] In another letter, a vassal king writes to Pharaoh, "My lord, just as I love the king my lord, so do the [the other kings]."[65] Turning to the Bible, we see the same sense of the word. According to 1 Kings 5:15, Hiram, king of Tyre, sent representatives to confirm covenant relations with the newly anointed Solomon, "for Hiram had always been a lover of David," that is, had always been loyal to him in covenant. To love God, then, may be understood not as an emotional or numinous disposition but simply as a noble command for steadfast loyalty. The converse is seen as well: ancient Near Eastern treaties speak of breach of covenant as an act of hate.[66]

Love and hate in the Decalogue bear these precise meanings, as in the references to those who "hate Me" (Exod 20:5) and those who "love Me" (Exod 20:6). Those who are said to love God are not necessarily those who reach an ecstatic and numinous experience of God's presence. To love God is simply to demonstrate fealty to Him through steadfast performance of His commandments. To violate those commandments is to breach the terms of the treaty or, in other words, to display disloyalty, here called "hate."

The terminology of suzerainty relations in the second millennium B.C.E. may also illuminate a very charged theological concept in the Bible, the notion of Israel as a chosen people. The biblical term used in reference to Israel as "chosen" is *sègullâ* (Exod 19:5).[67] In a Ugaritic document, a favored vassal of the king of Ugarit is called the *sglt* of his sovereign. Importantly, the term implies both subordination and distinction.[68] Indeed, this tension between distinction and subordination seems to be implicit in the first biblical reference to "chosenness." It is in the opening verses of the covenant narrative of Exodus 19: "Now, then, if you will obey me faithfully and keep My covenant, you shall be My treasured possession [*sègullâ* ] among all the peoples, for all the earth is mine" (19:5). Entering into covenant renders Israel a subordinate. But Israel is promised favored status among God's subordinates, when faithful to the terms of the subordination treaty.

Many of the Hittite subordination treaties also delineate the responsibilities of the sovereign toward the subordinate: protection against invasion; a pledge to honor the heir of the subordinate king; cementing the alliance through royal marriage; the grant of land; a pledge to support the subordinate king even if his own people request his deposal.[69] Typically, the sovereign pledges to furnish the subordinate with sustenance. Mutual affective and supportive gestures are often an integral part of these political treaties.[70] In like fashion, the Sinai narratives are explicit about God's responsibilities as sovereign to protect Israel the subordinate (e.g. Exod 20:7, 12; 23:20–33; Deut 6:10–11).

Even as the stipulations of the Sinai covenant may be seen to conform with the general form of Late Bronze Age subordination treaties, we may still observe the way this convention is not merely copied, but indeed is reworked in accordance with the theological agenda of the Sinai narratives. Within the Hittite treaties, the stipulations enjoined on the subordinate all relate to actions that directly serve the interests of the sovereign king. In the Sinai narratives, as we have seen, we indeed find prohibitions against serving foreign gods (Exod 20:3–4), resting on the Sabbath as a recognition of God's sovereignty in the world (Exod 20:8–11), and cultic obligations (Exod 20:21–23; 23:18–19), all of which could be said to reflect God's "personal interests." Nonetheless, we see that the scope of the stipulations enjoined on the "subordinate" (Israel) is greatly expanded. The second half of the Decalogue (Exod 20:13–14) and the better part of Exodus 21–23 address civil affairs of public welfare and justice, underscoring that the covenant is meant to usher in not only a religious order but a social one as well.

### Deposit of the Treaty in the Temple

The next typical element of the Hittite suzerainty treaty is a clause calling for a copy of the treaty to be deposited within the temple of the subordinate's deity, to demonstrate and affirm that the local deity of the subordinate is interested in the fulfillment of its terms. It also sends an implicit message to the inhabitants of the subordinate state that the treaty is now to occupy a central place within their value system. The same trope, again transformed mutatis mutandis to accord with the new theological agenda, appears in the Bible as well. The text of the treaty—or at least a part of it, the Tablets of Testimony—is deposited within the Ark of the Covenant within the Holy of Holies (Exod 25:21; 40:20; see Deut 31:26). In this fashion, Israel the subordinate symbolically recognizes the important place of the treaty within its own value system.[71] In the logic of the Hittite treaty, of course, the deposit of the tablets in the temple of the subordinate king's own god was a public display that that god attested to the binding nature of the treaty. Within the Sinai narrative, the god of the subordinate king is none other than the sovereign king, the Almighty.

If the tablet bearing the copy of the treaty was lost or stolen, it had to be replaced. In this vein, one Hittite king remarked to his subordinate, Talmi-Sharrumma of Aleppo—referring to him in the third person—"My father... made a treaty tablet for Talmi-Sharrumma, King of Aleppo, but the tablet has been stolen. I, the Great King, have written another tablet [for him], have sealed it with my seal, and have given it to him."[72] The apparent need for a replacement copy of a treaty tablet is well attested in the pentateuchal sources as well. The breaking of the Tablets of the Covenant by Moses necessitates the drafting of a new set of tablets (Exod 34:1–4). Whereas the Hittite king grants the treaty tablet royal legitimation by sealing it with his seal, the Tablets of the Covenant are consecrated by the fact that they are inscribed by God (Exod 32:15–16; 34:1, 28; Deut 10:1–4).

Expanding our focus from the Sinai narratives of Exodus to the structure of Deuteronomy, we may see the treaty elements I have identified, as well as others that are best represented in that book. Deuteronomy opens with a pedagogic history (Deut 1:1–3:29), followed by an expanded section containing a call for loyalty and extensive stipulations (Deut 4:1–26:19), and the recording of the covenant in written form (Deut 27:1–8; 31:24–26). There were, however, two other typical elements of the Hittite treaty form—always at the end—that come into play in the final chapters of Deuteronomy: *witnesses to the treaty* and *blessings and curses.*[73]

### Witnesses to the Treaty

Ancient Near Eastern suzerainty treaties typically included a long list of divine witnesses who were called on to enforce the treaty and to punish the subordinate in the event of violation. These were often gods of the natural world, and in the Late Bronze Age Hittite treaties, elements of the natural world itself were invoked, for example the skies, the earth, mountains, or rivers. Thus one representative text:

> The mountains, the rivers, the springs, the great sea, heaven and earth, the winds and the clouds. They shall be witnesses to this treaty and this oath. All the words of the treaty and oath which are written on this tablet—if Tette does not observe these words of the treaty and oath, but transgresses the oath, then these oath gods shall destroy Tette.[74]

The trope is again transformed, mutatis mutandis, in the biblical context. It would be incongruous, of course, for the Bible to call on other gods to bear witness to the treaty between God and Israel. Instead, we find the vestige of the earlier Near Eastern trope: it is not God who attests to Israel's commitment but the natural elements of heaven and the earth who are appointed by him to serve in this capacity (Deut 4:26, 30:19; 32:1; Isa 1:2; see Mic 6:1–2 with regard to mountains).[75] In the Sinai narratives of Exodus as well, the tablets are described as symbolic proof or public testimony of the covenant between man and God. The tablets are called simply "the testimony" (hā'ēdūt), and the Ark is referred to as the "Ark of the Testimony" (arōn hā'ēdūt; e.g., Exod 25:16, 25:21, 26:33–34).

*Blessings and Curses*

Finally, the Late Bronze Age treaties concluded with blessings that the gods would bestow on the subordinate in exchange for his loyalty and, conversely, curses that would befall him in the event of violation of the terms of the treaty. These were usually juxtaposed, and located at the end of the treaty, as here:

> If you...do not observe the words of this treaty, the gods...shall destroy you...they will draw you out like malt from its husk. As one does not get a plant from the midst of [tablet broken]...so you, together with any other wife whom you might take....And these gods...shall allot you poverty and destitution....Your name and your progeny...shall be eradicated from the earth. The ground shall be ice, so that you will slip. The ground of your land shall be a marsh of [tablet broken]...so that you will certainly sink and be unable to cross.
>
> If you observe this treaty and oath, these gods shall protect you... together with your wife...her sons and grandsons....And the land

of Mitanni shall...prosper and expand. And you...the Hurrians shall accept you for kingship for eternity.[76]

The curse/blessing trope appears in the Decalogue (Exod 20:5–6):

You shall not prostrate yourself to them nor worship them, for I am the Lord your God—a jealous God, who visits the sin of the fathers upon children to the third and fourth generations for my enemies. But who shows kindness for thousands [of generations] to those who love Me and observe My commandments.

Both in Leviticus 26 and Deuteronomy 28, similar conventions are employed. A series of blessings of prosperity and bounty open with the phrase "If you heed...then..." (Lev 26:3; Deut 28:1), followed by a longer, more elaborate series of curses, which likewise opens with the phrase "if you do not heed...then..." (Lev 26:14; Deut 28:15).[77]

I have focused thus far on covenantal passages in the Pentateuch. Yet much the same pattern emerges in Joshua 24, which tells of the covenant ceremony Joshua enacted in the name of God with the Israelites at the close of his career. The Hittite treaties reveal that an occasion to renew or reaffirm the treaty would arise when a new sovereign monarch or new subordinate monarch assumed the throne. With the generation of the Sinai covenant now departed, Joshua seeks to renew the covenant with Israel as it takes possession of the land. The renewal of the covenant opens with a historical prologue detailing the acts of favor that God had bestowed on Israel across the generations (Josh 24:1–13). The chapter continues by stating the commitments of loyalty and exclusive devotion that Israel is called on to ratify (Josh 24:14, 19, 23). The treaty is written down for posterity (Josh 24:26), and witnesses are called to testify to the commitment. In the place of divine witnesses, the people themselves are called as witnesses (Josh 24:23), as is a great stone monument erected in the shrine there (Josh 24:26). Joshua warns of a curse that will befall the people in the event of disobedience (Josh 24:20).[78]

The theological implications of all this are far-reaching. First of all, to summarize my element-by-element comparison between the Late Bronze Age suzerainty treaty and the covenantal narratives in the Bible, the notion of a "historical prologue" that precedes the actual covenant itself suggests that the relationship between God and man in the Bible is founded on gratitude and moral obligation for the salvation that He granted, and not merely as a function of His power over man. By invoking the language of "love," "hate," and "jealousy," these passages educate toward seeing God not just as a power but as a personality. And like the Hittite self-subjugation treaties, the pentateuchal covenant passages underscore the subordinate Israel's readiness to accede to the suzerainty treaty (Exod 19:8; 24:3; 24:7; Deut 5:24; see Josh 24:16–18).

But perhaps the greatest implication of casting the covenant between God and Israel in terms of the Late Bronze Age suzerainty treaty is the relative pedestal on which it places the human agent here, Israel. This implication has been dramatized by studies of the anthropology of honor as applied to treaty making in the ancient Near East. Consider the following relationships: a child in relation to his parent, the young in relation to the elderly, a slave in relation to his master, a subject in relation to his sovereign. These pairings are all social contexts in which persons of inferior status interact with those of superior status. Moreover, they are all relationships where there is a bestowal of honor, and it is bestowed unilaterally by the inferior figure to the superior one.[79]

In his study of honor and shame in ancient Near Eastern covenant relations, Saul Olyan has shown that whereas the master owes no honor to his servant, inscriptions from Mari and the Amarna archives reveal that honor is a commodity bestowed in both directions between sovereign and subordinate in political treaty making.[80] In this vein, we find in the El Amarna correspondence a letter to Pharaoh from one vassal complaining that he has received less honor from Pharaoh than has another vassal.[81] In one of the Hittite self-subjugation treaties, a subordinate king named Sunashshura of Kizzuwatna is mandated to appear at regular intervals in the court of the Hittite sovereign. The treaty reads, "Sunashshura must come before his majesty and look on the face of his majesty. As soon as he comes before his majesty, the noblemen of his majesty [will rise] from their seats. No one will remain seated above him."[82]

The visit of this Sunashshura to the Hittite court is hardly made in shame and debasement. He is received amicably and with distinction; the Hittite king's nobles must rise in his honor. There are indicators in the Hittite self-subjugation treaties, moreover, that even as the subordinate submitted to the sovereign, he still remained autonomous in relation to the kingdom of the sovereign. Nowhere in these treaties do we see that a sovereign could impose an heir after the death or abdication of a subordinate king or could ever rightfully annex a subordinate's territory, even in the event of the treaty being violated.[83]

In the ancient Near East, a variety of metaphors was typically invoked through which to articulate the human-divine encounter: metaphors of child encountering parent, of slave encountering master, and of subject encountering king. Common to all of these is that they are all relationships in which honor is bestowed unilaterally from inferior to superior. Indeed, each of these paradigms describes the disposition of man toward God in the Bible as well. Yet alongside these, I would claim, following Olyan, that the Bible sought complementary paradigms through which to articulate the human-divine encounter in a radically new way. It sought out the metaphor of Late Bronze Age treaty making, for in it honor was a commodity reciprocally bestowed between sovereign and subordinate. The implications are that within the biblical notion of covenant, God honors man even as man honors God.

## Who Is the "Subordinate King" of the Covenant?

One aspect of the parallel between the biblical covenant between God and Israel and Late Bronze Age political treaties has garnered, I submit, insufficient attention. To appreciate it, we need once again to turn to an analysis of the political treaties. The vast majority of the Late Bronze Age Hittite suzerainty treaties are unambiguously constructed as agreements between two *individuals*—the sovereign king—the king of the Hittites—and the subordinate king.[84] As the preamble of one of the treaties reads concerning the two monarchs, "They swore an oath to one another and concluded this treaty with one another."[85] To be sure, there are instances in these treaties in which the subordinate king is referred to metonymically. When the treaties routinely call on the subordinate king to return escaped fugitives to the land of the sovereign, the expectation is surely not that the subordinate king should personally apprehend the escapee or personally deliver him to the authorities of the sovereign. As a rule, the historical prologues attend to the interpersonal relationship between the two kings, and the blessings and curses likewise attend in pointed fashion to the person of the subordinate king, with virtually no attention to his subjects. The notion that the Hittite subordination treaty is between two kings and not between two peoples is well evidenced in two treaties in which the Hittite king states that in the event that the subjects of the subordinate king seek his deposal, the sovereign will remain loyal to him, against the wishes of the subordinate's people.[86]

Of the eighteen suzerainty treaties whose texts we have, only a single one is between a Hittite king as sovereign and an entire people, with no mention of a king.[87] The form of this treaty differs in significant ways from the treaties made with subordinate kings. This treaty has no historical prologue and no section delineating the blessings that will accrue to the subordinate for compliance. As noted, both Exodus and Deuteronomy contain narratives outlining the beneficence of the "sovereign king"—God—toward Israel. Put differently, the Sinai narratives resemble the form of the Late Bronze Age Hittite suzerainty treaty made with a subordinate king and not a subordinate people.

Within the biblical analogue, it is clear that the role of the sovereign is played by God. Who plays the role of the subordinate king? In the Pentateuch, it is true that the Israelites have a leader: Moses. Yet Moses may not be properly termed a king. He is never referred to by this term; his children are not his heirs. Moreover, nothing in the language of the covenant narratives suggests that it is Moses who is the vassal king and Israel his subjects. The covenant is never cast as a treaty between God and Moses. Rather, the implication of these passages is that God is forming this treaty, or covenant, with the people. It may be that in doing so, the Bible is conceptualizing a treaty between a sovereign (God) and a foreign people (Israel) and omitting the position of the subordinate king from the metaphor. In the next part of the discussion, I will suggest that this is decidedly not the case. The covenant narratives hew much more closely to the form of the political treaty between two individual monarchs than to the lone instance of a treaty between the Hittite king and a foreign people with no monarch at their helm.[88]

One is tempted to posit that the role of the subordinate king is played here by the corporate body of the people of Israel as a whole. Yet this is problematic, because within the Sinai covenant itself, God relates to individual Israelites. The nature of each and every one of the commandments of the Decalogue is such that it can be fulfilled, or transgressed, by an individual. Conversely, none of the commandments of the Decalogue requires a collective effort, as would be necessary to build a sanctuary, anoint a king, or engage in military conquest. Moreover, within the Decalogue, God distinguishes and differentiates between those who adhere to His covenant, and those who do not. He pledges to visit the guilt of fathers unto the third and fourth generations of those who "hate" Him, while showing kindness unto the thousandth generation of those who "love" Him (Exod 20:5–6). When God, as the sovereign, bestows honor, He does so selectively, and not only collectively. In 1 Sam 2:30, God says "those who honor me, I will honor, and as for those who despise me, they will be diminished, or dishonored.[89] This should not be taken to imply that God does not at all relate to Israel as a corporate body. Rather, it shows that the picture is a complex one, in which individuals are not automatically at all times subsumed within the identity of the collective.

Thus we may posit that to some degree, the subordinate king with whom God forms a political treaty is, in fact, the common man of Israel; that every man in Israel is to view himself as having the status of a king conferred on him—a subordinate king who serves under the protection of, and in gratitude to, a divine sovereign.

The proof of this may be seen in striking parallels between the stipulations and language used in the Hittite treaties regarding the subordinate king and the biblical laws and commandments that bind each and every common man of Israel. Several of the treaties mandate that as a show of fealty, the subordinate king must make regular appearances before the sovereign. The language here is instructive. Recall that in the aforementioned treaty that mandates the vassal Sunashshura's personal visit with the sovereign, it is a state visit replete with honor, as the Hittite king's nobles must rise in his presence.[90] Note also that the passage refers to the visitation as an act of "looking on the face of His Majesty"—a term used throughout the Bible to refer to a court appearance (e.g. Gen 43:3, 5, 23; Exod 10:28–29; 2 Sam 3:13, 14:32).

We find similar language in the stipulations of the covenant narrative of Exodus 19–24. In Exodus 23:17, the commandment of pilgrimage to the central shrine states, "three times a year, all of your males shall be seen by the face of *the Lord*—YHWH."[91] Nearly ubiquitous throughout the Bible is the notion that God may not be seen by mortals. Were they actually to behold God, they would die, as God explains to Moses, when Moses requests to see the face of God (Exod 33:20): "And God responded, you may not see my face, for no man may see me and live." Thus, it is highly incongruous to suppose that what was forbidden even once to Moses is in fact mandated for every male of Israel for generations. Moreover, the epithet "the Lord" (Heb. *hā-'adōn*), while attested elsewhere, is not commonplace in the Bible as a reference to YHWH. Yet when seen in the context of the Hittite suzerainty treaties, the meaning is clarified. The command that each Israelite male embark on pilgrimage is patterned after the requirement that a subordinate king visit the court of his sovereign, to see the face of his lord (master), that is, God. What is most instructive here is the fact that this is enjoined on all adult males. In the Hittite political treaties, of course, only the subordinate king is called on to visit the sovereign. Indeed, it would be beneath the dignity of the sovereign to receive all of the commoners subject to the subordinate king. Thus, the treaty imagery in the Bible does not bypass the subordinate king; the common man of Israel himself takes on aspects of a subordinate king. He is the one addressed by the covenant; he is the one on whom God has bestowed favor, and it is he who is enjoined to pay a fealty visit to the "court" of the divine sovereign.

We may see how the common man of Israel takes on aspects of the subordinate king of the Hittite political treaties with regard to treaty stipulations that mandate the periodic reading of the treaty within the subordinate king's court. In one treaty, forged with one Kupanta-Kurunta of Mira-Kuwaliya, the Hittite king states, "[This tablet which] I have made [for you, Kupanta-Kurunta], shall be read out [before you three times yearly]."[92] In another treaty, this time with a subordinate by the name of Alaksandu of Wilusa, the Hittite king states, "Furthermore, this tablet which I have made for you, Alaksandu, shall be read out before you three times yearly, and you, Alaksandu, shall know it."[93] Once again, we see a parallel stipulation in the Bible, but one that is extended to include all members of the children of Israel. In the Late Bronze Age suzerainty treaty, it is the subordinate king who is ultimately responsible to execute and follow the terms of the treaty, and thus he personally must be read its provisions. But the covenant between God and Israel is consecrated with each and every member of the polity, and thus each and every member must hear it read, because each and every member is responsible for its faithful implementation. In fact, "treaties," or the terms of the covenant between God and Israel, are read out before the whole people on a number of occasions. The first of these is at Sinai (Exod 24:3–4, 7–8):

> Moses went and repeated to the people all the commands of the Lord and all the rules; and all the people answered with one voice saying, "All the things that the Lord has commanded we will do!" Moses then wrote down all the commands of the Lord....Then [Moses] took the record of the covenant and read it aloud to the people. And they said, "All that the Lord has spoken, we will faithfully do!" Moses took the blood and dashed it on the people and said, "this is the blood of the covenant that the Lord now makes with you concerning all these commands."

The covenant is similarly read out to the entire people by Joshua at Shechem (Josh 8:30–35) and by Josiah during his reform (2 Kgs 23:2–3). The public readings of the laws in these instances are reported as one-time events. Yet a similar requirement is rooted in deuteronomic law as well (31:10–13):

> Every seventh year, the year set for remission, at the Feast of Booths, when all Israel comes to be seen by the face of YHWH your God in the place that he will choose, you shall read this Teaching aloud in the presence of all Israel. Gather the people—men, women and children, and the strangers in your communities—that they may hear and so learn to revere the Lord your God and to observe faithfully every word of this teaching. Their children too, who had not known, shall hear and learn to revere the Lord your God.

Many aspects of the covenant are enjoined only on the polity as a whole, for example, the command to erect a sanctuary (Exod 25:8). And intermediaries, such as Moses and the priesthood, still function in the mediation between the common man and the Almighty. Nonetheless, the parallels drawn here enable us to conclude that the common man of Israel was endowed by covenant theology with elements of the role of the subordinate king of the Late Bronze Age suzerainty treaties.

## Israel as the Spouse of God

The position I have been advancing is that in employing the structure of the Hittite political treaty, the biblical texts invoke a paradigm in which honor was a value reciprocally bestowed by each party, in contrast with the neighboring cultures of the ancient Near East that saw man in relation to the divine in various paradigms in which honor is bestowed unilaterally by inferior to superior. Biblical writings, however, invoke an additional paradigm from day-to-day affairs in which honor is reciprocally bestowed as a model for the encounter between God and Israel: the paradigm of marriage.[94] We need only look back at what we have seen thus far to understand how utterly transformative this is. In Mesopotamia, Ugarit, and Egypt, humankind was perceived as the servants of the kings. And in the human realm, the common man—a member of the dominated tribute-bearing class—was himself a subject, a servant, of the king and his extended dominant tribute-imposing class. To be sure, in these cultures, the gods were routinely seen to have spouses or consorts. Yet these were universally divine spouses—goddesses—thus forming an analogy between the cosmic family and the ruling family of the king. For these cultures to conceive of the marriage between a god and a human, or group of humans, would have been as unthinkable as for us to imagine the marital union of a human and a cat. Yet we find the marriage metaphor invoked time and again in the prophecies of Hosea, Isaiah, Jeremiah, and Ezekiel.[95] One of the most vivid and detailed uses of this metaphor is found in Ezekiel 16:4–14:

> (4) As for your birth, when you were born your navel cord was not
> cut, and you were not bathed in water…nor were you swaddled.
> (5) No one pitied you enough to do any one of these things for you
> out of compassion for you; on the day you were born, you were left
> lying, rejected, in the open field.…(7) I let you grow like the plants
> of the field; and you continued to grow up until you attained to
> womanhood, until your breasts became firm and your hair sprouted.
> You were still naked and bare (8) when I passed by you and saw that
> your time for love had arrived. So I spread My robe over you and
> covered your nakedness, and I entered into a covenant with you by
> oath—declares the Lord God; thus you became Mine. (9) I bathed
> you in water and washed the blood off you and anointed you with oil.

(10) I clothed you with embroidered garments.... (11) I decked you out in finery.... (13) You grew more and more beautiful and became fit for royalty. Your beauty won you fame among the nations, for it was perfected through the splendor which I set upon you—declares the Lord God.

The image is not an alternative to the metaphor of the political treaty but shares affinity with it. Marriage here (v. 8) refers to the Sinai covenant, according to one understanding of the parable, and indeed is here called a covenant as well. God's statement "I entered into a covenant with you by oath...thus you became Mine" (*va-tehiyî lî*) also parallels the language of the Sinai narrative "You shall be for me [*veheyîtem lî*] a treasured possession" (Exod 19:5) and "You shall be for me [*tihĕyû-lî*] a kingdom of priests and a holy nation" (Exod 19:6).[96] Indeed, the language invoked by God in his promise to deliver the Israelites from bondage and to bring them into the land of Israel (Exod 6:6–8) is suggestive of the marriage paradigm. Phrases such as "I shall take you," "I shall be for you," "I shall bring you into" are all laden with legal language that connotes marriage both in the Bible and elsewhere in the ancient Near East.[97]

Earlier we saw that terms in the Decalogue such as "those I love" (Exod 20:6) or the description of God as "jealous" (Exod 20:5) were understood as political terms, against the backdrop of the terminology of the suzerainty treaties. To "love" another was to be faithful to him, in response to his having held up his side of the agreement. Loyalty to a sovereign implicitly meant to the exclusion of treaties with other powers. Now we see that these terms may also be understood as expressions of the marriage paradigm for the God-Israel relationship.[98]

Just as the sovereign could bestow honor on a subordinate king within the sociodynamics of the Late Bronze Age political treaty, so, too, we may make a claim that in marriage, a husband bestows honor on his wife. In the passage cited earlier from Ezekiel 16, the prophet described the way God, the husband, had honored the young wife, Israel: "Your beauty won you fame among the nations, for it was perfected through the splendor [*hadar*] which I set upon you—declares the Lord God."[99] The verb form *hdr* is a synonym for the verb form of *kbd*, and is used in the command to pay honor to elders.[100] The paradigm of the political treaty as the basis for the covenant between God and Israel allowed me to suggest that the treaty God makes is with each and every member of the Israelite collective, endowing him to some degree with the status of a subordinate king. The marriage paradigm allows no such individuation. Nowhere do we find prophets who speak of God's marriage with individuals. Instead, it would seem that the "marriage" they speak of is solely with the collective Israel. The metaphor nonetheless holds implications for the metaphysical standing of the common man—indeed, for all members of the people of Israel. For all are engaged in a collective relationship with the Almighty in which honor is bestowed and is received.

As Yohanan Muffs has put it, the new idea in the Bible is not the idea of a single God—a notion that apparently had existed in Egypt in the fourteenth century B.C.E—but the idea of God as a personality who seeks a relationship of mutuality with human agents. In the neighboring cultures of the ancient Near East, man was merely a servant of kings. In the Bible, he is transformed into a servant king in relation to a beneficent sovereign, a wife in relation to her benefactor-husband. God seeks from Israel "love," in both the political sense of loyalty between parties to a treaty and in the sense of a faithful, intimate relationship between man and wife.[101]

The degree to which the Bible envisions an intimate relationship between the individual Israelite and the Almighty is distinct in the ancient Near East. To be sure, common people in all the other ancient Near East cultures engaged in personal, or "family," religion: a rich web of symbols, beliefs, and practices through which devotion was expressed to local patron and ancestral gods.[102] Yet religion of a national scale was one from which the common man was generally excluded. Religious laws for the masses are sparse within Hittite legal codes, and are entirely absent from Mesopotamian ones. The common man in these cultures had only a small role to play in the public worship of the deity, which was relegated entirely to the king and the priests. By contrast, God's interest in each and every member of the Israelite polity is expressed in the Sinai narrative of Exodus 19, which refers to the Israelites as a "kingdom of priests" (Exod 19:6).[103] The entire polity is called on to behave in priest-like fashion, and indeed, we find in the Bible parallels between laws that are specifically enjoined on the priestly class and analogous laws for the common man of Israel. Priestly proscriptions against cutting the hair at the corners of the head (Lev 21:4–5) as signs of mourning are matched with similar injunctions for the common Israelite as well (Lev 19:27–28).[104] The laws of holiness enjoined on each member of Israel concerning the consumption of meat (Exod 22:30; Deut 14:21) are similar to those elsewhere especially prescribed for the priests (Lev 22:8; Ezek 44:31). In Egypt, circumcision was a distinctive and obligatory mark of priesthood.[105] For the "kingdom of priests," the obligation throughout Israel is universal.

## Whose Interests Are Served by Covenant?

I have mentioned Peter Berger's claim that ancient religions could only be properly understood by asking the question cui bono—whose advantage is served by the cosmic beliefs the culture maintains? I have shown how the power structures and social hierarchy that governed other ancient Near Eastern cultures received legitimation through carefully systematized conceptualizations of the divine realm. Regarding Israel, when we employ the hermeneutics of suspicion and apply the test of cui bono to the biblical paradigms of the political treaty and marriage, what conclusions may we draw—who were the figures of biblical Israel who benefited from such metaphysical beliefs?[106] Was it the Israelite king? Covenant, it would seem, leaves the king out of the picture—the covenant was between God and the people of Israel. One can deliberate whether the covenant was with Israel as a corporate entity or also, as I have suggested, with each member of the polity. However, in the texts of Exodus, Deuteronomy, and Joshua that we saw it is untenable to claim that the Israelite king represents the subordinate party to the treaty. In each of these texts, the covenant is clearly conceived to be between God as the sovereign and the people as the subordinate.[107]

Nor, it would seem, did the notion of covenant serve to bolster other power interests such as the merchants or the gentry. Virtually the only mention of these groups in the Pentateuch is in terms of their responsibilities to the poor. One finds an emphasis on the priestly class in Leviticus, to be sure, but not at all in the covenant texts of, say, Exodus 19–24 or Joshua 24 or in the book of Deuteronomy, where priests are denied land ownership and share their status within the cult with the Levites.[108] It might be suggested that it was the prophets who stood to gain. Yet the references to groups of prophets in the Pentateuch are scant (see Num 11:23–29), and the criteria set out in Deuteronomy for validating an individual as a prophet are exacting in the extreme (Deut 18:15–22). Nor, as some have suggested, can the paradigm of covenant be said to represent the best interests of the state overall.[109] The systems I described in Mesopotamia, Ugarit, and Egypt may be said to represent state ideologies, in which the well-being of the state stood at the center of the gods' interests. By contrast, in the political treaty and marriage paradigms, it is hardly the greater glory of Israel that is cardinal to God's concerns. What is cardinal to God's concerns is the upholding of the political-marital relationship with which He engages Israel. When Israel is a faithful covenantal partner, God is only too pleased to ensure the welfare of the Israelite state. But conversely, when the covenant has been breached, God has no compunction about orchestrating the downfall of that state. Indeed, it must be admitted, that no immediate candidate jumps out of the pages of the Pentateuch as the interested party in the formulation of these new paradigms for the God-human encounter.[110]

The covenant and marriage paradigms, however, tell us much about the metaphysical standing of the common man within biblical thought, and the cosmic foundations of an egalitarian order. I opened this study by positing that from antiquity until the Renaissance, social and political orders were constructed and construed as serving some higher cosmic order, and not merely the protection of individuals. To understand how the Bible reformulated social and political thought in the ancient Near East, I claimed, we would need to engage in a comparative exploration of the structures of these societies as portrayed in the texts available to us and of how each was founded on metaphysical legitimation. Taking Mesopotamia, Ugarit, and Egypt as representative cultures, I noted how the logic of correspondences between the divine order and its earthly counterpart granted cosmic legitimation to the stratification of society, and the dominance of a tribute-imposing class over a tribute-bearing class. Covenant eschews this fundamental social divide by casting all of Israel as a subordinate king.

The covenant paradigm as ideological underpinning for an egalitarian order should prompt us to consider anew the role of human kingship in biblical thought. While some passages quoted earlier, like Psalm 2, glorified the role of the Davidic king, many passages in the Bible adopt a highly equivocal stance toward the notion of a human king. This equivocalness, the conventional wisdom goes, comes from the fear that the presence of a strongly sanctioned institution of monarchy would perforce marginalize the true and divine King of Kings.[111] Yet everything I have presented in this chapter suggests that the kingship of God stood only to gain from a religiously sanctioned earthly monarchy. When we look at neighboring cultures where the earthly king parallels the divine king, or is himself in some way a member of the divine realm, both divine kingship and human kingship are strengthened, in a symbiotic relationship. The divine analogue to the earthly power structure lends credence, validity, and metaphysical stature to that power. But the converse is no less true. The overpowering dominance of the earthly king in these cultures led to a conception of the gods as all-powerful. The less known divine sphere was illuminated by the better known human sphere. Nowhere in the literature of these cultures do we find that the presence of a strong king led to an attenuation in the belief of the masses in the gods as kings of a higher and more supreme order. The writings these cultures have left us, as well as the material finds we have unearthed, demonstrate that, in spite of the presence of well-entrenched monarchies—nay, perhaps precisely because of the presence of such political systems—the gods were securely at the focus of each and every one of these societies.

If much of biblical writing reveals an ambivalent attitude toward the notion of monarchy, I would suggest it is not because of a fear of the Almighty being marginalized. Rather, these texts reflect a fear that a strong monarchy would result in the marginalizing of the common man. By articulating the metaphysical paradigms of the God-human encounter in terms of a suzerainty treaty or marriage, the biblical texts portray a relationship in which honor can be reciprocally bestowed between God and Israel; indeed, between God and the common man of Israel. Only through the sublimation of the metaphysical standing of the monarchy in Israel could the biblical texts, particularly the Pentateuch, achieve a reformulation of social and political thought along egalitarian lines—a reformulation whereby the common man was transformed from a mere servant of kings into one who stands in honor before the Almighty as nothing less than a servant king.

Thus, the theology of covenant in the Pentateuch sets the stage, metaphysically speaking, for Israel to conceive of itself as a society devoid of the inherent and cosmically legitimated hierarchy found elsewhere. The theology, in turn, drives a host of reforms in the structure of the polity, its seats of power, and its laws of governance. Various passages throughout the Pentateuch could be referenced in this regard. Yet nowhere is the blueprint for the Israelite polity and its relationship with a monarch as fully developed as it is in the book of Deuteronomy, which we will read from a constitutional perspective in the next chapter.

# 2

# Egalitarian Politics

*Constitution, Class, and the Book of Deuteronomy*

Standing before his Congregational Church parish in Hampton Falls, New Hampshire, in early June 1788, Pastor Samuel Langdon prepared to speak to the weighty issue of the day. Only two weeks remained before he would serve as a representative to that state's constitutional convention. Eight states had already ratified the Constitution. If New Hampshire followed suit, it would be formally adopted as the law of the land. Searching for a text that would buttress his ardent support of ratification, the former Harvard College president opened his Bible to Deuteronomy chapter 4 and read aloud (Deut 4:5–8):

> Behold I have taught you statutes and judgments.... Keep therefore and do them; for this is your wisdom and your understanding in the sight of all the nations which shall hear all these statutes, and say, "Surely this great nation is a wise and understanding people."... What nation is there so great that hath statutes and judgments so righteous as all this law?

The parishioners heard Langdon go on to explicate the virtue of Deuteronomy as the basis of a law-based society with curbs on the corruptive influence of power as an integral part of its system. Bringing the lessons of Deuteronomy to bear on the momentous decision facing the nation, he remarked, "If I am not mistaken, instead of the twelve tribes of Israel we may substitute the thirteen States of the American union."[1]

The claim that constitutional thought has its roots in the Book of Deuteronomy is ancient indeed. Josephus (37–100 C.E.) referred to Deuteronomy as the *politeia*—regime plan or national constitution—of the Jewish people and implicitly suggested that the idea of a constitution is first found in the Bible and not in Greco-Roman sources, as his readers would have undoubtedly believed.[2] Most discussions of Deuteronomy's constitutional elements focus on Deuteronomy 16:18–18:22, the unit that broadly describes the powers of the judiciary, the priesthood, the monarchy, and the institution of prophecy. Moreover, these discussions routinely seek the historical setting within 1–2 Samuel and 1–2 Kings that ostensibly constitute the pretext for the formulations at hand. The law of the king (Deuteronomy 17:14–20) is said to reflect the times of, variously, Samuel, Solomon, Josiah, or the Babylonian exile.[3] The Book's plan for the centralization of the cult, ostensibly reflects the time of Hezekiah, or Josiah.[4] Deuteronomy, it is said, reflects northern influence— witness its mention of Shechem, its concern for social justice and emphasis of levitical and prophetic authority over against the king. Deuteronomy reflects southern influence, it is also said—witness its concern with the ark, a single sanctuary, and the idea of election. All scholarly attempts to address Deuteronomy's social and political agenda in toto have begun with a single axiom: because the text before us is multilayered, any explanation of its politics can be explained only as the tension among competing agendas throughout the history of its evolution and redaction.

Diachronic studies of this type are endowed with their own internal cogency and coherence. In this study, I suggest a contrasting approach: that one may read the *entirety* of Deuteronomy as a statement of the Book's constitutional principles. I execute this analysis through a synchronic reading of the text in its present canonical position, following the wilderness accounts of Exodus, Leviticus, and Numbers. Whatever theories may be adduced about the prehistory of Deuteronomy's various passages, the final form of the Masoretic Text may be assessed and analyzed at this canonical position as an integral whole. By largely divorcing the analysis of Deuteronomy's politics from the accounts of the books of Samuel and Kings, we allow the final form of the text to speak from the context of its canonical position, at the conclusion of the process of redaction. Deuteronomy is positioned in such a way that it follows the narrated time of the four books of the Pentateuch, invoking events recorded there, even as it sometimes reinterprets or adapts the telling of those accounts.

The ideal vision laid out by Deuteronomy does not accord fully with any account of the regime as depicted in 1–2 Samuel or in 1–2 Kings. Indeed, discrepancies between Deuteronomy and those narratives may reflect the difficulties inherent in the implementation of any ideal regime on the rough terrain of Realpolitik. As Plato and Aristotle noted, the noble proposals they raised for the ideal regime would inevitably be compromised by the exigencies of the moment and the baser human impulses inevitably at play in the establishment of a regime. At most, these thinkers averred, one could hope for a second-best regime. My aim is not to investigate Deuteronomy in light of the historiographic literature but to read Deuteronomy as a statement of principles and the broad contours of an ideal regime. To engage this reading, I wish to lay out a framework of political theory that will animate and facilitate my analysis.

## Deuteronomy's Dual Political Agenda: A Theoretical Framework

To read Deuteronomy politically is to discern two concomitant trends that cut across its chapters. The first trend concerns what Deuteronomy has to say about kingship. Observations are legion in the scholarly literature that the limitations of the Israelite king in Deut 17:14–20 are without parallel in the ancient Near East.[5] Nowhere else do we find legal curbs on the size of the military, the treasury, and the harem. It is likewise common within the scholarly literature to find discussions of kingship in relation to the other positions of authority that are listed alongside that of monarchy in Deut 16:18–18:20: the judiciary, the priesthood, and prophecy.[6] More recently, Bernard Levinson has expanded the discussion of kingship in Deuteronomy by drawing our attention to the spheres of activity that were routine for kings in the ancient Near East. He notes that across many of its chapters, Deuteronomy discusses the laws governing these activities within the Israelite polity, yet without any mention of the Israelite king. Put differently, what Levinson has shown us is that it is insufficient to read what Deuteronomy *says* about kingship; you have to read the whole book and read between the lines for what it *doesn't say* about kingship in order to understand the full impact of the statement.

In this chapter, I will take Levinson's approach, of seeing the powers of governance within the broader context of the book as a whole, one step further. In order to fully understand what Deuteronomy has to say about kingship, it is insufficient to enumerate the various spheres of activity in which Israelite kingship is limited or neutered in comparison to kingship elsewhere in the ancient Near East. Nor is it sufficient to demonstrate that some of these realms of power—such as the cultic and the judicial—are transferred to other hands.

To understand why these observations are insufficient, I will take a page from studies of the anthropology of political power in premodern societies.

The systems of monarchies and tyrannies in the ancient Near East that are rejected in Deuteronomy ruled by means of what may be called an *exclusionary power strategy*—one in which potentates seek to design political systems through the monopolization of the sources of power. They seek to control economic resources, for example the trade and control of luxury and prestige goods, as well as technological and military resources. They exploit ranked clan and descent groups, and they seek to otherwise dominate networks of subordinates. They seek to restrict access to the cult and to the supernatural.[7] An exclusionary power strategy is readily recognized as the basis of the most common political structure in premodern societies. But some premodern societies, anthropologists have found, eschew exclusionary power strategies. The alternative power structures found in these cultures share several interrelated characteristics that may be termed *collective* power strategies.

Collective power strategies divest a single ruler of the control of power. The various offices of power are subordinated to a bureaucratic management structure determined by a code of law and formally established standards of conduct.[8] Whereas the monopoly of power in a tyranny engenders a degree of cohesion within the polity through the use of force and the attendant fear it produces, the decentralization of power in a collective system necessitates the creation of new concepts and institutions to provide the basis for cohesion. Where collective power strategies predominate in archaic societies, it becomes essential that members of the society harbor a well-established and well-maintained notion of corporate solidarity as an integrated whole.[9] Such a society will need to develop codes of conduct that not only determine what bodies rule and how but also emphasize the immutable interdependence of subgroups and individuals generally. These codes of conduct will routinely receive manifest legitimation through ritual and numinous experiences.[10]

These comments from the field of anthropology parallel the empirical experience of Greek and Roman republican theorists. The Greek polis was universally grounded in a law-based system of mixed government. But what made the system cohesive was the notion of *citizenry*: the strong sense of fraternity, order, and responsibility shared by members of a common polity and their sense of striving for virtue, variously defined. As Cicero put it, "Of all fellowships, none is more serious and none more dear than that of each of us with the republic. Parents are dear, and children, relatives and acquaintances are dear, but our country has on its own embraced all the affections of all of us."[11] For classical political thinkers, cohesion through citizenry raised the question of *virtue*. Classical thinkers were keenly aware that in order to enable the corporate enterprise of a citizenry to provide the cohesion necessary to sustain an ordered society, it will be necessary to spur the citizenry to a set of dignified ideals that will shape and reflect the particular character of their community. These virtues, in turn, will dictate the traits of the ideal person, a citizen aware of his traditions and obligations.[12]

From here we may return to our discussion of kingship in Deuteronomy. It is insufficient to note the spheres of royal power that are denied the Israelite king; nor is it sufficient to note the other bodies to which various powers are shifted. Rather, these institutions must be seen within the broader context of the strong sense of citizenship that Deuteronomy seeks to create across its 34 chapters: how it calls forth unity within the society; how it mediates the relationships between different parts of the society; what collective institutions are granted ritual legitimation.[13] Most important, what are the competencies of citizenship, or what the Greeks would have called the specific set of virtues, that Deuteronomy seeks to foster within its citizens? It is within this broader conceptual and institutional fabric that the institutions of the regime are embedded. In summation, then, the first trend I will be identifying in my assessment of Deuteronomy's politics is more than just the attenuation of kingship. Rather, this will be identified as part of a broader agenda of the establishment of a collective power strategy and a rejection of the classic exclusionary power strategy exhibited elsewhere in the ancient Near East.[14]

But the political blueprint of Deuteronomy reveals a second, less noted, thrust: a rejection of tribal patriarchy as a primary structure of governance. Deuteronomy narrates the very end of the sojourn in the wilderness and assumes a familiarity with many of the events narrated in the books of Exodus, Leviticus, and Numbers. Deuteronomy seeks to attenuate the role of the tribal and clan hierarchy, which, those narratives tell us, played a dominant leadership role throughout that earlier period. To be sure, Deuteronomy does not eradicate the notion of tribes, just as it did not eradicate the notion of kingship. But in seeking to establish a collective power strategy, it sought to foster within Israel a more collective, national identity and corresponding bureaucratic form.

The two great thrusts of deuteronomic political thought—the rejection of the exclusionary power strategy, and the concomitant rejection of the primacy of tribal hierarchy—are integrally related. The strength of the clan structure lies in its reliance on familial qualities. As one grows older, one's status and, hence, one's power and authority, grow accordingly within the family. In a classic clan or tribal administrative structure, succession to a given post is determined by a ranking based on a classificatory system of relationships within the family. Power ties are based on blood ties, which creates great cohesiveness. There is no incentive for a junior member of the structure to revolt against the system, as his eventual advancement is systemically assured. The inherited positions mean that disloyalty and disruption are rarely seen within clan structured power systems.[15] Rank is ascribed rather than achieved. It is worth noting in this vein that whereas the rebellion of the Israelites against the central authority of Moses and Aaron is a ubiquitous motif in the wilderness narratives of the Pentateuch, we have not a single account of a struggle for control of power at the tribal level.

Historically, ancient and modern social and political organizations have struggled to win the transfer of allegiances from kin-based groups to larger collective bodies.[16] It is easy to see why. A clan or tribe member could be assured of advancement simply by dint of his seniority within the tribal framework. But republican bureaucratic frameworks feature institutions that are instrumental: positions are allotted not as a reward for patronage or seniority but as a means toward the end of good governance.[17] Thus, whereas extensive clan networks and patronage produce social capital that aids power brokers at the various levels of the tribal network, the very same networks emerge as a barrier to a more egalitarian, democratic, and efficient regime structure. Despite this barrier, in order to create a collective power strategy, Deuteronomy seeks to create a regime with just these qualities. An innate property of the notion of citizenship in a polity is a proclivity to perceive the individual in a universalistic fashion, without reference to his or her narrow, parochial, familial roles.[18] Again, the experience of the classical Greek theorists is illustrative. Aristotle notes that in order to strengthen the hold of the democracy at Athens, certain leaders sought to break the power of old kinship corporations and to create new social orders that would encourage citizens to see each other in a new, more collective light.[19] Rather than kinship ties, what would define people now would be more abstract ties of common religious norms, and particularly common laws. Citizenship, as opposed to tribal affiliation, represents an autonomous sphere, which seeks to address the needs and fulfillment of the broader community.[20] To speak of Deuteronomy's political agenda, then, is to speak of not only the rejection of an exclusionary power strategy but also—and less commonly identified—the adoption of a collective power strategy, with its emphasis on the people as a whole and its relatively egalitarian agenda, entailing the rejection of the traditional tribal hierarchy and kinship value system.

The Divestiture of Exclusionary Power in Deuteronomy

My point of departure in discussing collective power strategy in Deuteronomy is to review the way Deuteronomy strips kingship of many of the hallmarks that were standard for monarchs in the ancient Near East. As shown in chapter 1, the sanctity of primordialism permeated the institution of the monarchy in the ancient Near East. This sanctity gained concrete expression through the powers granted to the king in a wide range of spheres, powers that Deuteronomy dilutes with regard to the Israelite king: (1) the king as commander-in-chief; (2) the king as responsible for the cult; (3) the king as the benefactor of debt remission; and (4) the king as lawgiver.

## The King as Commander-in-Chief

In most ancient Near Eastern lands, the king's position as the supreme commander of the army was more than a primary sign of his royal power and prestige. It represented the capacity through which he served his god. He was expected to engage in warfare and to report to the gods about his successes on their behalf. One of the most ubiquitous genres of ancient Near Eastern literature is the battle report of a king to his god. An example from the octagonal clay prism that depicts the exploits of Tiglath-Pileser I (1114–1076 B.C.E.) will serve as an illustration:

> I destroyed the lands of Sarauš (and) Ammauš, which from
>     ancient times had not known submission, (so that they looked)
>     like ruin hills (created by) the deluge.
> I fought with their extensive army in Mt. Aruma,
>     and brought about their defeat.
> I laid out like grain heaps the corpses of their men-at-arms.
> I conquered their cities, took their gods, and brought out their
>     booty,  possessions (and) property.
> I burned, razed, (and) destroyed their cities (and) turned them into
>     ruin hills.
> I imposed the heavy yoke of my dominion on them (and)
>     made them vassals of Aššur, my lord.[21]

One of the primary motifs of Deuteronomy is the ensuing conquest of the Land of Israel and the regulated prosecution of battle through ritual and law. Deuteronomy 20:1–20 enumerates the laws of siege, engagement, prisoners of war, and booty taking. Significantly, Deuteronomy 20:1–10 concerns the preparations for battle, which feature an address to the troops by the priest, followed by further addresses by officers of high rank, followed by the commanding officers of each unit, who lead their troops out to battle. The highly ritualized prelude to battle is performed with no mention of the king.[22] Deuteronomy depicts the conquest of the land in many different terms: "When the Lord your God shall expand your borders" (12:20); " When the Lord your God shall rip out the nations whom you shall conquer" (12:29); "When the Lord your God shall bring you to the land and conquer it and remove from before you many nations" (7:1). None of these depictions mentions the king. Most striking, however, is the section that addresses the appointment of the king, and the occasion at which such an appointment may be made: "When you arrive in the land which the Lord your God will grant to you, and you conquer it and settle it, and you request, 'Anoint over me a king like all the nations around me,' you shall surely appoint a king" (17:14–15). Not only does the king play no role in the conquest of the land; a king may be requested only after the conquest has been completed![23]

The king's military capacity is further curtailed by the injunction against amassing horses and wealth (17:16–17). The quantum leap from an army based on foot soldiers to one that boasts a cavalry is dependent on the acquisition of horses and their maintenance even in peacetime, requiring the establishment of stables and the acquisition of sustenance. By proscribing a large number of horses, Deuteronomy essentially expresses its preference for a less potent army of foot soldiers.[24]

## King and Cult

Throughout the ancient Near East, among the most important duties that fell to the king were his cultic duties. In many cultures, including those of Egypt and Mesopotamia as well as of the Hittite and Phoenician kingdoms, the king was himself the high priest of the cult. Elsewhere, as in Ugarit, the priests were appointed by the king. In Mesopotamia, the building of temples to the gods was a constitutive act of kingship. Thus we find that Hammurabi, in the prologue to his code, puts forth his bona fides as a legitimate ruler to legislate and administer law through an enumeration not only of his conquests but of his cultic enterprises as well:

> At that time Anum and Enlil named me
> To promote the welfare of the people,
> Me, Hammurabi, the devout god-fearing prince...
> Hammurabi, the shepherd called by Enlil, am I...
> Who provides in abundance all sorts of things for [the cult center] Nippur-Duranki;
> The devout patron of [the temple of ] Ekur;
> The efficient king who restored Eridu to its place
> Who purified the cult of Eabzu.[25]

In contrast, Deuteronomy envisions no role for the king at the central shrine or indeed in any cultic activity whatsoever. More striking, perhaps, is that

Deuteronomy 12 prescribes that a temple be established, yet no mention is made of the king as its royal patron.[26]

### The King as the Benefactor of Debt Remission

Evidence from Mesopotamia from the middle of the third through the end of the first millennium B.C.E. attests to the royal practice of debt remission, the freeing of slaves, and the restoration of land to the original owners. These dispensations were often granted as a new king ascended the throne or immediately following the conquest of a new territory, and were intended to bolster the standing of the king in the eyes of the populace.[27] In Deuteronomy, however, debt remission and the freeing of slaves are detached from any royal decree. Rather than being enacted to serve the political needs of the ruler, these are enacted by law every seven years as a national obligation, without recourse to any action on the part of the king (15:1–7; 12–18).[28]

### The King as Lawgiver

In Mesopotamia, the kings were thought to be endowed with keen judicial insight. Hammurabi maintains that he was endowed by Šamaš, the sun god, with an acuity for justice and righteousness, as manifested in the laws he attributes to himself.[29] On the stele of the law code bearing his name, Lipit Ishtar curses the person "who will damage my handiwork...who will erase its inscription who will write his name on it."[30]

Alone among the literary works of the ancient Near East, the Hebrew Bible maintains that the law is of divine origin.[31] The king is neither the source of the law nor even its adjudicator, as judicial powers are granted to others in the polity as laid out in Deuteronomy 16:18–22 and 17:8–13, passages to which I will return shortly.[32] Moreover, the laws of the king pointedly subjugate him to the law: "he will make a copy of this Torah from before the levitical priests, and it shall be with him and he shall read from it all of his days so that he shall learn to revere the Lord his God, to safeguard all that is said in this Torah, and the precepts thereof he shall perform" (17:18–19). The Torah the king copies is a written legal document, or constitution, to which even the king is bound.[33]

### Deuteronomic Kingship in a Collective Power Strategy

As mentioned earlier, the positions of authority within a collective power structure cannot be understood in isolation. Their responsibilities, limitations, and interactions with each other and with the society they lead need to be understood in light of the virtues and ideals that are central to the society. The structures of the regimes in Athens and in Sparta, respectively, were to a large degree a reflection of what each society strived for, and how it perceived itself. In Sparta, citizens were dedicated to a military life, and virtue was achieved on the battlefield. Hence, authority rested in a military oligarchy. Within Deuteronomy, there are three virtues or characteristics of the polity that predominate and in turn shape and color the character of the various posts of authority. In this section, I lay these out and explore how they inform the peculiar notion of kingship in Deuteronomy 17:14–20.

I begin with the first element I discussed in chapter 1: Israel as a community in covenantal relationship with God. The center of divine attention in this relationship, I noted, was the people as a whole, and each individual person, not the leadership. From a literary standpoint, Deuteronomy is structured as a series of addresses to Israel as a collective "you": "*You* shall love the Lord your God with all your heart" (6:5); "*you* shall feast [in the temple] before the Lord your God, happy in all the undertakings in which the Lord your God has blessed *you*" (12:7).[34] There is a fundamentally egalitarian streak at play here. With the exception of priests and Levites (to whom I shall return shortly) no group is ascribed any preferred status. All men are equal before the Lord, because all share the status of the subordinate king of the suzerainty treaty, as I have shown.

This identity of each member of the polity has implications for Deuteronomy's portrayal of the regime of authority. While Deuteronomy enumerates specific offices, this "you" constitutes a fraternal and egalitarian citizenry that is the foremost political body in the polity. Deuteronomy specifies no formal framework for appointing leaders or representatives of any kind. Rather, it is this collective "you"—the covenantal community—that bears ultimate responsibility to choose a king and to appoint judges.[35] Indeed, it is to the covenantal community that the land is given, and it is the community at large that bears the responsibility for proper covenantal behavior.

As mentioned, the very installation of a king is contingent on the people ("you") initiating the request for one (17:14). Much attention has been focused on the prerequisite of Deuteronomy 17:15 that the king may not be an outsider.[36] But what seems no less informative is a second emphasis that stems from the wording of the injunction: "Be sure to set a king over yourself, *one of your own brethren*; you must not set a foreigner over you, one who is not *your brethren*." The "brethren" requirement not only excludes non-Israelites but also implies that any Israelite male may be appointed for the task. Lineage is of no concern here, because the only lineage that counts is that the candidate be one who stands in covenant with the Almighty—that is to say, everybody. He need only be a "brother," that is, a citizen like everyone else, a term mentioned twice in this verse. Potentially, any citizen may serve as king.[37]

The egalitarian thrust of these laws is taken further in the law restricting the number of wives the king may take (17:17). This injunction against maintaining a large number of wives has often been understood in light of the phrase that follows it, "so that his heart does not go astray," as a warning with reference to the corruptive cultural influence of non-Israelite wives.[38] Scripture, however, limits the number not of *foreign* women but of *all* women. The limitation may speak to the proclivity of ancient Near Eastern kings to engage in sexual escapades, as exhibited in the opening sequence of the Gilgamesh Epic. Insight may be further garnered from anthropological studies of exclusionary power strategies. In archaic societies, the king routinely sought to consolidate his power by marriage to upper-class families and clans and the establishment of kinship networks. If this were to be allowed in Israel, the influence of families of power would quickly eclipse that of the common families of Israel.[39] Thus the injunction against marrying widely may be understood as seeking to prevent the influence of cronyism—"so that his heart does not go astray."

Deuteronomy suggests a second element that is central to the newly forged citizenry: the ensuing military conquest of Canaan. For some republican thinkers, such as Montesquieu, the patriotism of a citizenry is achieved by the more noble means of social education, which is perceived to stand in opposition to martial discipline. It is when virtue ebbs that attachment to the common good is promulgated through the common enterprise of war.[40] For Greek republican thinkers, however, the more sublime and contemplative virtues were not necessarily at odds with military ones. Aristotle wrote:

> For men must be able to engage in business and go to war, but
> leisure and peace are better; they must do what is necessary and
> indeed what is useful, but what is honorable is better. On such
> principles children and persons of every age which requires educa-
> tion should be trained.[41]

Deuteronomy focuses on the importance of establishing a community of holiness in accordance with God's laws and exhortations. Yet for Deuteronomy, this does not stand in the way of establishing an order that is quite focused on military conquest.

We saw earlier that Deuteronomy prescribes legal parameters for the conduct of war in the Holy Land. But war and conquest generally are ubiquitous themes in Deuteronomy. The ideology of war—why it is being waged and toward what ends—is found in the sermons of 7:1–2, 17–26; 9:1–3; 31:3–8.[42] In the opening frame of the book, Moses recounts various experiences of the wilderness, all of which are conquests. Martial discipline within Deuteronomy is not a substitute for the fraternal cohesion of a virtuous citizenry but in fact a complement to it.

It is surely no coincidence, then, that the first law of the king is one that restricts the amassing of horses (17:16). This proscription continues the thread of egalitarian social considerations in the legislation of kingship in Deuteronomy. Were a royal chariot force to serve as the backbone of the nation's defense, it would inevitably emerge as an elite military class.[43] Indeed, the great jurist of Athens, Solon, extended preferred status to the members of the cavalry over other citizens. But what confers status in Deuteronomy is citizenship in the covenantal community—and this is shared by all.

The restriction against the amassing of horses concludes at the end of Deuteronomy 17:16 with a clause that has engendered much debate: "[he shall not] return the people to Egypt to amass horses, for the Lord has said to you, 'you shall not return that way again.'" One could well imagine a biblical injunction against ever returning to Egypt for any purpose. Yet this verse seems to limit "returning" to Egypt only if it is for the purpose of amassing cavalry horses. Moreover, the injunction speaks of returning "the people" for the purpose, when surely the acquisition and transport of horses could hardly require more than a tiny percentage of what is here termed "the people." There is cogency, therefore, in viewing the verse as a prohibition on the king from selling Israelite slaves to Egypt for the purpose of amassing horses, as this would represent an undoing of the Exodus, and would reduce the members of the community of Israel to the status of slaves.[44]

A third characteristic that animates the Israelite citizenry is that, like the Greek polis, it is law-based. The great twentieth-century political philosopher Friedrich Hayek saw Athenian political philosophy as the origin of the notion of equality before the law.[45] But it is already present in Deuteronomy. All public institutions—the judiciary, the priesthood, the monarchy, the institution of prophecy—are subordinated to the law. No institution is self-legitimating.[46] Moreover, the law is a public text, one read aloud before the entire nation (31:10–13). Its dictates are meant to be widely known, thus making abuse of power more obvious.

The requirement that the king engage in the study of the law (17:19–20) further extends the egalitarian thrust of the laws of the king. It also reflects the transformation of an ancient Near East practice of royal study, now in accordance with a collective power strategy. In ancient Egypt, in the Middle Kingdom especially, we find ethical wills that kings left their sons, wisdom teachings concerning the principles of good governance.[47] In Mesopotamia, the king was required to read texts concerning religion and cult, which, as noted, was a sphere under his responsibility.[48] What is distinct in Deuteronomy is that the king must copy and read from "this Torah"[49] about a wide range of issues, of which almost none pertains to kingship per se. In fact, the purpose of his study, "so that he may learn to revere the Lord his God to observe faithfully every word of this Torah as well as these laws," essentially places him on a par with the common citizen, whose responsibility in this regard is expressed elsewhere in Deuteronomy in identical terms (5:1; 6:6–8; 11:18–19).[50] Indeed, unlike in Mesopotamia, where the king was issued responsibility for the law, in Israel the entire community is the recipient of the law. The upkeep of the laws in Deuteronomy is a responsibility shared by every member of the society.[51]

Verse 20 sums up not only the purposes of the requirement to copy and study the Torah but also all of the laws of the king. When read together with the other laws of the king, the verse leads to a single conclusion: the king's responsibilities are essentially those required of every other Israelite citizen. As already noted, verse 17 says that the king must not let his heart sway—a phrase that is used with regard to compliance with God's wishes by all members of the Israelite polity (4:9). Here, in verse 17:20, it is said that the king must not "think himself high," just as the common Israelite is warned in identical language (8:14). The king must not "stray from the commandments neither right nor left," just as the Israelite citizen may not (5:29; 17:11; 28:14). He is "to learn to revere," "to do," and "to perform" the commandments, just as the Israelite citizen is to do (6:2; 10:12; 31:12). Even his reward is identical to that of the common Israelite: he should act in accordance with these precepts "so that he will merit long days" in his rule, a phrase that exactly parallels the phrase used to refer to the longevity promised the common Israelite for compliance with the commandments (6:2). The prerequisite for being a good Israelite king is to be a good Israelite citizen.

Reading the laws of the king in light of other deuteronomic passages shows how these laws are incorporated within the discourse of Deuteronomy's overall collective power strategy. In many cultures of the ancient Near East, the king was considered the son of God, with the implication of adoption, or election. Deuteronomy, too, speaks of the sons of God—but these statements refer to Israel as a whole (14:1; 32:6, 18) and pointedly not the king, even though the topos of the Israelite king as the elected son of God appears elsewhere (2 Sam 7:14–20; Ps 2:7). The royal ideology of the ancient Near East is here nationalized: as the "sons of God," all Israelites have the status elsewhere accorded only to the king.[52]

The opening narrative frame of Deuteronomy similarly portrays national leadership in a collective power strategy. While Deuteronomy speaks of no specific king, it expressly speaks of one dominant national leader—Moses—who served also as part priest, part judge, and part prophet. Deuteronomy 17 says nothing about how the king's leadership is to express and manifest itself but the book's narrative frame suggests a clue, one very much in keeping with collective power strategy. It portrays the leader, Moses, engaged in consultation with the people concerning issues of national policy. In chapter 1:9–18, Moses recounts the need he felt to decentralize his regime. He notes explicitly that he did not take unilateral action, but rather shared his musings on the subject with the people, suggested a plan, and then sought and received their approval. Several verses later, he tells of the converse situation: the people presented an initiative to Moses to send spies to scout out the land. Moses records that he was in favor of the idea and acquiesced. The picture that emerges is one of collective power par excellence. Moses emphasizes that in spite of his stature and authority, the right way to rule is by way of discussion and consensus between the ruler and the ruled. When reading the laws of governance of Deuteronomy within the framework of the book as a whole and its agenda of establishing a collective power strategy, the two narratives of Moses' leadership style are part of the message to any future leader: leadership according to Deuteronomy, even for a monarch, should be executed within a collective framework.

To summarize, the view of kingship within Deuteronomy is equivocal. Alone among the various powers delineated in Deuteronomy, kingship is viewed not as a necessary institution but as one that comes into being only in the wake of popular desire. Indeed, it is defined as an inherently foreign institution: "When you arrive in the land which the Lord your God will grant to you, and you conquer it and settle it, and you request, 'anoint over me a king *like all the nations around me*, you shall surely appoint a king'" (17:14–15). The fifteenth-century Spanish rabbinic commentator Don Isaac Abarbanel was correct in understanding that the entire institution is concessive in nature. Deuteronomy has its ideal vision, one that apparently does not require kingship. Yet it also incorporates flexibility in response to multiple sociopolitical needs. I will now explore how the additional powers of the deuteronomic regime play themselves out within the collective power strategy that the book employs.

The Power of the Priests/Levites

Far and away, it is the power of the priesthood that receives the most attention within Deuteronomy—in terms of both the number of references to the priests and Levites and the emphasis given the priesthood relative to that in the rest of the Pentateuch.[53]

While Deuteronomy envisions specific cultic roles for the priests and Levites at some points (with reference to priests—21:5, 26:4, 33:10), it describes these roles, for the most part, in the broadest terms: they "serve" at the central shrine (with reference to the Levites—9:8, 18:7; with reference to the priests—18:5, 21:5). It may be that Deuteronomy assumes that the priests and Levites execute many of the functions that are outlined elsewhere in the Pentateuch and there is no need to repeat all of them here.

I wish to suggest that the dearth of cultic detail ascribed to the priests and Levites in Deuteronomy may reflect a transformation of the primary role of the priesthood in accordance with a collective power strategy agenda. In Deuteronomy, a new emphasis is ascribed to the priesthood: the priests emerge as the guardians of the law, the constitution. This is seen at a number of junctures. We have already seen that the king is to write a copy of the law that is to be in the safekeeping of the priests (17:18). They also serve as members of the high tribunal (17:8–13) of law and justice. In other books of the Pentateuch, priests are not assigned a regular judicial role, and become involved only when cases need to be resolved by sacral means: oaths (Exod 22:7–10), ritual ordeal (Num 5:11–31), and Urim and Thummim (Exod 28:29–30). Yet in Deuteronomy, priests play a local judicial role in civil and criminal cases (19:17; 21:5).[54] Moses commands the priests to enact the septennial Hakhēl gathering, and to read before the nation the law he has vouchsafed to them (31:9–13). In addition to these ritually and legally sanctioned roles, the priests/Levites are given ad hoc responsibilities that center around the safeguarding of the law. It is the priests and Levites who join Moses in calling on the people to demonstrate fidelity to the law at 27:9–10. The Levites are given the law to place alongside the Ark of the Covenant (31:26). Verse 33:10 casts the Levites either as arbiters of the law, or its teachers.

At the same time the priests are empowered as the guardians of the law, the priesthood of Deuteronomy has four limitations that accord with a collective power strategy. In archaic states that practice a collective power strategy, ritual sanctifies and culturally reinforces an egalitarian spirit through numinous experience.[55] Group-oriented chiefdoms feature large architectural spaces suitable for group ritual.[56] These emphases may be seen in Deuteronomy's presentation of the temple, which focuses on the people's role there. Deuteronomy 12 calls for the building of the temple. Unlike elsewhere in the ancient Near East, it is not the king who is told to erect the temple. Nor is there any mention in that chapter of the cultic role of the priests. Rather, it is, again, "you" who are to build the temple (12:5–6). The "place that God chooses to establish His name" emerges as the place at which Israelites are to seek His presence (12:5), offer their sacrifices (12:6), and eat and rejoice before the Lord (12:7). In this first mention of the temple in Deuteronomy, the emphasis is entirely on the role of the people there. It is the people's shrine. Deuteronomy attends to cultic proceedings at several junctures (12:4–28, 14:22–27, 15:19–23, 16:1–18, 26:1–15). The common threads among all of these are two. First, they attend to the role of the people in participating in the cult and the way that participation is carried out. Second, these laws make no mention of the cultic role of the priests or Levites, with the exception of a single instance (26:5).[57] The emphasis on the role of the people in the cult is foreign to cultures where exclusionary power strategies prevail.

A collective power strategy, or what we may term a republican idea of mixed government with respect to the checked power of the priesthood, is evident here in a second way. Note that in Deuteronomy, the priesthood is joined by another institution within the regime in nearly every sphere of its activity. We noted earlier that the lines between priests and Levites throughout Deuteronomy are blurred, whereas in the Book of Numbers, the descendants of Aaron have exclusive rights to the priesthood, while other Levites merely assist them. The priests in Deuteronomy are always referred to as "levitical priests," or "the priests the sons of Levi," and never as "the priests the sons of Aaron." This terminology reflects the priestly sharing of powers and responsibilities across Deuteronomy. The supreme tribunal is indeed located at the temple, and is staffed by "the levitical priests" (17:9, 12). But it is staffed, as well, by "the judge of that time" (17:9, 12). The administration of justice in Deuteronomy 19:17 is likewise given over to priests and judges in concert. The prebattle hortatory proclamations to soldiers are made by priests in conjunction with officers (20:1–9). The enactment of the septennial festival of Hakhēl is entrusted to the priests in conjunction with the elders (31:9–10).

The third way that the collective power strategy checks the power of the priesthood concerns the role of the oracle and divination within Deuteronomy. Of all the cultic roles and tasks, the capacity to receive communication from the divine is the most sublime. Yet in Deuteronomy, the power to receive the oracle is mentioned with regard to the priest only once, at 33:10. In more explicit fashion, it is the domain of the prophet, who transmits God's commands and who correctly foretells events (18:9–22). Some assume that the role of the priests as the members of the supreme tribunal in difficult matters of law (17:8–13) in fact rests on the assumption that they consult oracular means.[58] Yet this is nowhere stated explicitly, and as we have seen, priests are not the sole members of the high tribunal: it includes as well "the judge of that time" (17:9, 12).[59] There is an enormous difference between the priestly power to adjudicate on the basis of oracular divination, such as the Urim and Thummim, and the priestly power in Deuteronomy to adjudicate on the basis of interpretation and application of the law and the examination of evidence. Divination by means of the Urim and Thummim is almost by definition a process that can have no control, no oversight, no inspection. Few priests will learn this art, and fewer still will have access to the breastplate to corroborate the findings. Divination has the potential to be an exclusionary source of power, par excellence. By contrast, authority that is rooted in the interpretation of a public text written in a language that is accessible to a wide audience limits the potential for domination by the priests, because their pronouncements may ultimately be measured against the spirit of the text itself. The public promulgation of the word of God at the septennial Hakhēl ceremony serves a like purpose. The fact that the law is made public contravenes the partisan interest of the priests and Levites in monopolizing control over the sacred texts.[60]

A collective power structure is exhibited, finally, in the allocation of land resources to priests and Levites. Chapter 17 has an interesting word play that encapsulates the issue at hand. Both the king and the priest are referred to as having been chosen by God (king, 17:15; priest/Levite, 18:5). Recall that Scripture mandates that the king must be "from amongst your brethren" (17:15). Yet the priest/Levite is described seven verses later as being "not among your brethren" (18:2). The priest/Levite is set apart, but not in status or entitlements. He is set apart from his brethren in his landlessness. Alone among Israelites, in Deuteronomy, Levites receive no land allotment. Instead, Scripture underscores at several junctures that the Levites subsist on the tithes and priestly gifts received from the people at large (12:12, 18–19; 14:22–29; 16:11, 14). It is instructive to note that the Levites apparently were so dependent on others that Scripture saw it fit to include them with the categories of the underprivileged (14:28–29).

While the general blueprint for Israelite society is egalitarian in nature, it must be admitted that the election of the priests and Levites contravenes this tendency. In the parlance of contemporary liberal discourse, we would say that opportunity of access to many precincts of the sanctuary is denied to the majority and available only to the chosen few. The election of the priests and Levites is justified within the Bible's terms, in ways at variance with other election theologies. The election of the priests and Levites is nowhere given metaphysical basis. Plato justified the hierarchy of Greek society on the grounds that the gods had differentiated the souls of different classes of persons.[61] The Bible knows of no such discourse, certainly not with respect to the priests and Levites. Their election is a reflection not of their innate status but of God's. As a sovereign king, He is worthy of an honor guard, of servants set aside as His attendants. It is in this vein that they are referred to as the legion of God (Num 4:3, 23, 30, 35, 39, 43), and are excused from the military responsibilities assigned to the legions of Israel. Aristotle presents a useful metaphor:

> Like the sailor, the citizen is a member of a community. Now, sailors have different functions, for one of them is a rower, another a pilot, and a third a look-out-man, a fourth is described by some similar term; and while the precise definition of each individual's virtue applies exclusively to him, there is, at the same time, a common definition applicable to them all. For they have all of them a common object, which is safety in navigation. Similarly, one citizen differs from another, but the salvation of the community is the common business of them all.[62]

The sailors do not serve identical functions. At the same time, note the role of the leader on the boat, the pilot. He is chief, but chief among sailors, in organic function, with their respective functions performed in complement to each other. The sailors are engaged in a collective effort whose purpose is the welfare of the community itself, and are all equally deserving of esteem. While the priests and Levites constitute a distinct class, that differentiation is subsumed within the larger organic mission that all members of the covenantal community of Israel share. All who fulfill their responsibilities are of equal esteem in the eyes of the Lord.

## The Judicial Power

Montesquieu saw the separation of the judicial power as vital, as the judicial power is "terrible among men," for it is through the judiciary that the government and the law most directly affect the citizenry.[63] He set down three postulates about the execution of justice that may be seen to animate Deuteronomy's view of the judiciary. First, adjudication must be based on the application of written laws and not on the arbitrary decision of the judge.[64] Second, only when the judiciary is fully independent of the other branches of the government will the regime be deemed moderate as opposed to despotic.[65] Third, the judiciary should be drawn from the body of the members of the people, without regard for rank or social standing.[66]

These three principles are at play within the chapters of Deuteronomy. The justice executed by the judges must be based on the law contained in the Torah (17:8–13). The supremacy of the law, however, is strikingly borne out in the procedures to be followed in the event that an issue of law proves too baffling.

Deuteronomy here makes no mention of priestly lots, Urim and Thummim on the "breastplate of justice" (see Exod 27:15–30; Lev 8:8), trial by ordeal (Num 5), or judicial oath before the divinity (see Exod 22:7, 10). What Deuteronomy emphasizes is that justice is determined by the interpretation and application of law alone.[67]

The appointment of judges as delineated in 16:18 addresses the judiciary's independence and its popular makeup. Oversight of the judicial sphere was a key attribute of kingship across the ancient Near East.[68] Yet in Deuteronomy, there is no indication that the king administers justice or appoints judges to their positions. Rather, "*You* shall appoint magistrates and clerks for your tribes in all the settlements that the Lord your God is giving you" (16:18).[69] It appears that anyone could be appointed a judge, without recourse to rank or social standing. More interesting, there is no precise mechanism prescribed for the appointment of judges. That is, Deuteronomy does not say anything about which representative bodies should make this decision, how many judges are to be appointed, or the hierarchy of the different levels of the judiciary. No doubt, such apparatuses existed. But had Deuteronomy enshrined them into law, those bodies would have become the focus. In omitting the precise mechanisms, Deuteronomy retains its focus on the citizenry as a whole—"*You.*" Even as representatives effect the appointment of judges, the ultimate authority and responsibility rests on the people.

A textual peculiarity in Deuteronomy 16:18–19 makes this evident. Verse 18 calls on "you" to appoint magistrates and clerks. "You," here as throughout Deuteronomy, refers to the collective of Israel. Even if the judges are chosen by a representative body, the very fact that the body is representative suggests that it is, in effect, the entire citizenry that is participating in the selection. Verse 19 however, uses the singular "you" three times in the following statement: "You shall not judge unfairly: you shall show no partiality; you shall not take bribes." The verse would seem to be addressing each judge himself. After all, it is only the judge who is now invested with power, and it is only the judges who are in a position to be corrupted. Nonetheless, the verse addresses the same collective body of Israel, "you," as was addressed in the previous verse, with its call to "you" to appoint magistrates and clerks. The Septuagint was sufficiently bothered by this that it changed the text such that the subject of the verse would refer to the appointed judges: "*They* shall not judge unfairly: *they* shall show no partiality; *they* shall not take bribes," and so on. One scholar, however, has suggested that the Masoretic Text may be defended. Since any Israelite may one day become a judge, all are forewarned: "*You* [singular] shall not judge unfairly," and so on. More compelling, however, is his suggestion that Scripture here addresses the entire polity, because it is the entire polity that is ultimately responsible for the proper administration of justice. If judges are corrupted, the people cannot hide behind a veil of innocence, wagging their fingers at the judges they themselves have appointed. The justice the judges practice is practiced on behalf of, and under the aegis of, the entire people.[70] The emphasis here provides an interesting variation on the idea of civic participation so central to Greek and Roman republican thought. For thinkers such as Plato and Aristotle, the ideal citizen is the one who participates in governance. As Pericles, the leader of Athens in the fifth century B.C.E., is reported to have said, "We do not say that a man who is not interested in politics minds his own business, but that he does not belong here at all."[71] Now, Deuteronomy does not maintain that every citizen should strive to assist in the affairs of public administration. Nonetheless, it does exhibit its own brand of civic participation: the collective is ultimately held responsible for the actions of its representatives, in this instance the judges; hence, "*You* shall not judge unfairly: *you* shall show no partiality; *you* shall not take bribes."

The emphasis of what Deuteronomy has to say about courts of law is less about legitimating the mechanisms of social control and more about assuring due process of law.[72] Scripture says little about the process by which judges are appointed, other than to say "You shall appoint magistrates and clerks" (16:18). It has much to say, however, about the pitfalls of this position of power (16:18–20):

> You shall appoint magistrates and officials in all of the settlements,
> in all of the tribes that the Lord your God is giving you, and they
> shall govern the people with due justice. You shall not judge unfairly:
> you shall show no partiality; you shall not take bribes, for bribes
> blind the eyes of the discerning and upset the plea of the just.
> Justice, justice shall you pursue.

Due process is the focus elsewhere as well. Capital crimes must involve scrutinizing inquiry (13:15; 17:4). Multiple witnesses are necessary to condemn an offender (17:6; 19:15). Procedures are laid down to identify and punish perjurers (19:15–21). The courts may not visit collective punishment on the family of the guilty (24:16). The law may not be slanted against the disadvantaged (24:17). Abuse of the corporal punishment system is to be prevented (25:1–4). All of these laws are well understood within the framework of a collective power strategy, where the protection of the citizenry is the focus.

## The Power of the Prophet

Regarding the jurisdiction of the prophet (18:15–22), we may see how this institution, too, is delicately woven into Deuteronomy's collective power structure. On the one hand, the prophet may be seen as a check on the power of the priest, for although the priest serves the cult, divine communication to the people is primarily transmitted through the person of the prophet. The prophet may also be seen to check the power of the king. The king is to be he "who is chosen by God" (17:15). Deuteronomy, however, is not explicit on how God makes His will known on this matter. Nonetheless, as several have noted, the elections of Saul and David by the prophet Samuel are narrated utilizing precisely this terminology of divine election (1 Sam 10:24; 16:8–10).[73] By doing so, the author of Samuel implicitly suggests that God chooses candidates for kingship through the agency of the prophet.

At the same time, the prophet's own power is checked as well. Deuteronomy identifies the potential prophet by saying, "I will raise for you a prophet *from your midst, from your brethren, like myself*," implying that he is not the member of any elite lineage, does not possess inherent powers, but rather, an ordinary citizen. Though the prophet receives divine communication, he never participates in the cult in order to communicate with the Lord. Nor does this inspired individual play any role whatever in the justice system. The emphasis on the citizenry as the ultimate authoritative body is seen here as well, as the prophet's validation is determined by the people (18:20–22), not by the priests, the king, the judges, the elders, or other prophets.

Notions of collective power were known elsewhere in the ancient Near East. Yet several elements of Deuteronomy's establishment of collective over exclusionary power are distinct in the broader regional and cultural context. Recent reappraisals of the political culture of Mari, a civilization located around the modern-day border between Syria and Iraq from the early second millennium B.C.E., reveal that the element of the collective political voice was often found in that culture. But this was the case in the local sphere of the *ālum*, the town or city, and was virtually unheard-of with regard to the *mātum*, the "land" or kingdom.[74] Deuteronomy, by contrast, envisions the application of a collective power strategy on a national scale. No less significant is the observation that while local-level polities in Mari practiced a form of collective governance, the evidence does not point to any conscious notion of equalizing all citizens.[75] Deuteronomy, however, provides a broad ideological base for the establishment an egalitarian citizenry, whose members achieve their status through the covenant with God.

The emphasis on the people as a whole as the focal point of the polity and as its ultimate guardians may seem to demand of the masses a level of virtue that is utopian. In this emphasis, however, a certain sociopolitical logic inheres, one that is well developed in the work of the late eminent sociologist Edward Shils.[76] For Shils, the more inegalitarian a society, the less likely it is that the masses, who inhabit the social periphery of that society, will intensely affirm the value system that has enthroned those above them, and the institutions they control. Shils points out that in contrast to such steeply hierarchical societies, the masses in the modern liberal society have come to feel that the central value system of the society is their very own, and have a strong sense of participation in its institutions of power. Citizens of modern liberal societies no longer see themselves as objects of the authoritative control of others. Rather, "the mass of the population have...come to share in the vital connection with the 'order' which inheres in the central value system and which was once thought to be in the special custody of the ruling classes."[77]

This dynamic, which Shils sees at play in the transition from premodern to modern societies, is at play in the transition in the politics of Deuteronomy—the transformation of an enslaved people to a responsible, proactive citizenry. Deuteronomy invokes the memory of the furnace of oppression (4:20), the torture (26:6) and the disenfranchisement (10:19) of Egypt, on more than 50 occasions. Deuteronomy's call to the people to become ennobled and assume responsibility is indeed a calling and a challenge. But it is also an offer: an offer of an opportunity to escape extreme marginalization and to share as central partners in the new order and to stand at its focus. Put differently, this call offers the people a stake in what is being established, in the hope that they will be capable of rising to the challenge.

To conclude this section on the divestiture of power from the figure of the king, and the creation of a collective power structure, I shall take a page from the sociology of agrarian societies. Gerhard Lenski notes that mountainous regions are better suited to republican regimes than river valleys and broad valleys. Because the topography naturally limits the economic surplus produced, and transportation problems are acute, it is difficult to amass in one location a quantity of surplus capable of sustaining a royal retinue. Moreover, the military forces necessary to uphold a major power have to be based on cavalry and horse-drawn chariots, both of which frequently prove impractical in mountainous areas.[78] In this light, it is of interest that Deuteronomy contrasts Israel's polity-to-be with the empire that Israel left behind in Egypt, in terms that emphasize their topographical distinction (11:8–12):

> Keep, therefore, all the Instruction that I enjoin upon you today, so
> that you may have the strength to invade and occupy the land which
> you propose to cross into and occupy, and that you may long endure
> upon the soil which the Lord swore to your fathers to give them and
> to their descendants, a land flowing with milk and honey. For the
> land which you are about to invade and occupy is not like the land of

Egypt from which you have come. There the grain you sowed could
be given drawn water like a vegetable garden; but the land you are
about to cross into and occupy, a land of hills and valleys, soaks up
its water from the rains of heaven. It is a land which the Lord God
looks after, on which the Lord your God always keeps His eye, from
year's beginning to year's end.

The dependence on divine grace is heightened, as the Israelite polity is to inhabit a region whose topography does not allow for the creation of abundant
economic surplus in predictable fashion, a factor that was a hallmark of the
founding of the great empires in the river basins of Mesopotamia and Egypt.

## Deuteronomy and the Rejection of Clan

I have thus far traced the contours of political thought in Deuteronomy that
reject exclusionary power in favor of collective power. As noted, however, re-
publics are susceptible to breakdown along lines of faction. A ubiquitous
theme in the annals of political history is the attempt to dissolve entrenched
kinship structures in an effort to forge a larger collective body. Speaking in the
terms of the narrated world of Deuteronomy, the collective strategy could take
hold only if there were an attendant weakening of the tribal hierarchy that fig-
ured so prominently during the trek in the wilderness. In biblical scholarship,
the amalgamation of the tribes into a federated whole is usually addressed
with reference to the formation of the monarchy under Saul and David and the
consolidation of the tribes into a national collective. I claim, however, that this
dynamic is equally at play in the political theory that animates the sermons
and laws of Deuteronomy.

To help us appreciate the way Deuteronomy negotiates the place of tribal
patriarchy in its new order, I will begin by surveying the role tribal hierarchy
plays in the wilderness regime within Exodus, Leviticus, and Numbers. I do so
specifically with reference to the institutions of the tribal chieftains (*nĕśi'îm*)
and the "elders." Each group is mentioned numerous times; at some junctures it
seems the two terms may be used interchangeably, at others not. I do not aim to
define and sort their respective responsibilities.[79] I will deal with the two groups
together, because my aim is simply to examine the place of tribal hierarchy
broadly within the wilderness community, as a foil for what I perceive as a series
of moves Deuteronomy makes to attenuate, if not eradicate, these institutions.

Chieftains and elders are routinely seen in several contexts in the wilderness. They relay the word of Moses to the people (elders, Exod 3:16; 4:29; 12:21;

*něśi'îm*, Num 10:4) and the feelings of the people to Moses (*něśi'îm*, Exod 16:2). They serve as representatives of the people at the Tabernacle (elders, Lev 9:1; *něśi'îm*, Exod 35:27; Num 7:2) and as representatives of the nation who accompany Moses on various occasions (elders, Exod 3:18; 18:12; 24:1, 9) and execute national administrative responsibilities such as the census and the apportionment of the land (elders, Num 11:16–30, *něśi'îm*, Num 1:1–19; 34:16–29; 36:2). All the census lists feature the name of the tribal chief as the military head of the tribe (Num 2:1–31; 3:24, 30, 32; 10:14–28). The role of the *nāś'î* is culturally reinforced through sacral legislation (Exod 22:27; Lev 4:22–26). On some occasions, a national political body called the *'ēdâ* convenes. This ad hoc body, vested with legislative and judicial powers, is comprised of tribal leaders (Num 35:12, 24–25; see Josh 22:16; Judg 21:10).[80] While these examples delineate the activities of the tribal heads, at least one instance demonstrates the functioning of lower levels of the hierarchy, the grievance brought on behalf of the daughters of Zelophehad (Num 36:1): "The family heads in the clan of the descendants of Gilead son of Machir son of Menasseh, one of the Josephite clans, came forward and appealed to Moses." Tribal and kinship structures, then, were the dominant political form of the desert regime.

It is striking that in Deuteronomy, many of these structures are simply absent. There is no mention of the *něśi'îm* at all, or of the ad hoc political body, the *'ēdâ*.[81] Moreover, a relatively lesser role is granted to the notion of tribe in Deuteronomy. As a federated bureaucratic structure, Deuteronomy seems to know of two units only: the nation and the city. Deuteronomy has little to say about a rung of hierarchy based around the social unit of the tribe. Verse 17:8 determines that if a matter is too difficult for the court "in your gate" (your city or town), then remedy may be found at the central court at the central sanctuary. There is no middle level of tribal court. The same two-tier, city-nation structure is exhibited in the law of the idolatrous city. Remedy of the situation devolves on "you"—the collective of Israel—and not, as one might expect, on the tribe, to rein in its own.[82] Nor does Scripture discuss the possibility of an "idolatrous tribe," akin to an idolatrous city but on a larger scale. The laws of distribution of charity reveal the same bureaucratic structure of city and nation: "when there emerges in your midst an indigent person, from one of your brethren, in one of your gates, in your land which God has given you, you shall not harden your heart," and so on (15:7). The implied "you" who is commanded to relieve this person's penury is the entirety of Israel, or the residents of that particular city. Within this structure, tribe members appear to have no greater mandate than anyone else to extend assistance.

The emphasis on the town over against the tribe is seen in the judicial realm as well. Various circumstances are recorded in which adjudication is carried out by town elders, not tribal elders: the cases of the rebellious son (21:18–21), the rape of the betrothed woman (22:21), and the unidentified corpse (21:5). One could aver that these issues are intrinsically local issues and that it is only fitting that they be adjudicated by town elders, not tribal elders. Yet levirate marriage is likewise adjudicated by town elders (25:5–10) and not a tribal court, even though the levirate marriage has direct consequences for the kinship structure of the tribe.[83]

Especially illustrative of Deuteronomy's two-tier, city-nation structure is the directive concerning the distribution of the cities of refuge. Here we find two passages: one that specifies the cities to be so designated in the Transjordan (4:41–43) and a general prescription for their distribution in the land of Canaan, west of the Jordan. In the passage that prescribes the cities to be set aside west of the Jordan, we read: "When the Lord cuts down the nations whose land the Lord your God gives, and you conquer them and reside in their cities, and in their houses, you shall designate for yourself *three cities within your land*" (19:1–2). Again, Deuteronomy knows only the whole territory of the nation and its cities. Tribal lines and hierarchy are irrelevant here. It is true that in the passage that describes the allotment in the Transjordan, the cities are identified by tribe (4:41–43). Yet Scripture seems less concerned here with having a city of refuge in each tribe and more with achieving the appropriate geographic dispersal of these cities. Hence, the cities are designated not just by tribe, but rather by geographic region: "[set aside] Betser *in the desert in the land of the plain* of Reuven, as well as Ramoth *in the Gilead* of Gad, as well as Golan *in the Bashan* of Menasseh."

The attempt to dissipate tribal identity is evident in Deuteronomy's rhetoric as well. We see in Deuteronomy a transformation of the valence of the word "fathers." In Numbers, especially, the word "fathers" is used in exclusive fashion (over 40 times) to refer to the tribal patriarchy in the phrase "house of the fathers," a reference to the kinship structure of the tribes. In sermons spoken to the people in Exodus, Leviticus, and Numbers, the word "fathers" as a reference to the patriarchs appears only a handful of times (Exod 3:15; 13:5, 11; Lev 26:42). In Deuteronomy, the trend is reversed. In the various sermons and laws, "your fathers" never refers to a tribal kinship structure but instead refers to the patriarchs (over 30 times).[84] The social purpose of this is to stress common ancestry and hence collective national identity, rather than identity fractured along clan and familial lines.

The notion that each citizen is called on to recognize a socioreligious identity that transcends kinship underlies the law of Deuteronomy 14:1–2:

> You are sons of the Lord your God. You shall not gash yourselves or
> shave the front of your heads in mourning for the dead. For you are a

> people consecrated to the Lord your God: the Lord your God chose
> you from among all other peoples on earth to be His treasured
> people.

The implication here is that although every individual has bloodlines that dictate his genealogical identity, that identity is superseded by Israel's collective filial relation to God. The use of the trope of the son- or sons-of-God in this fashion represents a further relocation of an ancient Near Eastern motif of royal theology within the covenantal theology of the Bible. As noted, throughout the ancient Near East, and indeed elsewhere in the Bible, kings were perceived as the adopted or elected "sons" of God. Deuteronomy makes no mention of the king in this capacity, and rather transfers this status of elected son to the collective polity of Israel.[85] Laws elsewhere in the Pentateuch generally refer to a fellow member of the community as a *rēʻâ* (e.g., Exod 22:6, 13; Lev 19:13, 16). The laws of Deuteronomy routinely substitute this with the word *'āḥ*, "brother," and in so doing appropriate the language of intimate and primary kinship now to refer to the bond of fellowship in the national community (e.g., Deut 15:7, 11, 12; 22:1–4).[86]

The ancien régime of patriarchy, though, is not altogether expunged from Deuteronomy. As I noted with regard to its equivocal treatment of kingship, Deuteronomy has its ideal vision. Yet it also incorporates the flexibility to answer multiple sociopolitical needs. The same is true with regard to the maintenance of some vestiges of the earlier kinship structures. Deuteronomy narrates the period immediately prior to the entry into the land, and seems to assume that patriarchy had served as the primary element of sociopolitical identity and bureaucratic structure in the wilderness, and perhaps even in slavery, and hence tribal patriarchy could hardly be extirpated at once. Deuteronomy therefore limits it and redirects it in accordance with a collective power strategy.

This is evident in the most detailed way in Deuteronomy's presentation of the judicial system and the hierarchy of its courts. Deuteronomy 1 opens by providing us with a baseline picture of the wilderness regime, entirely conceived along tribal hierarchical lines. Moses relates that, unable to handle the burden alone, he established the body of tribal chiefs (1:13). He then established a system of tribal magistrates and officers. He then takes these tribal officers and commands them (1:16), "Hear out your fellow men, and decide justly between any man and his brother, or his resident alien," implying that each tribe is to establish its own internal bureaucracy.[87]

Some scholars have suggested that the tribal judicial hierarchy described in chapter 1 remains in place as an unstated, yet assumed, part of Deuteronomy's vision of the judiciary, several elements of which we assessed above.[88] Yet there is a compelling reason to suspect otherwise. The kinship structures implicated in the offices of chiefs of thousands, hundreds, fifties, and tens that Moses recounts having established in the wilderness are nowhere else mentioned in Deuteronomy. Moreover, when Moses recalls the establishment of this bureaucracy, he tells the people, "*At that time* I said to you.... Pick from each of your tribes," and so on, implying the temporal circumstances of those events, events at a distance from the "today" of Deuteronomy.[89]

Many scholars, rightly in my view, see the judicial bureaucracy of Deuteronomy 16–17 as superseding the former structure, along what I have been describing as a collective power strategy. Here we find no references to the term *śarîm* ("officers," as in "officers of thousands," 1:15) or to the elders, but references instead to *šopṭîm*, "judges."[90] The structure described in Deuteronomy 1 is a reminiscence about the wilderness milieu of patriarchal-tribal hierarchy, where judicial powers were in the hands of tribal and family leaders.[91] The omission of the elders from much of the judicial bureaucracy in Deuteronomy's blueprint for civic life in the land of Israel represents a shift in sociopolitical direction. Because they attained their position by dint of seniority within their respective kinship structures, the elders were neither appointed by the emerging collective body of Israel nor responsible to it. Deuteronomy 16–17 breaks the link between the judiciary and the monarchy on the one hand and the judiciary and the tribal hierarchy on the other.[92]

The elders are not removed entirely, however, from the judicial process. They are retained in Deuteronomy to adjudicate matters that are naturally within their jurisdiction as senior members of the clan: clan and family law. Thus, town elders are ordained to adjudicate the cases of the rebellious son (21:19–20), the suspected adulteress (22:15–18), the levirate marriage (25:7–9), and the blood redeemer (19:11–13).[93] The elders are absent from cases of idolatry (13:2–19; 18:20–22 and esp. 17:2–7) and civil law (25:1–3).

The language and ideas of tribal hierarchy appear at several additional junctures throughout Deuteronomy. The thread that unites nearly all of these is that the tribal elders in these instances are assigned ad hoc roles alone, for the period of transition at hand and for the one that will follow Moses' demise. Virtually no permanent role—either in the political bureaucracy or through the sanction of ritual—is assigned either to the tribes qua tribes or to the tribal elders. The tribes as distinct structures are mentioned at two junctures: first, in connection with the blessings and curses to be recited at Mount Ebal on entry into the land (27:12–13), and second, as the recipients of Moses' blessings in Deuteronomy 33. These events are one-time affairs for this period of transition; neither receives permanent legitimation through the sanction of ritual.

The tribal elders appear at several convocations in which Moses exhorts the nation to faithful service (27:1, 29:9–10; 31:28). The elders, together with the priests, are to be the spiritual leaders after the death of Moses and are thus the natural candidates to ensure continued adherence to his exhortations.[94] It is only in this capacity of safeguarding the teaching of the law that the elders become enshrined in ritual law, the law of the septennial Hakhēl gathering (31:9–13). Other than in connection with family law, they play no role in the judiciary. They have no stated role in the military or in the cult, as had been the case during the wilderness period. It is instructive that on the death of Moses, Joshua assumes the mantle of leadership with no reference to a role to be played by the elders (34:9). Thus we see that the collective power structure of Deuteronomy is achieved by attenuating, though not eradicating, the rule of kingship on the one hand and the rule of kinship on the other.[95]

## Of Moses and Montesquieu

I have explored the various ways the vision of a collective regime dominates the political thinking of Deuteronomy over against that of two regnant models in the political landscape of the ancient Near East. As noted, Deuteronomy circumscribes monarchy in rejection of tyranny and at the same time delimits tribal patriarchy. Central to republican schemes—and Deuteronomy's is no exception—is the notion of a mixed government and a degree of separation of powers. To conclude this chapter, I will locate Deuteronomy's conception of a mixed government along the spectrum of theories of mixed government that have been proposed in the annals of western political thought. This leads to some remarkable conclusions.

The political philosophy of Deuteronomy represents an early and important chapter in the history of constitutional thought and the western notion of a constitutional monarchy. Seats of power in the ancient Near East—royal and cultic alike—invoked mythic origins for their status. In Deuteronomy, by contrast, the institutions of authority share a common origin, and are of equal provenance, status, and privilege, because all are created by the law, and accountable to it.[96]

To this we may add that Deuteronomy illustrates notions of separation of powers that have usually been considered quite recent. Classical Greek political thought understood that in the absence of a strong center in the figure of a monarch or a tyrant, factionalism threatened the stability of the polity. It was inevitable that the population would contain rich and poor, nobles and commoners. Classical theorists saw the solution as a balancing of power such that each faction within society would receive a share of the rule. What Aristotle called a "polity," or regime, was most often part oligarchy and part democracy.

Yet this balance of power was not the balance of institutions of government we are accustomed to today. Rather, the balance was achieved by allowing each of the socioeconomic factions a functioning role *within* each seat of government. Thus, in Polybius's conception, the legislative branch of government in the Roman republic was to consist of two bodies: the senate for the nobles and the assembly for the commoners, with each institution permanently enshrined in law.[97]

The notion that the effective division of power was predicated on its distribution across preexisting societal seats of power held sway across most of the history of republican thought, from Roman theorists through early modern thinkers. The modern notion of the separation of powers into three branches, executive, legislative, and judiciary, is credited to Montesquieu, in his 1748 work *The Spirit of the Laws*. Yet even in this seminal work, class and caste play a critical role in Montesquieu's conception of the effective division of governmental power.

Montesquieu was no more egalitarian than Polybius on this issue. Looking at the English model of his day, Montesquieu stated that the legislative power should consist of a body of hereditary nobles and of a body of commoners.[98] For Montesquieu, it was inconceivable to imagine a classless society and a regime where the division of powers was purely institutional and instrumental. Moreover, he saw hereditary nobility not as a necessary evil, or even as an immutable fact of life, but as a boon to effective government. The nobility, with its inherent wealth and power, would serve as a moderating force within government against the abuses of the monarch.[99] Moreover, the fact that the nobility's strength was derived from its own resources would endow its members with a sense of independence. This, together with developed education and time for reflection, would enable the nobles to contribute to effective government in a way members of the lower classes could not.[100]

It is precisely on this score of the relation between the separation of powers and the question of class that Deuteronomy stands distinct. For the first time in history, a division of at least some powers is articulated along lines of institution and instrument rather than of class and kinship, where office legitimizes preexisting societal seats of power. Not all seats of authority within Deuteronomy, of course, conform to this: the cult is in the hands of the tribe of the Levites, even as they remain economically dependent on the rest of the populace. At the same time, there is an egalitarian streak in the law of kingship, and on two levels. First of all, anyone who is "among your brethren" is eligible to be appointed king. Equally important, no tribe or other entity is sanctioned as the appointing body; the king is appointed by the collective "you." How that selection occurs, apparently, is an issue Deuteronomy deliberately leaves open, so as to imply that no body a priori has a greater divine imprimatur than any other. The tribal elders no longer represent the people at the cult and seem to have no function outside of arranging the Hakhēl convocation every seven years.

Most important is the statement Deuteronomy makes about judges and officers. For Montesquieu, what separates moderate from despotic regimes more than anything else is the independence of the judiciary, whose members are drawn from the common people.[101] Deuteronomy demonstrates remarkable accord with this. Deuteronomy is highly explicit concerning the authority through which each of the powers is determined. It is natural that God should choose to whom He wishes to convey His words, and thus the prophet is determined solely by God: "I will raise up a prophet for them from among their own people" (Deut 18:18). It is also natural that the priests, likewise, are chosen by God alone: "For the Lord your God has chosen [the priest] and his descendants to come, out of all your tribes, to be in attendance for service in the name of the Lord forever" (Deut 18:5). The king, however, is dually chosen, by the people he leads and by God whose people he leads: "you shall be free to set a king over yourself, one chosen by the Lord your God. Be sure to set as king over yourself one of your own people; you must not set a foreigner over you, one who is not your kinsman" (Deut 17:15). The judiciary, however, is chosen exclusively by human agents: "*you* shall appoint judges and officers in all the settlements that the Lord your God is giving to your tribes" (Deut 16:18). The egalitarian streak here is manifest, as in the case of the king, in dual fashion. Anyone may be appointed judge, and no less important, anyone, in theory, is eligible to participate in the process of appointing judges. One could easily imagine a dictate whereby any number of authoritative bodies would have a hand in appointing judges: the king, the priests, the elders, currently sitting judges, and/or the prophet. The judiciary in Deuteronomy is radically independent. Here, for the first time, is a view of public office as institutional and instrumental. The appointment of judges is mandated with the sole purpose of achieving the execution of justice, rather than the assignment of office to perpetuate the standing of a noble class. In this sense, this program is suggestive of the program that would appear only with the American founding fathers. Deuteronomy is a document in which heredity and class play little role in government—a document that has no word for class, caste, noble, or landed gentry.

# 3

# Egalitarianism and Assets

*God the Economist*

January 1, 1863, marked a monumental day in the legislative history of the United States, when two landmark pieces of legislation took effect. One was the Emancipation Proclamation, which freed all slaves who came under control of Union forces in the Civil War, liberating some 4 million slaves by 1865. While the Emancipation Proclamation extended civil equality, the Homestead Act, also enacted on that day, sought to create greater economic equality for millions of Americans. This act opened the Great Plains to mass settlement; nearly any man who was at least 21 years of age could acquire at virtually no cost a tract of 160 acres that would become his after five years of residence and farming. For 2 million new arrivals and other landless Americans, the Homestead Act was an opportunity to acquire assets and to bring equality of economic standing in line with equality before the law.[1] It underscored the philosophy that there is no equality without equity.

I have, to this point, examined the way a strand of thought in the biblical tradition, particularly the Pentateuch, sought an elevated position for the common man as the member of an ennobled and empowered citizenry. I have shown how this was achieved theologically through the notion of covenant and conceived politically in the Book of Deuteronomy. Ennoblement and empowerment, however, are not achieved in the theological or political realms alone. In this chapter, I examine how the law collections of the Pentateuch articulate a philosophy of riches with the social goal in mind of ensuring that a broad swath of the citizenry remain landed and economically secure. From these codes we may derive the western tradition's first articulation of a prescription for an economic order that seeks to minimize the distinctions of class based on wealth and instead seeks to ensure the economic benefit of the common citizen.

Each area of law I will examine has been the subject of comparative study with reference to parallel laws found elsewhere in the judicial corpora of the ancient Near East. The whole, however, is greater than the sum of the parts; laws that are uniformly treated as separate and independent, in fact, together make a larger statement about the theology and social reasoning that guide the distribution of assets in a covenantal society and reflect a concern to minimize extreme advantage.

## Analyzing Biblical Law Codes: Methodological Considerations

The source material that relates to economic activity in the Bible is vast and stems from many sources over many centuries. In seeking what I have been referring to as a strand of thought within the Bible that rejects hierarchy and seeks to promote egalitarianism, I focus on the law collections of the Pentateuch. One could, perhaps, adduce a theory of riches derived from narrated episodes, for example, the call to return items held in collateral in Nehemiah 5, the manumission of debt-slaves in Jeremiah 34, or the seizure of Naboth's vineyard by the wicked queen Jezebel in 1 Kings 21. Narrative stories, however, tell of a specific set of circumstances. Laws, by contrast, formulated to be prescriptive in nature over a variety of circumstances, more closely approximate a systematic approach. Any reading of the codes, however, is perforce predicated on a number of hermeneutical and methodological assumptions, and I shall lay mine out at the outset.

There is a well-trodden path in the scholarship on the law codes of the Hebrew Bible that represents an attempt to paint a whole picture, one that accounts for the sociohistorical origins of the law as well as its textual history. This scholarship routinely seeks to assign a given set of laws to specific hypothetical authors and/or editors.[2] A hypothesis is put forth to account for the evolutionary chronology of a given law; how a law, say, in the Book of Exodus undergoes reformulation and conceptual evolution as evidence in a parallel law, say, in the Book of Deuteronomy.[3] The form of the law in each source is explained from a sociohistorical perspective, or as the reflection of a particular ideology. The result is satisfying, because it offers a total picture: It places the law at hand in a specific sociohistorical context, and at the same time explains the variance among similar laws in legal sections of the Bible, while also accounting for the law's textual and conceptual development.

This well-trodden path, however, relies on a high degree of speculation at a great many turns. A methodological standard with which to address the questions of history and evolution surrounding the laws is sorely lacking. This is because of a dearth of sources we can reliably ascribe to the periods in question, as well as the absence of a consensus over first assumptions involved in tackling these questions.[4] Hence, a review of scholarship concerning the interconnection between the various laws of manumission of debt-servants in Exodus 21, Leviticus 25, and Deuteronomy 15 reveals a multitude of opinions on the subject.[5]

In this chapter, I will note the points of divergence among the various law corpora on a given issue, but also take a more conservative approach concerning our capacity to date the laws and to pinpoint their origins. I will not endeavor to locate the origins of the laws, their evolution, or their textual history, short of noting their affinity with what we know about socioeconomic conditions in tribal Israel.[6] Indeed, as I noted in the introduction, the narrative context of pentateuchal law confirms that the Pentateuch—in the form we have it in now—was meant to be read sequentially, as a whole. The embedding of law within narrative relegates the reading of law to the conventions of narrative, which is to say that it may be read as an integrated whole, whatever the prehistory of these texts and laws.[7] It is less secure to establish the origin and provenance of a law than to establish what I would call the social world of the text: the relations of social classes that the text assumes and the ideology it inculcates to guide these relations. Rather than seeking to locate a law's specific origins and its specific evolutionary trajectory, I will seek to analyze the laws in light of the geopolitical domain of the ancient Near East. The political and socioeconomic experience of many societies will serve as a resource for us to derive the implications of the economic laws of the Pentateuch. Some of these socioeconomic trends predate the biblical laws, some are contemporary with them, and some postdate them. My assumption, however, will be that because the laws are prescriptive and not ad hoc legislation for a one-time event, they aim to address a wide canvas of socioeconomic situations.

What we will see time and again is the way preexisting concepts and institutions in ancient Near Eastern culture are reworked according to a new agenda that advocates the attenuation of the socioeconomic hierarchy. I will be engaging the juridical corpora of those cultures in a comparative study, and here, too, I will make my methodological assumptions clear at the outset.

The role the law codes of the ancient Near East played in society is a subject of great debate. Rarely are they comprehensive in their treatment of the law. Moreover, it is far from clear that these "codes" served a juridical function: as has been famously noted, of the many thousands of Mesopotamian legal documents in our possession, not one cites the Code of Hammurabi, or any other "code," for authority. This in spite of the fact that the Code of Hammurabi was so esteemed that it was recopied for more than a millennium following its composition in the eighteenth century B.C.E. All of this suggests that ancient Near Eastern law codes were of a literary, rather than juridical, nature.[8]

Generally, three approaches to the law codes of the ancient Near East are adduced. Some scholars see them as idyllic collections of judicial problems and solutions. Others see them as thematic guides meant to serve judges, as juridical training texts. Yet others see them as the king's statements of self-justification to posterity or to the gods concerning the just character of his reign.[9] Whether these putative "laws" indeed served a statutory purpose or, as is more commonly accepted, were statements of juridical philosophy, we may legitimately see them as reflections of wider systems of thought and ideology. When we read a particular "law," it does not stand on its own, available for immediate interpretation, but must be understood as just one element of the culture in which it is embedded.[10]

Turning now to the nature of biblical law codes, a similar range of issues comes to the fore. The cases covered in these laws are far from comprehensive, and their formulations lack the scope and precision necessary for juridical rulings. Diachronic approaches have spawned a developed literature that seeks to trace the historical origins of these laws.[11] To understand, however, how the received form of the Bible frames and presents them, we do well to refer to the way I introduced them in chapter 1: the laws are, first and foremost, *treaty stipulations*. They are the conditions and mandates set down by the sovereign king YHWH for His treaty with the vassal Israel.[12] As such, they are prescriptive in nature, and are meant to be binding on the members of the covenantal community. It is on the basis of the fulfillment of these stipulations that Israel the vassal will be judged by the heavenly sovereign king, just as earthly sovereigns judged their vassals on the basis of their compliance with the treaty stipulations. It may well be, additionally, that Scripture intends that judges make quasi-statutory, analogical, or referential uses of some of these laws.[13] At the same time, it is clear that judges, perforce, must have also engaged a comprehensive oral law, or set of unwritten norms and social customs.

The nature of biblical law codes, it may be posited, is different from those of the ancient Near East. Only in the Bible is law presented as divine revelation, and only in the Bible do laws appear as treaty stipulations between a sovereign and a vassal. Moreover, we find that biblical law is often expressed in a paranetic or sermonic style, and is interwoven with narrative, homily, and hortatory passages, all uncharacteristic of ancient Near Eastern law. At the same time, these treaty stipulations share much in common with the terminology, formulation, and legal themes found in the law codes of the ancient Near East. While it remains unclear to what degree each set of laws was regarded as statutory and legislative in nature, we may nonetheless legitimately compare the laws of the Bible with those in the codes of the ancient Near East. For like those laws, the laws of the Bible may be rightly viewed as reflections of wider systems of thought and ideology, as the indexes of the blueprint of a civilization.[14]

## Economies Modern and Premodern

The task of adducing a theory of economic distribution from the laws of the Bible, however, is a daunting one. One is tempted to proceed by identifying the laws that deal with economic affairs, to assess their overall message, and to draw conclusions. Yet if we do so without an awareness of the mental divide between our world and the biblical world, we will be doomed to misunderstand. As the late Hungarian American economist Karl Polanyi noted, inhabitants of a commerce-based economic order, such as ours, stand at an enormous divide from those who lived in premodern society. Once upon a time, he noted, the economic order was merely a function of the social order in which it was subsumed. In the capitalist world we inhabit, however, the opposite is the case: social relations have become embedded in the economic system.[15] Several examples will illustrate this mental gulf. For us, the agents of production—land, labor, and capital—are impersonal, dehumanized entities. We buy and sell as anonymous economic agents. Any social relations between the buyer and seller of, say, a house or an automobile are merely incidental.

By contrast, in premodern economies, economic exchange is often an act of building a social relationship.[16] Sometimes norms of reciprocal exchange are governed by kinship and community to guarantee subsistence livelihood, particularly in tribal agrarian settings. At other times, the norms of the redistribution of wealth on the basis of class are dictated by caste membership.[17] Thus, in England, as late as the fourteenth or fifteenth centuries, land was not construed in the sense of a commodity that was freely salable, rent-producing property. Estates, manors, and principalities were emphatically not real estate in the commercial sense of today. Rather, inherited lands were the core of social life, the basis for prestige and status.[18] Nor was labor at this time any more salable. A country peasant was tied to his lord's estate. It was there that he tilled the lord's fields, ground his grains, and even served in his wars. The remuneration he received was not in the form of monetary payment. Rather, in return for his duties as a serf, he received benefits and protection from his lord. In the cities, an apprentice would enter the service of a master, but, as a rule, under predetermined conditions established by a guild.[19]

Another great divide between modern and premodern economies concerns the socioeconomic role of the family. In subsistence agriculture, production and consumption occur within the same social context, and there is limited exchange outside the family.[20] Economic roles and family roles all reside in the kinship structure, in the communal structures, and in the religious traditions that fortify both of these.[21] By contrast, in capitalist economies, the social setting for production (i.e. the workplace) and consumption (i.e. the home) are separated. In modern settings of economic production, individuals become isolated—geographically, temporally, and structurally—from their roles as members of a family.[22] Now the forces of the market command the movement of goods and services, rather than the religious, political, or familial sanctions that once governed economic activity.[23] More recent scholarship has claimed that Polanyi and his followers went too far, and that, in fact, throughout history market forces were always at play to a greater degree than Polanyi realized. But this criticism does not invalidate the observation that in premodern times, religious, political, and social mores influenced economic activity in ways and to a degree no longer prevalent in the capitalist West.[24]

Thus, in assessing the economic philosophy of the biblical legal collections, we need to be mindful that its terms can be properly construed only as a function of the larger social and, in this case, theological order within which it is embedded. Understanding what the Pentateuch has to say about lending and borrowing, taxation, and land tenure is not a matter of assessing several scattered verses, but of seeing those verses in relation to the wider social and theological statements within which they appear.

As noted in the introduction, this study is executed with the understanding that at many junctures throughout the history of the ancient Near East, the primary economic structure in society was the divide between the *dominant tribute-imposing class* and *the dominated tribute-bearing class*. One leitmotif in the biblical law codes is an attempt to restructure society in such a way that the exploitative role of tribute paid to a political elite is eliminated. I will show how the Bible's law codes have a tendency toward curbing the capacity to accrue great private wealth on the one hand while they radically transform both the theological and social role of tribute on the other.

A ubiquitous feature of the socioeconomic landscape of the ancient Near East was the danger the common man faced of falling into irreversible insolvency. Social stratification emerged as free citizens lost control over their means of production. A common pattern of this process was as follows. A peasant—a small landowner—resides on a small plot of privately owned lands, and engages in subsistence farming.[25] As his margins of profit are slim, he can go into debt for any number of reasons: personal illness, crop failure, taxation, or the monopoly of resources by the state or private elite. His first line of recourse is to procure a loan, which he can only get at high interest. The high interest renders him insolvent, so he is forced to sell or deliver family members into debt-slavery, to pay off the debt (see 2 Kgs 4:1–7; Neh 5:1–13). When this does not secure the means to pay off the debt, he has to resort to relinquishing or selling his own land (Neh 5:1–13)—his means of production—and, finally, to selling himself. Thus, he is compelled to enter the service of the state or some arrangement of feudal sharecropping for the landowning elite.[26] Indeed, records of debt-slavery in Mesopotamia emerge as early as the Ur III period (2050–1955 B.C.E.), and the institution was a permanent feature of the socioeconomic landscape of the ancient Near East.[27]

To counter this cycle, the biblical laws introduce a series of legal and conceptual reforms that together seek to achieve social equality—but of a very specific kind. It is not the egalitarianism developed since the French Revolution with its emphasis on the individual and inalienable human rights. Nor does this equality manifest itself in family organization, size of holdings, or amount of production. Rather, it takes the form of an economic system that seeks equality by granting communal and divine legitimation to respective households that assist one another in agrarian labor and granting relief to other households in need.[28] It envisions an association of free farmers and herdsmen, subsumed within a single social class, where the common ownership of the means of production is vested within extended kinship groups.[29] It is a system that rejects both statism and feudalism. Its rejection of statism is manifest in the fact that it is virtually tribute-free. Israel defined itself, according to the Pentateuch, in opposition to the empire of oppression, Egypt, but also in opposition to the centralized, bureaucratic states that populated the land of Israel[30] As shown in chapter 2, the Pentateuch largely rejects the monarchic principle as it was construed elsewhere, often with a religiously sanctioned central government, a professional army, and an elite class of charioteers. Instead, the biblical laws seek to advance a mode of production and an accompanying set of power relations that will build up the whole society, serving the greatest number of people, rather than a political or financial elite.[31]

While these laws have a social orientation, they are intimately bound up in theological notions as well. Only by appreciating the theology that stands behind these laws will we be able to fully construe their social implications. The economic policies that distinguished pentateuchal law from the norms of the ancient Near East were deep reflections of the theological differences I out-lined in chapter 1. Other cultures of the ancient Near East identified their gods as the creators of the world (in Egypt, Re and Atum; in Mesopotamia, Marduk, Ninurta, and Ashur, among others). Yet in these cultures, the divinity's rule over the resources of the world was refracted through that of the earthly king and his bureaucracy. In many quarters of the ancient Near East, the heavenly realm mirrored the earthly realm. Just as earthly kingship was legitimated by heavenly kingship, so, too, earthly hierarchy was legitimated by heavenly hier-archy, such that the distinctions among classes received cosmic sanction. The ultimate sovereignty of the gods manifested itself through the siphoning of resources from the dominated tribute-bearing class to the dominant tribute-imposing class, in accordance with the putative will of the gods. The Pentateuch, however, while mentioning the heavenly host, does not indicate the presence of a well-developed heavenly hierarchy, one that would ipso facto grant meta-physical legitimation to an order of haves and have-nots.[32] Absent a strong, centralized monarchical bureaucracy within the narrated world of the Pentateuch, the sovereignty of God is left unmitigated, unrefracted. All land, all persons are under His direct sovereignty.

A second theological postulate at work in these laws is that of God's iden-tity as the liberator of slaves. He forms a people out of those who were deemed to be people of no standing at all by the political and economic leaders who op-pressed them.[33] The egalitarian streak within pentateuchal laws accords with the portrayal of the exodus as the prime experience of Israel's self-understand-ing.[34] Indeed, no Israelite can lay claim to any greater status, because all ema-nate from the Exodus—a common seminal, liberating, and equalizing event. The twin notions of God's unmitigated sovereignty as creator and as liberator were notions that animated the measures the biblical law codes took to limit and curb the phenomenon of Israelite peasants descending into the cycle of insolvency.

In the sections that follow, I shall explore how the legal collections of the Pentateuch legislated to ensure that a broad swath of the citizenry remain landed, and economically secure. These laws, I will show, were invariably re-workings of preexistent norms and concepts in the juridical corpora of the ancient Near East. The reformulations invariably focused around two themes. In the first, the laws envision an economic order that minimizes the distinc-tions of class based on wealth. The second theme stems from the first. In order to ensure the establishment of a single-class society, the biblical laws under-score bonds of community and kinship.

The areas of law I will examine follow the natural economic order of the insolvency cycle described earlier:

1. *Land tenure.* I begin my exploration by assessing the laws concerning the ownership of land—the central means of production. The construction of the bulwark against insolvency begins with the enactment of laws that help the common man retain ownership of the land.
2. *Tithing.* While some causes of debt, such as crop failure, could not be legislated, protocols of taxation were one area that could be legislated to help the common man retain his solvency.
3. *Borrowing and interest.* Once in debt, a peasant could look for a loan as relief. Reforms in this realm made the terms of receiving a loan far more favorable to the borrower.
4. *Release edicts: an overview.* Edicts to alleviate debt and its consequences were legion in the ancient Near East. The biblical law collections reworked this concept in several important ways—theologically, socially, and economically.
5. *Debt release.* A primary element of the release edicts was the cancellation of debts. This is reworked in Deuteronomy to create a social and political dynamic that contrasts with that created elsewhere in the ancient Near East.
6. *Land redemption.* Another element of the ancient Near Eastern release edicts was land redemption. The institution is reworked theologically producing a far more liberating effect for the repatriated Israelite peasant.
7. *Manumission of debt-servants.* Exodus theology permeates the laws of manumission, as several stipulations set apart the laws of debt-servant release in the Bible from the prevailing norms found elsewhere.

For each of these areas, I will contrast the biblical law with the parallel norm in the ancient Near East, through an initial exploration of the theology that distinctly animates the reworking of the law in the Bible. From there, I will proceed to delineate the import of the law for Israelite society from a social and economic perspective.

## Land Tenure

Land was a primary means of production in agrarian society, and the legal collections, particularly those in Leviticus 25, reformulated ancient Near Eastern norms of land tenure in order to ensure that the Israelite peasant would retain his means of production.

To appreciate how the program of Leviticus 25 constitutes a striking break from ancient Near Eastern practices of land tenure, one must first consider the norms practiced elsewhere. Across the region, lands were held by varying combinations of actors or principals. Lands held by private individuals are attested, but were not the norm.[35] More often, lands were held communally, by, say, a tribe or a clan. But far and away the largest tracts of land were owned by the palace and by the temple.[36] The Pentateuch, in contrast, knows of no land-holding on the part of either the king or the cult. To be sure, when Deuteronomy speaks of a king (17:14–20), it implicitly must recognize that the king will have a residence; and elsewhere, residential areas are explicitly set aside for the members of the cult (Num 35:1–8; Lev 25:32). But neither the king nor the cult controls the means of production in this society—unlike the other agrarian societies throughout the ancient Near East. Instead, nearly all the land is turned over to the people themselves.[37]

To understand what it means in this context to say that the people had ownership of the land, however, we must first shed our modern understanding of "ownership" of land. For the most part, we relate to the ownership of land in absolute terms. The owner of a tract of land, be it an individual or a corporation, has the all the rights to that land—its development, its sale, and its produce. But in the ancient world, it was more common for land tenure to be conceived in terms of the parceling out of various rights. One person, say, an official, or a king, could own the land, while the rights to a portion of its yield could belong to someone else. Peasants had rights of usufruct, or "use-ownership" of the land they lived on, while title to the land belonged to the state.[38] Thus, in the New Kingdom in Egypt (c. 1550–1070 B.C.E.), for example, possession of lands was mediated through the usufruct of production. The official would take his share of the crop, and the actual field-worker would be subservient to him. The rights that were assigned to the service and production of others formed a multitiered system of recompense.[39] Similarly, lists of farmworkers at Ugarit suggest that the royal court had control of the land and that peasants were being paid for their work.[40]

The Pentateuch does not offer systematic guidelines regarding the issue of land tenure: how ownership was established and maintained, and how land was purchased.[41] The sole text that addresses in detail the legal status of the land held by individuals and clans is Leviticus 25. And here we may see how the notion of ownership of rights of production, rather than outright ownership of the land, comes into play. Like many other systems of land tenure in the ancient Near East, that of Leviticus 25 is predicated on the inalienability of the land outside of the family, in the recognition that absolute ownership of land was critical for economic security.[42] In Leviticus 25, however, the inalienability of property is presented with theological overtones. The ultimate owner of the land is God, and He grants rights to it to His people, Israel, as an everlasting holding, or in the legal terminology of the ancient Near East, as a land grant.[43] In the ancient Near East, a land grant represented a promise by a donor, often a king, to a recipient, in presupposition of the loyalty of the latter, or in recompense for services rendered.[44]

The theology of land grant by the divine king bears implications of a social and economic nature. Within the biblical scheme, the recipient of the land is Israel as a collective. Yet specific parcels of land are granted to individual families and clans (Lev 25:25–28; Ruth 4:3–6; Num 27:4, 11).[45] One central feature of this form of land tenure, in the Bible and elsewhere in premodern societies, is the feature that the land is not fully salable; you cannot sell it to whomever you want.[46] This has several ramifications. If one landowner has a good harvest and his neighbor does not, the temptation would naturally emerge for the successful landowner to buy out the land of his neighbor, effectively reducing the latter to dependency, while enabling the former to expand further his means of production (see Isa 5:8).[47]

Moreover, the collective ownership of the basic means of production— land, herds and flocks—by extended families served as a form of insurance against crop failure. Extended families were a structure of subclustered protective associations, subsumed under the further backing of the tribe.[48] What emerged were local and regional groupings of families entrusted to ensure each other's welfare.[49] The extended family (mišpaḥâ) constituted the risk-spreading context for the agricultural basis of the family.[50]

Anthropologists have noted that a key component of the success of this type of "insurance" in the form of clan-based mutual assistance is that the population needs to be immobile. That is, the mutual assistance bond among nested family groupings is only as strong as their geographic contiguity and cohesion. Hence, we may well understand from an economic perspective the call in Leviticus 25 for the redemption of tribal lands in the Jubilee year, a subject I will take up more broadly later. Mobility—the dissolution of this contiguity— would lead to a natural reluctance among neighboring landholders to share freely among themselves. In many primitive societies where the insurance principle is at work, mobility is quite restricted, and where mobility is high, the tendency toward reciprocal exchange tends to dissipate.[51]

To summarize, the laws of Leviticus 25 rework existing institutions in order to shore up the economic stability of the common man of Israel. In this first instance, we have seen how this is so with regard to norms of land tenure. No land in Israel is owned by the state, or the king, and very little by the temple, or by its officiants (Lev 25: 32–34). Rather, the land is held by individual families as a grant from the sovereign, in this case, God. The peasant's hold on the land is buttressed by two elements. The first is the cluster of family subunits that own the land, and offer a mutual assistance group for each other in time of need. The second element of the system is the limitation concerning the salability of the land. As it may not be sold in perpetuity, the peasant never runs the risk of being permanently alienated from the land, which is his means of production.

## Tithing

As noted, one element that could contribute to a peasant's descent into the cycle of insolvency was the burden of tribute or taxation, and here we may witness in the biblical laws a radical departure from norms prevalent elsewhere in the ancient Near East. Philology here is instructive for the comparison. Cognates of the Hebrew word for tithe, *ma'ăśer*, likewise connote activities of taxation elsewhere in the ancient Near East. In Ugarit, the *ma'šaru* or *mēšertu* was a payment consisting of a tenth of products of the field and on cattle. We similarly find a Babylonian tithe called *ešrû*.

What was the nature of these tithes? In our age, we readily distinguish between dues paid to a house of worship and taxes paid to the state. But in the documents that address the issue of tithing in the ancient Near East, it is not clear that such a distinction can be made. Tithes delivered to the temple precincts may well have been taxes for the state, and vice versa.[52] It is unclear whether in the ancient Near East it was meaningful to speak of a temple economy that stood independent of a state (i.e. royal) economy. In light of the religious legitimation given the court, as noted in chapter 1, we might do best to speak of the cult as the state temple, and of the king's regime as the sacral monarchy.[53] The distinction is not crucial here, however, since the tithing practices I am comparing—those of the cultures of the ancient Near East and those in the law codes of the Pentateuch—are ones broadly conceived as both tax tribute to the king and financial support of the cult.

In this regard, the Pentateuch laws stand distinct as they mandate tribute neither to the king nor to any other bureaucratic administration outside of the cult.[54] No regime, of course, would be able to function without taxing its populace; but such taxes, within the scheme of the law codes, apparently were to be levied without metaphysical sanction, as was so prevalent elsewhere. The freedom from religiously sanctioned tribute is an expression of the broader freedom from the monarchy I outlined in chapter 2. Instead, the Israelites are granted the liberty of the full and free use of their own labor products.[55] Again, the social policy is an extension of the theology. God the liberator seeks for Israel to live in freedom from its neighbors. Moreover, God the liberator seeks for each member of Israel to live in freedom without becoming the dependent of a wealthy elite class of rulers.

This departure emerges in bold relief when we consider some of the laws of tithing elsewhere in the ancient Near East. In Ugarit, the *ma'šaru* or *mēšertu* was a payment consisting of a tenth of the products of the field and the cattle. The military elites, or *maryannu*, were exempt from these taxes.[56] The biblical tithes were levied on all landowners, with no exemptions of any sort based on class or group distinctions. The texts surrounding the Babylonian tithe, *ešrū*, attest to the brutality that could follow when a tithe payment could not be made. In one instance, an individual who had defaulted on his tithe was made to surrender his offspring to the temple until he could pay off his debt through labor. Temples routinely found themselves with excess capital, which allowed them to engage in business enterprises, including a form of banking in which tithe produce was loaned out at high rates of interest.[57] Later sources, from the sixth century B.C.E., indicate that defaulters were made to borrow against their land or to deliver a member of their household into servitude or to pay late with interest.[58] While we know little about the tithing practices of ancient Egypt, it is clear that in the New Kingdom (c. 1550–1070 B.C.E.) the priesthood controlled an immense amount of land. We may assume that in Egypt and elsewhere, priestly consumption of wealth did not come at the expense of the ruling elites, but rather at the expense of the communal production the common people might otherwise have consumed.[59]

While tithes were given to the Levites and priests (Num 18:8–32; Deut 14:27, 18:3–5), these groups were given specifically designated residential holdings, and could not amass additional holdings. This restriction fundamentally alters the nature of the tithe. Precisely because Levites and priests could not hold agricultural lands, the tithes given to them were incorporated in a process of reciprocity. On the one hand, the priests and Levites are chosen— "drafted" may be a more precise term (see Num 4)—by God to serve as His attendants. The priests also represent a caste of teachers whose task it is to teach the laws to the entire people (Lev 10:11). Within Deuteronomy, I have shown, the priests are also cast more broadly, in a variety of ways, as the guardians of the law. On the other hand, they are essentially rendered dependents, and the payment of the tithes to them is a form of social security they receive (Num 4:23, 30, 35, 39, 43), because, unlike the rest of the people, they cannot earn their sustenance from land they inherit.[60]

As noted earlier, the Bible posits that God holds ownership over the entire land. At the same time, though, less surplus is demanded from the people of Israel for the cult than was customary in the imperial cults of the ancient Near

East.[61] In Mesopotamian cities, the temple was typically a complex administrative apparatus that controlled vast economic resources—principally vast stores of grain harvested from large tracts of land under temple control—and employed thousands of laborers. A text from Seleucid Uruk dating from the end of the first millennium B.C.E. indicates that a daily ration of half a ton of bread and fifty-four containers of beer and wine were brought as food offerings. Seventeen hundred milk cows out of a total herd of nearly ten times that size are recorded for the temple of Nanna and Ningal at Ur, from the Old Babylonian period. The temple at Nippur processed 350,000 sheep and goats annually.[62] By contrast, even on festivals, the Pentateuch never mandates community offerings in excess of a dozen or so animals a day.[63] So the scope of tribute is greatly minimized in the biblical law codes, and repercussions for failing to comply with its demands are entirely absent.

The biblical law collections reformulate norms of tithing in one additional way, seen in the laws of the tithes as they appear in Deuteronomy. Tithing in Leviticus speaks of support for the cult generally (Lev 27:30–33; see Gen 14:20; 28:22), and tithing in Numbers speaks of the practice in terms of a support mechanism for priests and Levites (Num 18:21–32). But in Deuteronomy the revision of the institution of tithing relative to the norms of the ancient Near East receives its greatest formulation.[64]

According to Deuteronomy, the recipient of the tithe in two out of every three years was none other than the Israelite producer himself, who was mandated to consume the tithe at the site of the central sanctuary (Deut 14:22–27). This mandate reflected a twofold agenda. The tithe here emerges as a means of providing the common people with a religious experience at the central sanctuary.[65] In the previous chapter, I highlighted the role cult can play in a collective power structure. In archaic states that practice a collective power strategy, ritual both sanctifies and culturally reinforces an egalitarian spirit through numinous experience[66] and group-oriented chiefdoms feature large architectural spaces suitable for group ritual.[67] Moreover, as the tithe constituted a tenth of his produce, it was inevitable that the pilgrim farmer would have far more grain at his disposal than he could consume. Sharing the surplus with other community members, and particularly with those in need, would be an inevitable outcome of this mandate.

In the third year, the tithe was given directly to the economically disadvantaged groups (Deut 14:27–29; 26:12–15). The writings of other ancient Near Eastern cultures show a general concern with alleviating the misery of such individuals. Yet the tithe of the third year in Deuteronomy represents the first known program of legislated taxation for a social purpose.[68]

Deuteronomy's notion of tithes—that for two out of three years surplus is shared broadly with the disadvantaged, and in the third year is given to them outright—is sound economics when seen in light of conceptions of redistributive economics in primitive societies. In modern capitalist societies, surplus earnings are placed into savings, and insurance policies are taken out to hedge against various forms of adversity. The laws of tithing may be construed as another element in a program of primitive insurance. In a premodern society, A will give some of his surplus in a good year to B, who may have fallen on hard times in exchange for B's commitment to reciprocate should their roles one day be reversed. This form of hunger insurance is especially attractive under two circumstances, both of which, for my purposes, were probably economic realities the law collections are intended to address, given climatic conditions in the land of Israel. The first is the difficulty of storing food long term. Food surplus cannot be simply and easily put aside for a later season of failed crops. The second is a relative scarcity of alternative goods for which the farmer can trade his agricultural surplus. The economy the laws envision includes no provisions about trade or merchant activity, and it is not clear what goods might have been available to a person with a surplus crop. Tithes, therefore, make good economic sense—as hunger insurance for all involved.

The sharing of excess in this kind of redistributive scheme is just one way premodern economies seek to bring about more ex post facto economic equality than the free market would. Generally speaking, sharing within the community and generosity toward other village members is a more highly valued trait in premodern than in modern society. Acts we moderns perceive as altruism may well reflect a socially mandated norm and the economic wisdom of informal insurance.[69]

The economic interdependence between the laws of land tenure and of tithing are further elucidated by insights from the anthropological literature. The success of redistributive mechanisms hinges on a key factor: individuals will be willing to share their surplus only within a social structure of members who continually interact with each other and share like propensities and prospects. In a word, they will be most willing to share in this fashion within the family. This creates a trade-off, from an economic perspective. On the one hand, the smaller and more geographically concentrated a kinship group is, the more likely its members are to be inclined to help each other. The problem from the standpoint of the efficacy of redistributive economics is that the nuclear family is small. Larger groups are better from an insurance standpoint, as is geographic dispersal. Hence, premodern societies devote much more in the way of linguistic, legal, and informational resources to delineating and maintaining kinship groups than do modern families. The desideratum, from an insurance standpoint, is that a kinship group should be as large and diverse as possible while still allowing kin group members to feel socially, politically, and existentially connected to one another.[70] Indeed, the extended legislation in the codes concerning family law (Lev 18, 20; Deut 22:13–29) is intended, in part, to legislate boundary limits that establish the bonds of kinship and of mutual responsibility.

We may now further appreciate the laws of land tenure in Leviticus 25, which highlight collective kinship ownership of patrimonial lands, in subclustered units. The size of these extended kin groups, spread out over a large region, reflects economic wisdom: bonds of familial solidarity are formed, enabling an individual to sacrifice for another with confidence that the measure will be reciprocated should the need arise. At the same time, the large size of the kin group and its dispersal over a large region are factors that help mitigate risk, from an insurance standpoint. Deuteronomy seeks to extend the risk base by attenuating tribal bonds in favor of national ones. Recall the terminology of national bonds noted in chapter 2—that the often-repeated term "brother" refers to a fellow Israelite, particularly in Deuteronomy.[71]

To summarize, the biblical law collections minimize the scope of religiously sanctioned taxation for purposes of supporting the crown, and even the cult. In Deuteronomy, instead, the tithes are recast as catalysts of a social program. Tithes afford the general populace the opportunity to engage in a collective numinous experience at the central shrine, which underscores the significance of all members, and fosters national cohesion. Tithes become transformed into a form of taxation in order to support a social agenda of caring for the disadvantaged. Finally, taxation through tithing emerges as a form of premodern insurance among a large pool of individuals bound by extended kinship ties and by a common ideology and purpose.

*Interest and Borrowing*

When a peasant found himself in dire straits financially, he would naturally seek a loan. A distinctive feature of biblical economic thinking, when seen against the backdrop of ancient Near Eastern law codes, is found in the laws concerning loans and interest. Throughout the ancient Near East, interest was allowed, although the law codes routinely limited it. It was common for interest on money loans to be set at 20 percent and on grain loans at 33.3 percent.[72] These were fixed rates that did not fluctuate as a reflection of actual economic returns, but seem to have been chosen for their ease of numerical calculation.[73] Alone among the cultures of the ancient Near East, the Bible issues prohibitions against charging interest (Exod 22:24; Lev 25:35–37; Deut 23:20–21; victuals at interest Deut 23:20; Lev 25:37; and anything else, Deut 23:20).[74] In Exodus 22:24 and Leviticus 25:35–37, the prohibition is stated with explicit reference to the poor. Yet in Deuteronomy 23:20, it is explicitly stated with reference to any Israelite.[75]

The prohibition on taking interest may be understood in the anthropological terms I discussed earlier. In primitive societies, such a law may be seen from the perspective of insurance. A loan is not considered a "favor" bestowed; rather, it simply constitutes the payment of an insurance claim, in that each member of the polity is duty bound to insure the others. To allow interest would be counter to the nature of the mutual responsibility members share toward each other.[76] That the prohibition against taking interest is a function of community building is very much evident in the language of the prohibition in Deuteronomy: "To a foreigner you may charge interest, but to your brother you shall not charge interest" (Deut 23:20). The charging of interest was not inherently immoral, as was suggested by Plato and Aristotle.[77] Rather it was a function of defining and bolstering identity within the collective brotherhood and of establishing the norms of responsibility that come with membership in it.

Other laws in the Bible demonstrate an awareness that, as the author of Proverbs wrote, "The rich rules over the poor, and the borrower is servant to the lender" (Prov 22:7; see Job 24:3).[78] Temples were frequent creditors in ancient Babylonia. The Šamaš temple served as a kind of bank that offered loans at interest.[79] This practice is not indicated with regard to the temple anywhere in the Bible.[80] The Code of Hammurabi deals extensively with pledges and cases of loan default.[81] Yet the limitations the Bible places on a creditor concerning the pledges he can take are singular in the legal codes of the ancient Near East: he may not possess it overnight and may not enter the house to seize it (Deut 24:10–13).[82] Items necessary for production may not be taken as pledges either (Deut 24:6). Moreover, the Laws of Eshnunna and the Code of Hammurabi provide sanctions against a debtor who becomes insolvent: he may be imprisoned and may have members of his family seized by the creditor.[83] Biblical law does not allow for the seizure of a person or his family in the event of forfeiture.[84] The creditor's right to repayment in all of these laws is subordinated to the economic survival and the personal dignity of the debtor.

To summarize, the prohibition against lending at interest to fellow citizens, nowhere else legislated, served the biblical agenda on a number of fronts. It closed an avenue through which the rich could accrue greater wealth at the expense of the needy. It fostered a sense of community and shared responsibility.

It further served as a boundary marker between those within the collective brotherhood and those who stood outside it.

### Release Edicts: An Overview

Financial insolvency could leave individuals in permanent straits with no hope of regaining their independence. This could manifest itself, as we saw, through a number of avenues. He could be in debt to a creditor for sums that would never realistically allow him to regain solvency. He could become alienated from his tribal or familial lands with no hope of ever regaining possession of them. He could resort to having to sell either himself or a dependent into debt-slavery, with no hope of ever being able to repurchase his freedom or theirs.

Throughout the ancient Near East, cultures routinely enacted relief edicts and releases that are the backdrop for biblical legislation in these regards. In Mesopotamia, we have evidence of these releases from as early as the middle of the third millennium B.C.E. until nearly the dawn of the Common Era. In the Old Babylonian period, roughly prior to the middle of the second millennium B.C.E., these edicts are often referred to as edicts that "establish *mīšarum*." *Mīšarum* edicts relieved private debts and state levies of the past, released debt slaves, and returned individuals to their alienated land. We have only a single complete text of such an edict.[85] But in contracts and other records—in greatest concentration from the Old Babylonian period—we have numerous references to such proclamations. They were normally made in the first year of a king's reign, but could be made at additional times. Whereas *mīšarum* edicts sought to restore the status quo ante, another form of royal release, *kidinnutu*, was a release from future taxes and levies.[86] In Egypt, amnesties were proclaimed for prisoners and debtors when a king ascended the throne, a practice documented from the period of the New Kingdom until the Hellenistic period. The same institutions existed in ancient Greece. On ascension, the Spartan king would release the populace from debts to the king and to the state.[87] Many charitable terms today have their origins in these practices. A proclamation of *philanthrōpa* by a Greek dynastic prince on his ascension was a call for the cancellation of debt taxes and the manumission of slaves.[88] A pardon of prisoners and rebels was called *amnestia*. What all these releases in all these periods and locales have in common is that they were edicts by the king—usually at the time of his coronation—and reflected his will to demonstrate his grace to the people and to reward loyal subjects.[89]

What motivated these enactments? Societies in the ancient Near East were heavily stratified, and it was inevitable that in many circumstances the rich got richer and the poor got poorer. While the various release edicts are depicted in the documents with a humanitarian "spin," in that they attest to the humanitarian nature of the king, they served political ends as well. When economic imbalances became extreme, the lack of equilibrium and viability could threaten social and political order. The edicts served to mitigate and address these threatening imbalances while earning the king a great deal of political capital with the people.[90] Moreover, by releasing debts, freeing debt-servants, returning lands to their original owners, and the like, the king inevitably was working to the detriment of the wealthy and the powerful, who may have been potential rivals.[91] The political implications of such release edicts are made explicit in Greek writings on the subject. Plutarch writes that when the Spartan ruler Agis sought to impose debt relief, his detractors considered the measure as nothing more than what we might call a Robin Hood scheme with clear political motivations: "By offering to the poor the property of the rich, and by distribution of land and remission of debts, he [bought] a large body-guard for himself, not many citizens for Sparta."[92]

These edicts are the backdrop of the biblical law codes that legislate debt release (Deut 15:1–7); land redemption (Lev 25:8–28), and the manumission of debt-slaves (Exod 21: 1–6; Lev 25:35–54; Deut 15:12–18). The Bible's reformulation of these laws begins with a fundamental departure from the norms of the ancient Near East: the decoupling of these releases from the political order. What determined the occasion of a release proclamation elsewhere was a royal decision, timed to suit the needs of the king. The Bible, however, regulates these proclamations by mandating them on a periodic basis. The implications of this are far-reaching. For one thing, such periodic scheduling means that the release proclamations are taken out of the hands of the king; indeed, in biblical law the king has no hand in declaring or implementing the release of debt, the manumission of slaves, or the redemption of tribal lands. As indicated in chapter 2, these are presented as a responsibility that devolves on the collective "you," and become the responsibility of creditors to debtors, masters to their servants, purchasers of land to sellers of land. Put differently, the legal mandate to engage in release is indeed a royal proclamation of release, akin to others found in the ancient Near East; the only difference is that the royal authority behind the proclamation is not a human king but the divine king.

The regular and periodic enactment of releases within the Bible's program highlights another critical difference between these norms and their ancient Near Eastern parallels. The *mīšarum* edicts were administrative acts, and as such were retrospective; they could only alter the state of affairs that already existed. The unscheduled and sudden nature of the enactments, it would seem, would be crucial to their efficacy. Like the devaluation of currency in modern times, proclamations of debt release cannot appear too predictable, or measures will be taken to circumvent them. The element of surprise is key to their effectiveness.[93] By contrast, the Bible addresses debt release as a statute that is prospective in nature, with the intention that the people will alter their affairs accordingly. Yet surely only a fool will extend a loan knowing that he would not be able to exact repayment. It would seem inevitable that credit would dry up within such a system.[94] Yet this goes precisely to the heart of a proper understanding of biblical "law": the treaty stipulations are themselves presented as a body of teaching. The purpose of biblical law is to shape and form the polity, not merely to address cases and provide remedy.

Because the biblical "laws" worked as not merely legal remedies but bodies of teaching, it is critical to note the interdependence of these laws with distinctly biblical notions of God's sovereignty as Creator. For what is remarkable about the release edicts of the Bible is the way they are integrated into and regulated by a unique system of calibrating time. It is well known that the intermingling of ethical and cultic provisions in the Bible is unknown in the legal corpora of the ancient Near East, where there is marked distinction between civil and criminal law on the one hand and ritual prescription on the other.[95] Elsewhere in the ancient Near East, the calendar was based on readily perceptible astronomical rhythms: the counting of days stemmed from observing the rising and setting of the sun; of months, from observations of the waxing and waning of the moon; of years, from observing the seasons and position of the sun. The ancient Near East, however, knew no calendar that operated around the notion of a week. To be sure, there are references in the literature of this region to periods of observance of a seven-day duration, say seven-day periods of mourning.[96] But there is no knowledge of a regular cycle of time known as a seven-day week. Units of time were functions of astronomical time, such as a day, a month, or a year.[97] The week is the invention of the Bible. This is significant, not simply because our contemporary demarcation of time revolves so centrally around the week, or because the week is convenient for adducing units of time longer than a day yet shorter than a month. The significance of the week lies in its origins. Uniquely, it is not a unit of time that emanates from nature. Neither the lunar month or even the solar year divides evenly into weeks. The only significance to the week is that the Bible ascribes to it. It represents not the cycles of nature but God's sovereignty, and dominion over nature; it represents the span of time in which God set nature into motion at Creation.

The Sabbath and the sabbatical cycle are deeply woven into pentateuchal legislation. These calendar cycles of seven gain manifest cultic expression— the counting of weeks between Passover and the Festival of Weeks; the special offerings on the weekly Sabbath; and so on. But no less pronounced is that the Sabbath principle's primary expression in biblical law is in regulating the schedule of the laws of social welfare.⁹⁸ This begins with the often-stated proclamation that rest is afforded the servant on the Sabbath day (Exod 20:10; 23:12; 31:14–15; Lev 23:3; Deut 5:14). In the seventh year—the "Sabbatical" year (Lev 25:4)—the field lies fallow and will yield food "for you, for your male and female slaves, for your hired and bound laborers who live with you" (Lev 25:6). Further, all of the releases are functions of the Sabbath principle, of God having rested on the seventh day. Hence, debt release is every seventh year (Deut 15:1); slaves are released after seven years of service (Exod 21:2; Deut 15:12), or, according to Leviticus, after counting seven cycles of seven years in the Jubilee year (Lev 25:8–9) debt-servants go free (Lev 25:40) and land reverts back to original owners (Lev 8–28).⁹⁹

Thus, the biblical law codes, in transforming release edicts theologically, neuter them as tools of political manipulation.

I turn now to examine the specifics of the Bible's reworking of the release edicts in three areas: debt release, land redemption, and manumission.

*Debt Release*

The particulars of the biblical laws of debt release, which reconfigure the pre-existing norms of the ancient Near East, are spelled out in Deuteronomy 15:1–6:

> (1) Every seventh year you shall practice remission of debts. (2) This shall be the nature of the remission: every creditor shall remit the due that he claims from his fellow; he shall not dun his fellow or kinsman, for the remission proclaimed is of the Lord. (3) You may dun the foreigner; but you must remit whatever is due you from your kinsmen. (4) There shall be no needy among you—since the Lord your God will bless you in the land that the Lord your God is giving you as a hereditary portion—(5) if only you heed the Lord your God and take care to keep all this Instruction that I enjoin upon you this day. (6) For the Lord your God will bless you as He promised you: you will extend loans to many nations, but require none yourself; you will dominate many nations, but they will not dominate you.

First, note the group entitled to debt release. The Edict of Ammiṣaduqa, to which I referred earlier as the only complete release text we have, states that the various debt releases outlined are only for Akkadians and Amorites, that is, the earliest known local inhabitants of the region. A typical clause, in this regard, reads:

"Whoever has given silver or barley to an Akkadian or an Amorite as an inter-est bearing loan...and had a document executed—because the king had in-voked *mīšarum* for the land, his document is voided."[100] In so delimiting the decree, the king saw it as a function of membership in his polity; strangers or foreigners would not be privileged by the dispensation. From a political per-spective, it is also clear that extending the release to foreigners would serve no interest of the king. His base of support is with the local inhabitants. It is in their eyes that he seeks to earn the reputation of *šar mīšarim* or "just king."

In the release passage of Deuteronomy 15, the political implications of debt release are entirely altered. As noted, because the edict is periodic and in no way associated with the king, it serves no political end of the king.[101] Moreover, ethnicity plays an even more dominant role and reflects Deuteronomy's overall emphasis on the establishment of an Israelite nation; the transactions that are addressed are those between "brothers" and "fel-lows." It is a practice that is explicitly not extended to others outside the nation. The economic viability of the policy is addressed as well: what is lost in can-celed debt for the sake of establishing brotherhood is compensated by the di-vine promise that profits will accrue from loans to be made to other nations, in a spirit of economic domination.

The decree also bears immediate consequences, for the establishment not only of brotherhood, but of egalitarian brotherhood. With the release man-dated to be enacted every seven years, the inequities of free trade would be leveled out on a more regular basis than elsewhere in the ancient Near East. For a society predicated on the principle of the rejection of hierarchy, there could be no more important legislation; equity is a vital component of equality. The release of debts, presumably to the poor, ensures the preservation of a relatively homogeneous society from an economic standpoint.[102] Indeed, this may be the intent of verse 4: "There shall be no needy among you." The verse may be read as a divine promise: faithfully fulfill these statutes, and I will as-sure the society prosperity. But it may also be read as a simple and natural outgrowth of the statutes: the release of debts every seven years serves as a hedge against the permanent development of an indigent underclass.

Yet this goes precisely to the heart of proper understanding of biblical law. The treaty stipulations are a body of teaching, and hence the necessity of verses 4–6, which do not add substantively to the legal injunctions of verses 1–3. Because this is a body of teaching, explanatory, ethical, religious, and historical motive clauses abound, and are melded into a single juridical cor-pus.[103] Debt release, like the other releases, is depoliticized, and placed in the realm of mutual responsibility between members of the brotherhood, serving as a catalyst for the forging of a society with no references to class distinctions.

## Land Redemption

The indigent peasant, according to Leviticus 25, could regain his land—his means of production—in one of two fashions. Either he or a kinsman had the option of buying back the land at any time (25:25–28).[104] The option that the seller maintains the right to buy back his property is attested in Neo-Assyrian documents, where the seller has the right to buy back his fields when he can afford to.[105] Alternatively, lacking the means, the individual would regain ownership of his land at the Jubilee (25:8–24).

What is most distinctive about the reworking of these laws in Leviticus 25 is their incorporation into a new theological matrix. In Mesopotamia, there is evidence of release with a theological agenda in mind. One early inscription reads that the king of Akkad "freed thirty-eight cities from corvée and from levy that they might serve on behalf of the temple of the god Šamaš alone."[106] In the first millennium B.C.E., the three holy cities of Nippur (holy to Enlil), Sippar (holy to Šamaš), and Babylon (holy to Marduk) were granted release from taxes and military service so that their inhabitants could serve their respective gods.[107]

This paradigm, whereby a city would receive a broad amnesty to serve a deity, is transformed in the release laws of Leviticus 25. Here, too, the release of land is expressed as being in the service of the Lord: "The land must not be sold beyond reclaim, for the land is Mine; you are but strangers resident with Me. Throughout the land that you hold, you must provide for the redemption of the land" (Lev 25:23–24).[108] The same stipulation is registered with regard to the manumission of servants. Israelites are to be freed, "For they are My servants, whom I freed from the land of Egypt; they may not give themselves over into servitude" (Lev 25:42); "For it is to Me that the Israelites are servants: they are My servants, whom I freed from the land of Egypt" (Lev 25:55). There is a strong theological connection between the laws of land redemption and the laws of manumission in the Jubilee year. What underlies the laws of manumission is the idea that an Israelite can hire out only years of service, not his person. What underlies the laws of land tenure and redemption is the idea that only years of produce may be sold, not outright ownership of the land in perpetuity. Both sets of laws are part of a single system of social welfare that derives from viewing ultimate ownership of all—people and land alike—as residing with God.[109] In the biblical formulation of Leviticus, release represents a transformation of the ancient Near Eastern paradigm. In Mesopotamia and in

Egypt,[110] when lands and residents were released from tribute and conscription, it was so that those resources could be dedicated to the cultic worship of a deity, in its temple. But within the release laws of Leviticus 25, the focus of the service of God is no longer expressed in cultic terms. Rather, the service of God is expressed as a fully released people returns to its fully released land to live out life in accordance with God's religious and ethical commandments.[111] The theological sanction to land redemption further ensures that the common man has a chance to return to economic viability.

*Manumission*

Manumission in the ancient Near East, as noted, was routinely effected through decrees of *mīšarum* or *andurārum*. As also noted, however, these decrees were not enshrined in law but were a function of royal decree. The enshrinement in the Bible of the institution within a legal framework meant that it would function prospectively: that both master and servant would know that the period of servitude would be finite, no matter what sum was still owed at the end of that period.

Of all ancient Near Eastern law collections, the Code of Hammurabi is the only one that addresses the manumission of slaves (Code of Hammurabi 117, hereafter CH).[112] In order to illuminate how the Bible's law codes transformed the institution of manumission, I will compare CH 117 and some of the laws of manumission that emerge from three biblical sections that address manumission, Exodus 21:1–11; Leviticus 25:8–13, 39–42, 47–55 and Deuteronomy 15:12–18.[113]

The Code of Hammurabi expresses enumerated and detailed concern for the maintenance of the existing social order, the protection of possessions and the smooth functioning of the economy. It lists several dozen laws, that govern trade and commerce. It underscores the need for the mobility of capital and the punctual observance of business agreements. How the biblical law codes stand out in this regard is evident in the laws of manumission. As noted, the biblical laws have a strong didactic element, and it is instructive to examine the rhetorical aspects of the laws: how they are phrased, and where they appear within the text of the Pentateuch. With the exception of the law prohibiting lending at interest, no other civil law is repeated as often throughout the Pentateuch as the law of manumission. The formulation and specifics of this law differ in each of the three law collections. Nonetheless, the aggregate rhetorical effect of apprehending the Pentateuch as a whole on this score is that the presence of this law in triplicate may be understood as a powerful message of the premium the Pentateuch places on ensuring a homogenous society of equally free citizens.

Notice as well the note on which Exodus 21 opens what is known as the Book of the Covenant, which Moses is said to have read to the Israelites at Sinai (24:7). The legal section of Exodus 21–23 encompasses many areas of torts and damages as well as religious law; yet it opens with the laws of manumission. These laws are not the most cardinal of laws, in terms of either their subject matter (loss of life, for example, is discussed in Exod 21:14–15) or their frequency of application. As rabbinic sources have pointed out, the placement of these laws at the beginning of the laws of the Book of the Covenant makes a statement about the importance of returning members of the Israelite polity to the status of full freedom.[114]

Moreover, this location is not in accord with the placement of laws of slaves in other ancient Near Eastern law codes: usually scattered in the latter parts or left to the end altogether.[115] This relegation to the later parts reflects the status of slaves in these cultures. In fact, in the Code of Hammurabi, a cardinal organizing principle is that in each area of law, say torts and damages, the structure of a section follows the hierarchy of the society, beginning with the highest level (those called the *awīlum*), with the laws relating to servants always at the end.[116] In the prologue to the Code of Hammurabi, the king declares his commitment to the values of *kittum u mīšarum*, "truth and justice." For the Mesopotamian mind, this is in no way undermined by the promulgation of a rigidly stratified, three-tier social hierarchy.[117]

Whereas both CH 117 and Exodus 21:1–6 address the period of service the debt-servant is to render, the biblical passage attends to an additional issue: a servant who wishes to remain in servitude (21:5–6). He is made to endure a branding of sorts: his ear is pierced. This rite—indeed, this legal circumstance of a debt-servant who wishes to remain in servitude—is without parallel in the legal codes of the ancient Near East.[118] The inclusion of such a stipulation in the biblical codes stems from its theology. Man is truly meant to be free; debt-servitude represents an anomaly, and should be viewed only as an exigency, a temporary state of affairs. The slave's preference for servitude represents a rejection of the freedom he has been accorded by the Exodus; he must therefore declare his desire to remain in servitude "before God" (21:6).

There is didactic value, further, in the unusual appellation used to describe the debt-slave as "a Hebrew slave" (*'ebed 'ibrî*) in 21:2.[119] Perhaps the appellation simply intends to distinguish between Israelite debt-servants, who are freed, and Canaanite ones, who are not. Alternatively, reading these laws as parts of the larger whole of the Pentateuch gives us license to examine the creation of semantic fields that span this particular law section and earlier pentateuchal narratives. Though the word ʿebed is often translated as "slave," in fact no distinct and exclusive term for "slave" exists. ʿEbed means a servant, a subordinate, an official, but does not connote ownership of the person, and does not indicate the duration of the status. More significant is the term ʿibrî, "a Hebrew." From a literary standpoint, the term used here—the one Moses used to address slaves recently redeemed from Egypt—harkens back to two contexts. One is a specific moment in the Joseph account, where we encounter the only other occurrence of the term ʿebed ʿibrî—in the accusations made to Potiphar by his wife about Joseph (Gen 39:17): "that ʿebed ʿibrî that you brought us made advances to me." It is clear that her remarks are meant as a derogatory and ethnic slur. The use of that very term here at the outset of the laws of manumission is intended to register a message to the potential debt-servant that he is to view his term as ad hoc and that his goal should be to return to the status of a free man. The second context the term harks back to is the one in which freedom for the Israelites had been demanded from the Egyptians in the name of the God of the ʿibrîm (e.g., Exod 5:3; 7:16); thus, the debtor snubs the salvation afforded him by the Exodus when he voluntarily seeks to remain in servitude (Exod 21:5–6). Indeed, while the passage detailing the servitude is six verses long, none of its particulars addresses the terms of the servitude itself; rather, all of its details address the terminus of the servitude, and the conditions under which the debtor will end it.[120]

According to the law of manumission in Deuteronomy, the creditor has to endow the debt-servant with severance pay at the end of his term of service (Deut 15:13–14). This law, too, both is cast in theological terms and carries social and economic implications. The severance the master is meant to pay is expressed in language that recalls the Exodus. The verse (Deut 15:13) "when you set him free, do not let him go empty-handed" (l'ō tĕšallĕḥenû rêqām) echoes the divine promise to Moses that the Israelites would depart Egypt bearing gifts from their former oppressors (Exod. 3:21), "And I will dispose the Egyptians favorably toward this people, so that when you go, you will not go away empty-handed" (l'ō tēlĕkû rêqām). Deuteronomy calls on the master to perform this gesture, saying (15:15), "Always remember that you were slaves in the land of Egypt and the Lord your God redeemed you; therefore I enjoin this commandment on you today."[121]

In these ways, the laws of manumission interrelate with the other laws I have examined—not only theologically but also from a purely economic standpoint. A man who became insolvent could, in theory, have a number of avenues open to him to relieve his debt. But I have shown already how some of these were legally limited. He could seek to sell his land; but the laws of land tenure and redemption severely limited this. He could borrow money; but there was no financial incentive for the lender to lend, as interest of any sort was prohibited, and according to Deuteronomy 15:1–6, the loan would be canceled in the sabbatical year. Under these circumstances, the capacity to sell his services of labor for an extended period of time could be an important avenue for the debtor to gain access to the capital he needed. Moreover, the capacity of the creditor to hold the servant for an extended period of time would provide incentive for him to invest in the worker and train him in a skill that would then translate into human capital he would take with him on his release.[122] The severance pay the servant receives according to Deuteronomy 15:14 must be in the form of sheep, or seed—commodities that can provide the means of production for a new start.

## Conclusions: Capitalism and Community

One of the enduring debates of modern political philosophy has centered around the question of the proper approach to the distribution of economic resources. It is often expressed as a debate between two standard-bearers: John Locke (1632–1704) and Jean-Jacques Rousseau (1712–1778). For us, who live in a capitalist society, Locke's arguments seem intuitive: he argued that it was in man's very nature to own and secure private property, and it was a primary purpose of government to secure those property rights. Rousseau, by contrast, was highly suspicious of private property. He felt that man's basic nature called for private property to be shared equally. He is famous for saying, "The first man who, having enclosed a piece of ground, bethought himself of saying 'this is mine,' and found people simple enough to believe him, was the real founder of civil society"—where "civil" society means anything but "civil" in the contemporary sense of the word: for Rousseau, it meant a society whose institutions corrupt the pure individual.[123] For Rousseau, private property was a destructive and egotistical institution that fostered greed.

Biblical writing rarely appears systematic when considered in contrast with the writings of the Greeks; but one can clearly detect a philosophy of riches that animates the Bible's laws concerning economic activity. One modern economist has determined that the biblical inhibition of the land and capital markets represents, in economic terms, the misallocation of resources, hence could only have slowed Israel's economic growth.[124] While perhaps true in strict economic terms, the claim stems from a capitalist bias.

What the economic laws of the Bible sought to achieve was an experiment with economic principles that existed elsewhere in the ancient Near Eastern social milieu. In many areas, peoples of a common status, members of a tribe or a clan, conducted their affairs placing a premium on strengthening mutual responsibility and kinship, following premodern modes of economic behavior. The Bible's economic laws sought to extend this sense of kinship and this form of economic activity to a national level, encompassing individuals who might be at a great divide, in terms of geography and in terms of kinship, but united in a common covenantal community. The biblical law collections sought to erect an economic order that was not centrally controlled, and indeed recognized the legitimacy of acquiring wealth. At the same time, they sought to ensure a modicum of social equality by placing a premium on the strengthening of relationships within the covenantal community and minimizing extreme advantage. These laws sought to ensure that all would have a chance to live honorably, mitigating against the establishment of a wealthy elite, while at the same time allowing the market to operate freely otherwise.[125]

Contemporary theorists have recognized that both capitalism and socialism may readily lead to a corroding of good values of citizenship. Capitalism fosters the making of money and implicitly removes the sin of greed from the social vocabulary. In today's societies, the moral and social orders are largely embedded in the economic one. Under such circumstances, we can readily see that mutual responsibility becomes endangered and the pursuit of self-interest becomes harmful rather than ameliorative. Socialism, on the other hand, can readily encourage sloth, as it fosters dependence on the provision of welfare by the state.[126] The solution, Francis Fukuyama avers, lies in the tempering of capitalism with some of the impulses that have been the study of this chapter:

> If the institutions of democracy and capitalism are to work properly, they must coexist with certain premodern cultural habits that ensure their proper functioning. Law, contract, and economic rationality provide a necessary but not sufficient basis for both the stability and prosperity of postindustrial societies; they must as well be leavened with reciprocity, moral obligation, duty toward community and trust...not anachronisms, but rather the sine qua non of modern society.[127]

# 4

# Egalitarian Technology

*Alphabet, Text, and Class*

The year is 1520. Across the wide swath of territory encompassing Christian Europe, and south and across the breadth of the Ottoman Empire, there is no a center of religious learning that is unfamiliar with Johannes Gutenberg's remarkable printing press, invented seventy years earlier, and the texts such presses have produced. Yet familiarity, apparently, does not always result in an embrace of the nascent technology. In fact, in some quarters, the opposite happens. In western Europe, Luther's thirty books have sold more than three hundred thousand copies in the space of just three years. For the first time in history, a great reading public has judged through a mass medium the validity of revolutionary ideas directed against an established institution, the Catholic Church.[1] In Catholic strongholds, the reception offered the opportunity to mass-produce texts is decidedly cooler. Here, no Bibles are printed in the vernacular languages, though the new technology is harnessed for the standardization of liturgy and Church practice. Farther to the south, in the Ottoman Empire, no religious texts at all are being printed for distribution. Indeed, to do so is considered a sin.[2]

These observations provide a key insight into the relationship between technology and culture. Changes in the technology of communication—such as the invention of the printing press or the internet—are widely understood as the key to explaining or even causing fundamental historical transformation.[3] Yet, advances in the technology of communication have diverse implications in diverse societies and periods. The effects a technology such as the internet or the printing press have in a particular culture is very much a function of its social institutions and prevailing ideologies.[4] The widespread circulation of texts in lands where the Reformation spread was, of course, no accident. Central to Reformation theology was the doctrine of *sola scriptura* (Latin, "by Scripture alone"), the notion that each individual Christian could accurately and authoritatively understand Scripture on his own terms, and should be encouraged to engage in personal Bible study in the vernacular. This doctrine, in turn, generated unusual—though at this point in time, by no means universal—pressure toward literacy. For Calvin, the members of the Church were to be "a priesthood of all believers."[5] Preaching in its varied aspects was to be undertaken by variously gifted individuals. This goal could not have been accomplished without fostering a learned and literate laity. By contrast, Catholic refusal to authorize vernacular alternatives to the Latin Vulgate meant that in Catholic countries, literacy remained the domain of the elite few.[6] The doctrine of *sola scriptura* and the ideas of empowering the individual predated Luther—they appear in the writings of the Oxford theologian John Wycliffe in the fourteenth century—but only the advent of the printing press allowed them to be spread and implemented.

In this chapter, I explore an earlier page in the history of the technologies of communication and the cultures in which they are employed. The revolution wrought by the printing press may be seen as a heuristic mechanism for understanding the implications of alphabetic texts in ancient Israel.[7] The adoption of the technology of the alphabetic script and its use in creating texts in ancient Israel was a function of a dynamic relationship between technology on the one hand and the theological and social mind frame of that culture on the other. The Pentateuch displays an attitude toward the dissemination of texts among the populace that is in sharp contrast to the relationship between texts and society we find elsewhere in the ancient Near East. It is a contrast, further, that reflects the egalitarian agenda the Pentateuch seeks to pursue, over against the entrenchment of class distinctions that is exhibited on this score in other cultures of the ancient Near East.

## Text and Class: Mesopotamia and Egypt

In today's modern cultures where literacy is nearly ubiquitous, access to texts of many kinds and the knowledge they contain is unfettered and, in theory, available to all. But in the ancient world, physical access to written texts and the skills necessary to read them were everywhere highly restricted. Indeed, in the cultures of the ancient Near East as well as ancient Greece, the production and use of texts was inextricably bound up with the formation of class distinctions: those who possessed the capacity to read and write were members of a trained scribal class who worked in the service of the ruling order.[8] Writing originated in the ancient Near East as a component of bureaucratic activity. Systems of writing were essential for the administration of large states and for the creation and propagation of compositions that were used to incise the key values of the culture on the hearts and minds of its royal elite.

However, the monopoly of access held by trained scribes was true of a particular kind of text. Most collections and archives from the ancient world include, perhaps even primarily, what we may term *documentary* texts—texts that were important only to the generation in which they were produced: correspondences, receipts, contracts, and the like. But then there were the texts that served neither documentary nor administrative function but rather were the cornerstones of cultural continuity and were passed on from one generation to the next. These would include works such as the Gilgamesh Epic, the Egyptian myth of Osiris, or, within the Greek context, the works of Homer and Euripides. These were texts whose creation, reading, and transmission were key instruments in the grounding of class distinctions; one scholar has termed them "long duration texts."[9]

In Mesopotamia, such texts were essentially composed for use exclusively within the domain of the elite scribal culture. Consider, for example, the setting in which the Babylonian creation myth of Enuma Elish would be accessed.[10] While today this text may be accessed by a wide reading audience (thanks to translation and print), this was hardly the case at the time of its composition and use. The tablets that bear this work (and, indeed, all other Mesopotamian texts in our possession) were located in temples or the foundations of palaces, or engraved in other inaccessible places, for example palace archives.[11] The text of Enuma Elish was never seen by the common man, but was read by the high priest on the fourth day of the new year festival, Akitu, in the presence of the statue of Marduk, in the inner sanctum of the temple. Its content focuses on the deeds of Marduk, and the reading of the account before the idol served to remind Marduk of his responsibilities toward the world to subdue the forces of chaos.[12]

That the setting for the transmission and retention of such long duration texts remained within the precincts of the elite is attested across the ages. One king of Ur, Shulgi (c. 2094–2047 B.C.E.), wished to establish his fame, but found stone inscriptions insufficient. Instead, he ordered:

> May my songs be (placed) in every mouth,
> May my poems never pass from memory!...
> To that end, I made the Wisdom-House-of-Nisaba resplendent
>     with scholarship, like heavenly stars,
> (So that) nothing (of these hymns) will ever pass from memory....
> Let them be played in the cult places![13]

Note that the venues for the perpetuation of the songs are not mass public ceremonies but the halls of study and the temples. One sees similar emphases on the sites of the elite as the venues for textual transmission in the Epic of Erra and Ishum (eighth century B.C.E.), in which the hero, Erra, states at the conclusion:

> "In the sanctuary of the god who honors this poem,
> may abundance accumulate,
> "But let the one who neglects it never smell incense.
> "Let the king who extols my name rule the world,
> "Let the prince who discourses the praise of my valor have no rival,
> "Let the singer who chants (it) not die from pestilence,
> "But his performance be pleasing to king and prince,
> "The scribe who masters it shall be spared in the enemy country
>     and honored in his own land,
> "In the sanctum of the learned, where they shall constantly invoke
>     my name, I shall grant them understanding." [14]

Again, this long duration text is meant to be the purview of the ruling class and its officials. Erra envisions his fame as being "the discourse of princes," performed by singers who chant it in the presence of kings and princes, and recited in the houses of learning.[15]

From time to time, Mesopotamian commoners did have access and exposure to such long duration texts, in the form of the display of monumental inscriptions. Yet the display of monumental writing was a display of royal power. Few could read the cuneiform writing. The alien nature of the script would naturally have served to affirm for the common man his place within the Mesopotamian hierarchy, that is to say, well below the place of the literate scribe and the court he serviced. This sense would be further corroborated by the relief that often appeared on the stele, depicting the gist of its written text, exalting the king who had promulgated the inscription.[16] Thus, the stele of the Code of Hammurabi bears an image of the divine gift of royal authority being granted to the king.[17]

In ancient Egypt, too, long duration texts were seen as the sole purview of the scribal class, and as instruments of the entrenchment of class distinctions. Priests and military officials of a certain rank were able to read and write the fairly intricate script and were trained to practice the art of drawing up written documents and to consult and study them.[18] Young princes were taught together in schools with the children of high officials. Writing was guarded and restricted in Egypt, as is shown in a work known as the *Admonitions of Ipuwer*, a mid-second-millennium eyewitness account of the devastation of Egypt at that time:

> Lo, the archives, its books are stolen,
> The secrets in it are laid bare.
> Lo, the magic spells are divulged,
> Spells are made worthless through being repeated by people.
> Lo, offices are opened,
> Their records stolen,
> The serf becomes an owner of serfs.
> Lo, [scribes] are slain,
> Their writings stolen,
> Woe is me, the grief of this time![19]

The tragedy for the author is compounded by the recognition that the common folk will now have access to the spells and that serfs will appropriate deeds of possession for themselves such that the "serf becomes an owner of serfs." It is estimated that throughout ancient Egyptian history, literacy probably never exceeded 1 percent of the entire population.[20]

The status literacy conferred on an individual is reflected in a Middle Kingdom (first half of the second millennium B.C.E.) schoolbook known as *The Satire of the Trades*. The composition tells of a father who escorts his son to the school for scribes, where the youngster will receive his initiation. The composition is presented as the words the father shares with his son about the virtues and rewards of the scribal profession, over against eighteen other professions the son might have chosen for himself. The father opens his remarks by stating:

> I have seen many beatings—
> Set your heart on books!
> I watched those seized for labor—
> There's nothing better than books!
> It's like a boat on water
> . . . .

> I'll make you love scribedom more than your mother,
> I'll make its beauties stand before you;
> It's the greatest of all callings,
> There's none like it in the land.

The father proceeds to catalogue the pains and drawbacks of other professions. A goldsmith, he claims, has "fingers like the claws of a crocodile" and "stinks more than fish roe." The reed cutter must travel to the delta to get arrows, and in the process suffers a terrible fate: "Mosquitoes have slain him, gnats have slaughtered him." A potter, the father says, "grubs in the mud more than a pig in order to fire his pots." Speaking in a manner that today could be described only as politically incorrect, the father derides the weaver as "worse off than a woman." As for the fisherman, "His is the worst of all jobs; he labors on the river, / Mingling with the crocodiles." He concludes:

> See, there's no profession without a boss,
> Except for the scribe; he is the boss.
> Hence, if you know writing,
> It will do better for you
> Than those professions I've set before you
> Each more wretched than the other.
> A peasant is not called a man,
> Beware of it![21]

As in Mesopotamia, the common folk in Egypt were exposed to royal texts from time to time. When a new king ascended the throne, messengers were dispatched with a communiqué that would be read publicly throughout the country. Its contents would include the new dating formula, policy pronouncements, and the new potentate's claims to legitimacy.[22] But these were not the long-duration texts that were the cornerstones of the culture, transmitted from one generation to the next, and only among the scribes and the ruling class they served.

## Text and Class: A Biblical View

The Pentateuch, it would seem, seeks out the promulgation, the oral publication, of its written texts. In Deuteronomy, Moses and Joshua are instructed to "write down these words and teach them to the children of Israel, that they should be fluent with it" (lit. "place it in their mouths," Deut 31:19). Scripture continues, "Moses wrote these words on that day and taught it to the children of Israel" (Deut 31:22). It is clear that the writing down was a stage in the process of dissemination. While not explicitly stated, the presence of a corps of instructors is implied, as Moses could not have been the only one involved in the process of instruction.[23]

A similar process is exhibited in Exodus 24:3–4: "Moses came and told the people all the words of the Lord and all the ordinances; and all the people answered with one voice, and said, 'All the words that the Lord has spoken we will do.' And Moses wrote down all the words of the Lord." Following the sacrificial ceremony, "Then he took the book of the covenant, and read it in the hearing of the people; and they said, 'All that the Lord has spoken we will do, and we will be obedient'" (24:7–8).[24] The use of text as a basis for wide-scale teaching is enshrined in the law of the septennial Hakhēl convocation: "When all Israel comes to appear before the Lord your God at the place that he will choose, you shall read this law before all Israel in their hearing. Assemble the people—men, women, and children, as well as the aliens residing in your towns—so that they may hear and learn to fear the Lord your God and to observe diligently all the words of this law" (Deut 31:11–12). Several other biblical narratives describe the public reading of passages from the Pentateuch to all Israel (Josh 8:32–35; 2 Kgs 23:1–3; Neh 7:72b–8:18 [ET 7:73b–8:18]). The Bible sees the oral-textual education system, whereby the literate read texts for the consumption of others, as encompassing the whole of Israel.

The evidence that the Pentateuch seeks to promulgate its texts goes beyond isolated passages and is deeply woven into its rhetorical fabric. The fact that much of the Torah speaks in the second person plural ("you shall...") implies that it is meant to be publicized. It stands apart from other law collections of the ancient Near East in that it regularly features motive clauses (e.g., Exod 22:20, "*You shall not* wrong a resident alien or oppress him, *for you* were resident aliens in the land of Egypt"), which suggest that the legal codes are to be viewed not only as law, but as a body of teaching; dissemination is of their essence.[25] The success of the venture of proclaiming Israel "a holy people" (Exod 19:6) hinges on the people's knowledge of the law and other teachings. The system of education that centered around the production and memorization of long-duration texts in Mesopotamia and Egypt is here radically transformed. In those cultures, the education system that surrounded texts was designed to create a literate scribal elite that stood in distinction from the commoners. Within the Pentateuch's vision, Israel is to become a "wise and discerning nation" (Deut 4:6) by virtue of the laws and teachings it has adopted, and thus stand distinct as a nation among the nations of the world. Israel is to become a "kingdom of priests" (Exod 19:6), a holy and educated minority within the world of nations.[26]

The Cambridge scholar Jack Goody has noted that a culture's willingness to disseminate its religious literature inevitably reflects an emphasis on the individual within that culture.[27] While it is anachronistic to speak of the post-Enlightenment construct of the "individual" within the Bible, a parallel phenomenon is exhibited in the evidence shown here. In earlier chapters I traced the way the Pentateuch sought to establish an egalitarian society whose core was the people as a whole, instead of a ruling elite, and in which citizens were empowered and ennobled. We now see that that accords with the impetus in the biblical vision to share the divine word with the people of Israel. It is telling that the Bible never depicts priests or scribes as jealous or protective of their writing skills. The notion of scribes feeling threatened lest "serfs become the owner of serfs" or that it is a tragedy if divine knowledge falls into the wrong hands, as Ipuwer put it in the Egyptian Middle Kingdom passage we saw above, is alien to biblical thought. Within the vision of the Pentateuch, reading and writing were not viewed as the exclusive domain of a scribal class and ruling court, as was the case for Israel's neighbors.[28]

## The Meaning and Purposes of Literacy in the Ancient World

To grasp the emphasis in the Pentateuch on writing texts and disseminating them, we first must set aside some of our modern conceptions about literacy. Our present-day identification of literacy with civilization as such was crystallized during the eighteenth century Enlightenment.[29] Indeed, the term "literacy" itself as referring to the capacity to freely read a written text is little more than a century old: according to the *Oxford English Dictionary*, the word first appeared only in 1883.[30] Today we would assume that literature is available only to the literate, but in premodern times this was hardly the case. Those who were exposed to texts and shaped by them numbered far more than those who had the actual capacity to read them. In his acclaimed study of literacy in medieval England, Michael Clanchy reminds us that "to read" in medieval times did not mean to set one's eyes to a text in silent meditation. Rather, much reading was done aloud, thus allowing the nonliterate to participate in the use of documents.[31] Charters in twelfth-century England routinely addressed "all those seeing and hearing."[32] The medieval recipient would listen to an utterance rather than scrutinize a document visually, as a modern literate person would.[33] The same was apparently true in ancient times as well. The Egyptian stele of Montuwoser, from the second millennium B.C.E., concludes: "Now as for everybody who will hear this stele, who is among the living, he will say, 'It is the truth.'"[34] We need not look, however, to medieval

England or even to ancient Egypt, to see that this was true in biblical Israel as well. A simple exercise in sociolinguistics will attest that reading in ancient Israel was fundamentally an experience of recitation, or proclamation aloud. In English, we have two highly distinct words, "to read" and "to call." The *Oxford English Dictionary* defines the verb 'to read' as "to inspect and interpret in thought any signs which represent words or discourse." "To call" is defined as "to utter one's voice loudly, forcibly and distinctly so as to be heard at a distance." Yet in Hebrew, these two verbs are designated by the same infinitive: *liqr'ō*. This implies that the dominant life-setting of *qĕrî'â*—"reading"—was recitation, as found in the verse "[Moses] took the record of the covenant and read it aloud to the people" (Exod 24:7).[35] In fact, nowhere in the Hebrew Bible is there reference to an individual reading silently to himself.[36] The norm in the Hebrew Bible is that texts are composed with the intent of later being read aloud.[37]

To access a long duration text in the ancient world was not merely to have the capacity to read it. The Mesopotamian and Egyptian literate accessed these texts as part of a broader oral-written mastery of the centerpieces of literature.[38] This mastery consisted of reading these key cultural texts and committing them to memory. The texts were the basis, the core curriculum, for the memorization and oral recitation of the tradition of a culture.[39] It was by mastering the key cultural traditions that scribes became the living repositories of the treasures of a culture. Master scribes could learn to compose new texts by accessing, echoing, and adapting the works they had internalized.[40] What mattered was not simply what was written on the clay tablets or sheets of papyri but what was written on the minds and hearts of the scribes and the elites they ministered to. Central to this practice of literacy is the interdependence of oral and written modes of communication and the assumption that written literature and oral recitation largely go hand in hand.[41] This form of literacy, with its emphasis on enculturation and socialization, was, by design, the domain of a distinct and separate class within the society. They formed a class whose responsibility was to establish the cornerstones of the culture in the minds and hearts of kings, ministers, and priests. When the Bible envisions Israel as "a nation of priests" (Exod 19:6) or as a "wise and discerning nation" (Deut 4:6), it is, in effect, reassigning the task of transmitting the culture to the whole of the people themselves. To be sure, the Bible throughout tells of priests and Levites who instruct the people (see Lev 10:8–10; Deut 17:9–12; 31:9–13; 33:10; 2 Chr 19:8–11). But the cultural treasure is there primarily for the people to hear, to internalize, and to transmit. Texts could reach a large audience in spite of a small readership, as attentive and responsive participation allowed the literate to instruct those who were not. Thus, in the passages from Exodus and

Deuteronomy cited earlier, there is no expectation that the Children of Israel as a whole will be able to read the words Moses has written. Deuteronomy even envisions the entire people learning to recite by heart the Song of Moses (Deut 32:1–43), in a process of writing for the sake of teaching a larger audience: "And now, write down for yourselves this song, and teach it to the Children of Israel placing it in their mouths" (Deut 31:19; see Deut 31:30, 32:44). The Israelites, in effect, are enjoined to engage in "writing" of a different sort. They are enjoined, as Proverbs 7:3b puts it, to "write [the teacher's directives] on the tablet of your heart."[42]

This conception of using texts for the enculturation of the broad polity of Israel may be understood in the context of the epigraphic finds from Iron Age Israel (c. 1200–500 B.C.E.). Though there are inscriptions of the alphabet (known as *abecedaries*) from as early as the twelfth century B.C.E., the epigraphic evidence points to a sharp rise in writing activity during the eighth and seventh centuries B.C.E. This coincides with the centralization of Judean society around Jerusalem, a growing government bureaucracy, and a more complex regional economy. The assorted correspondences, tax receipts, graffiti, and bullae attest to the widespread use of writing. Taken together, these finds reflect two levels of literacy. The simpler inscriptions of a word or a familiar phrase reflect so-called vulgar literacy, the capacity of many common folk to sign their names, read familiar words, and/or perform basic functions with letters. The longer texts we have should be seen as the products of trained scribes, who served the populace at large, in much the same way that today attorneys or accountants provide specialized services to people who need them.[43] The epigraphic evidence accords with the general picture of reading and writing in the Bible: virtually all writers and readers of longer texts in the Bible are officials who would have had literacy training, for example scribes, kings, priests, and officers. The assumption in these biblical depictions is that most of the population at large does not read and relies on literate professionals when in need of writing services.[44] At the same time, scribes served in various arenas: civil administration, trade, private records and correspondence, military installations, and private houses.[45] Few places would have lacked someone who could write, and few Israelites would have been unaware of writing.[46]

While the pentateuchal sources depict the reading of the texts in the presence of the people at large, other sources give us a glimpse of the mechanisms that may have been employed to promulgate texts in more localized and individual settings. A written text is used to teach an oral song in 2 Samuel 1:18–19: "[David] ordered that the Song of the Bow be taught to the men of Judah; it is written in the Scroll of Yashar. He said, 'Your glory, O Israel, lies slain.' "[47] The words of the prophet Jeremiah are read to an assembled gathering: "Then, in the hearing of all the people, Baruch read the words of Jeremiah from the scroll, in the house of the Lord, in the chamber of Gemariah son of Shaphan the secretary, which was in the upper court, at the entry of the New Gate of the Lord's house" (Jer 36:10). Isaiah (29:11–12) vents his frustration that his written words are rejected by the literate (*yôde'a sēfer*) and the illiterate (*'ăšer lo yād'a sēfer*) alike. The former are those capable of reading a written text bearing the prophet's sermon, and who seem to number a significant minority within the populace.[48]

The posting of a text for purposes of oral publication may be evident in the Book of Habakkuk. God commands the prophet Habakkuk (Hab 2:2) to inscribe his vision on tablets, "so that a town-crier may run with it."[49] To "run with it" here means to disseminate the message to a wider audience. This text presupposes a setting in which writing figures as the primary means of disseminating an oracle to a wider audience.[50] This understanding is supported by other biblical passages in which the trope of running stands as a metaphorical description of the medium through which God's works and words are announced. It is in this vein that Jeremiah can castigate prophets who promulgate falsehoods: "I did not send the prophets, yet they ran; I did not speak to them, yet they prophesied" (Jer 23:21; see Ps 147:15).[51]

Some have presumed that the prophets led circles of disciples, referred to by Scripture as "the sons of the prophets," who committed the words of the prophets to memory, and eventually edited them and wrote them down. Yet this notion is entirely speculative. The Bible nowhere links these "sons of prophets" and the transmission process of the prophets' sermons. In all the passages in which a prophet's words are committed to writing, it is the prophet himself who writes or dictates them. Inasmuch as the prophets could hardly convey their sermons to the people through speech alone, writing and public readings are to be taken as having been customary.[52]


## Alphabet and Class

The new role for the promulgation of texts within Israelite society envisioned in the biblical passages examined here was, in the first place, a revolution of ideology. I noted Goody's insight that a culture's willingness to disseminate its religious literature inevitably reflects an emphasis on the individual within that culture. But this revolution may well have been aided by an advance in the technology of communication: the development of the alphabetic script, and its use by biblical writers for purposes unknown before.

As noted, advances in the technology of communication yield diverse implications, depending on the social institutions and the prevailing ideologies of the particular cultures affected. This is no less true of advances in the technology of writing in the ancient Near East. The adoption of the technology of the alphabetic script and its use in creating texts in ancient Israel was a function of a dynamic relationship between technology and the theological and social mind frame of that culture.

The contrast between the restricted access to texts in Mesopotamia and Egypt and the unfettered access the Bible sets as an ideal for ancient Israel correlates with the complexity of the writing systems employed by each culture. To master a system such as Mesopotamian cuneiform or Egyptian hieroglyphics was no small task. To read what I called earlier a documentary source, for example an administrative order written in Akkadian, may have been within the capacity of various officials. But royal inscriptions, which were composed in Standard Babylonian, were much more difficult and could only be accessed by the most trained scribes.[53] Cuneiform writing typically employed six hundred or more signs, which could represent words, grammatical concepts (such as "plural") and syllables. Egyptian hieroglyphics also featured several hundred signs. Most of these were ideograms or groups of two or three consonants, as well as markers called determinatives that were used systematically to help classify and clarify the implication of a word. Some twenty alphabetic signs represented individual consonants. Neither cuneiform nor hieroglyphics fully converted speech into a semiotic system of writing. Rather, they were a mnemonic aid and, as indicated earlier, were used to record already familiar works that had been committed to memory.[54] Even students who memorized this limited number of central compositions would encounter in the texts themselves a sketchy notation of the compositions, works they had committed to memory through scribal training and apprenticeship.[55] Moreover, it was difficult to master the use of different writing surfaces and utensils, and to provide adequate storage facilities for the texts produced. Because the writing systems of these cultures were highly complex, even the literate would rarely access written texts with which they were not already familiar.[56] All these factors together ensured that literacy remained the privilege of an exclusive scribal class in the service of the king and temple. Indeed, the elite in these cultures had a vested interest in the status quo, which prevented others from gaining control of an important means of communication. Far from being interested in its simplification, scribes often chose to proliferate signs and values. The texts produced in Mesopotamia were composed exclusively by scribes and exclusively for scribal use—administrative or cultic, or in the training of other scribes.

The hallmark of the early history of the alphabet, by contrast, is that it was a medium of communication adopted by the lower strata of society and not the state apparatus. The first linear alphabetic inscription known to us is from the early second millennium B.C.E., at Wadi el-Hol in the eastern Egyptian desert.[57] What is most important and striking about this inscription is that it is a graffito and was produced by a commoner. This was at a time, of course, when the scribal class was still practicing the hieroglyphic system of writing. Other graffiti inscriptions dating from the sixteenth and fifteenth centuries B.C.E. have been found in the Sinai Desert, and reveal an alphabet similar to that found at Wadi el-Hol. By employing an alphabetic script, one could align a single consonantal sound (a phoneme) with one distinct sign (a grapheme), totaling somewhere between twenty-two and thirty letters, depending on the system. These inscriptions reflect experimentation both in the form of the letters and in the direction of writing and demonstrate that in the first half of the second millennium, standardization had yet to be achieved. This was mainly because no large state apparatus had yet adopted the alphabet as an official system of writing.[58] Indeed, the spread of writing outside state-sponsored institutions was occasioned in part by the invention of the alphabet. With the advent of the alphabet, it is no surprise that we begin to find inscriptions on potsherds, or ostraca, throughout the southern Levant. The writing attests to highly functional uses: names, lists, products—the type of inscription one would expect craftsmen, merchants, and landowners to create. At Ugarit, the alphabetic script was employed for the first time in the service of the textual cornerstones of a culture. The use here, however, did not alter the basic dynamic among literature, literacy, and class. In Ugarit, as in Mesopotamia and Egypt, access to the long-duration texts was an affair for the scribal elite.

Only in the rhetoric of the Bible is the message of the text addressed outward toward an entire people. We cannot know, in reality, to what extent these texts were actually propagated. We may posit, however, that the alphabetic script in which the Bible was written lent itself to the task of disseminating God's word more readily than would have been possible with texts produced in a culture founded on cuneiform. I noted earlier that there is evidence in Iron Age Israel, particularly in the eighth and seventh centuries, of so-called vulgar literacy. Because of the relative simplicity of the alphabet, the gap between the fully literate and those with a vulgar level of literacy would, perforce, have been narrowed, thus facilitating the transmission of the biblical texts broadly across the populace in the oral-written matrix described earlier.[59]

The printing press, I noted, brought nothing of its own accord; it brought change only when employed and exploited within the proper sociopolitical climate. The same holds true for the influence of the alphabet. There is no automatic tendency of the alphabet to promote universal literacy, and from there, democracy. While this may have been the dynamic at certain periods in Athens, it was certainly not true of other alphabetic cultures, such as imperial Rome, or the medieval Catholic states, where the circulation of alphabetic texts in Greek and Latin did little to hedge against the massive hierarchies endemic to these societies.[60] At the same time, through its simplicity, as evidenced by its common-folk origins, the alphabet was well suited to promote a social and religious platform that sought to promulgate and distribute texts among the general populace.

## The Diverse Implications of the Alphabetic Text

The willingness to publish and disseminate vernacular Bibles was highly dependent on the Reformation's stress on the individual and his worth; yet it was also well suited to a wide range of other doctrinal and societal planks of the Reformation platform. Looking to these further effects of the printing press as a heuristic mechanism, we may discern a link between a wide range of social and ideological institutions in the Biblical world and the centrality of the text and its use in educating a wide public.

It bears repeating that an advance in communication technology is not, in and of itself, always a blessing. Many scholars subscribe to the view that "power over texts allows power to be exercised through texts."[61] They note how writing and printing have been used to construct power in society, sometimes to highly destructive ends. Claude Lévi-Strauss declared that writing "seems to have favoured the exploitation of human beings rather than their enlightenment" and that "the primary function of written communication is to facilitate slavery."[62] Eisenstein rightly notes that the proliferation of printed materials led to a sharpening of acrimonious debate over theological issues, resulting in great carnage, and that the more efficient duplication of religious texts can be seen only as a mixed blessing.[63] Advances in communication technology, then, cannot be automatically traced to and associated with progress. Rather, their effects will depend on the social institutions and prevailing ideologies of the cultures with which they interface.

### The Rise of National Vernacular Literature

The distribution of printed texts in the early modern period is said to have occasioned the birth of modern citizenship in the nation-state. The vernacular

languages that were fashioned and standardized led to the creation of newspa-
pers and novels designed for a mass readership comprised of people in disparate locales who could now envision themselves as a public sharing a common
heritage, destiny, and range of religious, social, and political interests. People
could now imagine themselves as a political collective, and thus was born the
political "we."[64]

This phenomenon has been noted as illustrative of the role alphabetic
scripts played in the formation of national consciousnesses in the Late Bronze
Age (c. 1550–1200 B.C.E.) and Early Iron Age (c. 1200–1000 B.C.E.) in the Near
East. I noted earlier that the first uses of alphabetic script in the ancient Near
East were by members of the lower strata. The first use of the alphabetic script
for the purpose of high culture was in the Late Bronze Age in Ugarit. The alphabetic system, in time, succeeded in crowding out the syllabic cuneiform
system, restricting it more and more to its home territory; by the end of the
seventh century B.C.E., the reduced twenty-two-letter Canaanite alphabet had
become, through Greek and Latin, the source for all the European alphabets
and, via Aramaic, all the scripts of the East.[65]

The origins of this process at Ugarit are telling. It has been recently noted
that although Ugaritic scribes could compose texts in a broad spectrum of
languages, their use of alphabetic cuneiform Ugaritic is distinct: we have
found no foreign literature at Ugarit translated into this language, nor has any
of the literature composed in alphabetic cuneiform Ugaritic been found in
translation anywhere else.[66] The use of the alphabet in this way stands as a
watershed moment in the role and function of the alphabetic script. Prior to
this use at Ugarit, local mythology outside of Mesopotamia—as in the Hittite
empire of Anatolya, or in Emar to the east—had been composed in syllabic
cuneiform, a script that could be adapted to any language. Though the scribes
of Ugarit were fully familiar with this regnant system of writing high culture
in the ancient Near East, they chose to create a written language that was
particular—a step never before witnessed. Put differently, they created a written vernacular literature, and a local writing system in which to express it.[67]

The move reflects a desire to symbolize a distinctive identity that is reflective of the times. In the Late Bronze and Early Iron Age, new political identities
emerged among West Semitic peoples. We begin to see the written representation of "the people" (Amorite *li'mum*, Ugaritic *lu'mu*, Hebrew *'am*). The Ugaritic
literature signals the appearance within written literature of "the people" as a
political and religious unit. As noted in the opening chapter, the king was the
focus of ritual and history in Mesopotamia and in Egypt. In Ugarit, in the Late
Bronze Age, the ethnic group of the people begins to come into focus.[68]

The same peculiarity we see with Ugaritic language and writing and literature is apparent in the case of alphabetic Hebrew script and the literature of the Bible: no evidence has been found of foreign literatures that were translated into Hebrew during the Iron Age, and no part of the Hebrew Bible has been found translated into another language from that period. The Hebrew Bible is the first written history of a people, and as such may be said to reflect a new vernacular politics.[69] Some of the Ugaritic ritual texts refer to "the well-being of Ugarit," thus implicitly recognizing "Ugarit" as a religious and ethnic entity.[70] The Hebrew Bible, however, goes a step further and addresses itself to the people of Israel as audience and as active participants.[71] The printing press engendered the standardization of a written vernacular, rendering literary audiences into the citizens of political entities, leading to the rise of the modern nation-state. Likewise, the composition of the Hebrew Scriptures in the relatively simple system of the alphabetic script may have more readily allowed the creation of a diffusible vernacular literature designed to distinguish the local cultural universe from that of the surrounding environment.

## The Domestication of Religion

The availability of printed religious materials in the sixteenth century occasioned what may be termed the domestication of religion. The Reformation called on parents to conduct family services, to catechize children and apprentices, and to engage in Bible study in the home. What had formerly been the purview of the priest within the Church was now brought home. The Geneva Study Bible of 1599 notes "that masters in their houses ought to be as preachers to their families."[72] Husbands and fathers assumed new roles within Protestant households that Catholic family men entirely lacked.[73]

A parallel phenomenon is evident in the Bible's conception of the home. Popular family religion was endemic to the cultures of the ancient Near East, and usually entirely distinct from the worship of the state cult at the great temples.[74] In the Pentateuch, there is an emphasis on the home as a center of religious instruction and practice, alongside the worship that takes place at the central cult. Much, if not most, education in ancient Israel took place in the home. Family-based education ensured the cultural reproduction of the parent-teacher.[75] The home was the site of religious instruction (Deut 6:6–9; see 11:18–21):

(6) Take to heart these instructions with which I charge you this day.
(7) Impress [these words] on your children, recite them when you
stay at home and when you are away, when you lie down and when

you get up. (8) Bind them as a sign on your hand and them serve as a frontlet on your forehead; (9) inscribe them on the doorposts of your house and on your gates.

The hallmark of this education is the way it revolves around texts and their transmission. Opinions vary as to the precise referent of "these instructions" in the opening verse, but it is clear that they are some portion of the texts in which this commandment is embedded.[76] The dialogue between fathers and children about "these instructions" is picked up again in the next passage, at 6:20, "When in time to come your children ask you, 'What mean the decrees, laws, and rules that the Lord our God has enjoined upon you?'" The immersion of the child in an atmosphere wherein the texts are discussed—"when you stay at home and when you are away, when you lie down and when you get up"—provides context for the commandments enjoined in verses 8–9. Taken alone, these verses could be interpreted as amulets—that is, charms whose value is in the fact that they bear ceremonial, numinous writing.[77] Yet as they are embedded in a passage dedicated to education, it would seem that along with such ceremonial value, the texts that were bound and inscribed on the doorposts were texts that Deuteronomy envisioned would be read as well. This is not to say, as some have suggested, that the verse points to widespread literacy.[78] The surface area implied in these verses must certainly have been small, and it may be that Scripture assumes that since the populace would already be familiar with the text in question (by virtue of the mandate of vv. 6–7), they would have the capacity to read a brief inscription that was already known to them. This limited notion of literacy accords with norms of literacy among scribes in Mesopotamia and in Egypt noted earlier: even the literate would rarely access written texts they were not already familiar with.[79]

Some see these verses as evidence of a scholarly orientation or a predilection for wisdom that is unique to Deuteronomy.[80] However, the use of text in the education of children is evident in Exodus as well (Exod 13:8–9):

And you shall explain to your son on that day, "It is because of what the Lord did for me when I went free from Egypt." And this shall serve you as a sign on your hand and as a reminder on your forehead—in order that the Teaching of the Lord may be in your mouth—that with a mighty hand the Lord freed you from Egypt.

The "reminder" (Heb. *ziqqārôn*) is parallel to a similar "reminder" in the priestly vestments, a reminder expressed through inscription of writing (Exod 28:12). Moreover, this reminder shall serve "in order that the Teaching of the

Lord may be in your mouth," implying that it is an aid to committing to memory the lessons contained within it.[81]


## Text, Preservation, and Memory

The promulgation of texts in the early modern period was also understood to have ameliorative effects in terms of what we would today call "information protection." In 1791, Thomas Jefferson wrote to Ebenezer Hazard, an archivist who was gathering old and scattered documents pertaining to the early years of American history into what would become known as Hazard's Historical Collections. Encouraging Hazard in his efforts, Jefferson wrote:

> The lost cannot be recovered; but let us save what remains: not by
> vaults and locks which fence them in from the public eye and use,
> consigning them to the waste of time, but by such a multiplication of
> copies, as shall place them beyond the reach of accident.[82]

Jefferson here highlights the preservative potential of circulated printed copies. But more important, from a social perspective, is the point that this preservative nature of the printed word has a highly democratizing character. Information can be made more secure precisely by removing it from under lock and key and duplicating it for all to see. The notion that valuable data could be preserved best by being made public rather than by being kept secret ran counter to the traditional sensibilities of an earlier age.[83]

When Jefferson wrote that to put prized documents behind lock and key would subject them to "the waste of time" and "the reach of accident," he no doubt meant fire, flood, and perhaps even a worm endowed with a ravenous appetite. The creation of written copies of the prophetic sermons in their time, it is reasonable to assume, rendered a similar service. But the commitment of the prophetic sermons to writing had preservative implications of a far broader scope than those inherent in Jefferson's call to duplicate the historical documents Hazard was beginning to collect. Jefferson was concerned about the effects of the ravages time on the *documents*. The Bible employed writing to combat the effects of the ravages of time on the memory of the *people*.

Goody and Watt have written that in nonliterate societies, the individual has little perception of the past except in terms of the present. All beliefs and values, all forms of knowledge, are communicated between individuals in face-to-face contact and are stored only in human memory.[84] By contrast, they write, the annals of a literate society cannot but enforce a more objective recognition of the distinction between what was and what is. This argument has been well stated by Claude Lévi-Strauss:

> [Writing] can be thought of as an artificial memory, the development of which ought to lead to a clearer awareness of the past, and hence to a greater ability to organize both the present and the future.... Peoples with...writing...are able to store up their past achievements and to move forward with ever-increasing rapidity towards the goal they have set themselves, whereas [those without writing] being incapable of remembering the past beyond the narrow margin of individual memory, seem bound to remain imprisoned in a fluctuating history which will always lack both a beginning and any lasting awareness of an aim.[85]

While Lévi-Strauss goes on to doubt whether humans ever really do learn lessons from their written past, it is clear that the prophets intended that Israel should. In numerous instances, we find the prophets warning of doom and instructing that their prophecies be written down on public posts. In part, no doubt, these prophecies were written down so that the prophet's veracity and legitimacy would be established when the events foretold eventually unfolded. The written prophecies, however, would also enable future generations to judge their own times against the warnings and admonitions that had been spoken in an earlier age. God tells Isaiah to "write down a prophecy of doom on a tablet and to inscribe in a record, that it may be with them for future days" (Isa 30:8; see Deut 27:3, 8; Isa 8:1; Jer 30:2–3). On the eve of the Babylonian exile, God commands Jeremiah to acquire a parcel of land within Jerusalem and to draft a bill of purchase. The bill, Jeremiah is told, will serve as a sign that the exile will be of limited duration and that the exiles will, in fact, return and rebuild their homes. God instructs Jeremiah to place the deed of purchase into earthenware jars so that it will "last for a long time," so that Jeremiah's estate will have proof of the purchase. More important, the returnees will be able to view the bill as evidence of the unfolding events of redemption as having been foretold by the prophet in an earlier day (Jer 32:6–15). Moses writes down "the Book of the Torah" and charges the Levites to place it next to the Ark of the Covenant "so that it will be for a testimony" (Deut 31:24–25; see Exod 25:16, 21–22).[86] The narrative of 2 Kings 22:11 depicts how the discovered written text, "the Book of the Torah," brought Josiah to mourn, as he realized how far Israel had strayed from its dictates.

The relationship between the written medium and biblical theology is also deeply bound up with the biblical preoccupation with the concept of Exile. We have seen that the prophets understood that writing uniquely allows for a historical check—enabling, as Lévi-Strauss put it, people to develop "a clearer awareness of the past, and hence to arrive at a greater ability to organize both the present and the future." But it must be stressed that the Bible does not assume a static continuity for the Children of Israel within their land. Precisely the opposite is the case. There is hardly a book in the Pentateuch—the historiographic books or the prophetic books—that does not have the theme of exile at its center. As the thirteenth-century rabbinic exegete Nahmanides wrote in his opening gloss to the Pentateuch, the theme of exile in the Bible is implicit already in the story of the Garden of Eden, which concludes with the banishing of Adam and Eve from the Garden.[87] The biblical message, one that consistently threatens and then tells of upheaval, transience, and dislocation, is implicitly one that is aided by the medium of writing in order to survive. As Goody noted, because literate religions have a fixed point of reference, they are more resistant to change.[88] Moreover, the aspects of oral culture that cease to be of contemporary importance are likely to be eliminated by the process of forgetting. References to the land and to the temple, for example, would withstand the vagaries of exile and remain a part of the tradition until a time when those elements would again become relevant to the religious life of Israel because the tradition had been committed to writing. Indeed, we find in the books of Ezra-Nehemiah, composed with the return to the land of Israel after the Babylonian exile, an unprecedented emphasis on texts. The leader is now Ezra, who is a scribe, not a prophet. The books of Ezra-Nehemiah cite "the book of the Torah of Moses" some 30 times. All of this indicates that the role of the written text was instrumental in helping preserve the tradition during the period of the Babylonian exile.[89]

## From Image Culture to Word Culture

The distribution of religious texts may also be credited with abetting what is termed the sixteenth-century shift "from image culture to word culture," which took place in a fashion consistent with the spreading Reformation theology. Iconoclastic theology and practice, which reached its apex in the writings of John Calvin, ushered in a cultural shift from the visual to the verbal.[90] The pulpit replaced the altar. For Calvinists, religion suddenly became cerebral and allowed only the Word to stand as an image of the invisible reality of the spiritual dimension. The Bible, the written word of God, replaced the stained-glass window and the Mass as the primary didactic and liturgical focal point of faith and worship, and in turn presented a new and different basis for the common culture of the West.[91] By contrast, the Catholic Church heavily supported baroque statues and paintings throughout the seventeenth century; indeed, such images were deemed "the books of the illiterate."[92]

In the pagan religions of Mesopotamia, the idol was seen as an image that would embody the divinity when properly designed and cared for. In theory, a radically iconoclastic theology would have done away with any signs or symbols of the godhead. Indeed, this is what Islam tried to achieve. While God does speak to the Prophet, the Koran prescribes neither temple nor sacred space nor sacred objects. The Pentateuch, however, presents a middle position. To be sure, it proscribes graven images—of the true God, or of any false gods. Yet God's immanence in the world is reflected not only through His word— His prophecies—but also in tactile, visible fashion in His own handwriting engraved on the tablets. The tablets are written "with the finger of God" (Exod 31:18); the writing is the "writing of God, engraved on the tablets" (Exod 32:16). · While the tablets are not the subject of worship themselves, they do reside at the locus of sanctity in the spatial realm, within the Ark of the Covenant in the inner sanctum of the temple. These observations shed light on the accounts of God's writing on the tablets in Exodus and Deuteronomy. The locus of worship in the Sanctuary is not a graven image but the graven tablets that bear the signature of the Almighty. The sample of the divine word, written in the divine hand, tucked away in the Ark of the Covenant underscores the primary way Israel is to encounter the divine: through God's written word.[93]

The textualization of ancient Israel is well summarized by Josephus, writing after the close of the biblical period, in the first century C.E.:

> We have given practical proof of our reverence for our own
> Scriptures. For...it is an instinct with every Jew, from the day of his
> birth, to regard them as the decrees of God, to abide by them, and, if
> need be, cheerfully die for them. Time and again ere now the sight
> has been witnessed of prisoners enduring tortures and death in
> every form in the theatres, rather than utter a single word against the
> laws and allied documents....What Greek would endure as much for
> the same cause? Even to save the entire collection of his nation's
> writings from destruction he would not face the smallest personal
> injury. For to the Greeks they are mere stories improvised according
> to the fancy of their authors.[94]

Josephus may be suspected here of cultural grandstanding. Moreover, there is no question that the role of the text within Judaism was more entrenched in his era than it had been in preexilic Israel. Nonetheless, he describes well the centrality of the written text in the culture of Israel, a phenomenon whose roots certainly go back many centuries before.

Note, however, that Josephus claims that the role of the text in Jewish culture stands unique and that the same status is not accorded by the Greeks of his time to the texts of their own culture. To illuminate the revolutionary role the Bible accorded the text within society, I now turn to Greece in the Archaic and Classical periods, so as to cast a comparative light on the phenomena I have charted within biblical Israel.

## The Role of the Text in Ancient Greece

While the material I have surveyed suggests that the use of texts played a cardinal role in the Bible's view of Israelite society and in biblical theology, the evidence suggests a very different trend regarding the textualization of ancient Greece. I will briefly survey two periods here: the Archaic period, roughly 750–500 B.C.E., and the Classical period of Athens, roughly the fifth and fourth centuries B.C.E.

At the time that Isaiah and later Jeremiah were writing down their sermons for dissemination and the Book of Deuteronomy was calling for Israelites to convene every seven years for a mass reading of the law, Greece was still preliterate, and very few Greeks ever had contact with a text. The earliest Greek ostraca come from Ionia and are dated to the first half of the eighth century B.C.E.[95] Most of the one hundred or so inscriptions from the Archaic period simply serve to identify the owners of ceramic vessels.[96] Neither the stance of the letters nor their form is uniform, suggesting the absence of a standard at this time and that Greek writing is still in its formative stage. Some of the inscriptions are single lines of verse pertaining to drinking and dancing.[97] Laws began to be written down in the middle of the seventh century B.C.E.[98] They begin to be displayed in the sixth century B.C.E., with the public posting of Solon's decrees.

The evidence from the literary creations of the period support the same conclusions. Homer's *Iliad* and *Odyssey*, usually dated to the eighth century B.C.E., belong to a society that had little or no use of writing. Homer was an oral poet who composed in his head without writing. Most Greek literature was meant to be heard or even sung and was transmitted orally. There is still disagreement about how Homer's poetry eventually got written down, but this clearly was done in an early period when writing was barely known, if at all, and without the expectation of a wide readership.[99] The contexts in which writing appears in Homer are instructive. The earliest mention of writing in European literature is associated with a decidedly pejorative connotation. In book 6 of the *Iliad* (ll. 152–202), Proetus plots to have the innocent and valorous Bellerophon killed by framing him with a falsified letter. Writing continued to have sinister associations thereafter.[100] At the very least, we may say that none of the great epic material from this period either mentions the use of texts as a means for mass communication or exhibits any particular veneration for the written word. The epigraphic and literary evidence suggests that the percentage of Greeks who were literate before 600 B.C.E. was very small indeed.

This brings us to the Classical period, Athens in the fifth and fourth centuries B.C.E. Even at the height of Athens's power in the fifth century, few of its citizens would have had the opportunity, or even the need, to engage written texts.[101] Indeed, literacy seems never to have become a cause or subject of interest to democratic politicians; literacy and illiteracy often go unnoticed or unemphasized in Greek contexts.[102] The familiar genres of literature—speeches, recitations, and plays—were not available for villagers; the reading audience for these genres consisted of the highly educated, the wealthy, and their secretaries.[103] In one area, however, we may see how texts made an impact on even those who could not read them. Democracy in the late fifth century B.C.E. fostered an ideal of accountability, which mandated public access to the laws and records—an idea first voiced by the sixth-century B.C.E. jurist Solon.[104] Again we may see how technology and ideology go hand in hand. While the Greek alphabet had now become standardized, only in democratic Athens was writing publicly displayed. Oligarchies such as Sparta and Corinth cultivated secrecy, and no state documents were made public.[105]

The fourth century B.C.E. witnessed evolution in this regard. Writers such as Aristotle express a positive role for writing as a bulwark of justice and fairness.[106] Indeed, it is in the writings of Aristotle in the fourth century B.C.E. that one finds extensive discussion of literary and philosophical works in terms of the written text.[107] Written documents were not considered adequate proof by themselves in legal contexts until the second half of the fourth century B.C.E. The use of legal documents is taken to be an indicator of the evolved status of texts within a culture. As noted earlier, Jeremiah acquired his parcel of land via a bill of purchase, drafted and signed by witnesses (Jer 32:6–15), a sign of the established status accorded texts at the time the account was written.

The merits—or, perhaps, demerits—of textual writing in Athens in the early fourth century B.C.E. actually emerge as a subject of discourse in the writings of Plato. In the *Phaedrus*, Plato depicts a dialogue between Socrates and his young interlocutor, Phaedrus, concerning the ways to attain wisdom:

SOCRATES    Writing, Phaedrus, has this strange quality, and is very like painting; for the creatures of painting stand like living beings, but if one asks them a question, they preserve a solemn silence. And so it is with written words; you might think they spoke as if they had intelligence, but if you question them, wishing to know about their sayings, they always say only one and the same thing. And every word, when once it is written, is bandied about, alike among those who understand and those who have no interest in it, and it knows not to whom to speak or not to speak; when ill-treated or unjustly reviled it always needs its father to help it; for it has no power to protect or help itself.

PHAEDRUS   You are quite right about that, too.

SOCRATES   Now tell me; is there not another kind of speech, or word, which shows itself to be the legitimate brother of this bastard one, both in the manner of its begetting and in its better and more powerful nature?

PHAEDRUS   What is this word and how is it begotten, as you say?

SOCRATES   The word which is written with intelligence in the mind of the learner, which is able to defend itself and knows to whom it should speak, and before whom to be silent.

PHAEDRUS   You mean the living and breathing word of him who knows, of which the written word may justly be called the image.

SOCRATES   Exactly.... He who has knowledge of the just and the good will not, when in earnest, write them in ink, sowing them through a pen with words which cannot defend themselves by argument and cannot teach the truth effectually.... [Rather the wise man] writes to treasure up reminders for himself, when he comes to the forgetfulness of old age.... But nobler far is the serious pursuit of the dialectician, who, finding a congenial soul, by the help of science sows and plants therein words which are able to help themselves and him who planted them.[108]

The comments are well understood against Plato's life context. Within the confines of the Academy, which he founded in 387 B.C.E. for the systematic pursuit of philosophical research, one would naturally prefer the interpersonal medium. When the scope of one's horizons is limited to a select elite who live and learn in close confines, the argument Socrates puts forth here has merit. To be sure, Socrates does acknowledge the preservative potential of writing, but this is to be employed only by an aging dialectician suffering from memory loss. Otherwise, writing is the "bastard" alongside the legitimate son, "the living and breathing word of one who knows." The rhetorician, Lysias, was reprimanded for having offered speeches for sale in the market, treating an oration—a direct utterance of the soul—as a mere commodity.[109] In a subsequent section, Socrates goes on to tell his interlocutor, "No written discourse, whether in meter or in prose, deserves to be treated seriously."[110] Such a view of texts could hardly have found a place in the Pentateuch's view of society. Learning was not to be restricted to the elite. Rather, the communication of texts and their messages was envisioned as the key tool for exposing a broad society to the written word of God.

# 5

# Egalitarianism and the Evolution of Narrative

*The Rescue of Moses (Exodus 2:1–10)*
*and the Sargon Legend Compared*

During the Elizabethan period, Shakespeare wrote plays and Milton epic poems. Yet by the mid–eighteenth century, the novel had already emerged as the predominant form of literature being written in England. This shift in notions of *what* should be told in a story and *how* that story should be told is a reflection of philosophical and ideological developments. As an illustration of how ideology shapes both *what* is told in a story as well as *how* it is told, we may consider the rise of the modern novel. Tracing the dynamics of this evolution in a body of material readily familiar to us as literate English-speaking persons will equip us to understand a parallel literary phenomenon in ancient Israel: the evolution of biblical narrative.[1]

## Social Ideology and the Rise of the Modern Novel

Our contemporary notion of the novel as a fictional account of a fairly plausible drama portrayed through an extended prose narrative is a notion that only solidified among the reading and writing public in the beginning of the nineteenth century in Britain, with the writings of Jane Austen and Walter Scott.[2] But the novel first emerged as the new form of literature in England in the late seventeenth and early eighteenth centuries, replacing the modes of writing employed in the beginning of the seventeenth century in the plays of Shakespeare and the epic poems of Milton. The shift from these earlier forms of storytelling to the form of the novel, perhaps evidenced most famously—though by no means exclusively—in Swift's *Gulliver's Travels* (1726), was not merely the product of an aesthetic fashion. As already noted, the changing notions of what should be told in a story and how that story should be told reflect deep-seated changes unfolding in society.

The difference in content is palpable. For the likes of Chaucer, Spenser, Shakespeare, and Milton, storytelling is replete with tales of the miraculous, the supernatural, muses, and heavenly bodies. The emerging novels were suffused with Enlightenment thought. Descartes, in his *Discourse on Method* (1637), had set in motion a train of thought whereby truth was to be determined by the common individual, as opposed to received tradition.[3] The spirit of the times dictated that one could best make sense of the world through one's natural senses and rational faculties, that these provide one with a reliable and complete impression of it, and that in interpreting the world, one should be free from the shackles of collective tradition.[4] For the new genre of the novel, this meant devising plots that centered around the common experience, realms that had always played a subordinate role in the earlier literatures of epic and romance.[5]

But Enlightenment thought had ramifications not only for *what* would be narrated, but indeed *how*. It was a canon of earlier Renaissance writing that plots had to hew to traditional storylines and formulas. Nature was believed to be whole, eternal, and unchanging. Thus the works of Shakespeare, Milton, and the like reflect on legends, Scripture, and history, because all of these represent the classic, unchanging array of universal human experiences and predicaments. In Shakespeare, the figures and settings of disparate periods such as Troy, Rome, or the House of Tudor are all essentially undifferentiated. Indeed, Shakespeare died before the word "anachronism" appeared in the English language.[6] The novel bucks this trend by eschewing conformity to accepted models of plot. The primary criterion of the plot was now truth to individual experience. Relative to earlier genres, the novel has no set or standard form—a reflection of its attempt to mirror reality.[7]

An example of the new poetics developed in the novel can be seen in the names of the protagonists. Classical and Renaissance genres exhibit a preference for historical names or type-names that establish that the character is to be understood within the context of a canon or tradition rather than of his or her own age. But the eighteenth-century novel, following thinkers like Descartes, placed a premium on the thought processes within individual consciousness. So the novelist gave unprecedented attention to the personal identities of characters and gave them names that were more contemporary and related to the experiences they endured.[8]

The *how* of the novel's storytelling also involved its time frame. The genre of Greek tragedy had dictated that action be restricted to a time frame of twenty-four hours. Since the classical world viewed reality as reflective of time-less universals, teachings about the human condition could be drawn from the events of a single day no less well than from the duration of a life. The novel, by contrast, narrated events that unfolded over lengthy spans of time, some-times even a lifetime. Individuals were conceived for the first time as living out a historical and developmental process.[9] This change reflected a newer understanding that with fewer fixed universals, a person's character could in-deed change over time.[10]

Finally, perhaps the most significantly different *how* of the novel was in very mode of narration it employed in every sentence. The novel eschewed figurative eloquence in favor of a prose style that represented the prosaic real-ity on which it focused.[11]

## Social Ideology and the Evolution of Biblical Narrative

The emergence of the novel as an event in intellectual history can help us see in a new light how ancient Near Eastern modes of narration underwent trans-formation in the Hebrew Bible as a function of the new egalitarian ideologies, and how these transformations are evident both in *what* the biblical stories told and in *how* they told it.

The royal theology of the ancient Near East I examined in chapter 1 pro-vided a milieu for the creation of narrative compositions with two primary foci: gods and kings. Stories of the gods or the kings could take on many forms. Poetic myths detailed how the hidden forces of the human world were animated by the lives of the gods, their actions, and their dispositions.[12] In chapter 1, I presented a good example of this in the cosmogony Atrahasis, which told of the rivalry between the gods that led to the creation of humani-ty.[13] Epics, by contrast, focused on the actions of legendary heroes, usually kings.[14] The glorious acts of kings could also be found in other genres of litera-ture, such as dedicatory inscriptions, or commemorative compositions, often telling of the building of a temple or of a military escapade. They could also depict the career of a king, his traits, his feats and exploits. Annals or chroni-cles provided precise chronologies based on dated regnal years, and attended to a range of military and public projects undertaken by the king.[15] The audi-ences for all of these materials varied. The most important audience was the gods themselves—as evidenced by the fact that these texts have often been discovered in foundation deposits or other inaccessible locations. Myths were recited to remind the gods of their responsibilities. Details of a king's achievements on the battlefield made up a report to a deity about the king's activities on his or her behalf. Sometimes the materials were intended for a limited circle of court scribes and officials so that later generations of the elite would retain the memory of a king's great deeds.[16] Some commemorative inscriptions could also be for public reading to the members of the city.[17]

Biblical narratives were not written in a vacuum, and employ or adapt many of these genres. For example, Genesis 1–11 bears strong echoes of Mesopotamian mythic traditions concerning the creation of the world and the flood.[18] The epic motif in Mesopotamian and Egyptian literature of a fugitive hero finds parallels in the stories of Jacob, Moses, and David.[19] In the patriarchal narratives of Genesis, as in the Ugaritic narratives of Keret and Aqhat, the fatherly god is solicitous of his favorite human beings and takes a special interest in their desire for offspring.[20] Commemorative inscriptions of military campaigns share an affinity for a theological outlook on the outcome of warfare, as found in the historical books of Samuel-Kings.[21] The style of Mesopotamian king lists that establish chronologies of events is paralleled in the chronological style of the Book of Kings.[22]

However, narration in the Pentateuch accords with the covenant theology described in chapter 1, and appears to have been written with a different audience in mind: the people itself. Thus, in the Hebrew Bible generally, and the Pentateuch in particular, we find a new focus for narrative content: the story of a *people*, a nation, to be told and retold by that very people across their history. In the stories of the Pentateuch, the covenantal people would learn, not primarily about the exploits of their leaders, but rather about themselves as a collective in relationship with their sovereign deity: about their origins, their moments of greatness, and to an even greater extent, their moments of collective covenantal failing.[23] In this regard, the Hebrew Bible is the first literature before the Hellenistic period that may be termed a national history.[24] Since God addresses the people as a whole, and is concerned with their collective allegiance to Him as a subordinate king within the context of a political covenant, it is to be expected that the narratives included within the Pentateuch will focus on the affairs of the people as a whole: the Exodus from Egypt, the sin of the golden calf (Exod 32–34), the sin of the spies (Num 13–14), the Qoraḥ rebellion (Num 16–17), to name a few, are all stories whose focus is the collective life of Israel in the wilderness.

Yet, together with the accounts of the travails of the people as a whole, much narrative material in the Pentateuch is devoted to the characterization of individuals, particularly in the Book of Genesis. No doubt, this material may also be seen as national in perspective: it informs the audience of its

ancestral roots. This, in and of itself, was already an anomaly within the literature of the ancient Near East, as no other culture recorded its earliest beginnings to this extent.[25] Yet the narratives of the patriarchs in Genesis, and later
depictions, for example those of Moses and Jethro, are highly detailed charac-
terizations of individual protagonists, and go far beyond chronicling the names
of Israel's forefathers as in, say, in the genealogies of 1 Chronicles 1–10.

This sustained focus on the varied aspects of human character in the
Pentateuch may be seen as a reflection of the difference between polytheistic
religion, as exhibited in the cultures of the ancient Near East, and religion
predicated on the concept of covenant I delineated in chapter 1. Moreover, the
use of narratives focusing on the vivid characterization of individuals may be
seen as a reflection of the Pentateuch's unique formulation of the relationship
between the realm of the divine, nature, and humanity.

The ancients of the Near East knew that agriculture was a fragile enterprise. Sometimes the harvest was plentiful, but sometimes the crops failed
due to drought, pestilence, and the like. The question was how to make sense
of these unpredictable vicissitudes. The answer was to see in the vagaries of
nature the various interactions of divine forces. Ancients knew that animal
and human reproduction were dependent on the cohabitation of males and
females. Surely, then, they reasoned, the produce of the field might work in
the same way. Thus the Sumerians envisioned the fecundity of the field to be
the product of the sacred marriage of the god Dumuzi with the goddess
Inanna. Alternatively, if one year the rains were plentiful but in another the
fields were stricken with drought, the ancients interpreted these vagaries as
the result of battle between the divine forces that controlled the various elements. A year of good rainfall indicated that the storm god had defeated the
god of drought. Gods were envious beings that desired power and were perceived, as I noted, through the prism of what people saw in the affairs of human potentates. Earthly kings, too, desired power. And indeed, gods were
viewed in the same way as kings: The ancients well knew that a king who
emerged victorious in battle in one campaign could be defeated by a rival in
the next. Thus, ancient religion was really an attempt to articulate the interplay of heavenly forces and personalities. The drama that unfolded in the upper world between the divine forces and personages determined the fate of
mankind.[26]

In this cosmic drama, humans assumed the role of cheerleaders and fans
on the sidelines. Their support could spur the divine figures to the desired action and result. Enter the critical role of the recitation of myth and enactment
of ritual: to enable humans to participate in the divine ballgame, as it were.
When the divine forces engage in battle, man is there to collaborate with the

god who will later help him, through the agency of cultic ritual. When gods need to unite, as in the sacred marriage of Dumuzi and Inanna referred to earlier, cultic practices of song, dance, and performance allowed humans to experience and assist the perpetuation and fecundity of nature.[27] This conception of the vital role humans could play in bringing the gods to the desired action meant that participation in the cult was a vital and meaningful experience. Gods, men, animals, and nature all existed within a harmonious continuum. The presence of the gods was highly palpable, because they were immanent in nature. The Sumerian god Enki created the Tigris and Euphrates rivers by releasing into their beds a stream of his semen.[28] Hence, myth focused on the drama unfolding among the personages of the divine world, with little to say about the role of the human beings as they witnessed the goings-on. Indeed, the lack of interest in the inner stirrings of humans, their character, personality, and development, should not surprise us. As noted in chapter 1, humans—in Akkadian verse narrative, for example—existed solely to supply the material needs of the gods; their purpose in the world was defined in terms of ritual function. There was no need, therefore, to dwell on the evolution of the collective history of a people, or the moral and spiritual complexities of the human condition.

In the biblical conception of things, the relationship between man, nature, and God is radically reworked. Gone are the notions of material emanation from a divine creator whose seed, blood, or tears are the primordial elements of nature. The empiric and natural universe is no longer taken to be a throbbing and dynamic playing field for divine personages. There are no conflicting powers to be propitiated, no harmonizing forces, no interaction at all between divine figures. Now, it is God alone who guarantees victory in war, bounty in the fields, and the fecundity of the animals and the people. Moreover, God is transcendent over all natural phenomena, and not palpably manifest through them. For a person to conceive of divinity in this way thus entails a definite sacrifice, for it requires one to surrender the sense of a life lived in tangible and visible harmony with the cadences and vagaries of nature and the divine forces that govern them.[29]

Indeed, in the Bible the three-way relationship between humanity, nature, and God is redrawn. Nature and the course of events generally are no longer controlled by the interaction of divine figures. Rather, divine intervention in human affairs is determined by the course of human action.[30] Nature and history are determined by human behavior. Within this conception, humans move from the position of cheerleaders on the sidelines of the cosmic playing field to center stage. What happens to humans within covenant theology is entirely in their own hands (Deut 11:13–15):

If, then, you obey the commandments that I enjoin upon you this
day, loving the Lord your God and serving Him with all your heart
and soul, I will grant the rain for your land in season, the early rain
and the late. You shall gather in your new grain and wine and oil.
I will also provide grass in the fields for your cattle—and thus you
shall eat your fill.

Here, now, it is God who stands on the sidelines, coaching through His laws,
sermons and oracles, sometimes even as a cheerleader—but always adjudicating human activity and determining the fate of the human players.[31] Thus,
men are no longer simply the servants of the gods, but rather are charged with
the task of realizing His will. The Bible is the record of Israel's collective successes and failings at realizing that will.

To be sure, Mesopotamian cultures also believed that nature could be altered by the divine reaction to human behavior.[32] But the scrutinized behavior
that would determine the future of the Mesopotamian state never had to do
with the moral or spiritual fortitude of the population. Instead, disaster was
explained as either a failure to satisfy the cultic demands of the gods, or a failure on the part of the king in the affairs of state. The covenantal theology of
the Pentateuch, by contrast, places the onus on the moral and spiritual strength
of the people at large.

We are now in a position to see how this shift in ideology has such a profound impact on the Bible's narrative focus. Because the course of events—all
events, historical and natural—depends on Israel's behavior, each member of
the Israelite polity suddenly becomes endowed with great significance. The
behavior of the whole of Israel is only as good as the sum of each of its members. Each Israelite will need to excel, morally and spiritually. Each person becomes endowed with a sense of responsibility unparalleled in the literatures of
the ancient Near East.[33]

How will this moral and spiritual excellence be called forth? How will it
be taught? I have already shown how the legal materials of the Pentateuch
could serve as didactic tools. There is a limit, however, to the efficacy of an
apodictic command, such as "Thou shalt not steal." Such a demand does state
the desideratum in the clearest terms, but it gives no inkling of what might
make one steal, the inner world of a human being, and the struggle that one
might face in the contemplation of a theft. Consider the famous passage in
Augustine's *Confessions* (book 2) in which he dissects the motives and psychology that led him to steal from his neighbor's pear orchard when he was sixteen. The passage displays an acute awareness of how social pressure operates;
about how one will steal though one has no interest in the object itself, per se;

about the thrill of doing something wrong for its own sake, simply because it is forbidden; about theft as a masked quest for power. Put differently, what Augustine realizes is that the key to proper action is a thorough understanding of proper thought and feeling, and a nuanced understanding of human psychology. The command "Thou shalt not steal," in its stark simplicity, addresses none of this. It addresses the world of action, but not the inner world of thought and feeling that underlies all action. Each member of the Israelite polity is called on to excel morally and spiritually. The fate of Israel depends on it. Spiritual perfection, however, will only be a possibility if the Israelite citizenry can develop an awareness of the inner world of motive that stands behind proper action.

What Augustine sought to achieve though memoir and systematic self-reflection, the Pentateuch achieves through narrative characterization of its heroes and villains, their struggles and their tribulations. Here we find the principle of free choice, the sine qua non of ethics, at the fore. The examination of character—even when speaking of the Bible's greatest protagonists—is done with nary a trace of hagiography. The depiction of the biblical characters reflects the full complexity of the human condition. Motives are mixed, bearing and conduct are unpredictable, and patterns of behavior and their meaning remain opaque. Negative aspects of a protagonist's character are displayed openly alongside the positive ones.[34] Because the playing field that counts in the Bible is the human realm, it is no surprise that the nether world is deemphasized; the dead are no longer involved in the covenantal relationship.[35]

Narrative exploration of human character in the ancient Near East does not begin with the Bible, and there are some notable exceptions to the general assessment of ancient Near Eastern myth and epic I have offered here. The final, or what is known as the standard, version of the Gilgamesh Epic relates in great detail the story of the protagonist's education and progress to maturity.[36] Glory, friendship, lust, hubris, and frailty are among the elements of the human condition that are explored. Yet for all its humanity, the Gilgamesh Epic is at a great remove from mundane reality. Its protagonist himself is quasi-divine; most of his interlocutors are divine figures. His escapades take him to mysterious gardens and into interactions with mythic creatures.[37]

Also notable for their interest in character are the earliest surviving large-scale narratives in the ancient Near East, those from Ugarit. The tales of Aqhat and Keret focus on human actors. Yet interactions with the gods remove these tales, too, from the realm of the mundane. As the gods fly over the earth, they release agents to perform various tasks among humankind. The entire Aqhat epic revolves around a power struggle between the human protagonist, Danil, and the goddess Anat.[38] This stands in contrast to the stories found in the national literature that is the Hebrew Bible, a book of teaching to be read and heard by the people. While the stories of individuals in the Pentateuch include episodes of divine revelation and the occasional miracle, they are unparalleled in their focus on mundane human circumstances, when viewed in contrast with the myths and epics of the ancient Near East.

Earlier in this chapter, I mentioned how the rise of the novel in the eighteenth century occasioned not only a shift in *what* was narrated but also in the technique, the *how* of narration, and all as a function of the Enlightenment ideologies and sensitivities of the age. A similar dynamic is at play in the development of biblical narrative. Not only do these narratives about individuals exhibit a different focus in content, the *what*; their intense interest in personality and character development, in the complexity of the human condition, leads to more developed ways of telling a story—the *how*. Biblical storytelling builds on narratological techniques for the exploration of personality that were first used in the narrative epics of Ugarit in the Late Bronze Age (fifteenth to twelfth century B.C.E.).[39] The result is a mode of narration that stands in stark contrast to the one employed in the service of the royal theologies that predominated in the ancient Near East.

## The Rescue of Moses (Exodus 2:1–10) and the Sargon Legend

To illustrate the difference between narration in the service of royal theology and narration in the service of covenant theology, I will compare two narratives, one biblical and one Mesopotamian: the rescue of Moses in infancy by the daughter of Pharaoh (Exod 2:1–10) and the rescue of Sargon of Akkad as a foundling baby. The striking resemblance between these two will make their difference more apparent: the rhetorical features that are the hallmark of biblical narrative and its commitment to exploring character and the complexity of the human condition, over against the dominant mythic and epic traditions of the ancient Near East.

The Akkadian text known today as the "Sargon legend" is inscribed on a cuneiform tablet found in the great library at Nineveh of the Neo-Assyrian king Ashurbanipal (668–627 B.C.E.). Though several kings by the name of Sargon are known to us (Sargon I of the twentieth century B.C.E. and Sargon II of the late eighth century B.C.E.), the text known as the Sargon legend no doubt recounts the birth and rescue of the great Sargon of Akkad, who ruled Babylonia for over fifty years in the twenty-fourth century B.C.E. While there is debate about the original date of composition of the Sargon legend, most opinions favor the first millennium, on the basis of language content and style, and it may be that Sargon II commissioned the text that extols his namesake.[40] Sargon of Akkad, the first great conqueror of Mesopotamia, established a vast empire. The stories of his escapades continued to be told for two thousand years after his demise, not only in Mesopotamia but in Anatolia and Egypt as well. His name is mentioned in inscriptions, omens, and historical texts in Sumerian, Akkadian, Hittite, and perhaps also Hurrian.[41] With the possible exception of Gilgamesh, his position is unrivaled within the literary tradition of Mesopotamian historiography.[42] The Sargon legend includes the story of his rescue, followed by blessings to enable the future rulers of Akkad to share in his success:

> I am Sargon, the great king, king of Agade.
> My mother was a high priestess, I did not know my father.
> My father's brothers dwell in the uplands.
> My city is Zaupiranu, which lies on Euphrates bank.
> My mother, the high priestess, conceived me, she bore me in secret.
> She placed me in a reed basket, she sealed my hatch with pitch.
> She left me to the river, whence I could not come up.
> The river carried me off, it brought me to Aqqi, drawer of water.
> Aqqi, drawer of water, brought me up as he dipped his bucket.
> Aqqi, drawer of water, brought me up as his adopted son.
> Aqqi, drawer of water, set (me) to his orchard work.
> During my orchard work, Ishtar loved me,
> Fifty-five years I ruled as king.
> I became lord over and ruled the black-headed folk,
> I . . . [ ] hard mountains with picks of copper,
> I was wont to ascend high mountains.
> The [la]nd of the sea I sieged three times,
> I conquered Dilmun.
> I went up to great Der, I [ ],
> I destroyed [Ka]zallu and [ ].[43]

The Sargon legend has many similarities to the prose narrative of Exodus 2:1–10, which follows Pharaoh's decree that all male newborns be cast into the Nile:

> (1) A man of the house of Levi went and married the daughter of
> Levi. (2) The woman conceived and bore a son. She saw that he was
> good and she hid him for three months. (3) She could hide him no
> longer, and so she took for him a wicker basket and caulked it with
> bitumen and pitch. She put the child into it, and put it among the

reeds by the bank of the Nile. (4) His sister stationed herself at a distance, to learn what would befall him. (5) The daughter of Pharaoh came down to bathe in the Nile. Her maidens walked along the Nile. She saw the basket among the reeds and sent her slave girl, and she took it. (6) She opened, she saw him—the boy—and behold it was a baby crying. She spared his life, and she said, "From the children of the Hebrews is he." (7) His sister said to Pharaoh's daughter: "Shall I go, and call for you a Hebrew nurse, that she should nurse the child for you?" (8) Pharaoh's daughter said, "go," so the lass went and called the child's mother. (9) Pharaoh's daughter said to her, "Take this child and nurse it for me, and I shall pay your wages." So the woman took the child and nursed it. (10) The child grew up, and she brought him to Pharaoh's daughter, and he became for her as a son, and she named him Moshe, saying, "out of the water, I drew him."

Consider the motifs common to the two narratives. In both, the parents are mentioned anonymously. Both foundlings stem from priestly lineage on their mother's side: Moses' mother is from the tribe of Levi, the tribe that later in the Pentateuch emerges as the cultic caste of Israel, while Sargon's mother is a priestess. Both mothers give birth in secret. In both stories, the father is mentioned at the outset but quickly fades out of the picture, conspicuous in his absence from the subsequent story of rescue. In both, the child's mother places him in a basket lined with pitch. In both, the child is rescued from the river, is adopted by strangers, and comes under female guardianship: Moses under Pharaoh's daughter, Sargon under Ishtar. Both are compared to drawn water. Sargon exclaims, "Aqqi, drawer of water, brought me up as he dipped his bucket." Moses' very name is a derivation of the Hebrew word for drawing water—"'out of the water, I drew him (mĕšîtǐhû).'" Both foundlings receive divine election, rising to lead their peoples following a period of apprenticeship—Sargon as a gardener, Moses as a shepherd (Exod 3:1).[44]

Some scholars note differences in an attempt to discount any comparison between the two accounts. Sargon's mother, it is observed in this vein, seems to have conceived in illicit fashion, thus necessitating the child's abandonment, whereas Moses is conceived through legitimate parents, and is abandoned because he is hunted. Having established a significant difference between the two accounts, these scholars remove from the table any notion of comparison between them.[45] The similarities, however, seem too great to write off as mere coincidence.

I will begin my accounting of the similarities between the two stories by placing them within a wider comparative context. As many have noted, these two accounts represent only two instances of what folklorists call the type-story of the hero cast away in infancy.[46] The form is attested in written sources from as early as the first half of the second millennium. One count identifies seventy-two versions of this tale across ancient, medieval, and modern history.[47] The motif of an imperiled child of illustrious parents abandoned in infancy and raised by foster parents before rising to assume the mantle of leadership or the status of hero is a skeleton biography of Oedipus, Romulus, King Arthur, Snow White, Tarzan, and Superman.[48] Harry Potter is only the most recent reincarnation of the motif. In premodern versions, the structure of the tale usually includes the following seven elements: (1) a note that the infant was of noble birth; (2) an explanation for the abandonment; (3) preparations for the infant's exposure; (4) the act of exposure; (5) protection or salvation in an unusual manner (6) discovery and adoption; (7) a listing of the accomplishments of the hero.[49] One scholar has identified ten tales from premodern sources in which the abandonment occurs at a river or a riverbank, as in the Moses and Sargon stories.[50] The ubiquity of the motif suggests that it is rooted in a social reality. It is not uncommon for us today to hear news reports of infants abandoned near a garbage dumpster or at the entrance to a hospital emergency room. Infants are abandoned at locations where they will be noticed and, hopefully, cared for. In ancient times, no site was more the focus of day-to-day activity in riverine cultures than the river bank, where the chances were greatest that the child would be noticed and saved.

Like the Cinderella motif—found in such disparate places as Iran, Europe, Japan, among American Indians, and in ninth-century C.E. sources from China—the pervasiveness of the tale of the hero cast away in infancy across borders cultural and temporal suggests that oral transmission alone cannot explain its recurrence. Rather, it is best attributed to what Jung called the presence of archetypes within our collective unconscious: forms and symbols manifested within people across cultures, especially when they share common experiences, in this case the phenomenon of abandoned children. Motifs recur in independent fashion because they are universal. And when such events actually happen, people like to tell of them. Equally evident, however, are these stories' differences across cultures. Elements are present, or are not present, or appear in varying forms. As significant as the similarities are these differences, for they are often markers of precisely what sets apart a given culture as distinct. Over against the standard forms that are shared with other cultures, these differences highlight the values of a culture in bold relief.[51]

This conceptual framework enhances our insight into the comparison of the rescue narratives of Sargon and Moses. They are only two instances of a widely recurring tale.[52] We have ancient Near Eastern attestations of the foundling hero motif—in Egyptian literature, concerning Horus,[53] and in Hittite literature.[54] The pervasiveness of the tale no doubt reflects the fact that the social phenomenon of the exposed infant was not uncommon in the ancient world, due to economic necessity, the illegitimacy of a child, or a threat to a child's life.[55] Indeed, the legal sources from the ancient Near East that attest to the practice of adoption of an exposed child suggest that the phenomenon was not particularly rare.[56] A set of Mesopotamian texts known as the *ana ittišu* texts depicts cases that hew closely to the scenario described in Exodus 2:1–10: an abandoned child is found, given over to a wet-nurse for a set wage, weaned, and returned to the person who found the child. Formal adoption ensues, and includes the granting of a name.[57]

I turn now to a close comparison of the Sargon and Moses rescue accounts and an examination of how each reflects a distinct societal and ideological context. The overarching difference between the two is observable even before we begin to evaluate them element by element. The Sargon account is written in the first person, as is highly typical for royal narrative inscriptions, whereas the Moses account is written in third person, as is highly typical of biblical narrative. These two modes of narration evince deep ideological underpinnings.

First person narration can serve many different functions. In contemporary literature, we associate it with autobiography or memoir, and we see it as a vehicle for sharing introspection. In the context of the ancient Near East, this is rarely the case.[58] Rather, first person narration well suits the construction of an authoritarian personality. Nearly all the first person narration from the ancient Near East revolves around the feats and accomplishments of kings and sometimes other public figures, figures who dominated the populaces that served them.[59] First person narration by kings is ubiquitous in many of the genres of royal literature in the ancient Near East. In Mesopotamia, this could include royal inscriptions, compositions buried in the foundations of a temple (known as foundation deposits), letters by the king to the gods, annals, and historical epics. In Egypt, it is also seen in tomb inscriptions by high officials.[60] What underlies these first person compositions is a king's desire to gain acceptance, legitimacy, or sympathy, either from a deity or from the judgment of subsequent generations of the elite.

This spirit is everywhere apparent in the Sargon narrative. It opens with the declaration "I am Sargon, the great king, king of Agade." Every one of the twenty lines quoted here centers around a self-referential statement by Sargon about, and in celebration of, himself: "the river carried me off it brought me to Aqqi"; "Ishtar loved me." The poetics at work serve to convince the listener that Sargon was, indeed, divinely elected to rule. No less, they serve to convince that his authority is so total that he is entitled and empowered to tell the story himself. First person narration accords with royal theology: the subject matter is the king and his actions, the first person narration is that of the king himself. The point is to appease either the gods or members of the royal legacy.

By contrast, the Bible—in nearly universal fashion—depicts its narratives in the third person, as in the Moses rescue narrative.[61] I have pointed out that narrative in the Bible serves to articulate the subtleties of the demands of covenantal behavior in their fullest complexity, by illuminating the social imperatives and psychological forces at play in a given circumstance. Biblical narrative essentially sets forward a series of situations and scenarios that allows the reader or listener to fully empathize with the characters and, as it were, endure the experience, the challenges, and the dilemmas together with the protagonists.

The third person is especially appropriate in such narrative, for the first step toward achieving this effect is to dramatize the situations through third person narration. It neutralizes, as it were, the speaker or narrator as a discernable persona. Whereas the Sargon legend is presented as related by Sargon himself, the biblical stories are not presented as being related by any specific person; the narrator seems to practice what one scholar has called "drastic self-effacement."[62] He is, moreover, differentiated from the Almighty. God does not tell the story; in fact, God is a character in the Bible's stories. Rather, the narrator fades into the background, omniscient, yet not himself God.[63] The way the story's presentation seems to approach objectivity, without commentary, allows the reader to identify with the circumstances, as the protagonists of the story themselves do. The implicit omniscience of this mode of storytelling also allows the narrator to freely weave in and out of minds and to be privy to all relevant information—to help shape the moral dimensions of the dilemma at hand.[64]

A second sweeping difference between ancient Near Eastern royal inscriptions and biblical narrative concerns the role of the gods in the story. We think of the Bible as nothing if not a book of religious literature, a work that proclaims God's works in the world of ancient Israel. But when the Bible is set against the royal inscriptions, an unexpected phenomenon catches our attention. The gods are everywhere present in the royal inscriptions, and explicitly so—much more than in biblical narrative. In the Sargon legend, Sargon describes the overt providence bestowed on him by the goddess Ishtar following his rescue by Aqqi: "Aqqi, drawer of water, set (me) to his orchard work /

During my orchard work, Ishtar loved me / Fifty-five years I ruled as king." As noted, a palpable experience of the gods and goddesses was a hallmark of the world the ancients inhabited. In royal narrative inscriptions, there is little development of character, because essentially, the fortunes of the king are solely a product of the providence of the gods, or of the king's capacity to please them.

Surprisingly, by contrast, we note that the Bible makes relatively little *overt* mention of God in its narratives about individuals and their lives. The Moses rescue narrative is a case in point: God is nowhere explicitly mentioned. Seemingly, the hand of God is here. But it is behind the scenes, and not explicitly mentioned.[65] The issue is not merely semantic but deeply theological. Imagine the text of Exodus 2 slightly modified to include some overt references to God to accentuate His role in the story, say, somewhere around verse 5, "And God sent the daughter of Pharaoh down to bathe by the river." Were the text to make explicit what is only implicit, it would do so at great cost: the flood of divine presence in the story would drown out the possibility of seeing the characters' actions as autonomous choices. Acts of heroism, the moves made after agonizing inner struggle, would all be nullified. Instead, protagonists would be viewed as props made to act, marionettes animated by a divine puppeteer.[66] At one and the same time, from the biblical perspective, God implicitly guides events, while all the while the agents who act do so in utter freedom. The handling of divine intervention in the affairs of individuals in biblical narrative bears out the maxim of the rabbinic sage Rabbi Akiva of the second century C.E., who said, "Everything is foreseen on high, yet free choice is given."[67] A philosophical conundrum, it is an assumption that guides the poetics of biblical narrative.[68]

Turning now to a close reading of the Exodus account, we may see how biblical narrative, reflecting covenant theology, invests in developing its characters much more than does the Sargon legend, a product of ancient Near Eastern royal theology. Specific attention is brought to bear in the Exodus account on the trait of altruism. Calls for a kind heart, for kind treatment of the resident alien, abound in the Bible. The narrative of the rescue of Moses examines the complexity of motivation that enters into acts ostensibly performed out of an altruistic spirit.

Beginning our reading with verse 6, the key verse of the rescue scene, we note Scripture's handling of time. When Scripture wishes to cut through time quickly, it has no problem doing so—witness verse 2: "the woman conceived and she bore a son." In the Hebrew, nine months pass within the space of four words. Here in verse 6, however, the action of what must have transpired in the space of a few seconds is drawn out over five stages: (1) "She opened"

(6a); (2) "She saw him—the boy" (6b); (3) "And behold, it was a baby[69] crying" (6c); (4) "She spared his life" (6d); (5) "And she said, 'From the children
of the Hebrews is he'" (6e). One may read the elaboration here as coming
simply from an aesthetic desire to create suspense. But suspense could have
been just as effectively created, say, during the time the infant's sister kept
her watch, in verse 4. Rather, the five stages in verse 6 serve to detail the inner stirrings of Pharaoh's daughter, as she contemplates the extraordinary
sight before her.

Just what is her response? Herein lies the difficulty, the complexity, and
hence the beauty of the verse at hand. One may read her response as simply
one of compassion and conclude that this is the thrust and sweep of the verse
all the way through its five parsed segments. Yet surely it could not have been
that simple. She is, after all, Pharaoh's daughter, and the backdrop to the entire story is her own father's decree to kill all newborn Hebrew males (Exod
1:22). Instead, this verse opens up a range of possibilities for fathoming what
Pharaoh's daughter experiences at this fateful and critical moment. Usually
laconic in its style, Scripture here in verse 6 states the obvious (hence superflu-
ous) when it states, "She opened, *she saw him—the boy*—and it was a baby
(*na'ar*) crying." Remove the phrase "the boy" from the sentence, and you have
lost nothing by way of new information, as *"baby"* here, in the Hebrew, *na'ar*,
implicitly reveals the infant's gender to be male. It is obvious that once she
opens the basket, she will inevitably see the boy. What does Scripture wish to
stress when it says the obvious, that "She opened, *she saw him—the boy*—"?
Rather than looking for a single answer, we do better to seek an equivocal answer—one that embraces the ambiguities and inner contradictions of activity
and motivation. Perhaps the stressed seeing indicates that she took in the
gravity of the situation, and immediately realized what she later verbalizes at
the end of the verse—this is an Israelite boy, whose fate now rests in her
hands. Scripture expresses here in words what in cinematography would be
the equivalent of a studied close-up of her facial expression. Eyes bulged wide
open at the sight of the abandoned child; "she saw him—the boy."

"Seeing," however, within the narrative of Exodus 2, is a tagged and
charged term. This is the second time this baby has been "seen" in a sense
more profound than the mere optic phenomenon of neurons firing behind the
retina. Recall that on birth (v. 2), his mother *"saw* that he was good" and hid
him for three months. The "good"-ness that she *saw* is often taken to mean
that he was of exceptional physical beauty, or complexion.[70] If that is so, then
we understand that when Pharaoh's daughter "opened" and "she saw him,"
she saw precisely what the infant's mother had seen: "that he was good." Put
differently, the report "she saw him" suggests that beyond the moral quandary

that will tug her filial loyalties in one direction and her compassion in the other is an added dimension: she finds something in him that is attractive, something that predisposes her toward feeling sympathy for him.

The complexity of motivation continues through the remaining segments of verse 6. Not until the fourth segment (6d) does Scripture state "she spared his life." The sequence of the segments seems deliberate. Prior to that statement is the third segment (6c) "and behold, it was a baby crying." Only when she observes him crying is she moved to pity, and to spare his life—not before. Put differently, she experiences a sensual bombardment, which reaches its culmination with her resolution to spare the infant's life. Her initial encounter with the baby involves the sense of touch, as she takes the basket into her hands: "She saw the basket among the reeds and sent her slave girl, and she opened it." Then her experience of the foundling involves the sense of sight: "she opened, and she saw him—the boy—." Finally, to this is added the audile element of the baby's cries—"and behold it was a baby crying." The sensual overload of touch, sight, and sound leads her, finally, in the fourth segment, to resolve, against her responsibilities as daughter and as subject, to spare the child's life.

There is even more to this progression of response. Notice how the strategy of narration has subtly shifted. The first two segments are direct narration: "She opened"; "she saw him—the boy—." Direct narration for the third segment would have dictated the following syntax: "the baby cried." Instead we read *"and behold*, it was a baby crying." That word, "and behold" (Heb. *vě-hinnēh*) brings us into the inner subjectivity of the character, namely Pharaoh's daughter. The baby's cries are not reported to us from the objective, distanced perspective of the impersonal narrator; rather, the action is presented to us as perceived through the *interpretative thought process* of Pharaoh's daughter. The effect created of entering into her inner world is familiar to us from the realm of cinematography: the phrase "and behold" represents a shift of the camera's view. We should imagine the beginning of the verse (6a–6b) as being filmed at close range, such that we see both Pharaoh's daughter and the basket. When we reach 6c, "and behold, it was a baby crying," we no longer see Pharaoh's daughter; the camera is now perched over her shoulder, aimed downward at the basket. We see only the baby, just as she does. The word "behold" represents her own inner speech, her ruminations written out: "it is a baby crying!"

Such inner speech, or rumination (known formally as *free indirect discourse*) is a distinctive hallmark of biblical narrative, an innovation in literary convention that allowed, for the first time in ancient Near Eastern literature, the exploration of characters' inner thoughts and stirrings.[71] This exploration stems from a theory of action that understands that behind every action inner cognitive processes are at work. Proper covenantal behavior can only be achieved through an understanding and awareness of these processes. Thus, the attention in narratives such as this to the inner world from which action stems furthers the goal of educating toward proper conduct. The intense focus on the inner stirrings of Pharaoh's daughter inherent in the phrase "and behold, it was a baby crying" well suits my view that there is a progression in her response; that it is only after her sustained, multiple-stage encounter with the child, culminating with the intense experience of seeing him cry, that she resolves to spare his life.

The fifth segment (6e), "And she said, 'From the children of the Hebrews is he,'" is as multivalent as the act of gazing on him implied in the second segment (6b), "and she saw him." What is the import of this exclamation, following the resolve to spare his life, in the fourth segment? Two possible readings present themselves, and depend on the tone of voice we hear in her words. One possibility is to read the verse as rising in a crescendo—from tactility (verse 5e and 6a) to vision (6b) to audibility (6c) to inner resolve (6d), and finally to audible proclamation. In a burst of effusive sympathy and benevolence, she exclaims, "From the children of the Hebrews is he!"

Alternatively, we may read verse 6e as a backtracking of sorts. Having resolved to spare the infant's life in 6d, she now contemplates what she has decided, and finds herself in the throes of a dilemma. Caught between compassion for this helpless child and her filial and state loyalties, she wrings her hands and verbalizes the proximate cause of her tension-fraught predicament: "From the children of the Hebrews is he."

The investment in characterization in verse 6 stands in contrast with the parallel moment in the Sargon legend:

> The river carried me off, it brought me to Aqqi, drawer of water.
> Aqqi, drawer of water, brought me up as he dipped his bucket.

The character of Aqqi, who rescues Sargon from the river, is undeveloped and unexplored. We garner no insight into what Aqqi experiences as he saves the foundling, no explanation of his motivations or his concerns. If anything, it appears that his motivation might be to one day set the boy to work in the orchard. The emphasis at the moment of rescue is the same as it is throughout the legend: it is on Sargon, and the providence that guided his destiny, step by step; the text sets out to prove to the reader that Sargon is divinely protected and elected. His statement that "she left me to the river, whence I could not come up" underscores his utter helplessness, and the salvific providence that watches over him.

The exploration of altruism and the complexity of motivation are carried over into verse 7 of the Moses account, where we shift our focus to the child's sister, and the surprising initiative on which she embarks. In verse 4, we were told that she had stationed herself at a distance, "to learn what would befall him." Powerless to steer the child's fate, she hoped only to passively observe and discover what would be done to him by others: "to learn what would befall him." We are surprised, then, to see her take the initiative and advance a plan for his rescue. Ostensibly, verse 7 centers exclusively around Moses' sister. Yet within her proposal implications abound for the characterization of Pharaoh's daughter. Note that in her suggestion, the child's sister twice refers to the Egyptian princess: "Shall I go, and call *for you* a Hebrew nurse, that she should nurse the child *for you*?" She has grasped a vital component of the motivation driving Pharaoh's daughter's disposition toward the infant. The princess acts not exclusively out of compassion but out of some measure of self-interest as well.[72] Pharaoh's daughter has spared the baby because she wants it for herself. The baby's sister surmises that this is the card that must be played. Whatever she proposes must appear to be in the service of her interlocutor, and not first and foremost as an effort to save the baby. This is evident not solely from the repeated phrase "for you" in verse 7 but also from the dissonance between her proposed plan of action in verse 7 and the step she actually takes in verse 8. Having suggested calling a "Hebrew nurse" (v. 7), she proceeds instead to call "the child's mother" (v. 8). Had she revealed her intention to call the child's mother, the entire plan would have been undermined: Pharaoh's daughter—now attached to the child, and with designs of her own— would no doubt have been threatened. Her act of independence and courage is indeed the selfless act of a great heart. Yet Scripture through its exploration of her altruism demonstrates an awareness that additional motivations of self-interest may often accompany the altruistic act. These motivations do not nullify the greatness of the act; rather, they point to a more realistic and complex picture of human motivation.

That her compassion is intermingled with an element of self-interest and a desire to take possession of the child is evident at several more junctures in the narrative. She instructs the supposed Hebrew wet nurse to "take this child and nurse it *for me*" (v. 9).[73] The name she gives the baby in verse 10 also reveals the need she has to stake her claim on the foundling: "he became for her as a son, and she named him Moshe, for 'out of the water, I drew him.'"

Various interpretations have been offered of her statement in verse 9, "Take this child and nurse it for me, and *I* shall pay *your* wages." For the early medieval rabbinic sage R. Saadya Gaon, the offering of wages was a magnanimous gesture on her part. After all, the supposed Hebrew wet nurse was nothing but a slave.[74] For one modern scholar, in contrast, the offering of money indicates condescension.[75] Yet the element of the wages—indeed, much of what transpires in verses 7–10—is best understood against the legal context of the ancient Near East. The child's sister has initiated a process whereby Pharaoh's daughter will adopt the baby and his mother (unbeknownst to the princess) will serve as the formally hired wet nurse. Wet nurses were routinely contracted for their services in the ancient Near East, and the Moses narrative pays attention to many issues that arise in the legal literature of the time.[76] It would be mistaken to understand the "wages" here in strictly monetary terms, as remuneration for services rendered. Ancient Near Eastern nursing contracts, particularly from Mesopotamia, indicate that the suckling fee typically consisted of rations, such as barley, oil, wool, and only sometimes silver.[77] The "fee," then, is not only remunerative but also enables the wet nurse, by providing for herself, to provide the best nourishment for the infant. Many of the ancient written agreements address breach of contract, and reveal a concern that the wet nurse may abscond with the child. The treaties thus state in unequivocal terms that the right of possession belongs to the party that pays for the child's upkeep.[78] These legal concerns may well be reflected in the terms expressed in the statement "Take this child and nurse it for me, and I shall pay your wages." In paying the wages, Pharaoh's daughter is staking her legal claim to the child. The same Mesopotamian records indicate that when the child's support was being funded by an adoptive parent, the adoption process was concluded when the child was weaned, returned to the adoptive mother, and finally given a name by the benefactor, signaling the conclusion of the adoption process.[79] What Moses' sister has suggested, then, is a scheme whereby Pharaoh's daughter will adopt the infant.

While the adoption of baby Moses may conclude with the naming in verse 10, it appears that the maternal bond has already been established in verse 6. The verse is fraught with imagery that supports this contention. There is a syntactical irregularity, even more evident in the original Hebrew than the English translation, at the point in the narrative when she opens the basket: "She opened, she saw him—the boy—and behold it was a baby crying." Note that, even in English, this first clause of verse 6 is missing a direct object, and should properly read "she opened *it*" or "she opened *the basket*." From the context of the verse it is clear that she opened the basket, but syntactically the sentence is incomplete. The irregularity is even more pronounced in the original, because Hebrew ordinarily demands a direct object to complete the clause.[80] Absent the direct object, the words "She opened, she saw him—the boy—and behold it was a baby crying," are words that could well describe a birth scene. Childbirth is referred to elsewhere as the opening of the womb

(Gen 29:31; 30:22), and the literature of the ancient Near East abounds with imagery of the womb as a river.[81] So Pharaoh's daughter at this point experiences a profound, birth-like first encounter with the child.

Aside from Pharaoh's daughter and the child's sister, a third figure—often ignored in the scholarship—who is granted vivid characterization is the infant's mother. She appears in the nativity scene of verses 2–3 and again in her role as wet nurse in verses 9–10. The two scenes employ vastly different strategies of narration, both of which demonstrate the power of characterization in biblical narrative. Verses 2–3 take us into the inner world of a mother desperate to save her infant child:

> The woman conceived and bore a son. She saw that he was good
> and she hid him for three months. (3) She could hide him no
> longer, and so she took for him a wicker basket and caulked it with
> bitumen and pitch. She put the child into it, and put it among the
> reeds by the bank of the Nile.

Following the formulaic report of the birth, "the woman conceived and bore a son," the very first description of her is itself pregnant with meaning and gives a glimpse of her inner world: "She saw that he was good." "Seeing" of something "that it was good" may be read as an allusion to the account of Creation in Genesis 1, where at the end of each generative act, God "saw" what he had created, "and it was good." One modern commentator has suggested that the allusion here implies that "she looked on her child with a joy similar to that of God on His creation."[82] However we choose to understand the allusion, it is clear that the text seeks to convey something about her inner reaction to the baby's birth, and that it is something of great significance to her. Verse 3a, "She could hide him no longer," may in fact be redundant after verse 2d, in which we have already been told that the shelter was only of a three-month duration. But when verse 3a is included, it gives us a sense of the anguish, the despair that grips her as she struggles to determine a course of action. Indeed, the attention to technical detail here, "and so she took for him a wicker basket and caulked it with bitumen and pitch," demands elucidation, in light of the sparseness of detail in the rest of the passage. Surely, had we been spared the detail of the bitumen and the pitch, we would have assumed that the basket had been treated in some fashion; what purpose would be served by placing the child in a basket that would immediately sink? Rather, the flurry of detail attributed to the mother here intimates an attempt to compensate for her absolute powerlessness by engaging hyperactively in the small domain in which she does yet retain control to assist him. Anyone who has ever sent off a soldier to battle will immediately relate to the feeling. The anxious parent eagerly engages in doing the soldier's laundry, in stuffing his pockets with snacks of various sorts. But the activities, done out of love and caring, are really expressions of powerlessness, born out of the knowledge that there really is nothing one can do to keep one's loved one out of harm's way. The mother in these verses, in the same way, wishes to retain control over her special son, wishes, at the very least, to guide what will happen to him once he leaves her bosom but, alas, finds herself powerless. All that she can do is labor intensively, rubbing in the pitch and bitumen, themselves signs of the necessity of surrendering him to an unknown fate. The intensity of her connectedness with the child is nicely expressed in verse 2b: "she took for him a wicker basket," compensating for utter powerlessness by doing for him the little she can.

These two verses contrast with the parallel segment of the Sargon legend:

> She placed me in a reed basket, she sealed my hatch with pitch.
> She left me to the river, whence I could not come up.
> The river carried me off, it brought me to Aqqi, drawer of water.

Some sense of the mother's despair is evident in these lines as well, but this is not the dominant thrust. Rather, the Sargon legend focuses on the providence that ensures Sargon's rescue. Each line contains two self-referential clauses. The river is emphasized as a place of utter helplessness for him ("whence I could not come up") yet also as an entity that acts in almost autonomous fashion to facilitate his rescue: "The river carried me off, it brought me to Aqqi, drawer of water." As noted, the inner world expressed in these lines is that of the first person narrator, Sargon, as he reflects on the confluence of fortune that guided his fate.

The mother's sense of despair in the Moses account is underscored by her daughter's initiative in verse 4. It is only the sister who can bear to risk watching what could prove to be the baby's tragic end, and she establishes her vigil, apparently, unbeknownst to her mother. Evidently, the mother wishes no part of it, abandoning the child in an image reminiscent of the casting off of Ishmael by Hagar: "When the water was gone from the skin, she left the child under one of the bushes, and went and sat down at a distance, a bowshot away; for she thought 'Let me not look on as the child dies'" (Gen 21:15–16). For her to watch what would become of her infant son offers the possibility of witnessing his rescue, but also the risk of watching helplessly as he is killed. The mother rejects the option of engaging in emotional risk in order to attain certainty. By abandoning the child and departing, she opts, paradoxically, for the certainty of remaining in eternal doubt—she now knows for sure that she will never know what became of the child.

The narrative investment in the mother's inner world in these two verses is all the more stark in light of the treatment of her in verses 9–10. To depart from the text for a moment, imagine what comes over the mother as the story unfolds. One can only imagine the double joy for her of first learning from her daughter that the boy has been saved and then of the opportunity to once again hold him in her arms. What did she exclaim to her daughter, to her husband, or even to herself, when she learned of the rescue? On all these points, the text is silent. What did she feel as she took her baby back into her arms? In stark contrast to the intense characterization given her in verses 2–3, the text gives absolutely no sense here of her inner feelings: "Pharaoh's daughter said to her, "Take this child and nurse it for me, and I shall pay your wages." So *the woman* took the child and nursed it." There is a brutality here to the silencing the text enforces on her. Receiving her mandate from Pharaoh's daughter, she must stoically play the role assigned her: that of lactation machine, of robotic udder. We view the scene as perceived by Pharaoh's daughter: "*the woman* took the child and nursed it." She must absolutely quell all emotion, lest she be found out. The two halves of verse 9, in fact, reflect precisely this sentiment. It features a command by Pharaoh's daughter, "Take this child and nurse it for me," and a verbatim reiteration of its fulfillment: "So the woman took the child and nursed it." The nursing is carried out on terms dictated by Pharaoh's daughter. Scripture does not say she nursed "her son," but rather "the child," the term Pharaoh's daughter herself used to designate the infant.

The quashing of the mother's sentiments continues in the immediate passage to verse 10, and the return of the child to Pharaoh's daughter: "The child grew up, and she brought him to Pharaoh's daughter, and he became for her as a son, and she named him Moshe, for 'out of the water, I drew him.'" Consider what is omitted, flattened, in this dry and indifferent report. The period narrated at the beginning of verse 10 consisted of months—perhaps even years— of maternal joy, of bonding with the infant she caressed at her bosom, of watching his first smile, first laugh, first steps, first words. Yet each successive milestone must also have been for her like the sand that inexorably trickles through an hourglass. Forced to surrender him once at the age of three months, so, too, she will have to surrender him again. Yet these sentiments are nowhere here evident. What is so obviously true from a human standpoint, and so consonant with the tone and tenor of verses 2–3, is totally absent here. Her feelings are silenced, as she plays the part assigned her. The account is told from the perspective of the proprietress who has legal deed to the child. The outsourced lactation provider completes her services, and returns the child to its legal "mother": *and he became for her as a son.*

Further insight into the figure of the mother may be garnered from an unusual structural aspect of the entire passage. Observe the imbalanced way the narration in verses 1–10 employs speech to drive the action. Until the last clause of verse 6, the verse that depicts the moment of rescue, there is no speech whatsoever. Surely, the infant's mother must have spoken with the child's father; surely Pharaoh's daughter must have issued some sort of verbal command to her maidservant in sending her to fetch the basket in verse 5. The narration omits words that were undoubtedly spoken. To be sure, there is nothing unusual or startling about this; the narrator is under no obligation to report all that the protagonists of a story might have said. But the absence of speech in these verses stands out in bold relief when we notice that from the end of verse 6, all of the narration is driven by statements uttered by the protagonists. At the end of verse 6, Pharaoh's daughter speaks: "She spared his life, and *said*, 'From the children of the Hebrews is he.'" In verse 7, the infant's sister speaks to the Egyptian princess. In verse 8, the narrator could have done enough by informing us through narrative exposition that the princess acceded to the plan. Instead, the narrator includes the enunciation of the princess's assent: "Pharaoh's daughter said, 'go,' so the lass went and called the child's mother." In verse 9, the narrator could have reported through exposition that Pharaoh's daughter gave the infant over to the wet nurse, but again the plot is driven by speech: "Pharaoh's daughter said to her, 'Take this child and nurse it for me, and I shall pay your wages.' So the woman took the child and nursed it." The final act of speech is the naming of the child: "and she named him Moshe, *saying*, 'out of the water, I drew him.'"

None of these utterances in verses 6–10 constitute prayer or praise. Rather—without exception—they are acts of persuasion and exercise of power. Pharaoh's daughter's utterance at the end of verse 6, "and *she said*, 'From the children of the Hebrews is he,'" is the audible voice of her inner struggle, her efforts to shore up the resolve to violate her father's decree. In verse 7, the child's sister speaks in order to persuade Pharaoh's daughter to adopt her plan. In verses 8–9, Pharaoh's daughter ostensibly issues two orders. In verse 8, she commands the sister's action: "Pharaoh's daughter said, 'go,' so the lass went and called the child's mother." And in verse 9, she issues an order to the putative wet nurse: "Pharaoh's daughter said to her, 'Take this child and nurse it for me, and I shall pay your wages.' So the woman took the child and nursed it." Yet it is really the sister who has controlled the action and Pharaoh's daughter who has submitted to her plan.[83] The two orders Pharaoh's daughter issues are in reality mimicked reiterations of what the sister has suggested to her. The sister says (v. 7), "Shall I *go*, and call for you a Hebrew nurse?" Pharaoh's daughter parrots this, saying "go." In verse 7, the sister specifies: "that she should *nurse the child for you?*"—and this is the precise language Pharaoh's daughter employs in addressing the putative wet nurse: "Take this child and nurse it for me." Thus, there is a reversal. Pharaoh's daughter assumes the position of power, but unwittingly she is manipulated by the young maiden whose will and plan she executes. The final utterance, the naming of the baby, is a veritable speech act, a spoken enactment and exercise of power, for through it the baby is formally—even legally, as noted—stripped from his past, granted emancipation, and adopted by his new mother.[84] Speech, then, in this story is not merely a record of the words spoken during the unfolding of these dramatic events. Speech functions as a marked rhetorical tool that highlights the attempt at persuasion and the execution of power. It signals to us where power resides—primarily in Pharaoh's daughter, secondarily in the child's sister—and whence power has been stripped: the baby's mother, as evidenced in her silent anguish.

The employment of speech and the interaction between the figures in this narrative to illuminate character serves—as noted, in striking rhetorical contrast to the Sargon legend–to instruct by highlighting the multifaceted complexity of humans striving to achieve high moral and spiritual standing.

Some of the most astute insights into the story of the rescue of Moses have been made by a group of exegetes whose comments are nowhere written. Their perspective is expressed, rather, in the composition and colors of a painted canvas.[85] The story of the rescue of Moses was a theme revisited time and again by European masterpiece painters from the sixteenth through the eighteenth centuries. My interest in these paintings here is not art historical per se, but stems from certain painters' capacity to serve as biblical exegetes: they were close readers of the text. If we overlook the period dress and the tendency in these canvases to reduce the Nile, at times, to nothing more than a creek, we can discover interpretations that are not only true to the text but also illuminating of it in highly evocative ways.

Take, for example, the 1746 painting by William Hogarth of the return of Moses as a weaned child to Pharaoh's daughter of (fig. 5.1).

Notice particularly the way the child clutches at his mother's robe. Pharaoh's daughter, beaming at the prospect of her new possession, is entirely oblivious to the heart-rending trauma being experienced by mother and child. I find this painting evocative precisely because it gives voice to what is absent in the text. There can be no doubt that the separation of the child Moses from his mother was emotionally traumatic for each. And yet, as I noted earlier, the text silences this grief, because it is narrated from the perspective of Pharaoh's daughter. The "silencing" of the experience depicted in Hogarth's work is

FIGURE 5.1. *Moses Brought before Pharaoh's Daughter*, by William Hogarth (1746). ©
Coram Family in the care of the Foundling Museum, London/The Bridgeman Art
Library.

precisely Scripture's way of underscoring just how domineering is the authority of the Egyptian princess in this narrative.[86]

Proper consideration of this silenced yet searing moment, as depicted by
Hogarth, paves the way for understanding the continuation of the narrative in
verse 11: "Some time after that, when Moses had grown up, he went out to his
kinsfolk and witnessed their toil." Having been nurtured at a tender age by his
own mother, only to be taken away from her in early childhood, it is no wonder
that once Moses grows up he goes *out to his kinsfolk*; it would appear that the
visceral bonds developed in early childhood pushed him to seek a connection
with his roots.

While Hogarth's canvas portrays the moment at which Moses is returned
to Pharaoh's daughter, the most popular depiction among the European masters was the moment of rescue, verses 5–7. Their canvases makes us suddenly
aware of an element in the story that exegetes in print have almost entirely
ignored: the presence and influence of *the maidens*. Indeed, neither the handmaidens walking on the shore of the Nile nor the maidservant who fetches
the basket are given any speaking role in Exodus. Perhaps they, in fact, said

FIGURE 5.2. *The Finding of Moses,* by Gerrit de Wet (1650). Loan of the family Van Schaik–Van Eck van der Sluys to Museum Ons' Lieve Heer op Solder, Amsterdam.

nothing. But we would be mistaken to assume that in their silence they simply vanish from the story's main scenes. They are, rather, a presence. Even if we assume that the handmaidens are located at some distance from their mistress as she wades in the shallows, her personal maidservant would certainly have been aware of all that transpired, and certainly the infant's sister would not have gained access to the princess without the knowledge of those whose task it was to protect her.[87] Pharaoh's daughter, therefore, acts under the watchful eye of those who serve her; she is not alone with the basket.

What social pressure is exerted on the Egyptian princess as she acts under the scrutiny of her own servants? This issue, unconsidered in written commentaries, is a major theme of the visual ones. Consider the 1650 work by the Dutch painter Gerrit de Wet (fig. 5.2).

De Wet has closely read verse 5: "Her maidens walked along the Nile. *She* saw the basket among the reeds and sent her slave girl, and *she* took it." The basket was observable for all to see. Yet for others it was not worthy of notice. Only Pharaoh's daughter sensed that the sealed basket might carry a sensitive and vulnerable cargo. This painting—nay, this close reading of the verse— endows the princess with a sharpened acumen and distinctly acute sense of caring.

FIGURE 5.3. *The Finding of Moses*, by Francesco Zugno. Presented by Alfred de Pass, 1920. © The National Gallery, London.

Consider, alternatively, the painting by the eighteenth-century Italian Francesco Zugno (fig. 5.3).

Enrobed in white, Pharaoh's daughter is a heroine who stands in full view—and in contempt—of the Egyptian authorities (no doubt, the dog helps sniff out Israelite babies, to be done away with by the henchman). As she spares the infant's life, she is surrounded by her servants. Yet notice that for the most part, they look to her for clues as to what to do; they are deferential to her. They exert no social or moral pressure on her in either direction.

Not so in the painting by the Italian Orazio Gentileschi, a follower of Carracci (fig. 5.4).

In this work of around 1630, the maidens have decidedly weighed in on the side of the infant, as a dissenting princess expresses initial disapproval, pointing to the boy's circumcision. So, too, in the version by the Venetian artist Paolo Veronese of around 1570 (fig. 5.5).

A pensive princess stands with leg and elbow bent, as the servants clearly look for her favorable disposition concerning the child. Though Pharaoh's daughter is a princess and the baby's sister a slave-girl, the artist has cast them here on equal footing, standing at equal height, blurring the distinction between royalty and slavery, very much in keeping with the dynamics of verse 7, where the slave-girl manages an audience with the princess, who in turn adopts her advice and acts on it, as I noted, word for word, in verses 7–9.

FIGURE 5.4.    *The Finding of Moses,* by Orazio Gentileschi (1633). © Museo Nacional del Prado, Madrid.

While these paintings offer contrasting views of Pharaoh's daughter, I take all of them to be faithful to the text—not only individually and exclusively, as alternative interpretations, but in total as well. The story of the rescue of Moses by the daughter of Pharaoh showcases a courageous act of compassion, but one that was fraught with inner tension for the protagonist. Her great deed was executed through struggle, and motivated by a range of impulses, some altruistic and some self-serving.

The story of the rescue of Moses, finally, may be seen as a story of two hierarchies—one Hebrew and one Egyptian—that collide, destabilizing the place and role of all involved. From the top down, the Hebrew hierarchy appears in the form of three figures: the father, the mother, and the sister. The father is introduced vis-à-vis the mother in terms that are typical of the biblical discourse that establishes the primacy of the head of the household in the Israelite patriarchy: "A man of the house of Levi went and married the daughter of Levi."[88] Rounding out the lowest rung of the hierarchy is the daughter, whose natural role is to display filial loyalty and deference to her parents.

FIGURE 5.5. *The Finding of Moses*, by Paolo Veronese (1575). Andrew W. Mellon Collection. Image Courtesy of the Board of Trustees, National Gallery of Art, Washington.

From the top down, the Egyptian hierarchy also exhibits three levels: Pharaoh, the daughter of Pharaoh, and the maidens. It is true that Pharaoh plays no active role in this passage. Nonetheless, the king of Egypt is everywhere present in this story. It is his decree that sets up the entire scene. His daughter, second in the hierarchy within this story, is identified by his name only. Finally, we have the complement of maidservants mentioned in verse 5 who form the lowest rung of the Egyptian hierarchy here.

These two triadic hierarchies are concomitantly disrupted. The unraveling of the chain of prerogative begins in verses 2–3. With the boy's life in danger, the husband is not present. The wife has taken over jurisdiction to determine the fate of the child. No sooner has the father's ascendancy been eclipsed than the mother's is as well. For in verse 4, the sister acts on her own authority, and sets out to track the abandoned infant, apparently unbeknownst to her mother. The unraveling of the Hebrew hierarchy reaches its peak in verse 8, where it is the young daughter who summons her mother, and reassigns her to the role of wet nurse.

The rescue scene of verses 5–6 reveals the same dynamic of disruption within the story's hierarchy of Egyptian figures. The sovereign figure of Egypt is here likewise usurped by his subordinate—his daughter—who takes the issue of the fate of this Hebrew male child into her own hands. If Gentileschi (fig. 5.4) and Veronese (fig. 5.5) are correct in their painted interpretations of the story, then it is the lowest rung of the Egyptian hierarchy that may have tilted the balance in Moses' favor—the maidservants. Scrutinized by these other, ostensibly inferior, women as they dote on the Hebrew infant, Pharaoh's daughter capitulates, unable to execute the murder her filial responsibility calls for.[89]

The boundary between the two hierarchies is breached when Moses' sister, the lowest figure of the Hebrew hierarchy, enters into unmediated conversation with the princess of Egypt and prevails on her to perform her bidding. The two women who occupy the middle rung of their respective hierarchies, the "daughter of Levi" and the "daughter of Pharaoh" are brought face to face in the final two verses of the narrative, each one taking up an irregular and unnatural role. Pharaoh's daughter will assume the role of mother to a Hebrew child. Moses' mother will feign the role of a wet nurse in the service of the princess of Egypt. The crossing of boundaries and the blurring of hierarchy is encapsulated in the trajectory taken by the child at stake, who passes from Hebrew hands to Egyptian ones, back to Hebrew ones, and finally to Egyptian ones again.

The account of the rescue of Moses, in contrast with the Sargon legend, demonstrates that the narrative portions of the Pentateuch may be construed as a polemic against the hagiography of royal inscriptions and royal theology. Earthly kings—the central figures in ancient Near Eastern hierarchies—are a focus of the narratives of the Pentateuch, too. However, the narratives that portray kings in the Pentateuch universally do so in such a way as to humble the king, bringing him down from his pedestal. Kings can be defeated militarily either by God (Exod 14–15) or God's servants (Gen 14:14–16; Num 31:6–8). Kings could be made to sue for peace with the faithful (Gen 21:22–34). Kings could be "converted" and made to recognize God's dominion (Gen 14:18–20; 41:38–39). Kings could be humiliated before God or before his servants (Gen 12:17–20; 20:6–18; 26:8–11; Num 22–24). The actions of Pharaoh's daughter represent an act of disobedience against monarchic rule, such as the midwives of Exodus 1 (Exod 1:15–21) also perform. These stories are the harbingers of the tradition in which prophets challenge royal authority, as in Moses' stands before Pharaoh, Nathan's castigation of David (2 Sam 12:1–14), Elijah's censure of Ahab (1 Kgs 18) and Jeremiah's call to disobey the order of King Zedekiah (Jer 38:2; 37:13).[90]

The account produces the most dominant human figure of the entire Pentateuch, the man who will lead the Children of Israel. He is a man whose own lineage and upbringing are beyond hierarchy; he comes from no one class. As much a royal as he is a slave, Moses leaves the palace to cast his lot with his slave-kin, and to found for them an order where all are equal citizens under the sovereignty of the King of Kings.

# Conclusion

*Egalitarianisms Ancient and Modern*

This has been a book about an idea—the egalitarian impulse found in the warp and woof of the books of the Pentateuch. In a larger sense, however, this has been an exploration of an assumption: that we may fruitfully engage a religious text such as the Hebrew Bible in search of political teachings. That this line of inquiry has not been more developed within modern scholarship would seem to be rooted in particularly contemporary predispositions. The notion of the separation between church and state is fundamental to the functioning of pluralistic, multicultural democracies. Yet in a peculiar fashion, it would seem that this notion has conditioned our modes of thinking, corralling us into a philosophical bifurcation. Fitted with blinders that split religion and state into separate realms, we view our intellectual and cultural heritage accordingly. When we look for the ancient antecedents of our legal history, the earliest formulations of political science and the beginnings of constitutional theory, we look—in exclusive fashion—toward ancient Greece. And when we look for the earliest sources of our notion of monotheistic belief, moral teachings and individual piety, we look—again in exclusive fashion—toward the Hebrew Bible. This study has been a call to remove those blinders, and to see once again how the religious and the political in the Hebrew Bible must be viewed as part of an inseparable whole, if that work is to be properly understood.[1]

I have traced the way the passages of the Pentateuch transformed preexisting concepts and institutions in the social and political landscape of the ancient Near East in the service of a more egalitarian and communitarian ideal. In conclusion, I will try to locate the ideas developed in these pages on the map of notions of equality in the history of western thought. To trace the entire history of the idea of equality would be a daunting task in even a full-length study.[2] My purpose here is to adumbrate lines for future comparative study. I do so with three distinct periods in mind: Greek notions of equality, early Christian notions of equality, and modern notions of equality spawned by the great political theorists of the seventeenth and eighteenth centuries.

Theories and thought systems that espouse equality among persons may be seen to entertain three fundamental questions:

1. What is the basis for claiming that such equality exists? When we look around ourselves, it is evident that not all persons are equal. Some are more intelligent, some are physically stronger, some demonstrate a stronger moral fortitude—to name only a few measures of distinction readily evident. To proclaim the equality of a given set of persons, then, requires appeal to first principles that are not empirical, and are almost metaphysical in orientation.

2. What is it that gets equalized among putatively equal persons? Modern theories of equality display an array of competing conceptions and arguments: some emphasize the equality of *outcome* with regard to a set resource: economic resources, social status, political power. Other theories argue for equality of *opportunity*: opportunity for personal satisfaction, welfare, or social position.

3. How do these two issues—the metaphysical basis for claiming equality, and the way that equality is palpably felt and expressed—contribute to conceptions of the proper regime structure? Systems that espouse equality have always had to wrestle with the question of how to maintain social order. In a hierarchy, persons know their place, are predisposed to respect their station in life and, more important, the station assigned to the ruler, as ruler. Notions of equality leave open the question of how order is to be maintained and imposed when competing members view themselves as equals. Put differently, pure political equality is impossible, since all political relationships are inherently asymmetric.

These three issues typically operate concurrently with each other. The nonempirical basis for equality, the sense in which a system regards its members as equal, and the question of how hierarchy is to be maintained in spite of equality are issues that at all times are intimately related to one another, and therefore need to be examined conjointly.[3]

This book has charted the way one thought system—that of the Pentateuch—combines its answers to these questions. The hierarchical structure of ancient Near Eastern society is rejected on theological grounds. The equality of the members of the Israelite polity stems from their collective covenantal relationship with God, in which each member is endowed with the status of subordinate king before the sovereign King of Kings. This is the metaphysical basis on which the notion of equality is founded. The Israelites are "equalized," as it were, in their status before God as members of a covenantal community but, no less so, are equal in their standing before the law. In terms of economic resources, the Pentateuch envisions a system in which, inevitably, some accrue more wealth than others. While not seeking equality of outcome in terms of distribution of wealth as in socialist schemes, the economic laws of the Pentateuch strive to ensure that all members of the polity remain landed and economically secure, as shown in chapter 3. The combination of the theological basis offered in the Pentateuch for equality and the senses in which members are treated equally goes a long way toward addressing the third question: how is political order to be maintained in a polity of equals? The Pentateuch, we saw throughout, devotes great attention to the values and traits that must be instilled in the minds and hearts of the populace in order for them to rise to their covenantal obligations. The Pentateuch has a fundamentally optimistic view of human nature—it expects that an entire nation can behave in exemplary fashion with regard to one another and with regard to their sovereign king, God. Earthly kingship is greatly attenuated, and the various seats of power in Deuteronomy are all subject to the aegis and supervision of the people as a whole—"you." By investing greatly in the creation of a covenantal brotherhood of individuals bound by law and theology, the Pentateuch envisions an ideal society that holds together on the merits of its members, rather than on the basis of the authority of its power brokers.

Conceptions of equality within the thought of classical Greek thinkers contrast with the notions I have developed here of a homogeneous and egalitarian polity within ancient Israel.[4] The greatest philosophers of Athens, Plato and Aristotle, viewed the necessity of social hierarchy as absolutely axiomatic. Each person had their allotted station, and to break ranks was essentially a threat that could break society as well. What these thinkers understood intuitively was then given the sanction of religious legitimation. Plato cites a myth that was told to explain the basis for hierarchy: "All of you in the city are brothers, but the god who made you mixed some gold into those who are adequately equipped to rule, because they are most valuable. He put silver in those who are auxiliaries and iron and bronze in the farmers and other craftsmen."[5] So palpable were the differences between people that it seemed self-evident that their rights and assets should be differentiated accordingly. Aristotle demonstrated the logic behind this thinking:

> It is manifestly natural and beneficial for the body to be ruled by the soul...the same holds true of human beings with respect to the other animals...in addition, the relation of the male to the female is by nature that of better to worse and ruler to ruled. Things must also hold in the same way for all human beings. Thus those who are as widely separated from others as are soul and body or human and beast—and that is the condition of those whose work is the use of the body and from whom such work is the best there is—are slaves by nature. For them it is better to be ruled over by a master.[6]

The only way to maintain order was through a clearly sanctioned hierarchy of authority and subordination.[7]

While Aristotle and particularly Plato were affiliated with the aristocracy and championed oligarchic regimes, even the democrats of Athens likewise affirmed hierarchy as an organizing principle of authority. Citizenship in ancient Greece—even in democratic Athens—was denied to women, farmers, laborers, mechanics, freedmen, and metics (resident aliens). Only males with the proper pedigree, who underwent military training, could be granted citizenship, and these constituted no more than 20 percent of the population of Athens at any time. The denial of citizenship to so great a proportion of the population meant that the vast majority of the residents of Athens were the subjects of discrimination in terms of capacity to hold political office, receive justice equal to that of citizens in the courts, hold land, and participate in religious festivals.

While political equality was denied the vast majority of the residents of Athens, the equality that was established among those bearing citizenship may be set in fruitful comparison with the pentateuchal notions of equality I have explored. Regarding the three issues surrounding equality raised earlier, and how they interact, there are broad lines of comparison between the Greek thought and the thought of the Pentateuch. The appeal to theology—namely, that citizens were endowed by the gods with souls mixed with gold—provided the citizenry of Athens with a sense of brotherhood, divinely ordained. The citizens of Athens were equal in their standing before the law and in their access to public office. Particularly fascinating, in comparative perspective, are the institutions that helped sustain this sense of brotherhood and the way they are paralleled in the biblical context of the Pentateuch. In chapter 2, I examined Deuteronomy's prescriptions for the balancing of the various seats of power within the Israelite polity. Similar notions appear in a primary feature of classical Greek politics, the search for an alternative to despotism and the establishment of a mixed government. Prior to the sixth century B.C.E., during the Archaic period in both Greece and Rome, power was monopolized and routinely abused either by hereditary kings, oligarchs, or patricians. It was the Roman philosopher Cicero (106–43 B.C.E.) who gave us the term "republic," from the Latin words *res publica*, or "public things," "property of the public," by which he meant a regime devoted to the service of the people.[8] Though the term "republic," per se, originates in the first century B.C.E., the essential notion that the power of government should be exercised in the interests of the common good was already at play in Greece in the sixth century B.C.E. Variously throughout the Greco-Roman world, one finds systems of governance that feature monarchies, aristocracies, consulates, and magistrates. Forms of regime varied from polis to polis and from age to age; the particular governmental structures reflected the values and virtues toward which politics aimed, and at the same time channeled the movement toward those ends.[9] While classical Greek thinkers could differ on the precise form of the ideal regime, it was universally deemed essential that social forces and institutions be balanced against one another so that no entity dominated with its own particular interest.[10] While Plato in the third book of his *Laws* and Aristotle in the second book of his *Politics* speak abstractly about mixed regimes, Solon had already provided a constitution for Athens and, according to tradition, Lycurgus for Sparta, by the sixth century B.C.E.[11] The notion of a law-based polity, therefore, serves multiple tasks in the thought of classical Greece, as in the Pentateuch. It enables the creation of alternative power structures to tyranny, and at the same time encourages the forming of bonds of cohesion around a central set of rules established to promote the common good, granting citizens equal status before the law.[12]

Greek citizenship, like membership in the covenantal community of Israel, beckoned the citizen to excel at a set of traits and characteristics. Classical Greek thinkers attended keenly to the question of *virtue*. They stressed that for the corporate enterprise of a citizenry to provide the cohesion necessary to sustain social order, it would be necessary to spur the citizenry to a set of dignified ideals that would shape and reflect the particular character of their society. In turn, these virtues would dictate the traits of the model person, a citizen aware of his traditions and obligations.[13] Particularly for Aristotle, the purpose of the polis was to enable its citizens to attain virtue. "The political community must be set down as existing for the sake of noble deeds," he wrote, "and not merely for living together."[14] This notion was later abandoned by many modern republican theorists, starting with Machiavelli. For them, politics had nothing to do with the attainment of virtues but was about redressing human depravity and protecting people's rights to life, liberty, and property.[15] By contrast, Aristotle rooted political community in the human capacity to strive for moral excellence *(aretē)*. To live outside of a polis was to lack something vital to human flourishing. Such an individual was like an isolated piece of a larger mechanism.[16] The citizen drew his identity from his membership in the polis. Thus, to detach oneself from one's polis was just like separating a hand or foot from a whole body.[17]

The parallels between biblical and classical Greek conceptions of equality should not be overstated. As noted, the citizens of the Greek polis, in all ages, were only a small fraction of the total population. In each Greek city-state were a larger number of foreigners, slaves, and lower castes of society, for example the helots of Sparta. By contrast, the "citizenry" of Israel that is the biblical focal point seems far more inclusive, certainly of all male members of Israel and, on most points theological and legal, of the women as well. The Bible seems to assume at most points that foreigners, slaves, and other nonmembers of the polity are the minority. As in the Pentateuch, a cardinal feature of classical Greek political thought is the centrality of law. As Plato put it, "Wherever in a State the law is subservient and impotent, over the State I see ruin impending; but wherever the law is lord over the magistrates, and the magistrates are servants to the law, there I descry salvation and all the blessings that the gods bestow on States."[18] Yet for Greek thinkers, the law was, emphatically, the product of human wisdom, whereas for the Bible, the law is divine in origin. While Greek political thinking and practice did accord importance to the social role of religious ritual, the relationship between humans and God is much more central to the social and political thought of the Bible. Further, a hallmark of classical political thought, especially in Greece, was the notion of government as a highly participatory activity. As I mentioned, Pericles, the great leader of Athens in the mid–fifth century B.C.E., is reported to have said, "We do not say that a man who is not interested in politics minds his own business, but that he does not belong here at all."[19] While some voices in the Bible may exhibit an egalitarian streak concerning who may hold certain offices, and who may elect persons to these offices, the Bible nowhere puts forth an ideal of the citizen as one who actively participates in the affairs of government. The ideological distance between Athens and Jerusalem is great indeed.[20]

Equality was an important notion as well in the New Testament and the writings of the early Church Fathers. Once again, the nonempirical authority to which appeal is made is religious in nature. It is in the writings of Paul that, for the first time, equality is perceived as a notion that can theoretically embrace all of humanity: "For by one Spirit are we all baptized into one body, whether Jews or Greeks, whether slaves or free—and we were all given the one spirit to drink" (1 Cor 12:13); "There is neither Jew nor Greek; there is neither slave nor free; there is no 'male and female'; for all of you are One in Jesus Christ" (Gal 3:28). All are not equal at birth, but all can become so in the embrace of Jesus Christ.

The universal availability of equality within early Christian thought had a profound impact regarding the three issues of how to realize equality in society. The palpable sense of equality granted by belief in Jesus Christ was limited. Because the faith community was a highly scattered one, there are no prescriptions in the early Christian writings for norms and laws for the functioning of society. Hence, the equality proffered was one that could have no earthly manifestation.[21] Prior to the Fall, Church Fathers would aver, all had been deemed equal in all respects. In an unredeemed world, however, equality was to be found only in the eschatological community of faith, in the realm of the spirit, in standing before God—not in the realm of temporal social relations.[22] Paul, in fact, seems quite supportive of earthly hierarchical power structures. Governing powers, he writes, are "ordained by God," and to challenge their authority is to challenge divine authority (Rom 13:1–2; 1 Peter 2:13–15). Slaves should remain slaves because "Every one should remain in the state in which he was called" (1 Cor 7:20).[23] Placing a paramount value on the unity and moral authority of the church, the early Church Fathers preached obedience to the hierarchies that held power. This disposition predominated in Christian writings into medieval times. Under the influence of the structure of feudal society, the Church maintained that hierarchy was an essential in human affairs. The pope was vested as the ultimate authority in not only the spiritual but the temporal realm as well, with the clergy superior to the laity, and the nobility to their subjects.[24] Medievals harbored no thought whatever that society could make a conscious collective decision to refashion itself, or alter the structure of its political regimes. In the medieval mindset, the order of the world had been dictated on high, and a person was expected to accept his or her station in life, with roles and relations, obligations and privileges all predetermined.

During the Renaissance and the Reformation, thinkers began to consider how structures of power could be established anew to serve the purposes of a broader base of individuals. In the writings of Luther—and before him John Wycliffe of Oxford in the fourteenth century—the foundations of society and the bases of authority began to be questioned. These thinkers proclaimed the elevation of the individual as priest over himself, and called for the abolition of the papacy, thus ushering in the first disruption of the time-honored hierarchies. Under Reformation influence, equality before God reinforced equality of citizenship.

The metaphysical basis for equality underwent revision, as well as the sense in which people were now deemed equal. Increasingly, the appeal to first principles to justify the claim for equality came not solely from divine decree but from natural law.[25] The men who were termed equal by Thomas Hobbes (1588–1679) and John Locke (1632–1704) were conceived of as individuals, living in independence of one another before they ever entered association for common purposes. If the Pentateuch asserted the equality of all Israelites by virtue of the fact that all of them were liberated from bondage and all entered into covenant with the Almighty, these writers invoked a different source— scriptural, to be sure, but one that reflected new sensitivities concerning equality. Rather than finding the scriptural source for equality in the liberation and covenant passages of Exodus, they found it in Genesis—in the account of creation. All men were equal because they were created so by their Creator (with a capital *C*). As Jefferson would write in the Declaration of Independence: "all men are created equal and are endowed by their Creator with certain inalienable rights." Men, thus conceived, were equal not as they became formed into a community but prior to their entering community, as individuals.[26]

Equality, now based in natural law and in the divine act of creation, came to have a configuration significantly different from the one in the Pentateuch. It is true that, as in the Pentateuch, the sense of equality Locke assigned to individuals was as citizens, on equal footing in their relations to government, and to each other, and before the law.[27] For the Pentateuch, however, equality is born of a communitarian ideal. The equality between members of the Israelite polity is granted to them in order that they should collectively answer the higher calling of serving as subordinate kings in covenantal partnership. Individual rights exist, but they exist essentially to advance a collective good. Moreover, while the Pentateuch is aware of the possibility for people to behave in a depraved fashion, it passionately believes in their capacity to rise to great heights, spiritually and morally.

By contrast, because much of modern political thought sees persons as fully autonomous selves prior to the establishment of any community, the purpose of government is now found in the concept of agreement between individuals previously existing in independence of one another. As the agreement is made out of self-interest, so it is intended to protect the person and property of each contracting party. The state is now construed as instrumental to individual interests rather than as serving a higher, nobler calling. Writers such as Thomas Hobbes took a fundamentally pessimistic view of human nature, and assumed that the role of government was essentially to preserve the social order and guard against the abuse of power.[28]

To conclude, modern theorists view equality as the source of an entitlement: equal members of society are entitled to equality of outcome, such as wealth distribution, or equality of opportunity, for social status, political power, and the like. As I have shown, in its own way the Pentateuch also took measures that would allow early and more moderate notions of these forms of equality. Yet in one area, it may be seen that the Pentateuch stressed equality in a sense underemphasized in liberal rights discourse: equality of responsibility. As part of its communitarian ideal, the Pentateuch addressed "you," which, as we noted, was sometimes a collective plural and sometimes a call to each individual member of Israel. It did so with regard to not only the laws to be kept and the blessings to be bestowed but also the consequences to be suffered when Israel failed in her covenantal callings. A final avenue for further study would be to look for ways the egalitarian blueprint for the covenantal community of Israel can contribute to our thinking about the relation of rights to duties, the rights of individuals to the rights of groups, common goods and goals, and group relations in political theory.[29] In addressing and holding accountable a collective "you," it would seem that there is affinity between pentateuchal ethics and certain strands of existential political thought. This line of thinking rejects as myth the notion that values are things that each of us decides about independently of the group circumstances in which he or she finds herself. Rather, the collection of attitudes and dispositions within a community generate a climate in which individual behavior unfolds. The address of the collective "you" would seem to suggest that a culture binds its members by providing common experiences and viewpoints and creates an interconnectedness and interdependence among its members to a far greater degree than is often admitted in individual rights discourse.[30]

Where this may take us is not clear. But where we have come from is. If there was one truth the ancients held to be self-evident it was that all men were not created equal. If we maintain today that, in fact, they are endowed by their Creator with certain inalienable rights, then it is because we have inherited as part of our cultural heritage notions of equality that were deeply entrenched in the ancient passages of the Pentateuch.

# Notes

INTRODUCTION

1. See Fanya Oz-Salzberger, "The Jewish Roots of Western Freedom," *Azure* 13 (2002): 88–132. See earlier initial treatments in Gabriel Sivan, *The Bible and Civilization* (Jerusalem: Keter, 1973), 108–90; Abraham I. Katsh, *The Biblical Heritage of American Democracy* (New York: Ktav, 1977), 91–138. See also the brief remarks in Jean-Louis Ska, "Biblical Law and the Origins of Democracy," in *The Ten Commandments: The Reciprocity of Faithfulness*, ed. William P. Brown (Louisville, Ky.: Westminster John Knox, 2004), 146–58. The general topic is the subject of a new journal, *Hebraic Political Studies*, published by the Shalem Center, Jerusalem. See also discussion in Norman K. Gottwald, *The Politics of Ancient Israel* (Louisville, Ky.: Westminster John Knox, 2001), 255 n. 13.

2. William Shakespeare, *The Tempest*, act 2, scene 1.

3. The terminology is taken from Norman Gottwald, "Social Class as an Analytic and Hermeneutical Category in Biblical Studies," *JBL* 112:1 (1993): 6. In a similar vein, see I. J. Gelb, "From Freedom to Slavery," in *Gesellschaftsklassen im Alten Zweistromlandund den angrenzenden Gebeiten— XVIII: Recontre assyriogique internationale, München, 29. Juni bis 3. Juli 1970*, ed. D. O. Edzard, Bayerische Akademie der Wissenschaften, Philosophich-Historische Klasse, Sitzungsberichte, no. 75 (Munich: Verlag der Bayerischen Akademie der Wissenschaften, 1972), 92, and Daniel C. Snell, *Life in the Ancient Near East: 3100–332 B.C.E.* (New Haven, Conn.: Yale University Press, 1997), 146.

4. Michael Mann, *The Sources of Social Power*, 2 vols. (Cambridge: Cambridge University Press, 1986), 1:24.

5. While the terminology here is that of Gottwald, the phenomenon is considered endemic to premodern agrarian societies. See Gerhard E. Lenski, *Power and Privilege: A Theory of Social Stratification* (New York: Mc-Graw Hill, 1966), 243. For the structure of Mesopotamian society along these lines, see Gregory C. Chirichigno, *Debt-Slavery in Israel and the Ancient Near East*, JSOTSup no. 141 (Sheffield, England: JSOT Press, 1993), 49.

6. See discussion of class terms in the Code of Hammurabi in I. M. Diakonoff, "Slave-Labour vs. Non-Slave Labour: The Problem of Definition," in *Labor in the Ancient Near East*, ed. Marvin A. Powell (New Haven, Conn.: American Oriental Society, 1987), 2, and in Snell, *Life in the Ancient Near East*, 60.

7. Diakonoff, "Slave Labour," 3.

8. Gottwald, *Politics of Ancient Israel*, 147; Snell, *Life in the Ancient Near East*, 146–47.

9. Gottwald, *Politics of Ancient Israel*, 145.

10. Ibid., 132–33. On the rise of states in the ancient Near East see Charles R. Redman, *The Rise of Civilizations: From Early Farmers to Urban Society in the Ancient Near East* (San Francisco: Freeman, 1978), 177–322, and Mann, *Sources of Social Power*, 1:73–129.

11. Norman Gottwald, *The Tribes of Yahweh* (Maryknoll, N.Y.: Orbis Press, 1979), 391; Snell, *Life in the Ancient Near East*, 76; on feudalism in ancient Egypt and Mesopotamia see Rushton Coulborn, *Feudalism in History* (Princeton: Princeton University Press, 1956), 93–132.

12. Robert D. Miller II, *Chieftains of the Highland Clans: A History of Israel in the Twelfth and Eleventh Centuries* B.C. (Grand Rapids, Mich.: Eerdmans, 2005), xiv; for a summary of research on Iron Age I Israel, see xiii. For bibliography on the anthropological notion of tribe and application to the study of the ancient Near East, see Snell, *Life in the Ancient Near East*, 193 n. 38.

13. Mann, *Sources of Social Power*, 1:38.

14. D. B. Grusky, "Social Stratification," in *International Encyclopedia of the Social and Behavioral Sciences*, ed. Neil J. Smelser and Paul B. Baltes, 26 vols. (Amsterdam: Elsevier, 2001), 21:14446.

15. Howard Adelson, "The Origins of a Concept of Social Justice," in *Social Justice in the Ancient World*, ed. K. D. Irani and M. Silver (Westport, Conn.: Greenwood, 1995), 26.

16. Aristotle, *Politics* BK1 1254a20, trans. Benjamin Jowett, http://classics.mit .edu/Aristotle/politics.1.one.html.

17. Aristotle, *Politics* 3:9.

18. Adelson, "Origins of a Concept," 32.

19. Philip Pettit, *Republicanism: A Theory of Freedom and Government* (Oxford: Oxford University Press, 1997), 162.

20. See, for example, "The Protests of the Eloquent Peasant," trans. John A. Wilson, *ANET*, 400; "The Instruction of Ani," trans. John A. Wilson, *ANET*, 420–21; and "The Instruction of Amenemopet," trans. John A. Wilson, *ANET*, 421–24.

21. See Ziony Zevit, *The Religions of Ancient Israel: A Synthesis of Parallel Approaches* (London: Continuum, 2001); Susan Niditch, *Ancient Israelite Religion*

(New York: Oxford University Press, 1997); Susan Ackerman, *Under Every Green Tree: Popular Religion in Sixth-Century Judah* (Atlanta: Scholars Press, 1992).

22. Within the scholarship, there is debate as to how closely "biblical religion" may have approximated "Israelite religion." Some see biblical religion as the rarefied utopian ideal, the construct of an intellectual and spiritual elite, with relatively little bearing on the day-to-day reality of ancient Israelites. Others note that the Bible seems wholly concerned with the people, and does not bear the hallmarks of an esoteric faith. See discussions in S. A. Geller, "The God of the Covenant," in *One God or Many? Concepts of Divinity in the Ancient World*, ed. Barbara Nevling Porter (Chebeague, Me.: Casco Bay Assyriological Institute, 2000), 274, and in Moshe Greenberg, *Studies in the Bible and Jewish Thought* (Philadelphia: Jewish Publication Society, 1995), 112.

23. The general argument for this approach is contained in William W. Hallo, "Compare and Contrast: The Contextual Approach to Biblical Literature," in *The Bible in Light of Cuneiform Literature*, ed. William W. Hallo et al., Scripture in Context no. 3 (Lewiston, N.Y.: Edwin Mellen, 1990), 1–30. There is a voluminous literature on comparative methodology for the study of the Bible and the ancient Near East. For a recent bibliography see Marrti Nissinen, ed., *Prophecy in Its Ancient Near Eastern Context: Mesopotamian, Biblical, and Arabian Perspectives* (Atlanta: Society of Biblical Literature, 2000), 5 n. 4.

24. James W. Watts, *Reading Law: The Rhetorical Shape of the Pentateuch*, Biblical Seminar no. 59 (Sheffield, England: Sheffield Academic Press, 1999), 29.

25. The state of the scholarship is surveyed in Rolf Rendtorff, "Directions in Pentateuchal Studies," *Currents in Research: Biblical Studies* 5 (1997): 43–65. A good summary of the complex issues involved in the historical study of the origins of the Pentateuch is found in Gary N. Knoppers and Bernard M. Levinson, "How, When, Where, and Why Did the Pentateuch Become the Torah?" in *The Pentateuch as Torah: New Models for Understanding Its Promulgation and Acceptance*, ed. Gary N. Knoppers and Bernard M. Levinson (Winona Lake, Ind.: Eisenbrauns, 2007), 1–22.

26. Quoted in George Dalton, "Primitive Money," in *Tribal and Peasant Economies: Readings in Economic Anthropology*, ed. George Dalton (Garden City, N.Y.: Natural History Press, 1967), 44.

27. A voluminous literature is devoted to the role of the woman in the Bible and in the ancient Near East. The use of material finds as the basis for a reconstruction of women's lives in premonarchic Israel may be found in Carol Meyers, *Discovering Eve: Ancient Israelite Women in Context* (New York: Oxford University Press, 1988); a recent comprehensive overview of biblical images of women in the ancient Near Eastern context is found in Hennie J. Marsman, *Women in Ugarit and Israel: Their Social and Religious Position in the Context of the Ancient Near East*, Oudtestamentische Studiën no. 49 (Leiden: Brill, 2003); a survey of biblical law from the perspective of gender studies is in Cheryl B. Anderson, *Women, Ideology, and Violence: Critical Theory and the Construction of Gender in the Book of the Covenant and the Deuteronomic Law* (London: T & T Clark, 2004), and in *Gender and Law in the Hebrew Bible and the Ancient Near East*, ed. Victor H. Matthews, Bernard M. Levinson, and Tikva Frymer-Kensky, JSOTSup no. 262 (Sheffield, England: Sheffield Academic Press, 1998;

reprint, London: T & T Clark, 2004). A survey of a variety of feminist perspectives on the Bible is in Alice Bach, ed., *Women in the Hebrew Bible* (New York: Routledge, 1999). On the more equitable metaphysical status of women in the Bible relative to the standing ascribed to women in ancient Near Eastern literature, see Tikva Frymer-Kensky, *In the Wake of the Goddesses: Women, Culture, and the Biblical Transformation of Pagan Myth* (New York: Free Press, 1992), and *Reading the Women of the Bible: A New Interpretation of Their Stories* (New York: Schocken, 2002).

28. Transliteration throughout of Hebrew and other ancient Semitic languages follows the parameters of the *SBL Handbook of Style for Ancient Near Eastern Biblical and Early Christian Studies* (Peabody, Mass.: Hendrickson, 1999).

CHAPTER I

1. The trajectory presented here is based on Pierre Manent, *An Intellectual History of Liberalism*, trans. Rebecca Balinski (Princeton: Princeton University Press, 1995), 3–38.

2. Jerrold Seigel, foreword to Manent, *An Intellectual History of Liberalism*, viii.

3. Peter L. Berger, *The Sacred Canopy: Elements of a Sociological Theory of Religion* (Garden City, N.Y.: Doubleday, 1967), 31–38.

4. Paul Ricoeur, *Figuring the Sacred: Religion, Narrative, and Imagination* (Minneapolis: Fortress Press, 1995), 54. See also S. N. Eisenstadt, "Introduction: The Axial Age Breakthroughs—Their Characteristics and Origins," in *The Origins and Diversity of Axial Age Civilizations*, ed. S. N. Eisenstadt (Albany: State University of New York Press, 1986), 2–4.

5. See discussion with regard to ancient Near Eastern religions in J. David Schloen, *The House of the Father as Fact and Symbol: Patrimonialism in Ugarit and the Ancient Near East* (Winona Lake, Ind.: Eisenbrauns, 2001), 92.

6. Walter Brueggemann has posited that there are two trajectories of covenantal thought in the Hebrew Scriptures: first, our subject here, which he calls the "Mosaic liberation" tradition, and second, "the royal consolidation" tradition. See Brueggemann, "Trajectories in Old Testament Literature and the Sociology of Ancient Israel," *JBL* 98 (1979): 161–85.

7. See Jean Bottéro, *Religion in Ancient Mesopotamia*, trans. Teresa Lavender Fagan (Chicago: University of Chicago Press, 2001), 15; Thorkild Jacobsen, *The Treasures of Darkness: A History of Mesopotamian Religion* (New Haven, Conn.: Yale University Press, 1976), 77–79.

8. Jacobsen, *Treasures of Darkness*, 4; Bottéro, *Religion in Ancient Mesopotamia*, 51, 91, 220; Robert Karl Gnuse, *No Other Gods: Emergent Monotheism in Israel* (Sheffield, England: Sheffield Academic Press, 1997), 153.

9. Jacobsen, *Treasures of Darkness*, 81; Bottéro, *Religion in Ancient Mesopotamia*, 66, 115.

10. Bottéro, *Religion in Ancient Mesopotamia*, 98.

11. "Atrahasis," tablet I:76–98, trans. in Benjamin R. Foster, *From Distant Days: Myths, Tales, and Poetry of Ancient Mesopotamia* (Bethesda, Md.: CDL Press, 1995), 54–55 (all citations hereafter are to this translation).

12. "Atrahasis," tablet I:145–50, in Foster, *From Distant Days*, 56.

13. "Atrahasis," fragment, ll. a–k, in Foster, *From Distant Days*, 57–58.

14. A similar theme emerges in the Mesopotamian creation narrative *Enuma Elish*. In creating humanity, the god Marduk announces (tablet VI:5–8; see 29–37, 106–20):

> Blood I will mass and cause bones to be.
> I will establish a savage, "man" shall be his name.
> Verily, savage-man I will create.
> He shall be charged with the service of the gods
> That they might be at ease

See discussion in R. J. Clifford, *Creation Accounts in the Ancient Near East and in the Bible*, Catholic Biblical Quarterly Monograph Series no. 26 (Washington, D.C.: Catholic Biblical Association of America, 1994), 7, 92, and concerning the appearance of the trope in Sumerian creation epics, 13–53.

15. Bottéro, *Religion in Ancient Mesopotamia*, 207.

16. Mark S. Smith, *The Origins of Biblical Monotheism: Israel's Polytheistic Background and the Ugaritic Texts* (Oxford: Oxford University Press, 2001), 168–69.

17. G. A. Jonsson, *The Image of God: Genesis 1:26–28 in a Century of Old Testament Research*, trans. L. Svensden (Stockholm: Almquist & Wiksell, 1988), 219.

18. "Atrahasis," tablet I:344–350, in Foster, *From Distant Days*, 62.

19. Bottéro, *Religion in Ancient Mesopotamia*, 101

20. Jacobsen, *Treasures of Darkness*, 120.

21. W. G. Lambert and A. R. Millard, *Atra-hasis: The Babylonian Story of the Flood* (Oxford: Clarendon Press, 1969), 23.

22. See Tikva Frymer-Kensky, "The Atrahasis Epic and Its Significance for Our Understanding of Genesis 1–9," *Biblical Archaeologist* 40:4 (1977): 150–52.

23. See Lowell K. Handy, *Among the Host of Heaven: The Syro-Palestinian Pantheon as Bureaucracy* (Winona Lake, Ind.: Eisenbrauns, 1994).

24. Smith, *Origins of Biblical Monotheism*, 58

25. Ibid., 79.

26. Schloen, *House of the Father*, 350.

27. Indeed, some theoriphic names in Mesopotamia implied that Mesopotamians felt they could look to the gods for beneficence: *Šamaš-hatin*, "šamaš is protector"; *Šamaš-epiri*, "Šamaš takes care of me"; *Marduk-abi*, "Marduk is my father"; Bottéro, *Religion in Ancient Mesopotamia*, 39–40.

28. Schloen, *House of the Father*, 79, 94. Some of the patriarchal motifs concerning kingship in Ugarit were present in Egypt as well. Jan Assmann has demonstrated that in Egypt, the Pharaoh was considered the father of the nation, as procreator, provider, and educator. He was the mediator between the divine and human realms, as he was both the son of Amun, the sun god, and the father of the whole country. See Assmann, "Das Bild des Vaters im alten Ägypten," in *Das Vaterbild in Mythos und Geschichte*, ed. H. Tellenbach (Stuttgart: Kohlhammer, 1976), 12–49, and *Stein und Zeit: Mensch und Gesellschaft im alten Ägypten* (Munich: Wilhelm Fink, 1991).

29. Smith, *Origins of Monotheism*, 56.

30. Ibid., 45–46. On this meaning of *'inš 'ilm*, see Baruch A. Levine, review of *Le Culte à Ugarit* by Jean-Michel de Tarrogon, *Revue Biblique* 88 (1981): 246–47. The logic of correspondences was not limited to Semitic lands. The Olympian household of Zeus was conceived as being structured in the same manner as a Greek aristocratic household. Zeus was sovereign, as was the patriarch of the household. And in like fashion, various members of his family had designated areas of influence. See discussion and bibliography in Dale Launderville, *Piety and Politics: The Dynamics of Royal Authority in Homeric Greece, Biblical Israel, and Old Babylonian Mesopotamia* (Grand Rapids, Mich.: Eerdmans, 2002), 181.

31. For summary and discussion, see Jacobus Van Dijk, "Myth and Mythmaking in the Ancient Near East," in *CANE*, 3:1702–5.

32. For a discussion of the various views on the divinity of the Egyptian king see E. Hornung, *Conceptions of God in Ancient Egypt: The One and the Many*, trans. J. Baines (Ithaca, N.Y.: Cornell University Press, 1982) 140–42.

33. These statements with reference to Tuthmosis III are found in *Urkunden des ägyptischen Altertums* (Leipzig, 1903–39, Berlin, 1955–61) IV, 1236, 2; 165, 13, as cited in Hornung, *Conceptions of God in Ancient Egypt*, 139. In Mesopotamia, too, there is evidence that the king was awarded a degree of divine status, and thus his rule legitimated. From the time of Sargon of Akkad (c. 2300 B.C.E.), temples were erected for the worship of kings, and sculptures were made of them that incorporated typical iconographic hallmarks of divinity. See W. W. Hallo, "Texts, Statues and the Cult of the Divine King," in *Congress Volume Jerusalem 1986*, ed. J. A. Emerton (Leiden: Brill, 1988), 54–66.

34. For overview, see Ronald J. Leprohon, "Royal Ideology and State Administration in Pharaonic Egypt, in *CANE*, 1:273–87.

35. John Baines, "Restricted Knowledge, Hierarchy and Decorum: Modern Perceptions and Ancient Institutions," *Journal of the American Research Center in Egypt* 27 (1990): 19.

36. Henri Frankfort, *Kingship and the Gods: A Study of Ancient Near Eastern Religion as the Integration of Society and Nature* (Chicago: University of Chicago Press, 1948) 258–59.

37. Ibid., 7.

38. S. A. Geller, "The God of the Covenant," in *One God or Many? Concepts of Divinity in the Ancient World*, ed. Barbara Nevling Porter (Chebeague, Me.: Casco Bay Assyriological Institute, 2000), 309.

39. Frankfort, *Kingship and the Gods*, 341.

40. See the overview of covenant in the writings of Weber in Ernest W. Nicholson, *God and His People: Covenant Theology in the Old Testament* (Oxford: Clarendon Press, 1986), 38–42.

41. For a recent overview of this literature see Noel Weeks, *Admonition and Curse: The Ancient Near Eastern Treaty/Covenant Form as a Problem in Intercultural Relationships* (Edinburgh: T & T Clark, 2004), 6–10.

42. J. G. McConville, *Deuteronomy*, Apollos Old Testament Commentary, no. 5 (Leicester, England: Apollos, 2002), 24; Moshe Weinfeld, "Deuteronomy, Book of," in *ABD*, 2:169–70.

43. I substantiate this claim later in the discussion, in note 77. The Hittite suzerainty treaty texts are found in translation in Gary Beckman, *Hittite Diplomatic Texts*, ed. Harry A. Hoffner, Society of Biblical Literature Writings from the Ancient World Series, no. 7 (Atlanta: Scholars Press, 1999).

44. Weeks, *Admonition and Curse*, 152.

45. Ibid., 56.

46. Ibid., 170.

47. Implicit in this line of thinking is the assumption that treaty writing in Israel may reflect a general tendency to formalize treaties in writing in the mid- to late second millennium. This runs counter to Wellhausen's contention, adopted by many since, that covenant emerged in Israel only after the prophetic period. Yet it is likely that Wellhausen's position stems from a priori romantic assumptions concerning religion as it advances from its supposed primitive stages to its developed stages—assumptions that may be based in anachronism, and a certain set of disputable philosophical underpinnings.

48. Weeks, *Admonition and Curse*, 165. Support for such an approach may be garnered from Jeffrey Tigay's study of peripheral versions of Mesopotamian literary texts and their Mesopotamian originals. Tigay demonstrates that the peripheral texts not only differ in detail but also undergo modification in accordance with the theological and local interests of the peripheral culture. See Jeffrey H. Tigay, "On Evaluating Claims of Literary Borrowing," in *The Tablet and the Scroll: Near Eastern Studies in Honor of William W. Hallo*, ed. M. E. Cohen, D. C. Snell, and D. B. Weisberg (Bethesda, Md.: CDL Press, 1993) 250–55.

49. The pentateuchal materials I will be referencing are spread over chapters, sometimes with interruptions between them. For a source critic, these will be telltale signs that the work cannot be addressed synchronically. Yet once we identify the various elements of the Sinai narratives that bear resemblance to elements in the Hittite suzerainty treaties across a wide textual swath, the grounds on which the putative sources are identified becomes less convincing. See Weeks, *Admonition and Curse*, 154.

50. See Amnon Altman, *The Historical Prologue of the Hittite Vassal Treaties* (Ramat Gan, Israel: Bar-Ilan University Press, 2004), 43, 64. For text, see "Treaty between Mursili II of Hatti and Manapa-Tarhunta of the Land of the Seha-River," trans. in Beckman, *Hittite Diplomatic Texts*, 82–86. The present treaty is entry number 69 in Emmanuel Laroche, *Catalogue des textes hittites* (Paris: Klincksieck, 1971). Throughout the following discussion I shall cite the translation reference from Beckman's collection with a citation in parentheses to the entry number of the treaty in Laroche's collection.

51. For discussion and delineation of these two categories, see Altman, *Historical Prologue*, 132–38.

52. Ibid., 27; George E. Mendenhall and Gary A. Herion, "Covenant," *ABD* 1:1181.

53. "Treaty between Šuppiluliuma I of Hatti and Niqmaddu II of Ugarit, " sec. 2 (A obv. 9–28; B obv. 1'–2'), *CTH* 46; trans. in Beckman, *Hittite Diplomatic Texts*, 35; See discussion in Altman, *Historical Prologue*, 224. Similar circumstances appear to

be exhibited in the treaty between Šuppiluliuma I of Hatti and Tette of Nuhashshi, sec. 1 (A i 1–11), *CTH* 53; trans. in Beckman, *Hittite Diplomatic Texts*, 55.

54. "Treaty between Šuppiluliuma I of Hatti and Shattiwaza of Mitanni," sec. 6 (A obv. 48–58) *CTH* 51; trans. in Beckman, *Hittite Diplomatic Texts*, 44. See discussion in Altman, *The Historical Prologue*, 290.

55. See "Treaty between Tudhaliya IV of Hatti and Shaushga-muwa of Amurru," sec. 2 (A i 8–12), *CTH* 105; trans. in Beckman, *Hittite Diplomatic Texts*, 104.

56. Weeks, *Admonition and Curse*, 174.

57. Mendenhall and Herion, "Covenant," 1183.

58. "Treaty between Šuppiluliuma and Aziru," sec. 15 (iv. 21–26), *CTH* 49, trans. in Itamar Singer, "The Treaties between Hatti and Amurru," in *COS*, 2.17:95.

59. See similarly Exod 34:12, 15.

60. Mendenhall and Herion, "Covenant," 1179–80.

61. See Exod 34:14; Deut 4:24; 5:9; 6:15; Josh 24:19; Nah 1:2.

62. See Donald B. Redford, *Akhenaten: The Heretic King* (Princeton: Princeton University Press, 1984).

63. Maimonides, *Mishneh Torah, Laws of Repentance*, 10:3.

64. El-Amarna letter 138:71–73, trans. in William L. Moran, "The Ancient Near Eastern Background of the Love of God in Deuteronomy," *CBQ* 25 (1963): 79–80.

65. El-Amarna letter 53:40–44, trans. in Moran, "Ancient Near East Background," 79.

66. See discussion in Saul Olyan, "Honor, Shame and Covenant Relations in Ancient Israel and Its Environment," *JBL* 115 (1996): 210.

67. See elsewhere Deut 7:6, 14:2, 26:18, Ps 135:4. The word may also be related to the Akkadian word *sikiltu*, meaning possession, as found in 1Chr 29:3. See Eugene Carpenter, "*sĕgūllâ*," in *NIDOTTE*, 3:224.

68. See Claude F. A. Schaeffer, *Le Palais Royal d'Ugarit*, 5 vols. (Paris: Impr. Nationale, 1955), vol. 5, nos. 60:7, 12, and discussion, in Moshe Weinfeld, *Deuteronomy and the Deuteronomic School* (Oxford: Clarendon Press, 1972), 226 n. 2.

69. References to the commitments made by the sovereign Hittite kings to their respective vassals are summarized in tabular form in Altman, *Historical Prologue*, 151.

70. Dennis J. McCarthy, *Treaty and Covenant: A Study in Form in the Ancient Oriental Documents and in the Old Testament* (Rome: Biblical Institute Press, 1978), 128.

71. See discussion in Mendenhall and Herion, "Covenant," 1184; Altman, *Historical Prologue*, 184; Weinfeld, *Deuteronomy and the Deuteronomic School*, 63.

72. "Treaty between Muwattalli II of Hatti and Talmi-Sharrumma of Aleppo," sec. 2 (A obv. 3–8), *CTH* 75; trans. in Beckman, *Hittite Diplomatic Texts*, 93.

73. While source critics have traditionally attributed the extensive curse lists to Neo-Assyrian influence, the presence of these elements in Deuteronomy, while largely absent from Exodus (Exod 20:5–6 notwithstanding), may be explained as well through a synchronic reading of the pentateuchal narrative. At the outset of the relationship between God the sovereign and Israel the subordinate, the motivation to maintain the relationship is based on the sovereign's beneficence and the assumption that the subordinate will demonstrate due loyalty. The invocation of witnesses (Deut

27; 32) and the resort to threats of power in the form of curses (Deut 28) accord with the narrated time frame of Deuteronomy at the end of the sojourn in the wilderness; it looks back on a period during which Israel displayed a recidivist pattern of disobedience, and it looks forward to the tests and trials of conquest and subsequent prosperity. See Weeks, *Admonition and Curse*, 170–71.

74. "Treaty between Šuppiluliuma I of Hatti and Tette of Nuhashshi," sec. 17 (A iv 44'–57'), *CTH* 53; trans. in Beckman, *Hittite Diplomatic Texts*, 58.

75. We also find an instance in which it is Moses who bears witness against the people (Deut. 32:46): "Take to heart all the words to which I attest that I have enjoined on you today."

76. "Treaty between Šuppiluliuma I of Hatti and Shattiwaza of Mitanni," secs. 15–16 (A rev. 58–75), *CTH* 51; trans. in Beckman, *Hittite Diplomatic Texts*, 48.

77. See Mendenhall and Herion, "Covenant," 1181; Weinfeld, *Deuteronomy and the Deuteronomic School*, 116–46. As indicated earlier, the Neo-Assyrian vassal treaties and loyalty oaths also provide illumination of certain covenant passages, particularly those in Deuteronomy 27–29. Nonetheless, it will be clear that the Neo-Assyrian material alone does not provide the complete provenance, or even, I would claim, the primary one for understanding the context for covenant in Exodus, Joshua, and perhaps the rest of Deuteronomy as well. The historical prologue with its emphasis on the beneficence of the sovereign as the basis for the loyalty of the subordinate is a feature exclusive to the Hittite treaties and does not appear in the Neo-Assyrian ones. Blessings are matched with curses only in the Hittite treaties and never in the Neo-Assyrian ones. Instructions for deposition of the treaty and its periodic reading are likewise features found only in the Hittite materials and not in the Neo-Assyrian treaty or loyalty oath texts. Moreover, promises made by the sovereign king to the vassal and expressions of affection toward him—elements so cardinal in the Pentateuch's portrayal of God's disposition to Israel—are found only in the Hittite treaties, never in the Neo-Assyrian ones. The most up-to-date summary of this argument is in K. A. Kitchen, *On the Reliability of the Old Testament* (Grand Rapids, Mich.: Eerdmans, 2003), 283–94, and more broadly throughout Weeks, *Admonition and Curse*. See also discussions in Hayim Tadmor, "Treaty and Oath in the Ancient Near East: A Historian's Approach," in *Humanizing America's Iconic Book: Society of Biblical Literature Centennial Addresses 1980*, ed. Gene M. Tucker and Douglas A. Knight (Chico, Calif.: Scholars Press, 1980), 142–52; Mendenhall and Herion, "Covenant," 1179–1202; Weinfeld, *Deuteronomy and the Deuteronomic School*, 59–157.

78. A similar ritual of covenant renewal is found in the time of Josiah, in 1 Kgs 23.

79. I take the term "honor" in the sense defined by Julian Pitt-Rivers, one of the pioneers in the anthropology of honor. He defined the bestowal of "honor" as the recognition of the person's rank or status, and their entitlement to a permanent right of precedence marked by honorific insignia, expressed in modes of address, titles, and disposition of deference. See Pitt–Rivers, "Honor," in *International Encyclopedia of the Social Sciences*, 19 vols. (New York: Macmillan, 1968–91), 6:503.

80. Olyan, "Honor, Shame and Covenant Relations," 204.

81. El Amarna Letter 88:47, in *Die El-Amarna Tafeln*, ed. J. A. Knudtzon, 2 vols. (Leipzig: Hinrichs, 1907, 1915), 2:1177.

82. "Treaty between Tudhaliya II of Hatti and Sunashshura of Kizzuwatna," sec. 9 (A i 38–44), *CTH* 41 (Hittite), *CTH* 131 (Akkadian); trans. in Beckman, *Hittite Diplomatic Texts*, 19.

83. Altman, *Historical Prologue*, 138, 484.

84. See Beckman, *Hittite Diplomatic Texts*, treaties 2, 3, 7, 8, 9, 10, 11, 12, 13, 14, 15 (a parity treaty), 16, 17, 18. For the corresponding numbers in the *Catalogue des textes Hittites*, see the synoptic table of Hittite treaties in Beckman, 6–8.

85. "Treaty between Tudhaliya II of Hatti and Sunashshura of Kizzuwatna," sec. 1 (A i 1–4), *CTH* 41 (Hittite), *CTH* 131 (Akkadian); trans. in Beckman, *Hittite Diplomatic Documents*, 18.

86. See "Treaty between Mursili II of Hatti and Targasnalli of Hapalla," sec. 7 (obv. 41'–rev. 1), *CTH* 67; trans. in Beckman, *Hittite Diplomatic Documents*, 71, and "Treaty between Muwattalli II of Hatti and Alaksandu of Wilusa," sec. 5 (A i 57'–79'), *CTH* 76; trans. in Beckman, *Hittite Diplomatic Documents*, 88.

87. "Treaty between Arnuwanda I of Hatti and the Men of Ismerika," *CTH* 133; trans. in Beckman, *Hittite Diplomatic Texts*, 13–17. The treaty between Muwattalli II of Hatti and Talmi-Sharrumma of Aleppo (*CTH* 75, trans. in Beckman, *Hittite Diplomatic Texts*, 94) makes reference to a treaty an earlier Hittite king had made with residents of the region of Aleppo (sec. 10, A obv. 28–32). Another two are composed as treaties with the subordinate kings, yet in the course of these treaties, reference is made to the subordinate king's subjects. See "Treaty between Šuppiluliuma I of Hatti and Shattiwaza of Mitanni," *CTH* 51; trans. in Beckman, *Hittite Diplomatic Texts*, 42–48; "Treaty between Šuppiluliuma I of Hatti and Huqqana of Hayasa," *CTH* 42; trans. in Beckman, *Hittite Diplomatic Texts*, 26–34.

88. "Treaty between Arnuwanda I of Hatti and the Men of Ismerika," *CTH* 133; trans. in Beckman, *Hittite Diplomatic Texts*, 13–17. The treaty is imposed on the subordinates, and has no historical prologue in which the favor granted by the Hittite king is mentioned. Nor does it stipulate blessings that are to accrue to the subordinates in return for fulfillment of the terms of the treaty.

89. God likewise bestows honor on nonroyals in Ps 91:15 and esp. Isa 43:4. See Olyan, "Honor, Shame and Covenant Relations," 205.

90. See also "Treaty between Šuppiluliuma I of Hatti and Tette of Nuhashshi," sec. 3 (A ii 1–5): "Tette shall come yearly to My Majesty, his lord, in Hatti" (*CTH* 53; trans. in Beckman, *Hittite Diplomatic Texts*, 55). See also "Treaty between Šuppiluliuma of Hatti and Aziru of Amurru," sec. 1 [i 13]: "[You] Azira [must appear] yearly before My Majesty [your lord] in the land of Hatti" (*CTH* 49; trans. in Singer, "Treaties between Hatti and Amurru," 94.

91. See Exod 34:23; Deut 16:16.

92. "Treaty between Mursili II of Hatti and Kupanta-Kurunta of Mira-Kuwaliya," sec. 28 (I iv 1'–8'), *CTH* 68; trans. in Beckman, *Hittite Diplomatic Texts*, 81.

93. Treaty between Muwattalli II of Hatti and Alaksandu of Wilusa sec. 16 (A iii 73–83) (*CTH* 76; Beckman, *Hittite Diplomatic Texts*, 91). Another treaty, between

Šuppiluliuma I of Hatti and Shattiwaza of Mitanni, states (sec. 13, A rev. 35–53) that a duplicate tablet of the treaty "shall be read repeatedly, for ever and ever, before the king of the land of Mitanni and before the Hurrians," *CTH* 51; Beckman, *Hittite Diplomatic Texts*, 46.

94. See Tikva Frymer-Kensky, "The Wanton Wife of God," ch. 12 of *In the Wake of the Goddesses* (New York: Free Press, 1992), 144–52.

95. Hosea 2:4–10; Isa 1:21; 54:5–8; 57:3–10; 61:10–11; 62:4–5; Jer 2:2, 20; 3:1–5; 3:6–25; 13:27; 23:10; Ezek 16, 23.

96. These "covenant formulas" are explored in Rolf Rendtorff, *The Covenant Formula: An Exegetical and Theological Investigation*, trans. Margaret Kohl (Edinburgh: T & T Clark, 1998). On the relationship between the covenant formulas and marriage formulas in the Hebrew Bible and in the ancient Near East see Gordon Paul Hugenberger, *Marriage as Covenant: A Study of Biblical Law and Ethics Governing Marriage Developed from the Perspective of Malachi* (Leiden: Brill, 1994), 168–215; Seock-Tae Sohn, "I Will Be Your God and You Will Be My People": The Origin and Background of the Covenant Formula," in *Ki Baruch Hu: Ancient Near Eastern, Biblical and Judaic Studies in Honor of Baruch A. Levine*, ed. R. Chazan et al. (Winona Lake, Ind.: Eisenbrauns, 1999), 355–72.

97. Isaac B. Gottlieb, "Law, Love and Redemption: Legal Connotations in the Language of Exodus 6:6–8," *Journal of the Ancient Near Eastern Society of Columbia University* 26 (1999): 52–57.

98. God's desire for Israel is described in Deuteronomy (7:7; 10:15) as *ḥēšek*, a term normally connotative of sexual desire.

99. See Ignace I. Gelb et al., eds., *The Assyrian Dictionary of the Oriental Institute of the University of Chicago* (Chicago: Oriental Institute 1964–2006), 8:16, at the end of entry 3a, where the word *kabātu* is cited with reference to the name of a woman, Kab-ta-at-a-na-ha-wi-ri-sa, "She Is Important-for-Her Husband."

100. See Olyan, "Honor, Shame and Covenant Relations," 203 n. 6, who notes that in addition to *kbd*, verbal forms of the root *hdr* are attested occasionally (Lev 19:32 in reference to elders; Lam 5:12 in reference to elders; Prov 25:6 in reference to kings), and the noun *hdr* is paired frequently with *kbd* in poetry. Thus the verb *hdr* appears to be a synonym of the verb *kbd*. See Isa 35:2, Ps 8:6, Ps 21:6.

101. Y. Muffs, *Love and Joy: Law, Language, and Religion in Ancient Israel* (New York: Jewish Theological Society of America, 1992), 45. In the scholarship of biblical covenant parallels and precedents, one finds covenants established between a deity and a king; see Theodore J. Lewis, "The Identity and Function of El/Baal Berith," *JBL* 115 (2003): 404–10. Yet it is rare anywhere to find a covenant between a deity and a people. One possible parallel that is adduced is from the Phoenician Arslan Tash inscription; see David S. Sperling, "An Arslan Tash Incantation: Interpretations and Implications," *HUCA* 53 (1982): 1–10; Blane W. Concklin, "Arslan Tash and Other Vestiges of a Particular Syrian Incantatory Thread," *Biblica* 84 (2003): 89–99. The text there, however, hardly invokes the metaphor of political treaty with the breadth and scope demonstrated in the biblical passages examined here.

102. See Karel van der Toorn, *Family Religion in Babylonia, Syria and Israel: Continuity and Change in the Forms of Religious Life*, Studies in the History and Culture of the Ancient Near East, no. 7 (Leiden: Brill, 1996).

103. Moshe Greenberg, *Studies in the Bible and Jewish Thought* (Philadelphia: Jewish Publication Society, 1995), 377.

104. Ibid., 133.

105. Herman Te Velde, "Theology, Priests, and Worship in Ancient Egypt," *CANE* 3:1733. Jacob Milgrom has noted that the commandment to append tassels (*ṣîṣit*) to the hem is based on ancient Near Eastern practice whereby the more important the individual, the more elaborate the embroidery of the person's hem. The fringes, or tassels, were an identification tag of nobility. See Jacob Milgrom, "Of Hems and Tassels," *Biblical Archeological Review* 9 (1983): 61–65.

106. On this general issue see S. A. Geller, *Sacred Enigmas: Literary Religion in the Hebrew Bible* (London: Routledge, 1996), 174–77.

107. Though see 2 Kgs 23:1–4, where Josiah does seem to play an intermediate role.

108. Deuteronomy 18:1–2. On the equality of rights between priests and Levites in Deuteronomy, see Richard D. Nelson, *Deuteronomy: A Commentary* (Louisville, Ky.: Westminster John Knox, 2002), 228–32; Mark Leuchter, "The Levite in Your Gates: The Deuteronomic Redefinition of Levitical Authority," *JBL* 126:3 (2007): 417–36.

109. Nicholson, *God and His People*, 200.

110. Peter Berger himself had recognized that the dynamics of cui bono failed to adequately explain biblical conceptions of God and man. Yet his one-sentence explanation of this, chalking it up to God's "utter transcendence" (*Sacred Canopy*, 35), hardly does justice to the issue.

111. John L. McKenzie, *A Theology of the Old Testament* (Garden City, N.Y.: Doubleday, 1974), 267–317; Walter Eichrodt, *Theology of the Old Testament*, trans. J. A. Baker, 2 vols. (London: SCM Press, 1961), 1:441.

CHAPTER 2

Portions of this chapter appeared previously as Joshua Berman, "Constitution, Class, and the Book of Deuteronomy," *Hebraic Political Studies* 1:5 (2006) 523–48.

1. Samuel Langdon, "The Republic of the Israelites: An Example to the American States," in *God's New Israel: Religious Interpretations of American Destiny*, ed. Conrad Cherry (Englewood Cliffs, N.J.: Prentice-Hall, 1971), 98. See discussion in S. Dean McBride Jr., "The Polity of the Covenant People: The Book of Deuteronomy," *Interpretation* 41 (1987): 231.

2. See Josephus Flavius, *Antiquities of the Jews*, 4.184, 193, 198, 302, 310, and particularly 4.312, and discussion in McBride, "Polity of the Covenant People," 229–30. For later Jewish sources that sought to see in Deuteronomy a blueprint for a Jewish polity, see Daniel Elazar, *Covenant & Polity in Biblical Israel* (New Brunswick, N.J.: Transaction Press, 1995), 196. For a discussion of fifteenth- to eighteenth-century western political theorists who saw Deuteronomy as a blueprint for constitutional thought, see Fania Oz-Salzberger, "The Jewish Roots of Western Freedom,"

*Azure* 13 (2002): 88–132. On the question of whether *politeia* should be construed in Josephus as "constitution" or simply as "form of government," see Bernard M. Levinson, *"The Right Chorale": Studies in Biblical Law and Interpretation*, Forschungen zum Alten Testament no. 54 (Tübingen: Mohr-Siebeck, 2007), 55–56.

3. On Samuel, see Baruch Halpern, "The Uneasy Compromise: Israel between League and Monarchy," in *Traditions in Transformation: Turning Points in Biblical Faith*, ed. Baruch Halpern and Jon D. Levenson (Winona Lake, Ind.: Eisenbrauns, 1981), 82–83; Baruch Halpern, *The Constitution of the Monarchy in Israel* (Chico, Calif.: Scholars Press, 1981), 225–35. On Solomon, see Marvin A. Sweeney, "The Critique of Solomon in the Josianic Edition of the Deuteronomistic History," *JBL* 114 (1995): 609–22. On Josiah, see Mark Leuchter, *Josiah's Reform and Jeremiah's Scroll*, Hebrew Bible Monographs no. 6 (Sheffield, England: Sheffield Phoenix Press, 2006), 33–46. On the Babylonian exile, see N. Lohfink, "Die Sicherung der Wirksamkeit des Gotteswortes durch das Prinzip der Schriftlichkeit der Tora und durch das Prinzip der Gewaltenteilung nach den Ämtergesetzen des Buches Deuteronomium (Dt. 16, 18–18,22)," in *Studien zum Deuteronomium und zur deuteronomistischen Literatur I*, ed. N. Lohfink, Stuttgarter biblische Aufsatzbände no. 8 (Stuttgart: Katholisches Bibelwerk, 1990), 305–23.

4. See R. H. Lowery, *The Reforming Kings: Cult and Society in First Temple Judah* JSOTSup no. 120 (Sheffield, England: JSOT Press, 1991).

5. For comparative studies of kingship in the Hebrew Bible and the ancient Near East see John Day, ed., *King and Messiah in Israel and the Ancient Near East: Proceedings of the Oxford Old Testament Seminar* (Sheffield, England: Sheffield Academic Press, 1998); Dale Francis Launderville, *Piety and Politics: the Dynamics of Royal Authority in Homeric Greece, Biblical Israel and Old Babylonian Mesopotamia* (Grand Rapids, Mich.: Eerdmans, 2003); Bernard Levinson, "The Reconceptualization of Kingship in Deuteronomy and the Deuteronomic History's Transformation of Torah," *VT* 51 (2001): 511–34.

6. Moshe Greenberg, *Studies in the Bible and Jewish Thought* (Philadelphia: Jewish Publication Society, 1995), 51–62; Douglas Knight, "Political Rights and Powers in Monarchic Israel," *Semeia* 66 (1995): 93–117; Norbert Lohfink, "Distribution of the Functions of Power: The Laws Concerning Public Offices in Deuteronomy 16:18–18:22," in *A Song of Power and the Power of Song: Essays on the Book of Deuteronomy*, ed. Duane L. Christensen (Winona Lake, Ind.: Eisenbrauns, 1993) 336–55; Jean-Marie Carriére, *Theorie du Politique dan le Deuteronome: Analyse des unites, des structures et des concepts de Dt 16, 18–18, 22* (Frankfurt am Main: Peter Lang, 2001).

7. The theoretical discussion here is based on Richard E. Blanton, "Beyond Centralization: Steps toward a Theory of Egalitarian Behavior in Archaic States," in *Archaic States*, ed. Gary M. Feinman and Joyce Marcus (Santa Fe: School of American Research Press, 1998), 147; see in this regard Patricia Dutcher-Walls, "The Circumscription of the King: Deuteronomy 17:16–17 in Its Ancient Social Context," *JBL* 121 (2002): 607.

8. Blanton, "Beyond Centralization," 146–47; Dutcher-Walls, "Circumscription of the King," 607.

9. Dutcher-Walls, "Circumscription of the King," 608.

10. Blanton, "Beyond Centralization," 150, 164.

11. Cicero, *On Duties*, trans. E. M. Atkins (Cambridge: Cambridge University Press, 1991), 23; see Iseult Honohan, *Civic Republicanism* (London: Routledge, 2002), 38.

12. Peter Riesenberg, *Citizenship in the Western Tradition: Plato to Rousseau* (Chapel Hill: University of North Carolina Press, 1992), 34. See, in particular, the funeral oration ascribed to Pericles in Thucydides, *The Peloponnesian War*, 2:34–46. Some scholars question the historicity of the oratory. Yet even if viewed as propaganda spun by Thucydides himself, the text highlights his own sense that there are virtues particular to being an Athenian that are worth inculcating.

13. By "citizen" I mean a member of the community who is endowed with rights and bound by responsibilities, who embraces a political identity based on ideals, culture, and history that identify the individual with society. In the Bible, such an individual may be referred to via a number of appellations, as I delineate below. I do not use the term "citizen" as an exclusive reference to the Hebrew term *'ezrāḥ*, which is often translated as "citizen" but refers to the community member only with respect to his or her cultic duties toward God. See *NIDOTTE*, 1:344–45. On citizenship, see Anthony R. Brunello, "Citizenship Rights and Responsibilities," in *International Encyclopedia of Government and Politics*, ed. Frank N. Magill (London: Fitzroy Dearborn, 1996), 1:181–84.

14. See comments in a similar, if less developed, vein in Norman Gottwald, *The Tribes of Yahweh* (Maryknoll, N.Y.: Orbis Press, 1979), 614.

15. Ronald M. Glassman, *Democracy and Despotism in Primitive Societies: A Neo-Weberian Approach to Political Theory* (Millwood, N.Y.: Associated Faculty Press, 1986), 120.

16. See George E. Mendenhall, *The Tenth Generation: The Origins of the Biblical Tradition* (Baltimore: Johns Hopkins University Press, 1973), 179. At the risk of editorializing, I note that as of this writing, current events well illustrate this phenomenon. In both Iraq and the autonomous Palestinian territories, nascent national movements are struggling to overcome the draw and security of deeply rooted alternative tribal and sectarian frameworks. The phenomenon is well documented with regard to post-Soviet Kazakhstan in Ian Bremmer and Cory Welt, "The Trouble with Democracy in Kazakhstan," *Central Asian Survey* 15:2 (1996): 179–99.

17. Glassman, Democracy and Despotism, 120.

18. Ulrich K. Preuss, "Two Challenges to European Citizenship," *Political Studies* 44:3 (1996): 535.

19. Aristotle, *Politics*, bk. 6, 1319b23–27.

20. Preuss, "Two Challenges," 535.

21. "Aššur prism of Tiglath-Pileser I," cylinder A (III.73–87), trans. A. Kirk Grayson, *Assyrian Royal Inscriptions*, 2 vols. (Wiesbaden: Harrassowitz, 1972–76), 2:10.

22. Nor is the king mentioned in any of the other deuteronomic sections pertaining to war; see 21:11–14, 23:9–14; 24:5.

23. Evidence from Mycenae and Cyrene shows that there were ancient Greek monarchies where kingship was not based on military power. See Anselm C.

Hagedorn, *Between Moses and Plato: Individual and Society in Deuteronomy and Ancient Greek Law*, FRLANT no. 204 (Göttingen: Vanderhoeck & Ruprecht, 2004), 146–54.

24. Shemaryahu Talmon, "Kingship and the Ideology of the State," in *World History of the Jewish People*, ed. Ben-Zion Netanyahu, 8 vols. (Tel Aviv: Massadah, 1963–), 4:13–14; A. D. H. Mayes, *Deuteronomy* (Grand Rapids: Eerdmans, 1979), 272, notes that the agenda of attenuating royal prestige by limiting the number of horses accords with other biblical references that suggest that the possession of wealth and horses denies a person the capacity to trust in God (Isa 2:7–9; Mic 5:9).

25. "Code of Hammurabi," I:24–30; 46–64, trans. Theophile J. Meek (*ANET*, 164). In the prologue to the Code, Hammurabi claims to have engaged in temple building or sacrificial offerings on behalf of some twenty deities. See discussion in Halpern, *Constitution of the Monarchy in Israel*, 30–31.

26. Levinson, "Reconceptualization of Kingship," 523. The separation of monarchy and cult, however, is distinctly deuteronomic. Many kings are seen offering sacrifices, most notably Solomon (1 Kgs 8:5), and indeed Solomon is the driving force in the construction of the First Temple (1 Kgs 6–8). No protest is registered against kings anywhere in the prophetic literature for performing cultic activities. Elsewhere in the Hebrew Bible this objection is registered only in 2 Chr 26:16–20, with reference to Uzziah.

27. On the practice of *andurārum* see Moshe Weinfeld, *Social Justice in Ancient Israel and in the Ancient Near East* (Jerusalem: Magnes, 1995), 75–96, and for bibliography on this practice, see Richard D. Nelson, *Deuteronomy: A Commentary* (Louisville, Ky.: Westminster John Knox Press, 2002), 192 n. 3.

28. Levinson, "Reconceptualization of Kingship," 529. See further on this in the next chapter.

29. Epilogue to the Code of Hammurabi, xxivb 76, 80–90; xxvb 10–20, 70–80; 95–100. See the discussion in Moshe Greenberg, "Some Postulates of Biblical Criminal Law," in *Yehezkel Kaufmann Jubilee Volume*, ed. Menahem Haran (Jerusalem: Magnes Press, 1960), 9–10.

30. Translated by S. N. Kramer (*ANET*, 161). See the discussion in Levinson, "Reconceptualization of Kingship," 514. For other assessments of the components of royal prestige that are attenuated in Deuteronomy see Gary Knoppers, "The Deuteronomist and the Deuteronomic Law of the King: A Reexamination of a Relationship," *ZAW* 108 (1996): 329–46.

31. In Egypt, we do not find statements of authorship and promulgation of the laws made by the kings themselves, as we find in Mesopotamia. Rather, we find that the Egyptian king was beholden to *maat*, a sense of right and wrong that would be adjudicated by the gods, even as the laws of Egypt themselves are never attributed a direct divine source. See Ronald J. Leprohon, "Royal Ideology and State Administration in Pharaonic Egypt," in *CANE*, 1:274.

32. Outside of the Pentateuch, however, we do find that executing justice is a task given to the king. See, for example, 1 Kgs 3:16–28; Ps 72:1–4.

33. Nelson, *Deuteronomy*, 225.

34. To be sure, "you" in Deuteronomy sometimes refers to individuals. But this does not preclude understanding much of the book's message as being addressed to

the polity as a whole. On the singular and plural addresses in Deuteronomy and their implications for both diachronic and synchronic readings, see Moshe Weinfeld, *Deuteronomy 1–11*, AB no. 5 (New York: Doubleday, 1991), 15–16.

35. Nelson, *Deuteronomy*, 214.

36. See discussions in Duane L. Christensen, *Deuteronomy 1:1–21:9*, Word Biblical Commentary no. 6A (Nashville, Tenn.: Thomas Nelson, 2001); Mayes, *Deuteronomy*, 272; Peter C. Craigie, *The Book of Deuteronomy* (Grand Rapids, Mich.: Eerdmans, 1976), 254.

37. The genealogical qualification of the king as portrayed here is distinct to Deuteronomy. The covenant with the Davidic line, established in 2 Sam 7, emerges as the dominant portrayal of kingship and blood lines in biblical literature.

38. Craigie, *Deuteronomy*, 256; Mayes, *Deuteronomy*, 272–73; Christensen, *Deuteronomy 1:1–21:9*, 384.

39. Dutcher-Walls, "Circumscription of the King," 609; Nelson, *Deuteronomy*, 224.

40. Charles de Secondat Montesquieu, *Spirit of the Laws*, 11:13, 17; Thomas L. Pangle, *Montesquieu's Philosophy of Liberalism* (Chicago: University of Chicago Press, 1973), 121.

41. Aristotle, *Politics*, bk. 7, 1333a41–1333b5, trans. Benjamin Jowett, http://classics.mit.edu/Aristotle/politics.7.seven.html.

42. Nelson, *Deuteronomy*, 245.

43. Ibid., 225; Gottwald, *Tribes of Yahweh*, 212.

44. Jacob Liver, "King, Kingship," in *Biblical Encyclopedia*, 8 vols. (Jerusalem: Bialik Institute, 1950–88), 4:1103 (in Hebrew).

45. F. A. Hayek, *The Political Ideal of the Rule of Law* (Cairo: National Bank of Egypt, 1955), 6–9.

46. Levinson, "Reconceptualization of Kingship," 532.

47. Moshe Weinfeld, "'Temple Scroll' or 'King's Law,'" *Shnaton* 3 (1978–9): 224 (in Hebrew); see texts in *ANET*, 414–20.

48. Weinfeld, "Temple Scroll," 226.

49. Opinions vary as to which passages are subsumed under this phrase. See Jeffrey H. Tigay, *Deuteronomy* (Philadelphia: Jewish Publication Society, 1996), 5.

50. Ibid., 168.

51. Shalom M. Paul, *Studies in the Book of the Covenant in Light of Biblical and Cuneiform Law* (Leiden: Brill, 1970), 38.

52. Levinson, "Reconceptualization of Kingship," 513, 530–31.

53. The differentiation within Deuteronomy between Levites and priests as a distinct group of Aaronite descendants is a complex question, and has garnered much scholarly attention. Whereas in Leviticus and Numbers the priests are designated "the sons of Aaron," in contradistinction to other members of the tribe of Levi, Deuteronomy never refers to the priests in this fashion and, in fact, often uses the phrase "levitical priests." In this section, I address the role of the cultic personnel in Deuteronomy—the Levites as well as the priests—as a group distinguished from the rest of the people. Because I am addressing the general status and powers of the cultic personnel, rather than the individual powers of priests as opposed to Levites,

I will not review the issue, which is beyond the scope of this chapter. For a summary of the positions on this issue, see Mark Leuchter, "The Levite in Your Gates: The Deuteronomic Redefinition of Levitical Authority," *JBL* 126:3 (2007): 417–36; Christensen, *Deuteronomy 1:1–21:9*, 389–90; Nelson, *Deuteronomy*, 231 n. 4.

54. Tigay, *Deuteronomy*, 164. The judicial role of priests is also reflected in Ezek 44:24 and possibly in Isa 28:7 and 1 Kgs 8:31–32.

55. Blanton, "Beyond Centralization," 164.

56. Ibid., 150.

57. I take the role ascribed to the priests in 21:5 to be of a judicial nature, as implied by the verse itself.

58. Lohfink, "Distribution of the Functions of Power," 349; Nelson, *Deuteronomy*, 221.

59. Lohfink, "Distribution of the Functions of Power," 349; Levinson, "Reconceptualization of Kingship," 52; Robert Wilson, *Prophecy and Society in Ancient Israel* (Philadelphia: Fortress, 1980), 160; Christensen, *Deuteronomy 1:1–21:9*, 376; Mayes, *Deuteronomy*, 267.

60. Greenberg, *Studies in the Bible and Jewish Thought*, 56.

61. Plato, *Republic*, 415a.

62. Aristotle, *Politics*, bk. 3, 1276b21–29, trans. Benjamin Jowett, http://classics .mit.edu/Aristotle/politics.3.three.html.

63. Montesquieu, *Spirit of the Laws*, 11:6; Pangle, *Montesquieu's Philosophy of Liberalism*, 132; Judith N. Shklar, *Montesquieu* (Oxford: Oxford University Press, 1987), 88.

64. References to the Torah as written law, to which the community appeals for juridical decision, are legion in the Book of Ezra. Early hints at this view of the law are found in Deuteronomy. See discussion concerning the history of the promulgation of the written law as statutory in Michael LeFebvre, *Collections, Codes and Torah: The Re-Characterization of Israel's Written Law* (New York: T & T Clark, 2006), 55–95.

65. Montesquieu, *Spirit of the Laws*, 11:6; Shklar, *Montesquieu*, 81.

66. Montesquieu, *Spirit of the Laws*, 11:6.

67. Levinson, "Reconceptualization of Kingship," 522.

68. Thus in literature from Ugarit, the king, Keret, is reproached for failing to hear the cases of widows and orphans; see M. Dietrich, Otto Lorenz, and J. Sanmartin, eds., *The Cuneiform Alphabetic Texts from Ugarit, Ras Ibn Hani and Other Places* (Münster: Ugarit, 1995), 1.16.VI.43–50. Hammurabi claims in the prologue to the Code that Marduk appointed him so that "the strong might not oppress the weak" (i.27–44). See discussion of the contrast between Deuteronomy and the prevailing norms elsewhere on this issue, in Levinson, *"The Right Chorale,"* 76–77.

69. Elsewhere, however, Scripture emphatically does place justice in the hands of the king. See 2 Sam 14:1–24; 1 Kgs 3:16–28; Ps. 72:1.

70. Tigay, *Deuteronomy*, 160. See also McBride, "Polity of the Covenant People," 240.

71. Thucydides, *The Peloponnesian War*, trans. R. Warner (Hammondsworth, England: Penguin, 1972), 147.

72. McBride, "Polity of the Covenant People," 238.

73. J. Milgrom, "The Ideological and Historical Importance of the Office of the Judge in Deuteronomy," in *Isac Leo Seeligmann Volume: Essays on the Bible and the Ancient World*, ed. Alexander Rofé and Yair Zakovitch, 3 vols. (Jerusalem: E. Rubinstein, 1983), 3:134; Tigay, *Deuteronomy*, 166.

74. On the topic of collective power at Mari see Daniel E. Fleming, *Democracy's Ancient Ancestors: Mari and Early Collective Governance* (Cambridge: Cambridge University Press, 2004).

75. Fleming, *Democracy's Ancient Ancestors*, xiv.

76. For the following, see Edward Shils, *Center and Periphery: Essays in Macrosociology* (Chicago: University of Chicago Press, 1975), 3–16.

77. Ibid., 16.

78. Gerhard E. Lenski, *Power and Privilege: A Theory of Social Stratification* (New York: McGraw-Hill, 1966), 197.

79. See H. Reviv, *The Elders in Ancient Israel: A Study of a Biblical Institution* (Jerusalem: Magnes, 1989); Jacob Milgrom, "Priestly Terminology and the Political and Social Structure of Pre-Monarchic Israel," *Jewish Quarterly Review* 79 (1978): 65–81.

80. Jacob Milgrom, *Numbers* (Philadelphia: Jewish Publication Society, 1989), 335.

81. Within my synchronic reading of Deuteronomy, in its final form, as the fifth book of the Pentateuch, I have read this switch of terminology as a reflection of an evolution of the structure of the regime. Diachronic readings of Deuteronomy will typically see these terms as typical of Priestly vocabulary, while Deuteronomy utilizes different words and concepts.

82. This is seen in Judges 20, when the tribes of Israel demand that the tribe of Benjamin discipline the inhabitants of Gibeah for their crime against the concubine.

83. There is a tendency in the scholarship to view Deuteronomy as championing collective identity at the expense of local institutions, as in the following statement: "Deuteronomy stresses the homogeneity of the people, Israel, and attempts to impose upon this undivided people the social control elements of a 'shame-culture...an attempt to impose a common code of moral indignation throughout the country, a cultural identity that outstrips the obligations of kinship—the obligations of the village—in its claim on individual loyalty'"; Baruch Halpern, "Jerusalem and the Lineages in the Seventh Century B.C.E.: Kinship and the Rise of Individual Moral Liability," in *Law and Ideology in Monarchic Israel*, ed. Baruch Halpern and Deborah W. Hobson, JSOTSup no. 124 (Sheffield, England: Sheffield Academic Press, 1991), 75. But this view is in error. Deuteronomy, in fact, stresses the importance of villages; the attenuation of patriarchal hierarchy is at the level of the tribe.

84. On this, I am following the position of Norbert Lohfink, *Die Väter Israels im Deuteronomium: Mit einer Stellungnahme von Thomas Römer*, Orbis biblicus et orientalis no. 111 (Freiburg, Switzerland: Universitätsverlag, 1991).

85. While the status of the tribe is diminished within Deuteronomy—indeed there are no laws that adjudicate tribal affairs—we see that Deuteronomy does place a

premium on laws concerning the nuclear family (the better parts of Deuteronomy 21–22, 24:1–5). Naomi Sternberg takes the often-recognized superior status accorded to women in Deuteronomy to be a function of this effort to buttress the family unit rather than as a desire by Deuteronomy to better the lot of women qua women. See Steinberg, "The Deuteronomic Law Code and the Politics of State Centralization," in *The Bible and the Politics of Exegesis*, ed. David Jobling et al. (Cleveland: Pilgrim Press, 1991), 161–70.

86. Victor P. Hamilton, "'āh," in *NIDOTTE*, 1:348.

87. Notice that in the second episode, he recounts the mission of the spies. Moses again highlights the prominence of the tribal hierarchy in the wilderness (1:22–23): "Then all of you came to me and said, "Let us send men ahead to explore the land for us and bring back word.... I approved of the plan, and so I selected twelve of your men, one from each tribe.""

88. Christensen, *Deuteronomy 1:1–21:9*, 22; Craigie, *Deuteronomy*, 97–98; Tigay, *Deuteronomy*, 11–12; Moshe Weinfeld, "Judge and Officer in Ancient Israel and the Ancient Near East," *Israel Oriental Society* 7 (1977): 65–88; J. G. McConville, *Deuteronomy*, Apollos Old Testament Commentary no. 5 (Leicester, England: InterVarsity Press, 2002), 287.

89. Nelson, *Deuteronomy*, 19.

90. Milgrom, "Ideological and Historical Importance," 133, notes that in eighth-century texts, however (e.g. Hosea 13:10; Isa 1:23, 26; 32:1), *śar* and *šopēṭ* are interchangeable.

91. Alexander Rofé, "The Law about the Organization of Justice in Deuteronomy (16:18–20; 17:8–13)," *Bet Miqra* 21 (1976): 200 (in Hebrew); Bernard M. Levinson, *Deuteronomy and the Hermeneutics of Legal Innovation* (New York: Oxford University Press, 1997), 124–27. S. R. Driver also sees this group as superseded by the later structure of Deut. 16; Driver, *A Critical and Exegetical Commentary on Deuteronomy* (Edinburgh: T & T Clark, 1965), 18–19. Deut 1:6–18 employs language found in Exod 18:13–26, Num 11:11–17, and Deut 16:18–20. For an examination of the way Deuteronomy reworks these narratives in accordance with deuteronomic ideology, see Marc Zvi Brettler, *The Creation of History in Ancient Israel* (London: Routledge, 1995), 65–70; Nelson, *Deuteronomy*, 19–20.

92. Bernard M. Levinson, *Deuteronomy and the Hermeneutics of Legal Innovation* (New York: Oxford University Press, 1997), 126; Nelson, *Deuteronomy*, 215; in a similar vein, see Tigay, *Deuteronomy*, 160.

93. Milgrom, "Ideological and Historical Importance," 136; Moshe Weinfeld, *Deuteronomy and the Deuteronomic School* (Oxford: Clarendon Press, 1972), 234. Other scholars see the reworked role of the elders in Deuteronomy as a sign of layered strata of legal materials. For a succinct review of the claims, see Levinson, "The Right Chorale," 72 n. 52.

94. Tigay, *Deuteronomy*, 247; Craigie, *Deuteronomy*, 327. As several scholars have noted—Nelson, Deuteronomy, 341, Tigay, *Deuteronomy*, 277, Duane L. Christensen, *Deuteronomy 21:10–34:12*, Word Biblical Commentary 6B (Nashville, Tenn.: Thomas Nelson, 2001), 717—the convocation at 29:9–10 serves to downplay the role of the

elders. The elders are summoned along with everyone else, including women, children, and wood-choppers. The covenant is established with each individual member of Israel regardless of social rank.

95. The shifting responsibilities and identities ascribed to the "elders" may be understood in light of Daniel Fleming's observations concerning the use of the term in Mesopotamian legal writings. Fleming notes that it is erroneous to consider the elders as a standing institution, individuals who execute set tasks and assemble on a regular basis. Rather than an individual title or post, "elder" should be considered a broad classification of status. "Elder" indicates senior leadership with various connotations determined according to the particular political circumstance. Fleming notes that in Mesopotamian literature the references to elders even in a particular locale "shows an enormous fluidity of both written application and political reality"; Fleming, *Democracy's Ancient Ancestors*, 190.

96. See discussion in Levinson, *"The Right Chorale,"* 81–82.

97. Pangle, *Montesquieu's Philosophy of Liberalism*, 118–20.

98. Montesquieu, *Spirit of the Laws*, 11:6.

99. Shklar, *Montesquieu*, 87.

100. Pangle, *Montesquieu's Philosophy of Liberalism*, 129.

101. Montesquieu, *Spirit of the Laws*, 11:6; Shklar, *Montesquieu*, 81.

## CHAPTER 3

1. On the Homestead Act see Heather Cox Richardson, *The Greatest Nation of the Earth: Republican Economic Policies During the Civil War* (Cambridge, Mass.: Harvard University Press, 1997).

2. A typical discussion of this nature concerning the various laws of manumission may be found in Gregory C. Chirichigno, *Debt-Slavery in Israel and the Ancient Near East*, JSOTSup no. 141 (Sheffield, England: JSOT Press, 1993), 22–24, with extensive bibliography. See Bernard M. Levinson, "The Birth of the Lemma: The Restrictive Reinterpretation of the Covenant Code's Manumission Law by the Holiness Code (Leviticus 25:44–46)," *JBL* 124:4 (2005): 617–39, and most recently, Bernard M. Levinson, *Legal Revision and Religious Renewal in Ancient Israel* (Cambridge: Cambridge University Press, 2008). For differing views concerning the evolution of the Torah's usury laws see E. E. Neufeld, "The Prohibitions against Loans at Interest in Ancient Hebrew Laws," *HUCA* 26 (1955): 363–64, who posits a date in the eighth century B.C.E. Yet see Jeffrey H. Tigay, *Deuteronomy* (Philadelphia: Jewish Publication Society, 1996), xxi, who rightly points out that in a source from that century, we would expect to find laws about merchants, artisans, professional soldiers, commerce, real estate, written contracts, commercial loans, and more, none of which are addressed by Deuteronomy's codes.

3. For a recent study in this vein concerning the relationship between the law of manumission in Exodus 21:2–6 and Deuteronomy 15:12–18, see Bernard M. Levinson, "The Manumission of Hermeneutics: The Slave Laws of the Pentateuch as a Challenge to Contemporary Pentateuchal Theory," in *Congress Volume Leiden 2004*, ed. André Lemaire, VTS no. 109 (Leiden: Brill, 2006), 281–324.

4. For a comprehensive review of the complexities involved see Gary N. Knoppers and Bernard M. Levinson, "How, When, Where, and Why Did the Pentateuch Become the Torah?" in *The Pentateuch as Torah: New Models for Understanding Its Promulgation and Acceptance*, ed., Gary N. Knoppers and Bernard M. Levinson (Winona Lake, Ind.: Eisenbrauns, 2007), 1–22.

5. For a recent review of the scholarship see Levinson, "Manumission of Hermeneutics," 282–91.

6. Many scholars see a strong affinity between the societies described in the law codes and the economy of the land of Israel that arises from material finds from the tribal period. See Martin Noth, *The Laws in the Pentateuch and Other Studies*, trans. D. Ap-Thomas (Philadelphia: Fortress, 1966), 33, 60; H. Eberhard von Waldow, "Social Responsibility and Social Structure in Early Israel," *CBQ* 32 (1970): 184–85. Thus, the stipulations that distinguish between sale of agricultural lands and of residential houses, as delineated in Lev 25: 29–34, accurately reflect the settlement patterns of the majority of Israelites who settled in the highlands and lowlands of Canaan. See Chirichigno, *Debt Slavery*, 351.

7. See James W. Watts, *Reading Law: The Rhetorical Shaping of the Pentateuch*, Biblical Seminar no. 59 (Sheffield, England: Sheffield Academic Press, 1999), 29.

8. See Raymond Westbrook, "Biblical and Cuneiform Law Codes," *Revue Biblique* 92 (1985): 247–64; and especially Jean Bottéro, *Mesopotamia: Writing, Reasoning, and the Gods*, trans. Zainab Bahrani and Marc Van De Mieroop (Chicago: University of Chicago Press, 1992), 156–84.

9. See a recent overview of the issue in Michael LeFebvre, *Collections, Codes and Torah: The Re-Characterization of Israel's Written Law* (New York: T & T Clark, 2006), 1–30.

10. See Moshe Greenberg, *Studies in the Bible and Jewish Thought* (Philadelphia: Jewish Publication Society, 1995), 27; Shalom Paul, *Studies in the Book of the Covenant in Light of Biblical and Cuneiform Law* (Leiden: Brill, 1970), 1, 42 (reprinted with a foreword by Samuel Greengus [Eugene, Ore.: Wipf & Stock, 2006]); E. A. Speiser, "The Biblical Idea of History in Its Common Near Eastern Setting, *Israel Exploration Journal* 7 (1957): 202.

11. See overview in LeFebvre, *Collections, Codes and Torah*, 31–54.

12. As Bernard Jackson, *Studies in the Semiotics of Biblical Law*, JSOTSup no. 314 (Sheffield, England: Sheffield Academic Press, 2000), 121–41, has noted, we find four categories of use for written law in the preexilic period: monumental use (see Deut 27:1–8; Josh 8:30–35); repository within the sanctuary (see Deut 31:25–30); didactic use (see Josh 1:7–8; 2 Chr 17:7–9), and in ritual reading (see Deut 31:10–13; Josh 8:34–35). All of these are well understood in light of my exploration of Late Bronze Age treaty stipulations in chapter 1. As noted, the stipulations had to be recorded on tablets; the tablets had to be placed within the vassal's temple; and the stipulations had to be read out periodically before the vassal.

13. Michael Fishbane, *Biblical Interpretation in Ancient Israel* (Oxford: Clarendon Press, 1985), 95.

14. See Edward Greenstein, "Bible: Biblical Law," in *Back to the Sources: Reading the Classic Jewish Texts*, ed. Barry W. Holtz (New York: Summit, 1984), 84; J. M.

Hamilton, *Social Justice and Deuteronomy: The Case of Deuteronomy 15*, Society of Biblical Literature Dissertation Series no. 136 (Atlanta: Scholars Press, 1992), 8. On ancient Near Eastern legal collections as theoretical reflections on ethical issues, and the need to see them in literary terms, see Bernard M. Levinson, "The Right Chorale: From the Poetics to the Hermeneutics of the Hebrew Bible," in *"The Right Chorale": Studies in Biblical Law and Interpretation*, Forschungen zum alten Testament no. 54 (Tübingen: Mohr-Siebeck, 2007), 31.

15. See George Dalton, ed., *Primitive, Archaic, and Modern Economies: Essays of Karl Polanyi* (Garden City, N.Y.: Doubleday, 1968), 71.

16. Daryll Forde and Mary Douglas, "Primitive Economics," in *Tribal and Peasant Economies: Readings in Economic Anthropology*, ed. George Dalton (Garden City, N.Y.: Natural History Press, 1967), 23; George Dalton, "Subsistence and Peasant Economies in Africa," in Dalton, *Tribal and Peasant Economies*, 157.

17. Neil J. Smelser, "Toward a Theory of Modernization," in Dalton, *Tribal and Peasant Economies*, 33.

18. Robert L. Heilbroner, *The Worldly Philosophers: The Lives, Times and Ideas of the Great Economic Thinkers* (1953; New York: Simon and Schuster, 1980), 25.

19. Ibid., 26.

20. Smelser, "Toward a Theory of Modernization," 33.

21. Ibid., 40.

22. Ibid., 40.

23. Ibid., 34.

24. See C. C. Lamberg-Karlovsky, "The Archaeological Evidence for International Commerce: Public and/or Private Enterprise in Mesopotamia?" in *Privatization in the Ancient Near East and Classical World*, ed. Michael Hudson and Baruch A. Levine, Peabody Museum Bulletin no. 5 (Cambridge, Mass.: Harvard University Press, 1996), 73.

25. It would appear that alongside royal estate holdings, some form of private ownership of land was extant in all periods and places in the ancient Near East, with the possible exception of Egypt, where all lands may have been considered to be the property of the king. See Daniel C. Snell, *Life in the Ancient Near East: 3100–332 B.C.E.* (New Haven, Conn.: Yale University Press, 1997), 125–28, and the extended bibliography in Chirichigno, *Debt Slavery in Israel*, 35 n. 1.

26. Chirichigno, *Debt Slavery in Israel*, 51; Norman Gottwald, *The Tribes of Yahweh* (Maryknoll, N.Y.: Orbis Press, 1979), 212.

27. Chirichigno, *Debt Slavery in Israel*, 54. Many scholars have identified this cycle of political economy at work in Israel in the eighth and seventh centuries B.C.E. See Jeffrey A. Fager, "Land Tenure in the Biblical Jubilee: A Moral World View," *HAR* 11 (1987): 60; Chirichigno, *Debt Slavery in Israel*, 126; Bernhard Lang, "The Social Organization of Peasant Poverty in Biblical Israel," in *Anthropological Approaches to the Old Testament*, ed. Bernhard Lang, Issues in Religion and Theology no. 8 (Philadelphia: Fortress Press, 1985), 87; Marvin L. Chaney, "Bitter Bounty: The Dynamics of Political Economy Critiqued by the Eighth-Century Prophets," in *The Bible and Liberation: Political and Social Hermeneutics*, ed. N. K. Gottwald and

R. A. Horsley (Maryknoll, N.Y.: Orbis, 1993), 250–63; Marvin L. Chaney, "Whose Sour Grapes? The Addresses of Isaiah 5:1–7 in the Light of Political Economy," *Semeia* 87 (1999): 105–22; I. Hahn, "Representation of Society in the Old Testament and the Asiatic Mode of Production," *Oikumene* 2 (1978): 27–41.

28. I follow closely in this section Gottwald's description of the Bible's communitarian mode of production. See Norman Gottwald, "Social Class as an Analytic and Hermeneutical Category in Biblical Studies," *JBL* 112:1 (1993): 7.

29. Gottwald, *Tribes of Yahweh*, 613; Greenstein, "Bible: Biblical Law," 96; Paul, *Studies in the Book of the Covenant*, 44.

30. J. D. Levenson, "Poverty and the State in Biblical Thought," *Judaism* 25 (1976): 232.

31. Norman K. Gottwald, "The Prophetic Critique of Political Economy: Its Ground and Import," in *The Hebrew Bible in Its Social World and Ours*, ed. Norman K. Gottwald (Atlanta: Scholars Press, 1993), 362. According to Snell, *Life in the Ancient Near East*, 87, it is likely that in Israel, free peasants constituted the largest group in any period.

32. For a discussion of the correlation between social justice and monotheism, see Robert Karl Gnuse, *No Other Gods: Emergent Monotheism in Israel* (Sheffield, England: Sheffield Academic Press, 1997), 230.

33. Gnuse, *No Other Gods*, 257; Gottwald, "Prophetic Critique," 353.

34. Levenson, "Poverty and the State," 232; Greenstein, "Bible: Biblical Law," 96.

35. Although the notion of personal ownership of land is self-evident today, it seems to have had its origins in the ancient Near East in the palace sector. A ruler's property could be exempted from the redistributive norms that governed most lands. The ruler would then be able to bestow these lands on various groups with ties to the palace, with the result that certain tracts of land became hereditary legacies. Private property seems to have been quite widespread at Nuzi in the late second millennium, B.C.E. See Maynard Paul Maidman, "Nuzi: Portrait of an Ancient Mesopotamian Provincial Town," in *CANE*, 2:931–47. For an overall history of the privatization of lands in the ancient Near East see Michael Hudson, "Introduction—Privatization: A Survey of the Unresolved Controversies," in Hudson and Levine, *Privatization in the Ancient Near East*, 1–32, and Michael Hudson, "The Dynamics of Privatization from the Bronze Age to the Present," in Hudson and Levine, *Privatization in the Ancient Near East*, 33–72. With regard to day to day commodities, however, it is clear that individuals would obtain items from private craftsmen who produced them for purchase or barter within a market economy.

36. With regard to Egypt see David O'Connor, "The Social and Economic Organization of Ancient Egyptian Temples," in *CANE*, 1:319–29. With regard to Mesopotamia, see Norman Yoffee, "The Economy of Ancient Western Asia," in *CANE*, 3:1387–99.

37. Jeffrey A. Fager, *Land Tenure and the Biblical Jubilee: Uncovering Hebrew Ethics through the Sociology of Knowledge*, JSOTSup no. 155 (Sheffield, England: JSOT Press, 1993), 88.

38. Fager, *Land Tenure and the Biblical Jubilee*, 24.

39. Christopher J. Eyre, "Work and the Organisation of Work in the New Kingdom," in *Labor in the Ancient Near East*, ed. Marvin A. Powell (New Haven, Conn.: American Oriental Society, 1987), 212.

40. Snell, *Life in the Ancient Near East*, 71.

41. Likewise, few are the narratives across the entire Bible that offer a detailed account of how land transactions were enacted. See Gen 23:4–18; Jer 32:6–14.

42. Fager, *Land Tenure*, 26.

43. Baruch A. Levine, *Leviticus* (Philadelphia: Jewish Publication Society of America, 1989), 270.

44. Moshe Weinfeld, *Deuteronomy and the Deuteronomic School* (Oxford: Clarendon, 1972), 74. Attestations to land grants in the kingdoms of Judah and of Israel are found in 1 Sam 22:7–8; 2 Sam 19:30; 1 Kgs 21. See Baruch A. Levine, "Farewell to the Ancient Near East: Evaluating Biblical References to Ownership of Land in Comparative Perspective," in Hudson and Levine, *Privatization in the Ancient Near East*, 229–33.

45. D. C. Hopkins, *The Highlands of Canaan: Agricultural Life in the Early Iron Age* (Sheffield, England: Almond Press, 1985) 257. See also S. Kaufman, "A Reconstruction of the Social Welfare Systems of Ancient Israel," in *In the Shelter of Elyon: Essays on Ancient Palestinian Life and Literature in Honor of G. W. Ahlström*, ed. W. Boyd Barrick and John R. Spencer (Sheffield, England: Sheffield Academic Press, 1984), 280. For a discussion of how land is to be divided within the tribe, according to biblical sources, see Levine, "Farewell to the Ancient Near East," 223–52. See also Baruch A. Levine, "The Clan-Based Economy of Biblical Israel," in *Symbiosis, Symbolism, and the Power of the Past: Canaan, Ancient Israel and Their Neighbors from the Late Bronze Age through Roman Palestina*, ed. William G. Dever and Seymour Gitin (Winona Lake, Ind.: Eisenbrauns, 2003), 445–53.

46. Indeed, most societies of the ancient Near East limited the absolute right of individuals to buy or sell land at will. See Jeffrey A. Fager, "Land Tenure in the Biblical Jubilee," 59; Chirichigno, *Debt Slavery in Israel*, 335.

47. See discussion in Richard A. Posner, "Theory of Primitive Society with Special Reference to Law," *Journal of Law and Economics* 23 (1980): 32.

48. Gottwald, *Tribes of Yahweh*, 613.

49. Ibid., 315–16.

50. Hopkins, *Highlands of Canaan*, 261.

51. Posner, "Theory of Primitive Society," 17. Indeed, as George Dalton "Traditional Production in Primitive African Economies," in Dalton, *Tribal and Peasant Economies*, 67, has noted, in many parts of agricultural Africa, people acquire land rarely through purchase and most often through kinship right. The need for kinship contiguity provides the rationale for the restriction placed on the daughters of Zelophehad, barring them as women landowners to marry outside the tribe (Num 36).

52. The few references within the Ugaritic texts point without exception to the king as recipient of the tithes. See Michael Heltzer, *The Rural Community in Ancient Ugarit* (Wiesbaden: Reichert, 1976), 35. Elsewhere, both in the Hebrew Bible and in almost all ancient Near Eastern sources, tithes are delivered to the temple or sanctuary.

See H. Jagersma, "The Tithes in the OT," *Oudtestamentische Studiën* 21 (1981): 123. In Israel as well, the distinction between the royal and temple tithes is not always clear, since temples were ispo facto royal temples (Amos 7:13) and the kings controlled their treasuries (1 Kgs15:18; 2 Kgs 12:19; 18:15) and were responsible for their maintenance (2 Kgs 12:7–17; 22:3–7; Ezek 45:17; 2 Chr 31:3–6). See Jacob Milgrom, *Cult and Conscience: The Asham and the Priestly Doctrine of Repentance* (Leiden: Brill, 1976), 57. For an overview of tithing in the Bible and its relationship to tithing in the ancient Near East, see Moshe Weinfeld, "Tithing in the Bible: Its Monarchic and Cultic Background," *Be'er Sheva* 1 (1973) 122–31 (in Hebrew).

53. See discussion in Jagersma, "Tithes in the OT," 123.

54. This is decidedly not the case throughout the Bible, however. In 1 Sam 8:15–17 and 1 Kgs 4:7, the tithe is a tax collected through the legal claim of the kingdom as sacral monarchy, belonging to God and the king together. See Frank Crüsemann, *The Torah: Theology and Social History of Old Testament Law*, trans. Allan W. Mahnke (Minneapolis: Fortress, 1996), 217.

55. Gottwald, "Prophetic Critique," 351; Crüsemann, *Torah*, 221.

56. I. Mendelsohn, "Samuel's Denunciation of Kingship in the Light of Akkadian Documents from Ugarit," *Bulletin of the American Schools of Oriental Research* 143 (1956): 17–22; Jagersma, "Tithes in the OT," 121.

57. Milgrom, *Cult and Conscience*, 58.

58. Ibid., 62.

59. Gottwald, *Tribes of Yahweh*, 695.

60. On the primary identity of the priests as ministers and stewards of God, see Peter J. Leithart, "Attendants of Yahweh's House: Priesthood in the Old Testament," *JSOT* 85 (1999): 3–24. For an overview of priesthood throughout the Hebrew Bible see Richard D. Nelson, *Raising Up a Faithful Priest: Community and Priesthood in Biblical Theology* (Louisville, Ky.: Westminster/John Knox Press, 1993), and Lester L. Grabbe, *Priests, Prophets, Diviners, Sages: A Socio-Historical Study of Religious Specialists in Ancient Israel* (Valley Forge, Pa.: Trinity Press International, 1995), 41–65.

61. Gottwald, *Tribes of Yahweh*, 696.

62. John F. Robertson, "The Social and Economic Organization of Ancient Mesopotamian Temples," in *CANE*, 1:444–46.

63. Occasions mentioned elsewhere in the Bible, however, indicate that major cultic events could involve massive economic resources (see 1 Kgs 8:5).

64. Whereas rabbinic exegesis has sought to see the tithe laws of Deuteronomy as augmenting those in the other books of the Pentateuch, modern scholarship has tended to view the laws as mutually exclusive, as a revision of the entire institution of tithing. See Crüsemann, *Torah*, 217–24; Nelson, *Deuteronomy*, 184–85; Tigay, *Deuteronomy*, 141–42. Modern scholars also debate whether all the pentateuchal tithes were obligatory or only those in Deuteronomy. See Milgrom, *Cult and Conscience*, 63, and Tigay, *Deuteronomy*, 141.

65. Tigay, *Deuteronomy*, 142.

66. Blanton, "Beyond Centralization," 164.

67. Ibid., 150. There is much debate among modern commentators concerning the notion of centralization of the cult in Deuteronomy and its relationship to the seventh-century cultic reforms enacted by Hezekiah and Josiah. See arguments in J. G. McConville, "Deuteronomy's Unification of Passover and Maṣṣōt: A Response to Bernard M. Levinson," *JBL* 119 (2000): 47–58. Specifically, some see the centralization program as depicted in Deuteronomy 12–14 as reflective of an economic agenda that actually serves the interests of the bureaucracy and the urban merchants. See W. Eugene Claburn, "The Fiscal Basis of Josiah's Reforms," *JBL* 92 (1973): 11–22. In the synchronic reading I propose here of the final form of Deuteronomy, the program for the centralization of the cult needs to be seen as a part of a whole that includes the prohibition on the king amassing excessive wealth. I explain the laws of tithing here in that context—that of a collective power strategy, as outlined in chapter 2.

68. Crüsemann, *Torah*, 217. Employing a hermeneutics of suspicion, Harold V. Bennett, *Injustice Made Legal: Deuteronomic Law and the Plight of the Widows, Strangers and Orphans in Ancient Israel* (Grand Rapids, Mich.: Eerdmans, 2002), claims that these laws originated as a way to guarantee the material benefit of the officials who drafted them. His, theory, however, rests on a particular historical location for these laws, in his opinion the ninth-century Omiride dynasty. In examining Deuteronomy as an integrated whole, however, after final redaction, it is clear that the Book's rhetoric extols the humanitarian virtues of these laws.

69. Posner, "Theory of Primitive Society," 14.

70. Ibid., 12–13.

71. On the term "brother" in the Hebrew Bible, see *NIDOTTE*, 1:345–348. On the use of "brother" for "member" of a tribe, or nation, see Gerhard von Rad, "Brothers and Neighbor in the Old Testament," in von Rad, *God at Work in Israel*, trans. John H. Marks (Nashville, Tenn.: Abingdon, 1980), 183–93.

72. R. Maloney, "Usury and Restrictions in Interest-Taking in the Ancient Near East," *CBQ* 36 (1974): 1–20; Tigay, *Deuteronomy*, 217. Higher rates were known as well. See G. R. Driver and John C. Miles, *The Babylonian Laws*, 2 vols. (Oxford: Clarendon Press, 1952), 1:173–77. While these high rates were given official sanction, the law codes of Mesopotamia also offer protection to the indigent: a lender who charged in excess of the maximum rate could lose his capital (Code of Hammurabi 90; *ANET*, 169). See discussion in Cyril S. Rodd, *Glimpses of a Strange Land: Studies in Old Testament Ethics* (Edinburgh: T & T Clark, 2001), 144.

73. Michael Hudson, "The Dynamics of Privatization from the Bronze Age to the Present," in Hudson and Levine, *Privatization in the Ancient Near East*, 47.

74. The writer of a letter from Ugarit, after discussing some business affairs, concludes by stating that the money he owes the addressee as a loan should not bear interest, as "we are each of us gentlemen." See "A Loan between Gentlemen," trans. J. Nougayrol (*ANET*, 629). The writer, however, does not refer to normative law but rather seems to suggest the practice in an ad hoc fashion.

75. E. E. Neufeld, "Prohibitions against Loans," 364–65. A point debated within the scholarship to these passages concerns the extent to which the biblical law codes sought to prohibit lending at interest. Neufeld maintains that there is a distinction

between the source in Exod 22:24, which may be read as proscribing the charging of interest to the poor, and Deut 23:20, which may be read as prohibiting interest outright, under any circumstances. Others maintain that all the sources apply equally to all members of the polity, and that the verse in Exodus simply depicted poverty as a likely scenario in which one would seek a loan. Hillel Gamoran has astutely noted that not a single biblical passage in which lending is mentioned seems to be a case of a commercial loan, and that out of the sixteen biblical passages that address interest, thirteen explicitly indicate that the borrower is indigent, whereas the rest are silent on this issue. See Hillel Gamoran, "The Biblical Law against Loans on Interest," *JNES* 30 (1971): 127–34, and discussion in Rodd, *Glimpses of a Strange Land*, 144–47.

76. Posner, "Theory of Primitive Society," 15; Morris Silver, *Prophets and Markets* (New York: Barnes and Noble, 1983), 236.

77. Aristotle, *Nicomachaen Ethics*, bk 5.1133a; *Politics*, bk 2.1258b; Plato, *Laws*, bk 5.742c.

78. Other passages that take a negative view of lending at interest include Ezek 18:5–9; Ps 15:5; Prov. 28:8.

79. Maloney, "Usury and Restrictions," 15.

80. Neufeld, "Prohibitions against Loans," 379.

81. See Driver and Miles, *Babylonian Laws*, 1:208–21.

82. Leon Epsztein, *Social Justice in the Ancient Near East and the People of the Bible* (London: SCM Press, 1986), 127.

83. Epsztein, *Social Justice*, 124; Driver and Miles, *Babylonian Laws*, 1:208–21.

84. Elsewhere in the Bible, however, there is evidence that this may have been practiced in ancient Israel. See Amos 2:6 and 2 Kgs. 4:1–7.

85. On this, see J. J. Finkelstein, "The Edict of Ammiṣaduqa: A New Text," *RA* 63 (1969): 45–64. The complete text is found in *ANET* (trans. J. J. Finkelstein), 526–28.

86. Another release edict that could effect debts and slaves, proclamations of *andurārum* are also frequently attested within the Mesopotamian literature. An overview of edicts of *mīšarum* and of *andurārum* is found in Hamilton, *Social Justice and Deuteronomy*, 48–56, and in Moshe Weinfeld, *Social Justice in Ancient Israel and in the Ancient Near East* (Jerusalem: Magnes Press, 1995), 75–96.

87. Herodotus, *Histories*, VI:59.

88. Weinfeld, *Social Justice*, 145–46.

89. Ibid., 77.

90. Michael Hudson highlights the political motivation of release edicts in more dramatic terms. In Mesopotamia, communally owned lands would be allocated to citizens in order to support their families. In return for rights to work the land and a sense of self-sufficiency, citizens owed the state military service or service in the execution of public works. If a citizen sold his land, or borrowed against it, his status as a citizen would be compromised, and he would no longer bear the same military and labor obligations to the palace. When large numbers of citizens lost their autonomy over the land due to debt burdens, it was the palace that ultimately suffered. Land redemption was a way of restoring the land to the citizens—and the

citizens' labors, in turn, back to the palace. See Michael Hudson, "Land Monopolization, Fiscal Crises and Clean State 'Jubilee' Proclamations in Antiquity," in *A Philosophy for a Fair Society*, ed. Michael Hudson, G. J. Miller and Kris Feder (London: Shepheard-Walwyn, 1994), 36–40.

91. Marvin L. Chaney, "Debt Easement in Israelite History and Tradition," in *The Bible and the Politics of Exegesis: Essays in Honor of Norman K. Gottwald on His Sixty-fifth Birthday*, ed. David Jobling et al. (Cleveland: Pilgrim, 1991), 130–31.

92. Plutarch, *Lives: Agis and Cleomenes*, 7:7, trans. Bernadotte Perrin (Cambridge, Mass.: Harvard University Press, 1913), 10:19. See similar sentiments in Roman times, in Cicero, *Duties*, 2, 78–80. See discussion in Weinfeld, *Social Justice*, 11.

93. Raymond Westbrook, "Jubilee Laws," *Israel Law Review* 6 (1971): 220.

94. Raymond Westbrook, "Social Justice in the Ancient Near East," in *Social Justice in the Ancient World*, ed. K. D. Irani and M. Silver (Westport, Conn.: Greenwood, 1995), 160.

95. William W. Hallo, "New Moons and Sabbaths: A Case Study in the Contrastive Approach," *HUCA* 48 (1977): 16.

96. *The Tale of Aqhat*, in *Corpus des Tablettes en Cunéiformes Alphabétiques*, ed. A. Herdner, Mission de Ras-Shamra (Paris: Geuthner, 1963), 17.1.16 (trans. H. L. Ginsburg, *ANET*, 150); *Epic of Gilgamesh*, Old Babylonian version 10.2.5–9 (trans. E. A. Speiser, *ANET*, 90); *Curse of Agade*, II:199, in *The Curse of Agade*, ed. J. S. Cooper (Baltimore: Johns Hopkins University Press, 1983), 59. On the notion of a calendrical week in the Hebrew Bible and in the ancient Near East, see Jeffery Tigay, "šābûʿă," in *Biblical Encyclopedia*, 8 vols. (Jerusalem: Bialik Institute, 1950–88), 7:468–79 (in Hebrew).

97. Different systems were adduced for breaking down the month into smaller units in Mesopotamia. See Hallo, "New Moons and Sabbaths," 12–13.

98. Ibid., 15; M. Tsevat, "The Basic Meaning of the Biblical Sabbath," *ZAW* 84 (1972): 448; Benjamin Uffenheimer, "Myth and Reality in Ancient Israel," in *The Origins and Diversity of Axial Age Civilizations*, ed. S. N. Eisenstadt (Albany: State University of New York Press, 1986), 150–53.

99. For a discussion of accounts of the historical background of the Jubilee year legislation, see Fager, *Land Tenure and the Biblical Jubilee*, 24–34.

100. "The Edict of Ammiṣaduqa," text C, ll. 27–34, trans. J. J. Finkelstein (*ANET*, 526).

101. While debt release is mentioned explicitly only here in this passage in Deut 15, some understand that debt release was implicit within the laws of the Jubilee year at Lev 25:41; Jacob Milgrom, *Leviticus: A Book of Ritual and Ethics* (Minneapolis: Fortress Press, 2004), 301, contra Tigay, *Deuteronomy*, 467. In this understanding, the motif of the royal decree of manumission is transformed, as it is now God who authorizes the freedom announced in Lev 25:41, giving the reason for the freedom: "For they are My slaves, whom I freed from the land of Egypt" (Lev 25:42).

102. Nelson, *Deuteronomy*, 192.

103. Paul, *Studies in the Book of the Covenant*, 100–101; Hamilton, *Social Justice and Deuteronomy*, 84. Indeed, the address formulation (such as "*you* shall . . ." or

"when *you* … ") that is endemic to all of the biblical codes is exceptional in the cuneiform juridical corpora. As noted earlier, this rhetorical device is characteristic of ancient Near Eastern treaty texts, underscoring the covenantal nature of the God-Israel relationship. The purpose of the biblical laws is to shape and form a society, and not merely to provide examples of case law. Hence the ideal of underscoring the I-Thou relationship established through these laws between God and Israel. See Paul, *Studies in the Book of the Covenant*, 123, and "Formulaic Patterns of Law in Israel and Mesopotamia," Paul, *Divrei Shalom: Collected Studies of Shalom M. Paul on the Bible and the Ancient Near East 1967–2005* (Leiden: Brill, 2005) 49–50.

104. Though if a kinsman redeemed the land, he would take control of it until the Jubilee year, at which point it reverted to the control of the original family member, thus ensuring that the redeemer would receive recompense for his expenditure.

105. Weinfeld, *Social Justice in Ancient Israel*, 95.

106. Inscription of Manishtushu, king of Akkad (twenty-second century B.C.E.), cited in ibid., 16; see further discussion of this text, 80. See a similar dispensation regarding Ishmedagan of Isin (1953–1935 B.C.E.), 82 and n. 27.

107. See texts in ibid., 80–81.

108. The notion of an extended territory being defined as sacred space is explored in Steven Grosby, "Sociological Implications of the Distinction between 'Locality' and 'Extended Territory' with Particular Reference to the Old Testament," *Social Compass* 40:2 (1993): 179–98, reprinted in Steven Grosby, *Biblical Ideas of Nationality: Ancient and Modern* (Winona Lake, Ind.: Eisenbrauns, 2002), 69–91.

109. Sara Japhet, "The Relationship between the Legal Corpora in the Pentateuch in Light of Manumission Laws," in *Studies in Bible 1986*, ed. S. Japhet, Scripta Hierosolymitana no. 31 (Jerusalem: Magnes, 1986) 85–86.

110. See Weinfeld, *Social Justice in Ancient Israel*, 16.

111. Ibid., 16.

112. On manumission in Mesopotamia, see Chirichigno, *Debt Slavery in Israel*, 55–96. As noted at the beginning of this chapter, it is highly uncertain to what degree the laws detailed in the Code of Hammurabi provide an accurate picture of Mesopotamian legal practice. Not a single Mesopotamian document attests that this law was ever enforced. See W. F. Leemans, "Quelques considerations à propos d'une etude récente du doit du Proche-Orient ancien," *Bibliotheca Orientalis* 48 (1991): 414–20.

113. As noted, there is great scholarly debate about the interrelationship among these three sections. In this study I will assume, as do the majority of scholars, that the three sections above all speak about Israelite debt servants. Bernard Levinson has argued convincingly that in Leviticus 25, the debtor does not actually become a servant, but rather adopts indenture ("Birth of the Lemma," 617–39). The distinction, however, does not change the overall picture of manumission laws of the Pentateuch when seen over against those of the ancient Near East. For a synchronic appraisal of the law of manumission in the three codes that seeks to identify the tensions as different facets of a broader educational agenda, see Mordechai Breuer, *Pirkei*

*Mo'adot*, 2 vols. (Jerusalem: Horeb, 1986) 1:16–21 (in Hebrew). Issues surrounding the manumission of debt servants are narrated in Jer 34:8–16 and Neh 5:1–13.

114. See *Midrash Shemot Rabbah* 30:15, and the commentary of the thirteenth-century rabbinic exegete Nachmanides (1194–1270) to Exod 21:2. See discussion in Levinson, "*The Right Chorale,*" 59 n. 23.

115. Chaney, "Debt Easement," 135.

116. In this vein, see the laws of torts, which address injury according to this hierarchy at several junctions, for example in secs. 197–99, 204–14, 215–17.

117. Eckart Otto, "Soziale Restitution und Vertragsrecht: *Mīšaru(m), (an) durāru(m), kirenzi parā tarnumar, šemitta und derôr* in Mesopotamia, Syrien, in der Hebräischen Bibel und die Frage des Rechtstransfers im Alten Orient," *RA* 92 (1998):140 n. 64; Levinson, "*The Right Chorale,*" 58. In several other laws governing the treatment of indentured servants in the Book of the Covenant, we find that these individuals are granted a much higher standing vis-à-vis free men than they are in the Code of Hammurabi, particularly in cases of assault and battery. See J. J. Finkelstein, *The Ox That Gored: Transactions of the American Philosophical Society Held at Philadelphia for Promoting Useful Knowledge 71:2* (1981) (Philadelphia: American Philosophical Society, 1981) 37, 40.

118. Chirichigno, *Debt Slavery in Ancient Israel*, 255.

119. For a discussion of the possible relationship between the appellation '*ibrî* 'and *h(_)apiru* slavery in the ancient Near East see Chirichigno, *Debt Slavery in Ancient Israel*, 201–6; Meir Sternberg, *Hebrews between Cultures: Group Portraits and National Literature* (Bloomington: Indiana University Press, 1998) 431–45; Paul, *Studies in the Book of the Covenant*, 47.

120. See exegesis in this vein in Benno Jacob, *Exodus: The Second Book of the Bible*, trans. Walter Jacob and Yaakov Elman (Hoboken, N.J.: Ktav, 1992) 611–12. In this section on manumission, I am assuming that all the pentateuchal laws on this issue speak only with regard to the Israelite debt servant. Indeed, while there are other servant laws in the Book of the Covenant, I assume that the term '*ebed*, on its own, refers to a foreign chattel-slave, not to an Israelite debt-servant. The Pentateuch denotes a member of the Israelite community who is a debt-servant through either the designation '*ibrî*—as it does in Exodus (21:2) and in Deuteronomy (15:12)—or the appellation "brother," as in Lev 25:35–44. Thus, the tort laws of Exod 21:20–21, 26–27, 32, the laws of coveting and of rest on the Sabbath (Exod 20:10, 17 = Deut 5:21), and the law of the fugitive slave (Deut 23:15–16) all refer exclusively to the foreign chattel-slave. Concerning tort law, and Sabbath law, the '*ebed 'ibrî* inhered the same status as any other member of the Israelite polity. See discussion of the issue and a review of opinion in Chirichigno, *Debt Slavery*, 182–84.

121. In Leviticus 25:39–43, the debtor is not made a formal servant but rather assumes the status of a resident hireling, such that all of his wages pay off his debt. Because the impoverished Israelite is not "enslaved," there is no provision for manumission by a redeemer. When the debtor, however, has had to sell himself to a foreigner, the redeemer is obligated to buy back the debtor's liberty (Lev 25:47–55).

122. This economic analysis of debt-servitude in the Bible is taken from Silver, *Prophets and Markets*, 72. It is interesting that according to CH 117, the debtor goes

out after three years, whereas according to Exod 21:2 and Deut 15:12, the servant works for six years prior to release. According to the economic implications of extended servitude laid bare here, it is possible to see the longer term of service in the biblical passages as serving the interests of the debtor.

123. See Jean-Jacque Rousseau, "Discourse on Inequality," trans. G. D. H. Cole, in Rousseau, *Social Contract and Discourses* (1913; reprint, London: Phoenix, 1990), 84.

124. Silver, *Prophets and Markets*, 242.

125. Indeed, the eighth century B.C.E. prophet Amos addresses himself precisely to a society that has fallen out of kilter along these lines. See Amos 2:6–8; 4:1; 8:4–6. See discussion of the implications of biblical ethics for a globalized economy in Jonathan Sacks, *The Dignity of Difference: How to Avoid the Clash of Civilizations* (London: Continuum, 2003), 151–52.

126. See discussion in Derek Heater, *A Brief History of Citizenship* (New York: New York University Press, 2004), 206.

127. Francis Fukuyama, *Trust: The Social Virtues and the Creation of Prosperity* (London: Hamish Hamilton, 1995), 11.

CHAPTER 4

1. Elizabeth L. Eisenstein, *The Printing Press as an Agent of Change: Communications and Cultural Transformation in Early Modern Europe*, 2 vols. (Cambridge: Cambridge University Press, 1979), 1:303–4.

2. Ibid., 1:335.

3. Mogens Trolle Larsen, introduction to *Literacy and Society*, ed. K. Schousboe and M. T. Larsen (Copenhagen: Akademisk Forlag, 1989), 7.

4. See discussion in Larsen, introduction, 9–10, and a broader discussion of the topic in Brian Street, *Literacy in Theory and Practice* (Cambridge: Cambridge University Press, 1984).

5. Eisenstein, *Printing Press*, 1:310.

6. Ibid., 1:333.

7. The following discussion builds on initial avenues of comparison between the role of the alphabet in ancient Israel and the role of the printing press in early modern Europe in Jonathan Sacks, *The Dignity of Difference: How to Avoid the Clash of Civilizations* (London: Continuum, 2002), 125–41.

8. On the general topic, see David Carr, *Writing on the Tablet of the Heart: Origins of Scripture and Literature* (Oxford: Oxford University Press, 2005).

9. Ibid., 19. Loosely, one may think of a literary canon, though some object to the use of the term with reference to Mesopotamian culture. See Victor Hurowitz, "Canon and Canonization in Mesopotamia," in *Proceedings of the Twelfth World Congress of Jewish Studies: Division A—The Bible and Its World*, ed. Ron Margolin (Jerusalem: World Union of Jewish Studies, 1997), 1–12; William W. Hallo, "The Concept of Canonicity in Cuneiform and Biblical Literature: A Comparative Appraisal," in *The Biblical Canon in Comparative Perspective*, ed. K. L. Younger, W. W. Hallo, and B. F. Batto (Lewiston, N.Y.: Edwin Mellen, 1991), 1–19.

10. See translation in *ANET*, 60–72.

11. A. Leo Oppenheim, *Ancient Mesopotamia: Portrait of a Dead Civilization* (Chicago: University of Chicago Press, 1964), 26.

12. Aaron Demsky, "Literacy," in *Oxford Encyclopedia of Archaeology in the Ancient Near East,* ed. Eric M. Meyers, 3 vols. (New York: Oxford University Press, 1997), 3:367–68.

13. Cited as "Shulgi Hymn E," in J. Klein, *The Royal Hymns of Shulgi King of Ur: Man's Quest for Immortal Fame,* Transactions of the American Philosophical Society Held at Philadelphia for Promoting Useful Knowledge, vol. 71, pt. 7 (Philadelphia: American Philosophical Society, 1981), 18–21. See discussion in Victor Hurowitz, "Spanning the Generations: Aspects of Oral and Written Transmission in the Bible and Ancient Mesopotamia," in *Freedom and Responsibility,* ed. R. M. Geffen and M. B. Edelman (New York: Ktav, 1999), 13.

14. "The Epic of Erra and Ishum," tablet V 48–56, trans. in Benjamin R. Foster, *Before the Muses: An Anthology of Akkadian Literature* (Bethesda, Md.: CDL Press, 1993), 804.

15. Victor Hurowitz ("Spanning the Generations," 21–25) is of the opinion that in fact, the transmission of long duration texts was intended for the masses as well. He derives this from the following passage from the Erra epic:

"Let this poem stand forever, let it endure till eternity,
"Let all lands hear it and praise my valor,
"Let all inhabitants witness and extol my name." (Erra Tablet V 58–61)

Hurowitz also cites the prologue of the Code of Hammurabi, which states, "he instructed me to lead the people justly and teach them proper conduct." The archeological record, however, has produced no record of scribes or other teachers involved in such a process of mass instruction, which surely would have been a regular and monumental undertaking. It seems that when such compositions speak of fathers instructing sons, or of "all lands" hearing and praising, or "all inhabitants" extolling, the all-inclusive discourse refers to those who count—the members of the ruling class. One does find in Neo-Assyrian materials letters, for example, that of Sargon II (eighth century B.C.E.), that would be read to the public in a ceremony of a communal nature. But this was for immediate consumption, not retention and transmission among the populace from one generation to the next. See A. Leo Oppenheim, "The City of Assur in 714 BC," *JNES* 19 (1960): 133–47. Peter Machinist questions whether such ceremonies, in fact, constituted any form of education at all. See Peter Machinist, "Assyrians on Assyria in the First Millennium BC," in *Anfänge politischen Denkens in der Antike: Die nahöstlichen Kulturen und die Griechen,* ed. Kurt Raaflaub and Elisabeth Müller-Luckner (Munich: Oldenbourg, 1993), 102.

16. Machinist, "Assyrians on Assyria," 101

17. William Schniedewind, *How the Bible Became a Book* (Cambridge: Cambridge University Press, 2004), 37. See further Irene Winter, "Royal Rhetoric and the Development of Historical Narrative in Neo-Assyrian Reliefs," *Studies in Visual Communication* 7 (1981): 12–13; Jacob Klein, "On Writing Monumental Inscriptions in the Ur III Scribal Curriculum," *RA* 80 (1986): 1, 6–7; Joan Goodnick Westenholz, "Thoughts on Esoteric Knowledge and Secret Lore," in *Intellectual Life of*

*the Ancient Near East,* ed. Jirí Prosecky, Comple Rendu, Recontre Assyriologique Internationale 43 (Prague: Oriental Institute, 1998), 456.

18. H. te Velde, "Scribes and Literacy in Ancient Egypt" in *Scripta Signa Vocis: Studies about Scripts, Scriptures and Languages in the Near East presented to J. H. Hospers,* ed. H. L. J. Vanstiphout et al. (Groningen: Forsten, 1986), 253.

19. Miriam Lichtheim, *Ancient Egyptian Literature,* 3 vols. (Berkeley: University of California Press, 1976) 1:155. Redford notes that the protectiveness with which spells were guarded would dictate that there would be an incentive not to train an excess of lector priests. An excess of individuals trained in the science, thereby making it more widely available, would by necessity diminish its mystique. See Donald B. Redford, "Scribe and Speaker," in *Writings and Speech in Israelite and Ancient Near Eastern Prophecy,* ed. Ehud Ben Zvi and Michael H. Floyd, SBL Symposium Series no. 10 (Atlanta: Society of Biblical Literature, 2000), 154, n. 33.

20. John Baines, "Literacy and Ancient Egyptian Society," *Man* 18 (1983): 584.

21. "Dua-Khety or the Satire on the Trades," trans. Miriam Lichtheim, in *COS,* 1.48:122–25.

22. C. J. Eyre, "Is Egyptian Historical Literature 'Historical' or 'Literary'?" in *Ancient Egyptian Literature: History and Forms,* ed. A. Loprieno, Probleme der Ägyptologie no. 10 (Leiden: Brill, 1996), 426–27.

23. Other episodes during the monarchic period where prophecies are written down for the purpose of public consumption are found in Jer 29:1–23 and 36:2–3 (see also Isa 8:1; Jer 30:2). The Book of Chronicles records (2 Chr 17:7–9) that the Judean King Jehoshaphat undertook a movement of religious revival through the agency of "officers" and "Levites" who "taught in the province of Judea, and with them was the Book of the Law of God, and they traversed all the cities of Judea and instructed the people." As with much of the material found in Chronicles but not in Samuel-Kings, some scholars regard such material as historically reliable while others see it as originating with the Chronicler himself, sometime after the return of Ezra.

24. For discussion of the parameters of the Book of the Covenant see James W. Watts, *Reading Law: The Rhetorical Shaping of the Pentateuch* (Sheffield, England: Sheffield Academic Press, 1999), 16.

25. Moshe Greenberg, *Studies in the Bible and Jewish Thought* (Philadelphia: Jewish Publication Society, 1995), 52–54.

26. Carr, *Writing on the Tablet of the Heart,* 172.

27. Jack Goody, *The Logic of Writing and the Organization of Society* (Cambridge: Cambridge University Press, 1986), 2.

28. Sean Warner, "The Alphabet: An Innovation and Its Diffusion," *VT* 30 (1980): 87.

29. Rosalind Thomas, *Literacy and Orality in Ancient Greece* (Cambridge: Cambridge University Press, 1992), 2.

30. Michael T. Clanchy, "Reading the Signs at Durham Cathedral," in Schousboe and Larsen, *Literacy and Society,* 141.

31. Michael T. Clanchy, *From Memory to Written Record: England 1066–1307* (1979; London: Edward Arnold, 1993) 219.

32. Ibid., 202.

33. Ibid., 214–20.

34. Christopher Eyre and John Baines, "Interactions between Orality and Literacy in Ancient Egypt," in Schousboe and Larsen, *Literacy and Society*, 109.

35. See Daniel Boyarin, "Placing Reading: Ancient Israel and Medieval Europe," in *The Ethnography of Reading*, ed. Jonathan Boyarin (Berkeley: University of California Press, 1993), 12–16; Jeffrey Tigay, *Deuteronomy* (Philadelphia: Jewish Publication Society, 1996), 169; Schniedewind, *How the Bible Became a Book*, 48. This finding underscores the emerging consensus within scholarship that the tendency to see a society as either literate or oral is oversimple and misleading. See Thomas, *Literacy and Orality*, 4. On the subtle interplay between literacy and orality see further Ruth Finnegan, *Literacy and Orality: Studies in the Technology of Communication* (Oxford: Basil Blackwell, 1988).

36. Isaac Rabinowitz, *A Witness Forever: Ancient Israel's Perception of Literature and the Resultant Hebrew Bible* (Bethesda, Md.: CDL Press, 1993), 27. One might suggest that the king, according to Deut 17:19, is enjoined to read to himself. The verse, however, may imply that he needs to recite the Torah aloud. Alternatively, as Ben-Zvi suggests, *qār'ā* may imply that it is read on his behalf, but not necessarily by him, as is seen concerning the verb *katab*, where one is considered to have written, even if someone else incises the words on his behalf. See Ehud Ben-Zvi, "Introduction: Setting an Agenda," in Ben-Zvi and Floyd, *Writings and Speech in Israelite and Ancient Near Eastern Prophecy*, 7.

37. Rabinowitz, *A Witness Forever*, 31.

38. Carr, *Writing on the Tablet of the Heart*, 13, 116.

39. For extensive bibliography on the relation between orality and textuality see ibid., 7 n. 15.

40. Ibid., 159.

41. Edward L. Greenstein, "Some Developments in the Study of Language and Some Implications for Interpreting Ancient Texts and Cultures," in *Semitic Linguistics: The State of the Art at the Turn of the Twenty-First Century*, ed. Shlomo Izre'el, Israel Oriental Studies 20 (Winona Lake, Ind.: Eisenbrauns, 2002), 462; Hurowitz, "Spanning the Generations," 11.

42. Michael H. Floyd, " 'Write the Revelation (Hab 2:2): Re-imagining the Cultural History of Prophecy," in Ben-Zvi and Floyd, *Writings and Speech in Israelite and Ancient Near Eastern Prophecy*, 137.

43. See the assessment in Schniedewind, *How the Bible Became a Book*, 48–63. Some scholars, though, conclude from the evidence that greater widespread literacy during the early Iron Age cannot be ruled out. See Richard S. Hess, "Literacy in Iron Age Israel," in *Windows into Old Testament History*, ed. V. Philip Long (Grand Rapids, Mich.: Eerdmans, 2002) 82–95.

44. References to use of texts in legal, annalistic, letter-writing, and other contexts are widespread (e.g. Deut 24:1–4; see Jer 32:10–12; Isa 50:1) See Carr, *Writing on the Tablet of the Heart*, 116–24.

45. Floyd, " 'Write the Revelation," 136.

46. Alan R. Millard, "An Assessment of the Evidence for Writing in Ancient Israel," in *Biblical Archaeology Today: Proceedings of the International Congress on*

*Biblical Archaeology, Jerusalem, April 1984,* ed. Janet Amitai (Jerusalem: Israel Academy of Sciences and Humanity, 1985), 308, and in agreement with him, Ian M. Young, "Israelite Literacy: Interpreting the Evidence," *VT* 48 (1998): 241 n. 12. There is great debate about the extent of literacy in ancient Israel; I have adopted here the consensus emerging today, that those who could read were in the minority, and were probably trained scribes. On the extent of literacy within ancient Israel see Menahem Haran, "On the Diffusion of Literacy and Schools in Ancient Israel," in *Congress Volume 1986,* ed. J. A. Emerton, VTS no. 40 (Leiden: Brill, 1988), 81–95, for a more minimalist interpretation of evidence, and Millard, "An Assessment of the Evidence," 301–12, for a more maximalist one. Some scholars, most notably Lemaire, *Les Écoles et la Formation de la Bible Dans L'Ancien Israël* (Fribourg: Editions Universitaires, 1981), have argued for the existence of a system of schools in ancient Israel, though the issue has been hotly contested. See David W. Jamieson-Drake, *Scribes and Schools in Monarchic Judah: A Socio- Archeological Approach* (Sheffield, England: Almond Press, 1991), and James L. Crenshaw, *Education in Ancient Israel: Across the Deadening Silence* (New York: Doubleday, 1998), 4 n. 6, for an exhaustive bibliography on the subject, as well as Ben-Zvi, "Introduction: Setting an Agenda," 5, n. 8.

47. Carr, *Writing on the Tablet of the Heart,* 132–33.

48. In one postexilic narrative, the Levites assume a preeminent role in promulgating the texts and its lessons to the wider populace (Neh 8:7–8): "Also Jeshua, Bani, Sherebiah, Jamin, Akkub, Shabbethai, Hodiah, Maaseiah, Kelita, Azariah, Jozabad, Hanan, Pelaiah, the Levites, helped the people to understand the law, while the people remained in their places. So they read from the book, from the law of God, with interpretation. They gave the sense, so that the people understood the reading."

49. I have adopted here the translation of Joachim Schaper, "Exilic and Post-Exilic Prophecy and the Orality/Literacy Problem," *VT* 55: 3 (2005): 333, where the participle *qōr'ē* is taken to refer to a town crier who publicly exclaims the text contained on the tablets. See further Joachim Schaper, "The 'Publication' of Legal Texts in Ancient Judah," in *The Pentateuch as Torah: New Models for Understanding Its Promulgation and Acceptance,* ed. Gary N. Knoppers and Bernard M. Levinson (Winona Lake, Ind.: Eisenbrauns, 2007), 225–36.

50. Michael H. Floyd, "Prophecy and Writing in Habakkuk 2:1–5," *ZAW* 105 (1993): 462–81, esp. 473, 477.

51. See Jer 8:8, an admittedly difficult verse, where it is implied that the enemies of the prophet utilize writing to spread their interpretation of the law of the Lord.

52. Yehezkel Kaufmann, *The Religion of Israel,* trans. Moshe Greenberg (London: Allen & Unwin, 1961), 355–61. Kaufmann notes (361) that we often find that significant speech is then committed to writing. God first speaks the Decalogue and only later sets it down on the tablets. Moses rehearses the laws to the people, then writes them in a book (Exod 24:3–8). Samuel proclaims the law of the king to the people and then composes it in writing (1 Sam 8:9; 10:25). Ezekiel is charged first to tell Israel the plan of the temple, and afterward to write it in their sight (Ezek 43:11). See also the discussion in Floyd, "Prophecy and Writing," 467.

53. Machinist, "Assyrians on Assyria," 101.

54. Schniedewind, *How the Bible Became a Book*, 36.

55. Carr, *Writing on the Tablet of the Heart*, 81.

56. Ibid., 6.

57. See discussion in Schniedewind, *How the Bible Became a Book*, 38; Seth L. Sanders, "What Was the Alphabet For? The Rise of Written Vernacular and the Making of Israelite National Literature," *Maarav* 11 (2004): 31.

58. Sanders, "What Was the Alphabet For," 44.

59. Schaper, "Exilic and Post-Exilic Prophecy," 335.

60. The overly glorious case for the alphabet in this vein, within biblical studies, is found in Frank Moore Cross, "The Invention and Development of the Alphabet," in *The Origins of Writing*, ed. Wayne M. Senner (Lincoln: University of Nebraska Press, 1990), 77–90. See discussion of this issue in Sanders, "What Was the Alphabet For," 34–35.

61. Alan K. Bowman and Greg Woolf, "Literacy and Power in the Ancient World," in *Literacy and Power in the Ancient World*, ed. Alan K. Bowman and Greg Woolf (Cambridge: Cambridge University Press, 1994), 8.

62. Claude Lévi-Strauss, *Tristes Tropiques*, trans. J. and D. Weightman (New York: Atheneum, 1974), 299.

63. Eisenstein, *Printing Press*, 1:318.

64. See Benedict Anderson, *Imagined Communities: Reflections on the Origin and Spread of Nationalism* (1983; reprint, London: Verso, 1991), and Sanders, "What Was the Alphabet For," 31.

65. Demsky, "Literacy," 364–65. For more on the development of the alphabet see Alan R. Millard, "The Infancy of the Alphabet," *World Archaeology* 17 (1986): 390–98; Godfrey R. Driver, *Semitic Writing: From Pictograph to Alphabet* (1948; reprint, London: Oxford University Press, 1976), and Joseph Naveh, *An Early History of the Alphabet* (Jerusalem: Magnes Press, 1982).

66. Sanders, "What Was the Alphabet For," 33.

67. Ibid., 46.

68. Ibid., 27.

69. Ibid., 27.

70. See "The Ritual for National Unity," trans. in Dennis Pardee, *Ritual and Cult at Ugarit* (Atlanta: Society of Biblical Literature, 2002), 77–83.

71. Sanders, "What Was the Alphabet For," 54.

72. *Geneva Study Bible of 1599*, comment to Gen 17:23.

73. Eisenstein, *Printing Press*, 1:424.

74. See Karel van der Toorn, *Family Religion in Babylonia, Syria and Israel: Continuity and Change in the Forms of Religious Life*, Studies in the History and Culture of the Ancient Near East no. 7 (Leiden: Brill, 1996), 2.

75. Carr, *Writing on the Tablet of the Heart*, 130.

76. Some take this to refer to the two previous verses, Deut 6:4–5. Others favor seeing this as a reference to the Decalogue, while others still prefer a broader interpretation that it refers to the whole of the Torah taught at Moab. See discussion in Jean-Pierre Sonnet, *The Book within the Book: Writing in Deuteronomy* (Leiden: Brill, 1997) 52–55; Carr, *Writing on the Tablet of the Heart*, 135.

77. As understood by Moshe Weinfeld, *Deuteronomy 1–11*, AB no. 5 (New York: Doubleday, 1991), 342.

78. E.g. Millard, "An Assessment," 308.

79. Carr, *Writing on the Tablet of the Heart*, 6.

80. See discussion in van der Toorn, *Family Religion in Babylonia, Syria and Israel*, 361.

81. See in less explicit fashion Exod 13:16; Benno Jacob, *The Second Book of the Bible: Exodus*, trans. Walter Jacob (New York: Ktav, 1992), 368.

82. Cited in Julian Boyd, "These Precious Monuments of…Our History," *American Archivist* 22:2 (1959): 175–76.

83. Eisenstein, *Printing Press*, 1:116.

84. Jack Goody and Ian Watt, "The Consequences of Literacy," in *Literacy in Traditional Societies*, ed. Jack Goody (Cambridge: Cambridge University Press, 1968) 29.

85. Lévi-Strauss, *Tristes Tropiques*, 298. See in similar terms comments by Goody and Watt ("Consequences of Literacy," 34): "In non-literate societies, the individual has little perception of the past except in terms of the present, whereas the annals of a literate society cannot but enforce a more objective recognition of the distinction between what was and what is."

86. For a survey of opinions about the content of "the Book of the Torah" referred to in Deut 31:24–25, see Sonnet, *Book within the Book*, 156–57.

87. Nahmanides, commentary to Genesis, 1:1. For English translation see Charles B. Chavel, ed., *Ramban (Nachmanides): Commentary on the Torah—Genesis* (New York: Shilo, 1971) 18–20.

88. Goody, *Logic of Writing*, 2.

89. On the importance of texts in Ezra-Nehemiah, see Tamara Cohn-Eskenazi, *In an Age of Prose* (Atlanta: Scholars Press, 1988).

90. A distinct emphasis on the importance of observing the injunction against idolatry (the Second Commandment) is found in Calvin's *Institutes of the Christian Religion* (1536), a comprehensive and systematic manual of Protestant dogmatic theology, the single most important manual produced during the Reformation.

91. Carlos M. V. Eire, *The War against the Idols: The Reformation of Worship from Erasmus to Calvin* (Cambridge: Cambridge University Press, 1986), 315–17; Eisenstein, *Printing Press*, 1:366.

92. Eisenstein, *Printing Press*, 1:67.

93. The representational role of the written tablets was first formulated in slightly different terms by Aaron Demsky, "Writing in Ancient Israel," pt. 1, "The Biblical Period," in *Mikra: Text, Translation, Reading and Interpretation of the Hebrew Bible in Ancient Judaism and Early Christianity*, ed. M. J. Mulder (Assen, Netherlands: Van Gorcum, 1988), 18–19, and later in Susan Niditch, *Oral World and Written Word: Ancient Israelite Literature* (London: SPCK, 1996), 80. For all of their aura and mystique, the Tablets of the Covenant, it should be pointed out, quickly fall out of the focus of biblical theology. Outside of the pentateuchal narratives of the receipt of the tablets and their installation within the Ark of the Covenant, there is only a single reference to them throughout the rest of the Hebrew Bible (1 Kgs 8:9). They are never read from

or displayed; indeed, they go unmentioned even when the Ark is captured and opened by the Philistines and subsequently returned to Israel (1 Sam 4–6).

94. Josephus Flavius, *Contra Apion*, 1.42–44, in *Josephus*, trans. H. S. J. Thackeray, 9 vols. (London: Heineman, 1926) 1:179–81. See Josephus's comments in a similar vein in Contra Apion 2:171–83. For discussion see M. D. Goodman, "Texts, Scribes and Power in Roman Judaea," in Bauman and Woolf, *Literacy and Power in the Ancient World,* 99–108.

95. William Harris, *Ancient Literacy* (Cambridge, Mass.: Harvard University Press, 1989), viii; William D. Whitt, "The Story of the Semitic Alphabet," in *CANE,* 4:2390; Thomas, *Literacy and Orality,* 58.

96. Harris, *Ancient Literacy,* 46.

97. Thomas, *Literacy and Orality,* 58.

98. Ibid., 66–72.

99. Ibid., 12; Harris, *Ancient Literacy,* 49

100. Harris, *Ancient Literacy,* 37.

101. Thomas, *Literacy and Orality,* 8.

102. Harris, *Ancient Literacy,* 62.

103. Ibid., 35; Thomas, *Literacy and Orality,* 11.

104. Thomas, *Literacy and Orality,* 145. See now the wide-ranging comparison of the promulgation of written law in Athens and in postexilic Judah in Gary N. Knoppers and Paul B. Harvey Jr., "The Pentateuch in Ancient Mediterranean Context: The Publication of Local Law Codes," in Knoppers and Levinson, *Pentateuch as Torah,* 105–44. See also on the status of written law in ancient Greece, Anselm C. Hagedorn, *Between Moses and Plato: Individual and Society in Deuteronomy and Ancient Greek Law,* FRLANT no. 204 (Göttingen: Vanderhoeck & Ruprecht, 2004), 62–89.

105. Thomas, *Literacy and Orality,* 144.

106. Ibid., 130. See Aristotle, *Politics,* bk 3.1286a 9–17; 1287b 5–8; 2.1270b 28; Euripides, *Suppliants,* 433.

107. Thomas, *Literacy and Orality,* 92.

108. Plato, *Phaedrus,* 275d–276d. This translation is based on the 1914 translation of Harold North Fowler, http://plato.evansville.edu/texts/fowler/phaedrus14.htm.

109. Graeme Nicholson, *Plato's Phaedrus: The Philosophy of Love* (West Lafayette, Ind.: Purdue University Press, 1999), 78; for a broad discussion of the status of writing in fifth- and fourth-century Athens, see 75–88; and W. K. C. Guthrie, *A History of Greek Philosophy,* 4 vols. (Cambridge: Cambridge University Press, 1969–86), 4:56–66.

110. Plato, *Phaedrus,* 277e. This translation is based on the Fowler translation, http://plato.evansville.edu/texts/fowler/phaedrus15.htm.


CHAPTER 5

1. Some broad lines of comparison between the rise of the novel and the rise of biblical narrative are suggested in Robert S. Kawashima, *Biblical Narrative and the Death of the Rhapsode* (Bloomington, Ind.: Indiana University Press, 2004), 192.

2. John Richetti, introduction to *The Cambridge Companion to the Eighteenth-Century Novel*, ed. John Richetti (Cambridge: Cambridge University Press, 1996), 1.

3. Ian Watt, *The Rise of the Novel* (Berkeley: University of California Press, 1967), 14.

4. Watt, *Rise of the Novel*, 12.

5. Richetti, introduction, 4.

6. Watt, *Rise of the Novel*, 23.

7. Ibid., 13.

8. Ibid., 18.

9. Ibid., 24.

10. Ibid., 23.

11. Michael McKeon, *The Origins of the English Novel, 1600–1740* (Baltimore: Johns Hopkins University Press, 1987), 2; Watt, *Rise of the Novel*, 27.

12. For an overview of the various uses of the term *myth* generally and within biblical studies particularly, see Richard G. Walsh, *Mapping Myths of Biblical Interpretation* (Sheffield, England: Sheffield Academic Press, 2001).

13. For an overview of ancient Near Eastern myth, see W. G. Lambert, "Myth and Mythmaking in Sumer and Akkad," in *CANE*, 3:1825–35.

14. Edward L. Greenstein, "The God of Israel and the Gods of Canaan: How Different Were They?" *Proceedings of the World Congress of Jewish Studies* 12 (1999): A:56*.

15. John Van Seters, "The Historiography of the Ancient Near East," in *CANE*, 4:2433–44.

16. Ibid., 2434.

17. See A. Leo Oppenheim, "The City of Assur in 714 BC," *JNES* 19 (1960): 133–47.

18. For an overview and several articles detailing these comparisons, see Richard S. Hess and David Toshio Tsumura, eds., *I Studied Inscriptions from before the Flood*, Sources for Biblical and Theological Study no. 4 (Winona Lake, Ind.: Eisenbrauns, 1994).

19. See Victor H. Matthews and Don C. Benjamin, eds., *Old Testament Parallels: Laws and Stories from the Ancient Near East* (1991; reprint, New York: Paulist Press, 1997), 129–33; Gary A. Rendsburg, "Notes on Genesis xxxv," *VT* 34 (1984): 361–66.

20. Matthews and Benjamin, *Old Testament Parallels*, 66–81; Greenstein, "God of Israel and the Gods of Canaan," 56*-57*.

21. Simon B. Parker, *Stories in Scripture and Inscription: Comparative Studies on Narrative in Northwest Semitic Inscriptions and the Hebrew Bible* (New York: Oxford University Press, 1997), 43–74.

22. For overview see Bill T. Arnold and Bryan E. Beyer, *Readings from the Ancient Near East: Primary Sources for Old Testament Study* (Grand Rapids, Mich.: Baker Academic, 2002), 150–59.

23. In the historical books of Judges, Samuel, and Kings, however, the trend is reversed, and the stories about the people seem subordinated to the tales about Israel's leaders.

24. Van Seters, "Historiography of the Ancient Near East," 2433.

25. See Norman Gottwald, *The Politics of Ancient Israel* (Louisville, Ky.: Westminster John Knox, 2001), 152, 159.

26. Tikva Frymer-Kensky, *In the Wake of the Goddesses: Women, Culture and the Biblical Transformation of Pagan Myth* (New York: Free Press, 1992), 86. See also H. and H. A. Frankfort, *The Intellectual Adventure of Ancient Man: An Essay on Speculative Thought in the Ancient Near East* (Chicago: University of Chicago Press, 1946), 7; Benjamin Uffenheimer, "Myth and Reality in Ancient Israel," in *The Origins and Diversity of Axial Age Civilizations*, ed. S. N. Eisenstadt (Albany: State University of New York Press, 1986), 140–42.

27. Frymer-Kensky, *In the Wake of the Goddesses*, 86, 91.

28. See discussion of the epic "Enki and the World Order," in Kawashima, *Biblical Narrative*, 200.

29. Henri Frankfort, *Kingship and the Gods: A Study of Ancient Near Eastern Religion as the Integration of Society and Nature* (Chicago: University of Chicago Press, 1948), 343.

30. Frymer-Kensky, *In the Wake of the Goddesses*, 103.

31. Ibid., 107.

32. On the role of the divine in human affairs in Mesopotamia see Bertil Albrektson, *History and the Gods: An Essay on the Idea of Historical Events as Divine Manifestations in the Ancient Near East and Israel* (Lund: CWK Gleerup, 1967).

33. Walther Eichrodt, *Man in the Old Testament*, trans. K. and R. Gregor Smith (London: SCM Press, 1951), 9; Frankfort and Frankfort, *Intellectual Adventure of Ancient Man*, 371.

34. Meir Sternberg, *The Poetics of Biblical Narrative: Ideological Literature and the Drama of Reading* (Bloomington, Ind.: Indiana University Press, 1985), 38; David Damrosch, *The Narrative Covenant* (San Francisco: Harper & Row, 1987), 40.

35. Damrosch, *Narrative Covenant*, 123; Stephen A. Geller, *Sacred Enigmas: Literary Religion in the Hebrew Bible* (London: Routledge, 1996), 311.

36. See Peter Machinist, "On Self-Consciousness in Mesopotamia," in Eisenstadt, *Origins and Diversity of Axial Age Civilizations*, 194.

37. For the text of the Gilgamesh Epic (trans. E. A. Speiser), see *ANET,* 72–99, and for a summary and overview of interpretation, see William Moran, "The Gilgamesh Epic: A Masterpiece from Ancient Mesopotamia," in *CANE,* 4:2327–36.

38. For text of the Aqhat epic, see M. D. Coogan, *Stories from Ancient Canaan* (Louisville, Ky.: Westminster, 1978), 32–47, and for the text of Keret, see 58–74.

39. See discussion in S. A. Geller, "The God of the Covenant," in *One God or Many? Concepts of Divinity in the Ancient World*, ed. Barbara Nevling Porter (Chebeague, Me.: Casco Bay Assyriological Institute, 2000), 310–12. For an overview to the scholarship concerning the rise of biblical narrative from its ancient Near Eastern precursors, see Kawashima, *Biblical Narrative and the Death of the Rhapsode*, 1–8. While biblical narrative advances the art of characterization, it may properly be seen to have its roots in the poetics that govern Ugaritic epic. For an overview of standard rhetorical tools of biblical narrative that are already exhibited in Ugaritic literature, see Edward L. Greenstein, "On the Genesis of Biblical Prose Narrative," *Prooftexts* 8 (1988): 347–54, and in greater detail in his "The Relationship between

Biblical Narrative and Ancient Canaanite Narrative," in *Essays on Hebrew Literature in Honor of Avraham Holtz*, ed. Zvia Ben-Yosef Ginor (New York: Jewish Theological Seminary of America, 2003), 9–31 (in Hebrew).

40. Brian Lewis, *The Sargon Legend: A Study of the Akkadian Text and the Tale of the Hero Who Was Exposed at Birth* (Cambridge, Mass.: ASOR, 1980), 91–101; B. R. Foster, *From Distant Days: Myths, Tales and Poetry of Ancient Mesopotamia* (Bethesda, Md.: CDL Press, 1995), 165. On the possibility of Sargon II commissioning the composition, see Benjamin R. Foster, "The Birth Legend of Sargon of Akkad," in *COS*, 1.133:461.

41. Lewis, *Sargon Legend*, 125.

42. Ibid., 109.

43. Foster, "Birth Legend of Sargon," in *COS*, 1:461.

44. William H. C. Propp, *Exodus 1–18*, AB no. 2 (New York: Doubleday, 1998), 155. Propp also notes that each account resonates with the Flood traditions of its respective culture. This is evident in the narrative of Exodus 2, where the term for basket, *tēbâ*, is found elsewhere, only in the context of the flood narrative of Gen 6–9.

45. M. Cogan, "A Technical Term for Exposure," *JNES* 27 (1968): 133–35. See also Brevard S. Childs, "The Birth of Moses," *JBL* 84 (1965): 115–18; Moshe Greenberg, *Understanding Exodus* (New York: Melton Research Center, 1969), 198–99; Benno Jacob, "The Childhood and Youth of Moses, the Messenger of God," in *Essays in Honour of J. H. Hertz*, ed. I. Epstein et al. (London: Edward Goldston, 1944), 245.

46. See discussion in Lewis, *Sargon Legend*, 149.

47. Ibid., 152–95.

48. Propp, *Exodus 1–18*, 155.

49. Lewis, *Sargon Legend*, 211–215.

50. Donald B. Redford, "The Literary Motif of the Exposed Child," *Numen* 14 (1967): 225.

51. See discussion in Propp, *Exodus 1–18*, 158; Otto Rank, *The Myth of the Birth of the Hero*, trans. Gregory C. Richter (New York: Brunner, 1952), 4. See, generally, Susan Niditch, *Folklore and the Hebrew Bible* (Minneapolis: Fortress Press, 1993).

52. It is not my purpose here to discuss the historicity of either tale, as we lack the empirical finds to make such assessments on scientific footing. It should also be pointed out that when we discuss the rhetorical aspects of "tales" or "stories," we in no way impugn their status as the possible bearers of historical accuracy. Fact may be crafted in literary fashion, and fiction may be cast as a newspaper article. On this point see Sternberg, *Poetics of Biblical Narrative*, 23–34. The discussion here pertains to the poetics of the accounts before us and to the way they communicate their message.

53. See discussion in Propp, *Exodus 1–18*, 155–56.

54. William W. Hallo, *The Book of the People*, Brown Judaica Series no. 225 (Atlanta: Scholars Press, 1991), 130–32.

55. Redford, "Literary Motif of the Exposed Child," 211.

56. Lewis, *Sargon Legend*, 267.

57. George W. Coats, *Exodus 1–18* (Grand Rapids, Mich.: Eerdmans, 1999), 27. In the collection of *ana ittišu* documents, one Assyrian text (III, col. 3, ll. 38–44)

describes the adoption of an abandoned child found on a river during the first half of the eleventh century B.C.E. See discussion in Shemaryahu Talmon, ed., *Shemot* (Tel-Aviv: Davidzon Etti, 1993), 29 (in Hebrew).

58. A rare example of internal thought and introspection in Mesopotamian literature is found in the Akkadian story of King Idrimi of Alalakh, II:10–12. See discussion in Edward L. Greenstein, "Autobiographies in Ancient Western Asia," in *CANE*, 4:2426–28. That this story is thoroughly atypical of Mesopotamian literature was already noticed by A. Leo Oppenheim, review of *The Statue of Idri-mi* by Sidney Smith, *JNES* 14 (1955): 199–200.

59. Greenstein, "Autobiographies in Ancient Western Asia," 2431. See also Miriam Lichtheim, *Ancient Egyptian Autobiography Chiefly of the Middle Kingdom: A Study and an Anthology* (Freiburg, Germany: Universitatsverlag, 1988); Tremper Longman III, *Fictional Akkadian Autobiography: A Generic and Comparative Study* (Winona Lake, Ind.: Eisenbrauns, 1991).

60. Van Seters, "Historiography of the Ancient Near East," 2433–44.

61. First person narration, however, is found in part of the book of Ezra and in all of Nehemiah, as well as in brief sections of Ecclesiastes and in some narrative stretches of the prophetic literature. See discussion in Sternberg, *Poetics of Biblical Narrative*, 86–87.

62. Ibid., 118. When I refer to Sargon as the speaker, I am leaving aside the historical question of whether Sargon of Akkad actually dictated this composition. Instead, I am referring solely to the narratological question of voice within the piece, and its ramifications for communication of message.

63. The argument for the omniscience of the narrator in biblical narrative is made in extensive fashion in Sternberg, *Poetics of Biblical Narrative*, 84–128. See critique of this point in Lynn Poland, "Defending Biblical Poetics," *Journal of Religion* 68 (1988): 426–34.

64. On the depersonalization of the biblical narrator, see Kawashima, *Biblical Narrative and the Death of the Rhapsode*, 9–16, and Sternberg, *Poetics of Biblical Narrative*, 58–83.

65. See discussion in Childs, "Birth of Moses," 116.

66. See discussion in Simon Parker, *The Pre-Biblical Narrative Tradition: Essays on the Ugaritic Poems Keret and Aqhat* (Atlanta: Scholars Press, 1989), 230–32.

67. M. Avot 3:19.

68. There are however, some notable exceptions to this narratological strategy, whereby Scripture adds an expositional note that God has steered events. See, e.g., Exod 9:12; 10:20, 27; Judg 14:4; 1 Kgs 12:15.

69. Though the Hebrew here, *na'ar* usually refers to a "youth"; when speaking of a minor, it can connote an infant as well. See Judg 13:8; 2 Sam 12:16, and Propp, *Exodus 1–18*, 151.

70. Propp, *Exodus 1–18*, 149.

71. A precursor of this is seen in the early lines of the Keret epic, where Keret "sees his lineage destroyed" and then weeps—where "seeing" indicates inner thought, utilizing the standard word for observing any event. Biblical "behold" is lexically distinct from "seeing." On free indirect discourse in biblical narrative see

Kawashima, *Biblical Narrative and the Death of the Rhapsode*, 78–87; Sternberg, *Poetics of Biblical Narrative*, 52–53. On the uses of the particle *hinnēh*, see Tamar Zewi, "The Particles הנה and והנה in Biblical Hebrew," *Hebrew Studies* 37 (1996): 35–37; Simcha Kogut, "On the Meaning and Syntactical Status of הנה in Biblical Hebrew," *Scripta Hierosolymitana* 31 (1986), 133–54; Adele Berlin, *Poetics and Interpretation of Biblical Narrative* (Sheffield, England: Almond Press, 1983), 62–63, 91–95.

72. Umberto Cassuto, *A Commentary on the Book of Exodus*, trans. Israel Abrahams (Jerusalem: Magnes Press, 1967), 20.

73. Ibid., 20.

74. See discussion in Greenberg, *Understanding Exodus*, 41.

75. J. S. Ackerman, "The Literary Context of the Moses Birth Story (Exod 1–2)," in *Literary Interpretations of Biblical Narratives*, ed. K. R. R. Gros Louis et al. (Nashville, Tenn.: Abingdon, 1974), 1:93.

76. Carol Meyers, *Exodus* (Cambridge: Cambridge University Press, 2005), 41; Marten Stol, *Birth in Babylonia and the Bible: Its Mediterranean Setting* (Groningen: Styx, 2000), 181–90; Mayer I. Gruber, *Motherhood of God and Other Studies* (Atlanta: Scholars Press, 1992), 92–95.

77. Meyers, *Exodus*, 182; Childs, "Birth of Moses," 113. Although the Hebrew word for "monetary wage" is *śākar*, as here, most instances of the word in the Hebrew Bible connote not a monetary salary but recompense of all sorts, human and divine.

78. Childs, "Birth of Moses," 112.

79. Ibid., 112; Coats, *Exodus 1–18*, 27. Propp (*Exodus 1–18*, 152) notes that the phrase used here in v. 9, "and he became for her as a son" (*va-yehî lâ le-ben*), is the language of adoption used with regard to Mordecai as standing in loco parentis in Esther 3:7. Indeed, an Egyptian record from the eleventh century B.C.E. tells of a woman who adopted the child of a female slave and emancipated him to make him her heir. See Greenberg, *Understanding Exodus*, 200; A. H. Gardiner, "Adoption Extraordinary," *Journal of Egyptian Archaeology* (1940): 23–28.

80. Note that among the ancient versions, the Samaritan Pentateuch places the objectival suffix on the first verb rather than on the second. In place of the Masoretic Text version, "She opened, she saw *him*—the boy," the Samaritan version reads "She opened *it* (*va-tiftaḥa*), she saw (*va-tir'eh*) the boy." See Propp, *Exodus 1–18*, 144.

81. See sources in Propp, *Exodus 1–18*, 158; see also Rank, *Myth of the Birth of the Hero*, 69–70.

82. Benno Jacob, *The Second Book of the Bible: Exodus*, trans. Walter Jacob and Yaakov Elman (Hoboken, N.J.: Ktav, 1992), 25.

83. Gordon F. Davies, *Israel in Egypt: Reading Exodus 1–2*, JSOTSup no. 135 (Sheffield, England: Sheffield Academic Press, 1992), 109.

84. Many have noted that the only proper name indicated in the story is the name Moses and that all the other characters remain anonymous. This is usually taken as an indication of the centrality of the infant, and the great stature that awaits him. I would suggest that only the name Moses is included because its function as a name is fundamentally unique. The name given a child is usually a reflection of the parents' hopes, prayers, and aspirations. The granting of the name Moses, uniquely,

represents the exercise of power, as it caps the adoption process, severing him from his roots.

85. On the nexus between biblical interpretation and pictorial representation see J. Cheryl Exum, *Beyond the Biblical Horizon: The Bible and the Arts* (Leiden: Brill, 1999).

86. Observe a similar dynamic in the way Scripture handles the sale of Joseph, and the anguish he suffered. In a moment of introspection, as they are manhandled by the viceroy of Egypt, the brothers reflect and exclaim, "surely we are guilty for what we did to our brother, for we witnessed his distress as he pleaded with us, as we turned away with indifference" (Gen 42:21). The comment is made in retrospect. And yet in the narrative that depicts the sale itself, Gen 37:24–28, Joseph is silent—or, more to the point, he is silenced by the narrative, as it works to project their indifference and insouciance to his suffering.

87. This, contra Greenberg, *Understanding Exodus*, 40, and the medieival rabbinic exegete Rashi to verse 5, who follows *b. Sotah* 12b.

88. See similar formulaic introductions that establish the primacy of the male in the patriarchal household: Judg 19:1; 1 Sam 1:1–2; 1 Sam 25:2–3; Ruth 1:1–2.

89. Note the following comment by the rabbis concerning the pressure that the maidens may have exerted on Pharaoh's daughter (*Midrash Shemot Rabbah* 1:23): "They said to her: 'Your highness! It is the norm when a king issues a decree, that even when no one else fulfills it, his immediate family nonetheless will. How then do you violate your own father's decree?'" The implicit understanding in this midrashic expansion of the text is that even as they stand silently, the maidens weigh in with an opinion and an expectation: they expect the princess to obey her father's decree. Here, too, the maidens are transferred from a position of servility to one of judgment over Pharaoh's daughter. Here, too, the natural hierarchy is destabilized.

90. See Frank Moore Cross, *Canaanite Myth and Hebrew Epic: Essays in the History of the Religion of Israel* (Cambridge, Mass.: Harvard University Press, 1973), 223–29; Yoram Hazony, "The Jewish Origins of the Western Disobedience Tradition," *Azure* 4 (Summer 1998): 28–40.

CONCLUSION

1. The examination of Greek political thought to the exclusion of biblical and ancient Near Eastern traditions is critically discussed in Daniel E. Fleming, *Democracy's Ancient Ancestors: Mari and Early Collective Governance* (Cambridge: Cambridge University Press, 2004), xi, and in Bernard Levinson, "Deuteronomy's Conception of Law as an 'Ideal Type': A Missing Chapter in the History of Constitutional Law," *Maarav* 12:1–2 (2005): 87–89, and in Yoram Hazony, "The Jewish Origins of the Western Disobedience Tradition," *Azure* 4 (1998): 26–27, 42–45.

2. Sketches of this history are found in Henry Phelps Brown, *Egalitarianism and the Generation of Inequality* (Oxford: Clarendon Press, 1988), and in Louis P. Pojman and Robert Westmoreland, eds., *Equality: Selected Readings* (New York: Oxford University Press, 1997).

3. Other questions that are typically at the center of discussions of equality are listed in Pojman and Westmoreland, *Equality*, 11–13.

4. The field of comparative study between Greek and Hebrew political thought is at a relatively young stage. The most wide-ranging study to date has been Anselm C. Hagedorn, *Between Moses and Plato: Individual and Society in Deuteronomy and Ancient Greek Law*, FRLANT no. 204 (Göttingen: Vanderhoeck & Ruprecht, 2004); for a history of efforts in this regard see 14–38.

5. Plato, *Republic*, bk 3.415a, trans. in G. M. A. Grube, *Plato: Republic* (Indianapolis: Hackett, 1992), 91.

6. Aristotle, *Politics* bk 1, 1254b4–19, trans. in Peter L. Phillips Simpson, *The Politics of Aristotle* (Chapel Hill: University of North Carolina Press, 1997), 15–16.

7. Brown, *Egalitarianism and the Generation of Inequality*, 246.

8. Matthew Westcott Smith, "Republicanism," in *International Encyclopedia of Government and Politics*, ed. Frank N. Magill (London: Fitzroy Dearborn, 1996), 2:1172; Iseult Honohan, *Civic Republicanism* (London: Routledge, 2002), 32.

9. Harvey C. Mansfield, *Taming of the Prince: The Ambivalence of Modern Executive Power* (New York: Free Press, 1989), 71.

10. Honohan, *Civic Republicanism*, 5.

11. Biancamaria Fontana, *The Invention of the Modern Republic* (Cambridge: Cambridge University Press, 1994), 9.

12. Honohan, *Civic Republicanism*, 36.

13. Peter Riesenberg, *Citizenship in the Western Tradition: Plato to Rousseau* (Chapel Hill: University of North Carolina Press, 1992), 34. See, in particular, the funeral oration ascribed to Pericles by Thucydides, *The Peloponnesian War*, 2:34–46. Some scholars question the historicity of the oratory. Yet even if viewed as propaganda spun by Thucydides himself, the text highlights his own sense that there are virtues particular to being an Athenian that are worth inculcating.

14. Aristotle, *Politics*, bk 1, 1281a2–4, trans. in Simpson, *Politics of Aristotle*, 94.

15. Smith, "Republicanism," 1173.

16. Aristotle, *Politics*, bk 1, 1253a6.

17. Ibid., bk 1, 1253a18; Honohan, *Civic Republicanism*, 20.

18. Plato, *Laws*, bk 4, :715d, trans. R. G. Bury, www.persues.tufts.edu/cgibin/ptext?lookup=plat.+Laws+4.715d.

19. Thucydides, *Peloponnesian War* (Hammondswoth, England: Penguin, 1972), 147.

20. A monograph-scale work comparing political structures in biblical Israel and Homeric Greece is that of Dale Launderville, *Piety and Politics: The Dynamics of Royal Authority in Homeric Greece, Biblical Israel, and Old Babylonian Mesopotamia* (Grand Rapids, Mich.: Eerdmans, 2002). Launderville's work in large part seeks that which is common across cultures. Tellingly, his focus in biblical writings is on monarchy as portrayed in the historiographic books and in the prophetic literature; there is little discussion of kingship in Deuteronomy, where the depiction of kingship stands in contrast with notions of kingship outside of Israel.

21. In smaller communities of the faithful, however, equality could emerge as a cardinal principle for the structure of communal life. Luke writes that the disciples,

following the word of Peter, established a brotherhood based on communist ideals: resources were pooled and redistributed each according to his need (Acts 2:44–45; 4:32–35). See K. Lake, "The Communism of Acts 2 and 4–6 and the Appointment of the Seven," in *The Beginnings of Christianity*, ed. F. J. Foakes-Jackson and K. Lake, 5 vols. (1920–33; reprint, Grand Rapids, Mich.: Baker, 1979), 5:140–50; D. L. Mealand, "Community of Goods and Utopian Allusions in Acts ii–iv," *Journal of Theological Studies* 28 (1977): 96–99.

22. See discussion in Sanford A. Lakoff, "Christianity and Equality," in *Equality*, ed. J. Roland Pennock and John W. Chapman, Nomos no. 9 (New York: Atherton Press, 1967), 115–33.

23. On Pauline views of the state and authority see, Michael V. Jackson, " 'Be Subject': Paul and the State," *Baptist Quarterly* 40:1 (2003): 36–47; Paul David Feinberg, "The Christian and Civil Authorities," *Master's Seminary Journal* 10:1 (1999): 87–99.

24. Lakoff, "Christianity and Equality," 127.

25. Though natural law became broadly adopted as the basis for the claim of equality in the modern period, the notion is already found in Roman times in the writings of Cicero, who determined that all stood equal before the law because all were endowed with reason. See Brown, *Egalitarianism and the Generation of Inequality*, 24–25.

26. Honohan, *Civic Republicanism*, 36.

27. See for example John Locke, *Two Treatises on Government*, 2.54, and discussion in Brown, *Egalitarianism and the Generation of Inequality*, 61. Even here, however, the beneficiaries of equality were of a limited group. While early modern thinkers like Locke eschewed the exercise of arbitrary power and the preserve of privilege, the beneficiaries of their notions of equality were white men of substance, to the exclusion of women, blacks, and for the most part, the common laborer.

28. See Thomas Hobbes, *Leviathan*, pt. 2, *Of Commonwealth*.

29. See in this regard, David Novak, *Covenantal Rights: A Study in Jewish Political Theory* (Princeton: Princeton University Press, 2000).

30. See in this vein Karl Jaspers, *The Question of German Guilt*, trans. E. B. Ashton (New York: Dial Press, 1947); Larry May, *Sharing Responsibility* (Chicago: University of Chicago Press, 1992); Jonathan Sacks, *To Heal a Fractured World: The Ethics of Responsibility* (New York: Schocken Books, 2005).

# Select Bibliography

Ackerman, J. S. "The Literary Context of the Moses Birth Story (Exod 1–2)."
In *Literary Interpretations of Biblical Narratives*, ed. K. R. R. Gros Louis
et al., 74–119. Nashville, Tenn.: Abingdon, 1974.

Ackerman, Susan. *Under Every Green Tree: Popular Religion in Sixth-Century
Judah*. Atlanta: Scholars Press, 1992.

Adelson, Howard. "The Origins of a Concept of Social Justice." In *Social
Justice in the Ancient World*, ed. K. D. Irani and M. Silver, 25–40.
Westport, Conn.: Greenwood, 1995.

Albrektson, Bertil. *History and the Gods: An Essay on the Idea of Historical
Events as Divine Manifestations in the Ancient Near East and Israel*. Lund:
CWK Gleerup, 1967.

Altman, Amnon. *The Historical Prologue of the Hittite Vassal Treaties*. Ramat
Gan: Bar-Ilan University Press, 2004.

Anderson, Benedict. *Imagined Communities: Reflections on the Origin and
Spread of Nationalism*. 1983. Reprint, London: Verso, 1991.

Anderson, Cheryl B. *Women, Ideology, and Violence: Critical Theory and the
Construction of Gender in the Book of the Covenant and the Deuteronomic
Law*. London: T & T Clark, 2004.

Arnold, Bill T., and Bryan E. Beyer, eds. *Readings from the Ancient Near East:
Primary Sources for Old Testament Study*. Grand Rapids, Mich.: Baker
Academic, 2002.

Assmann, Jan. "Das Bild des Vaters im alten Ägypten." In *Das Vaterbild in
Mythos und Geschichte*, ed. H. Tellenbach, 12–49. Stuttgart: Kohlhammer,
1976.

———. *Stein und Zeit: Mensch und Gesellschaft im alten Ägypten*. Munich:
Wilhelm Fink, 1991.

Bach, Alice, ed. *Women in the Hebrew Bible.* New York: Routledge, 1999.

Baines, John. "Literacy and Ancient Egyptian Society." *Man* 18 (1983): 572–99.

———. "Restricted Knowledge, Hierarchy and Decorum: Modern Perceptions and Ancient Institutions." *Journal of the American Research Center in Egypt* 27 (1990): 1–23.

Beckman, Gary. *Hittite Diplomatic Texts.* Ed. Harry A. Hoffner. Society of Biblical Literature Writings from the Ancient World Series, no. 7. Atlanta: Scholars Press, 1999.

Bennett, Harold V. *Injustice Made Legal: Deuteronomic Law and the Plight of the Widows, Strangers and Orphans in Ancient Israel.* Grand Rapids, Mich.: Eerdmans, 2002.

Ben-Zvi, Ehud. "Introduction: Setting an Agenda." In *Writings and Speech in Israelite and Ancient Near Eastern Prophecy,* ed. Ehud Ben-Zvi and Michael H. Floyd, 1–29. Symposium Series no. 10. Atlanta: Society of Biblical Literature, 2000.

Berger, Peter L. *The Sacred Canopy: Elements of a Sociological Theory of Religion.* Garden City, N.Y.: Doubleday, 1967.

Berlin, Adele. *Poetics and Interpretation of Biblical Narrative.* Sheffield, England: Almond Press, 1983.

Blanton, Richard E., "Beyond Centralization: Steps toward a Theory of Egalitarian Behavior in Archaic States." In *Archaic States,* ed. Gary M. Feinman and Joyce Marcus, 135–72. Santa Fe: School of American Research Press, 1998.

Bottéro, Jean. *Mesopotamia: Writing, Reasoning, and the Gods.* Trans. Zainab Bahrani and Marc Van De Mieroop. Chicago: University of Chicago Press, 1992.

———. *Religion in Ancient Mesopotamia.* Trans. Teresa Lavender Fagan. Chicago: University of Chicago Press, 2001.

Bowman, Alan K., and Greg Woolf. "Literacy and Power in the Ancient World." In *Literacy and Power in the Ancient World,* ed. Alan K. Bowman and Greg Woolf, 1–16. Cambridge: Cambridge University Press, 1994.

Boyarin, Daniel. "Placing Reading: Ancient Israel and Medieval Europe." In *The Ethnography of Reading,* ed. Jonathan Boyarin, 10–37. Berkeley: University of California Press, 1993.

Boyd, Julian. "These Precious Monuments of…Our History." *American Archivist* 22:2 (1959): 175–76.

Bremmer, Ian, and Cory Welt. "The Trouble with Democracy in Kazakhstan." *Central Asian Survey* 15:2 (1996): 179–99.

Brettler, Marc Zvi. *The Creation of History in Ancient Israel.* London: Routledge, 1995.

Breuer, Mordechai. *Pirkei Mo'adot,* 2 vols. Jerusalem: Horeb, 1986 (in Hebrew).

Brown, Henry Phelps. *Egalitarianism and the Generation of Inequality.* Oxford: Clarendon Press, 1988.

Brueggemann, Walter. "Trajectories in Old Testament Literature and the Sociology of Ancient Israel." *JBL* 98 (1979): 161–85.

Brunello, Anthony R. "Citizenship Rights and Responsibilities." In *The International Encyclopedia of Government and Politics,* ed. Frank N. Magill, 2 vols., 1:181–84. London: Fitzroy Dearborn, 1996.

Carpenter, Eugene. "sĕgŭllâ." In *NIDOTTE*, 3:224.

Carr, David. *Writing on the Tablet of the Heart: Origins of Scripture and Literature.* Oxford: Oxford University Press, 2005.

Carriére, Jean-Marie. *Theorie du Politique dan le Deuteronome: Analyse des unites, des structures et des concepts de Dt 16,18–18,22.* Frankfurt: Peter Lang, 2001.

Cassuto, Umberto. *A Commentary on the Book of Exodus.* Trans. Israel Abrahams. Jerusalem: Magnes Press, 1967.

Chaney, Marvin L. "Debt Easement in Israelite History and Tradition." In *The Bible and the Politics of Exegesis: Essays in Honor of Norman K. Gottwald on His Sixty-Fifth Birthday*, ed. David Jobling et al., 127–39. Cleveland: Pilgrim, 1991.

————. "Bitter Bounty: the Dynamics of Political Economy Critiqued by the Eighth-Century Prophets," in *The Bible and Liberation: Political and Social Hermeneutics*, ed. N. K. Gottwald and R. A. Horsley, 250–63. Maryknoll, N.Y.: Orbis, 1993.

————. "Whose Sour Grapes? The Addresses of Isaiah 5:1–7 in the Light of Political Economy." *Semeia* 87 (1999): 105–22.

Chavel, Charles B., ed. *Ramban (Nachmanides): Commentary on the Torah—Genesis.* New York: Shilo, 1971.

Childs, Brevard S. "The Birth of Moses." *JBL* 84 (1965): 109–22.

Chirichigno, Gregory C. *Debt-Slavery in Israel and the Ancient Near East.* JSOTSup no. 141. Sheffield, England: JSOT Press, 1993.

Christensen, Duane L. *Deuteronomy 1:1–21:9.* Word Biblical Commentary no. 6A. Nashville, Tenn.: Thomas Nelson, 2001.

Claburn, W. Eugene. "The Fiscal Basis of Josiah's Reforms." *JBL* 92 (1973): 11–22.

Clanchy, Michael T. "Reading the Signs at Durham Cathedral." In *Literacy and Society*, ed. K. Schousboe and M. T. Larsen, 149–70. Copenhagen: Akademisk Forlag, 1989.

————. *From Memory to Written Record: England 1066–1307.* 1979. Reprint, London: Edward Arnold, 1993.

Clifford, R. J. *Creation Accounts in the Ancient Near East and in the Bible.* Catholic Biblical Quarterly Monograph Series, no. 26. Washington, D.C.: Catholic Biblical Association of America, 1994.

Coats, George W. *Exodus 1–18.* Grand Rapids, Mich.: Eerdmans, 1999.

Cogan, M. "A Technical Term for Exposure." *JNES* 27 (1968): 133–35.

Cohn-Eskenazi, Tamara. *In an Age of Prose.* Atlanta: Scholars Press, 1988.

Concklin, Blane W. "Arslan Tash and Other Vestiges of a Particular Syrian Incantatory Thread." *Biblica* 84 (2003): 89–99.

Coogan, M. D. *Stories from Ancient Canaan.* Louisville, Ky.: Westminster, 1978.

Coulborn, Rushton. *Feudalism in History.* Princeton: Princeton University Press, 1956.

Craigie, Peter C. *The Book of Deuteronomy.* Grand Rapids, Mich.: Eerdmans, 1976.

Crenshaw, James L. *Education in Ancient Israel: Across the Deadening Silence.* New York: Doubleday, 1998.

Cross, Frank Moore. *Canaanite Myth and Hebrew Epic: Essays in the History of the Religion of Israel.* Cambridge, Mass.: Harvard University Press, 1973.

———. "The Invention and Development of the Alphabet." In *The Origins of Writing*, ed. Wayne M. Senner, 77–90. Lincoln: University of Nebraska Press, 1990.

Crüsemann, Frank. *The Torah: Theology and Social History of Old Testament Law.* Trans. Allan W. Mahnke. Minneapolis: Fortress, 1996.

Dalton George. "Primitive Money." In *Tribal and Peasant Economies: Readings in Economic Anthropology*, ed. George Dalton, 254–81. Garden City, N.Y.: Natural History Press, 1967.

———. "Subsistence and Peasant Economies in Africa." In *Tribal and Peasant Economies: Readings in Economic Anthropology*, ed. George Dalton, 155–68. Garden City, N.Y.: Natural History Press, 1967.

———, ed. *Primitive, Archaic, and Modern Economies: Essays of Karl Polanyi.* Garden City, N.Y.: Doubleday, 1968.

Damrosch, David. *The Narrative Covenant.* San Francisco: Harper & Row, 1987.

Davies, Gordon F. *Israel in Egypt: Reading Exodus 1–2.* JSOTSup no. 135. Sheffield, England: Sheffield Academic Press, 1992.

Day, John, ed. *King and Messiah in Israel and the Ancient Near East: Proceedings of the Oxford Old Testament Seminar.* Sheffield, England: Sheffield Academic Press, 1998.

Demsky, Aaron. "Writing in Ancient Israel." Pt. 1. "The Biblical Period." In *Mikra: Text, Translation, Reading and Interpretation of the Hebrew Bible in Ancient Judaism and Early Christianity*, ed. M. J. Mulder, 1–20. Assen, Netherlands: Van Gorcum, 1988.

———. "Literacy." In *Oxford Encyclopedia of Archaeology in the Ancient Near East*, ed. Eric M. Meyers, 3 vols., 3:362–69. New York: Oxford University Press, 1997.

Diakonoff, I. M. "Slave-Labour vs. Non-Slave Labour: The Problem of Definition," in *Labor in the Ancient Near East*, ed. Marvin A. Powell, 1–3. New Haven, Conn.: American Oriental Society, 1987.

Dietrich, M., Otto Lorenz, and J. Sanmartin, eds. *The Cuneiform Alphabetic Texts from Ugarit, Ras Ibn Hani and Other Places.* Münster: Ugarit, 1995.

Driver, Godfrey R. *Semitic Writing: From Pictograph to Alphabet.* 1948. Reprint, London: Oxford University Press, 1976.

Driver, G. R., and John C. Miles. *The Babylonian Laws.* 2 vols. Oxford: Clarendon Press, 1952.

Driver, S. R. *A Critical and Exegetical Commentary on Deuteronomy.* 1901. Reprint, Edinburgh: T & T Clark, 1965.

Dutcher-Walls, Patricia. "The Circumscription of the King: Deuteronomy 17:16–17 in its Ancient Social Context." *JBL* 121:4 (2002): 601–16.

Eichrodt, Walther. *Man in the Old Testament.* Trans. K. and R. Gregor Smith. London: SCM Press, 1951.

———. *Theology of the Old Testament.* Trans. J. A. Baker. 2 vols. London: SCM Press, 1961.

Eire, Carlos M. V. *The War against the Idols: The Reformation of Worship from Erasmus to Calvin.* Cambridge: Cambridge University Press, 1986.

Eisenstadt, S. N., ed. *The Origins and Diversity of Axial Age Civilizations.* Albany: State University of New York Press, 1986.

Eisenstein, Elizabeth L. *The Printing Press as an Agent of Change: Communications and Cultural Transformation in Early Modern Europe*. 2 vols. Cambridge: Cambridge University Press, 1979.

Elazar, Daniel. *Covenant and Polity in Biblical Israel*. New Brunswick, N.J.: Transaction Press, 1995.

Epsztein, Leon. *Social Justice in the Ancient Near East and the People of the Bible*. London: SCM Press, 1986.

Exum, J. Cheryl. *Beyond the Biblical Horizon: The Bible and the Arts*. Leiden: Brill, 1999.

Eyre, Christopher J. "Work and the Organisation of Work in the New Kingdom." In *Labor in the Ancient Near East*, ed. Marvin A. Powell, 5–47. New Haven, Conn.: American Oriental Society, 1987.

———. "Is Egyptian Historical Literature 'Historical' or 'Literary'?" In *Ancient Egyptian Literature: History and Forms*, ed. A. Loprieno, Probleme der Ägyptologie no. 10, 426–27. Leiden: Brill, 1996.

Eyre, Christopher, and John Baines. "Interactions between Orality and Literacy in Ancient Egypt." In *Literacy and Society*, ed. K. Schousboe and M. T. Larsen, 91–114. Copenhagen: Akademisk Forlag, 1989.

Fager, Jeffrey A. "Land Tenure in the Biblical Jubilee: A Moral World View." *HAR* 11 (1987): 59–68.

———. *Land Tenure and the Biblical Jubilee: Uncovering Hebrew Ethics through the Sociology of Knowledge*. JSOTSup no. 155. Sheffield, England: JSOT Press, 1993.

Feinberg, Paul David. "The Christian and Civil Authorities." *Master's Seminary Journal* 10:1 (1999): 87–99.

Finkelstein, J. J. "The Edict of Ammiṣaduqa: A New Text." *RA* 63 (1969): 45–64.

———. *The Ox that Gored*. Transactions of the American Philosophical Society Held at Philadelphia for Promoting Useful Knowledge, vol. 71, pt. 2 (Philadelphia: American Philosophical Society, 1981), 1–89.

Finnegan, Ruth. *Literacy and Orality: Studies in the Technology of Communication*. Oxford: Blackwell, 1988.

Fishbane, Michael. *Biblical Interpretation in Ancient Israel*. Oxford: Clarendon Press, 1985.

Fleming, Daniel E. *Democracy's Ancient Ancestors: Mari and Early Collective Governance*. Cambridge: Cambridge University Press, 2004.

Floyd, Michael H. "Prophecy and Writing in Habakkuk 2:1–5." *ZAW* 105 (1993): 462–81.

———. "Write the Revelation' (Hab 2:2): Re-Imagining the Cultural History of Prophecy." In *Writings and Speech in Israelite and Ancient Near Eastern Prophecy*, ed. Ehud Ben-Zvi and Michael H. Floyd, 103–43. SBL Symposium Series no. 10. Atlanta: Society of Biblical Literature, 2000.

Fontana, Biancamaria. *The Invention of the Modern Republic*. Cambridge: Cambridge University Press, 1994.

Forde, Daryll, and Mary Douglas. "Primitive Economics." In *Tribal and Peasant Economies: Readings in Economic Anthropology*, ed. George Dalton, 13–28. Garden City, N.Y.: Natural History Press, 1967.

Foster, Benjamin R. *Before the Muses: An Anthology of Akkadian Literature*. Bethesda, Md.: CDL Press, 1993.

———. *From Distant Days: Myths, Tales, and Poetry of Ancient Mesopotamia*. Bethesda, Md.: CDL Press, 1995.

Frankfort, H., and H. A. Frankfort. *The Intellectual Adventure of Ancient Man: An Essay on Speculative Thought in the Ancient Near East*. Chicago: University of Chicago Press, 1946.

Frankfort, Henri. *Kingship and the Gods: A Study of Ancient Near Eastern Religion as the Integration of Society and Nature*. Chicago: University of Chicago Press, 1948.

Frymer-Kensky, Tikva. "The Atrahasis Epic and Its Significance for Our Understanding of Genesis 1–9." *Biblical Archaeologist* 40:4 (1977): 147–55.

———. *In the Wake of the Goddesses: Women, Culture, and the Biblical Transformation of Pagan Myth*. New York: Free Press, 1992.

———. *Reading the Women of the Bible: A New Interpretation of Their Stories*. New York: Schocken, 2002.

Fukuyama, Francis. *Trust: The Social Virtues and the Creation of Prosperity*. London: Hamish Hamilton, 1995.

Gamoran, Hillel. "The Biblical Law against Loans on Interest." *JNES* 30 (1971): 127–34.

Gardiner, A. H. "Adoption Extraordinary." *Journal of Egyptian Archaeology* (1940): 23–28.

Gelb, I. J. "From Freedom to Slavery." In *Gesellschaftsklassen im Alten Zweistromland und den angrenzenden Gebeiten—XVIII: Recontre assyriogique internationale, München, 29. Juni bis 3. Juli 1970*, ed. D. O. Edzard. Bayerische Akademie der Wissenschaften, Philosophich-Historische Klasse, Sitzungs-berichte, no. 75. Munich: Verlag der Bayerischen Akademie der Wissenschaften, 1972.

Geller S. A. *Sacred Enigmas: Literary Religion in the Hebrew Bible*. London: Routledge, 1996.

———. "The God of the Covenant." In *One God or Many? Concepts of Divinity in the Ancient World*, ed. Barbara Nevling Porter, 273–319. Chebeague, Me.: Casco Bay Assyriological Institute, 2000.

Glassman, Ronald M. *Democracy and Despotism in Primitive Societies: A Neo-Weberian Approach to Political Theory*. Millwood, N.Y.: Associated Faculty Press, 1986.

Gnuse, Robert Karl. *No Other Gods: Emergent Monotheism in Israel*. Sheffield, England: Sheffield Academic Press, 1997.

Goodman, M. D. "Texts, Scribes and Power in Roman Judaea." In *Literacy and Power in the Ancient World*, ed. Alan K. Bowman and Greg Woolf, 99–108. Cambridge: Cambridge University Press, 1994.

Goody, Jack. *The Logic of Writing and the Organization of Society*. Cambridge: Cambridge University Press, 1986.

Goody, Jack, and Ian Watt. "The Consequences of Literacy." In *Literacy in Traditional Societies*, ed. Jack Goody, 27–68. Cambridge: Cambridge University Press, 1968.

Gottlieb, Isaac B. "Law, Love and Redemption: Legal Connotations in the Language of Exodus 6:6–8." *Journal of the Ancient Near Eastern Society of Columbia University* 26 (1999): 52–57.

Gottwald, Norman K. *The Tribes of Yahweh* (Maryknoll, N.Y.: Orbis Press, 1979).
———. "The Prophetic Critique of Political Economy: Its Ground and Import." In
  *The Hebrew Bible in Its Social World and Ours*, ed. Norman K. Gottwald, 349–64.
  Atlanta: Scholars Press, 1993.
———. "Social Class as an Analytic and Hermeneutical Category in Biblical Studies."
  *JBL* 112:1 (1993): 3–22.
———. *The Politics of Ancient Israel*. Louisville, Ky.: Westminster John Knox, 2001.
Grabbe, Lester L. *Priests, Prophets, Diviners, Sages: A Socio-Historical Study of Religious
  Specialists in Ancient Israel*. Valley Forge, Penn.: Trinity Press International, 1995.
Grayson, A. Kirk. *Assyrian Royal Inscriptions*. 2 vols. Wiesbaden: Harrassowitz,
  1972–76.
Greenberg, Moshe, "Some Postulates of Biblical Criminal Law." In *Yehezkel
  Kaufmann Jubilee Volume*, ed. Menaham Haran, 5–28. Jerusalem: Magnes Press,
  1960.
———. *Understanding Exodus*. New York: Melton Research Center, 1969.
———. *Studies in the Bible and Jewish Thought*. Philadelphia: Jewish Publications
  Society, 1995.
Greenstein, Edward. "Bible: Biblical Law." In *Back to the Sources: Reading the Classic
  Jewish Texts*, ed. Barry W. Holtz, 83–108. New York: Summit, 1984.
———. "On the Genesis of Biblical Prose Narrative." *Prooftexts* 8 (1988): 347–54.
———. "Autobiographies in Ancient Western Asia." In *CANE*, 4:2421–32.
———. "The God of Israel and the Gods of Canaan: How Different Were They?"
  *Proceedings of the World Congress of Jewish Studies* 12 (1999): A:47*–58*.
———. "Some Developments in the Study of Language and Some Implications for
  Interpreting Ancient Texts and Cultures." In *Israel Oriental Studies 20: Semitic
  Linguistics: The State of the Art at the Turn of the Twenty-First Century*, ed. Shlomo
  Izre'el, 441–79. Winona Lake, Ind.: Eisenbrauns, 2002.
———. "The Relationship between Biblical Narrative and Ancient Canaanite
  Narrative." In *Essays on Hebrew Literature in Honor of Avraham Holtz*, ed. Zvia
  Ben-Yosef Ginor, 9–31. New York: Jewish Theological Seminary of America,
  2003 (in Hebrew).
Grosby, Steven. *Biblical Ideas of Nationality: Ancient and Modern*. Winona Lake, Ind.:
  Eisenbrauns, 2002.
Gruber, Mayer I. *Motherhood of God and Other Studies*. Atlanta: Scholars Press, 1992.
Grusky, D. B. "Social Stratification." In *International Encyclopedia of the Social and
  Behavioral Sciences*, ed. Neil J. Smelser and Paul B. Baltes, 26 vols., 21:14446.
  Amsterdam: Elsevier, 2001.
Guthrie, W. K. C. *A History of Greek Philosophy*. 4 vols. Cambridge: Cambridge
  University Press, 1969–86.
Hagedorn, Anselm C. *Between Moses and Plato: Individual and Society in Deuteronomy
  and Ancient Greek Law*. FRLANT no. 204. Göttingen: Vanderhoeck & Ruprecht,
  2004.
Hahn, I. "Representation of Society in the Old Testament and the Asiatic Mode of
  Production." *Oikumene* 2 (1978): 27–41.

Hallo, William W. "New Moons and Sabbaths: A Case Study in the Contrastive Approach." *HUCA* 48 (1977): 1–18.

———. "Texts, Statues and the Cult of the Divine King." In *Congress Volume Jerusalem 1986*, ed. J. A. Emerton, 54–66. Leiden: Brill, 1988.

———. "Compare and Contrast: The Contextual Approach to Biblical Literature." In *The Bible in Light of Cuneiform Literature*, ed. William W. Hallo et al., 1–30. Scripture in Context no. 3. Lewiston, N.Y.: Edwin Mellen, 1990.

———. *The Book of the People.* Brown Judaica Series no. 225. Atlanta: Scholars Press, 1991.

———. "The Concept of Canonicity in Cuneiform and Biblical Literature: A Comparative Appraisal." In *The Biblical Canon in Comparative Perspective*, ed. K. L. Younger, W. W. Hallo, and B. F. Batto, 1–19. Lewiston, N.Y.: Edwin Mellen, 1991.

———. *The Context of Scripture.* 3 vols. Leiden: Brill, 1997–.

Halpern, Baruch. *The Constitution of the Monarchy in Israel.* Chico, Calif.: Scholars Press, 1981.

———. "The Uneasy Compromise: Israel between League and Monarchy." In *Traditions in Transformation: Turning Points in Biblical Faith*, ed. Baruch Halpern and Jon D. Levenson, 77–85. Winona Lake, Ind.: Eisenbrauns, 1981.

———. "Jerusalem and the Lineages in the Seventh Century B.C.E.: Kinship and the Rise of Individual Moral Liability." In *Law and Ideology in Monarchic Israel*, ed. Baruch Halpern and Deborah W. Hobson, 11–107. JSOTSup no. 124. Sheffield, England: Sheffield Academic Press, 1991.

Hamilton, J. M. *Social Justice and Deuteronomy: The Case of Deuteronomy 15.* Society of Biblical Literature Dissertation Series no. 136. Atlanta: Scholars Press, 1992.

Handy, Lowell K. *Among the Host of Heaven: The Syro-Palestinian Pantheon as Bureaucracy.* Winona Lake, Ind.: Eisenbrauns, 1994.

Haran, Menahem. "On the Diffusion of Literacy and Schools in Ancient Israel." In *Congress Volume 1986*, ed. J. A. Emerton, 81–95. VTS no. 40. Leiden: Brill, 1988.

Harris, William. *Ancient Literacy.* Cambridge, Mass.: Harvard University Press, 1989.

Hayek, F. A. *The Political Ideal of the Rule of Law.* Cairo: National Bank of Egypt, 1955.

Hazony, Yoram. "The Jewish Origins of the Western Disobedience Tradition." *Azure* 4 (Summer 1998): 17–74.

Heater, Derek. *A Brief History of Citizenship.* New York: New York University Press, 2004.

Heilbroner, Robert L. *The Worldly Philosophers: The Lives, Times and Ideas of the Great Economic Thinkers.* 1953. Reprint, New York: Simon and Schuster, 1980.

Hess, Richard S. "Literacy in Iron Age Israel." In *Windows into Old Testament History*, ed. V. Philip Long, 82–95. Grand Rapids, Mich.: Eerdmans, 2002.

Hess, Richard S., and David Toshio Tsumura, eds. *I Studied Inscriptions from Before the Flood.* Sources for Biblical and Theological Study no. 4. Winona Lake, Ind.: Eisenbrauns, 1994.

Honohan, Iseult. *Civic Republicanism.* London: Routledge, 2002.

Hopkins, D. C. *The Highlands of Canaan: Agricultural Life in the Early Iron Age.* Sheffield, England: Almond Press, 1985.

Hudson, Michael. "Land Monopolization, Fiscal Crises and Clean State 'Jubilee' Proclamations in Antiquity." In *A Philosophy for a Fair Society*, ed. Michael Hudson, G. J. Miller, and Kris Feder, 139–68. London: Shepheard-Walwyn, 1994.

———. "The Dynamics of Privatization from the Bronze Age to the Present." In *Privatization in the Ancient Near East and Classical World*, ed. Michael Hudson and Baruch A. Levine, 33–72. Peabody Museum Bulletin no. 5. Cambridge, Mass.: Harvard University Press, 1996.

———. "Introduction: Privatization: A Survey of the Unresolved Controversies." In *Privatization in the Ancient Near East and Classical World*, ed. Michael Hudson and Baruch A. Levine, 1–32. Peabody Museum Bulletin no. 5. Cambridge, Mass.: Harvard University Press, 1996.

Hugenberger, Gordon Paul. *Marriage as Covenant: A Study of Biblical Law and Ethics Governing Marriage Developed from the Perspective of Malachi*. Leiden: Brill, 1994.

Hurowitz, Victor. "Canon and Canonization in Mesopotamia." *Proceedings of the World Congress of Jewish Studies* 12 (1999) Part A: Bible Studies: 1–12.

———. "Spanning the Generations: Aspects of Oral and Written Transmission in the Bible and Ancient Mesopotamia." In *Freedom and Responsibility*, ed. R. M. Geffen and M. B. Edelman, 11–30. New York: Ktav, 1999.

Jackson, Bernard. *Studies in the Semiotics of Biblical Law*. JSOTSup no. 314. Sheffield, England: Sheffield Academic Press, 2000.

Jackson, Michael V. "'Be Subject': Paul and the State." *Baptist Quarterly* 40:1 (2003): 36–47.

Jacob, Benno. "The Childhood and Youth of Moses, the Messenger of God." In *Essays in Honour of J. H. Hertz*, ed. I. Epstein et al., 245–59. London: Edward Goldston, 1944.

———. *Exodus: The Second Book of the Bible*. Trans. Walter Jacob and Yaakov Elman. Hoboken, N.J.: Ktav, 1992.

Jacobsen, Thorkild. *The Treasures of Darkness: A History of Mesopotamian Religion*. New Haven, Conn.: Yale University Press, 1976.

Jagersma, H. "The Tithes in the OT." *Oudtestamentische Studiën* 21 (1981): 116–28.

Jamieson-Drake, David W. *Scribes and Schools in Monarchic Judah: A Socio-Archeological Approach*. Sheffield, England: Almond Press, 1991.

Japhet, Sara. "The Relationship between the Legal Corpora in the Pentateuch in Light of Manumission Laws." In *Studies in Bible 1986*, ed. S. Japhet, 63–89. Scripta Hierosolymitana no. 31. Jerusalem: Magnes, 1986.

Jaspers, Karl. *The Question of German Guilt*. Trans. E. B. Ashton. New York: Dial Press, 1947.

Jonsson, G. A. *The Image of God: Genesis 1:26–28 in a Century of Old Testament Research*. Trans. L. Svensden. Stockholm: Almquist & Wiksell, 1988.

Katsh, Abraham I. *The Biblical Heritage of American Democracy*. New York: Ktav, 1977.

Kaufman, S. "A Reconstruction of the Social Welfare Systems of Ancient Israel." In *In the Shelter of Elyon: Essays on Ancient Palestinian Life and Literature in Honor of G. W. Ahlström*, ed. W. Boyd Barrick and John R. Spencer, 277–86. Sheffield, England: Sheffield Academic Press, 1984.

Kaufmann, Yehezkel. *The Religion of Israel*, Trans. Moshe Greenberg. London: Allen & Unwin, 1961.

Kawashima, Robert S. *Biblical Narrative and the Death of the Rhapsode*. Bloomington: Indiana University Press, 2004.

Kitchen, K. A. *On the Reliability of the Old Testament*. Grand Rapids, Mich.: Eerdmans, 2003.

Klein, J. *The Royal Hymns of Shulgi King of Ur: Man's Quest for Immortal Fame*. Transactions of the American Philosophical Society Held at Philadelphia for Promoting Useful Knowledge. vol. 71, pt. 7. Philadelphia: American Philosophical Society, 1981.

———. "On Writing Monumental Inscriptions in the Ur III Scribal Curriculum." *RA* 80 (1986): 1–7.

Knight, Douglas. "Political Rights and Powers in Monarchic Israel." *Semeia* 66 (1995): 93–117.

Knoppers, Gary. "The Deuteronomist and the Deuteronomic Law of the King: A Reexamination of a Relationship." *ZAW* 108 (1996): 329–46.

Knoppers, Gary N., and Paul B. Harvey Jr., "The Pentateuch in Ancient Mediterranean Context: The Publication of Local Law Codes." In *The Pentateuch as Torah: New Models for Understanding Its Promulgation and Acceptance*, ed. Gary N. Knoppers and Bernard M. Levinson, 105–44. Winona Lake, Ind.: Eisenbrauns, 2007.

Knoppers, Gary N., and Bernard M. Levinson. "How, When, Where, and Why Did the Pentateuch Become the Torah?" In *The Pentateuch as Torah: New Models for Understanding Its Promulgation and Acceptance*, ed. Gary N. Knoppers and Bernard M. Levinson, 1–22. Winona Lake, Ind.: Eisenbrauns, 2007.

Knudtzon J. A., ed. *Die El-Amarna Tafeln*. 2 vols. Leipzig: Hinrichs, 1907.

Kogut, Simcha. "On the Meaning and Syntactical Status of הנה in Biblical Hebrew." *Scripta Hierosolymitana* 31 (1986): 133–54.

Lake, K. "The Communism of Acts 2 and 4–6 and the Appointment of the Seven." In *The Beginnings of Christianity*, ed. F. J. Foakes-Jackson and K. Lake, 5 vols., 5:140–50. 1920–33. Reprint, Grand Rapids, Mich.: Baker, 1979.

Lakoff, Sanford A. "Christianity and Equality." In *Equality*, ed. J. Roland Pennock and John W. Chapman, 115–33. Nomos no. 9. New York: Atherton Press, 1967.

Lamberg-Karlovsky, C. C. "The Archaeological Evidence for International Commerce: Public and/or Private Enterprise in Mesopotamia?" In *Privatization in the Ancient Near East and Classical World*, ed. Michael Hudson and Baruch A. Levine, 73–108. Peabody Museum Bulletin no. 5: Cambridge, Mass.: Harvard University Press, 1996.

Lambert, W. G. "Myth and Mythmaking in Sumer and Akkad." In *CANE*, 3:1825–35.

Lambert, W. G., and A. R. Millard. *Atra-hasis: The Babylonian Story of the Flood*. Oxford: Clarendon Press, 1969.

Lang, Bernhard. "The Social Organization of Peasant Poverty in Biblical Israel." In *Anthropological Approaches to the Old Testament*, ed. Bernhard Lang, 83–99. Issues in Religion and Theology no. 8. Philadelphia: Fortress Press, 1985.

Laroche, Emmanuel, ed. *Catalogue des textes Hittites*. Paris: Klincksieck, 1971.

Launderville, Dale. *Piety and Politics: The Dynamics of Royal Authority in Homeric Greece, Biblical Israel, and Old Babylonian Mesopotamia*. Grand Rapids, Mich.: Eerdmans, 2002.

Leemans, W. F. "Quelques considerations à propos d'une etude récente du doit du Proche-Orient ancien." *Bibliotheca Orientalis* 48 (1991): 414–20.

LeFebvre, Michael. *Collections, Codes and Torah: The Re-Characterization of Israel's Written Law*. New York: T & T Clark, 2006.

Leithart, Peter J. "Attendants of Yahweh's House: Priesthood in the Old Testament." *JSOT* 85 (1999): 3–24.

Lemaire, André. *Les écoles et la Formation de la Bible Dans L'Ancien Israël*. Fribourg, Germany: Editions Universitaires, 1981.

Lenski, Gerhard E. *Power and Privilege: A Theory of Social Stratification*. New York: Mc-Graw Hill, 1966.

Leprohon, Ronald J. "Royal Ideology and State Administration in Pharaonic Egypt. In *CANE* 1:273–87.

Leuchter, Mark. *Josiah's Reform and Jeremiah's Scroll*. Hebrew Bible Monographs no. 6. Sheffield, England: Sheffield Phoenix Press, 2006.

Leuchter, Mark. "The Levite in Your Gates: The Deuteronomic Redefinition of Levitical Authority." *JBL* 126:3 (2007): 417–36.

Levenson, J. D. "Poverty and the State in Biblical Thought." *Judaism* 25 (1976): 230–41.

Levine, Baruch A. Review of *Le Culte à Ugarit*, by Jean-Michel de Tarrogon. *Revue Biblique* 88 (1981): 246–47.

———. *Leviticus*. Philadelphia: Jewish Publication Society of America, 1989.

———. "The Clan-Based Economy of Biblical Israel." In *Symbiosis, Symbolism, and the Power of the Past: Canaan, Ancient Israel and Their Neighbors from the Late Bronze Age through Roman Palestina*, ed. William G. Dever and Seymour Gitin, 445–53. Winona Lake, Ind.: Eisenbrauns, 2003.

Levinson, Bernard M. *Deuteronomy and the Hermeneutics of Legal Innovation*. New York: Oxford University Press, 1997.

———. "The Reconceptualization of Kingship in Deuteronomy and the Deuteronomic History's Transformation of Torah." *VT* 51 (2001): 511–34.

———. "The Birth of the Lemma: The Restrictive Reinterpretation of the Covenant Code's Manumission Law by the Holiness Code (Leviticus 25:44–46)." *JBL* 124:4 (2005): 617–39.

———. "The Manumission of Hermeneutics: The Slave Laws of the Pentateuch as a Challenge to Contemporary Pentateuchal Theory." In *Congress Volume Leiden 2004*, ed. André Lemaire, VTS no. 109, 281–324. Leiden: Brill, 2006.

———. *"The Right Chorale": Studies in Biblical Law and Interpretation*. Forschungen zum Alten Testament no. 54. Tübingen: Mohr-Siebeck, 2007.

———. *Legal Revision and Religious Renewal in Ancient Israel*. Cambridge: Cambridge University Press, 2008.

Lévi-Strauss, Claude. *Tristes Tropiques*. Trans. J. and D. Weightman. New York: Atheneum, 1974.

Lewis, Brian. *The Sargon Legend: A Study of the Akkadian Text and the Tale of the Hero Who Was Exposed at Birth.* Cambridge, Mass.: ASOR, 1980.

Lewis, Theodore J. "The Identity and Function of El/Baal Berith." *JBL* 115 (2003): 401–23.

Lichtheim, Miriam. *Ancient Egyptian Autobiography Chiefly of the Middle Kingdom: A Study and an Anthology.* Freiburg, Germany: Universitatsverlag, 1988.

Lichtheim, Miriam. *Ancient Egyptian Literature.* 3 vols. Berkeley: University of California Press, 1976.

Liver, Jacob. "King, Kingship." In *Biblical Encyclopedia*, 8 vols., 4:1080–1111. Jerusalem: Bialik Institute, 1950–88 (in Hebrew).

Lohfink, N. "Die Sicherung der Wirksamkeit des Gotteswortes durch das Prinzip der Schriftlichkeit der Tora und durch das Prinzip der Gewaltenteilung nach den ämtergesetzen des Buches Deuteronomium (Dt. 16, 18–18,22)." In *Studien zum Deuteronomium und zur deuteronomistischen Literatur I*, ed. N. Lohfink, Stuttgarter biblische Aufsatzbände no. 8, 305–23. Stuttgart: Katholisches Bibelwerk, 1990.

———. "Distribution of the Functions of Power: The Laws Concerning Public Offices in Deuteronomy 16:18–18:22." In *A Song of Power and the Power of Song: Essays on the Book of Deuteronomy*, ed. Duane L. Christensen, 336–55. Winona Lake, Ind.: Eisenbrauns, 1993.

———. *Die Väter Israels im Deuteronomium: Mit einer Stellungnahme von Thomas Römer.* Orbis biblicus et orientalis no. 111. Freiburg, Germany: Universitätsverlag, 1991.

Longman, Tremper, III. *Fictional Akkadian Autobiography: A Generic and Comparative Study.* Winona Lake, Ind.: Eisnebrauns, 1991.

Lowery, R. H. *The Reforming Kings: Cult and Society in First Temple Judah.* JSOTSup no. 120. Sheffield, England: JSOT Press, 1991.

Machinist, Peter. "On Self-Consciousness in Mesopotamia." In *The Origins and Diversity of Axial Age Civilizations*, ed. S. N. Eisenstadt, 193–202, 511–18 Albany: State University of New York Press, 1986.

———. "Assyrians on Assyria in the First Millennium BC." In *Anfänge politischen Denkens in der Antike: Die nahöstlichen Kulturen und die Griechen*, ed. Kurt Raaflaub and Elisabeth Müller-Luckner, 77–104. Munich: Oldenbourg, 1993.

Maidman, Maynard Paul. "Nuzi: Portarit of an Ancient Mesopotamian Provincial Town," In *CANE*, 2:931–47.

Maloney, R. "Usury and Restrictions in Interest-Taking in the Ancient Near East." *CBQ* 36 (1974): 1–20.

Manent, Pierre. *An Intellectual History of Liberalism.* Trans. Rebecca Balinski. Princeton: Princeton University Press, 1995.

Mann, Michael. *The Sources of Social Power.* 2 vols. Cambridge: Cambridge University Press, 1986.

Mansfield, Harvey C. *Taming of the Prince: The Ambivalence of Modern Executive Power.* New York: Free Press, 1989.

Marsman, Hennie J. *Women in Ugarit and Israel: Their Social and Religious Position in the Context of the Ancient Near East.* Oudtestamentische Studiën no. 49. Leiden: Brill, 2003.

Matthews, Victor H., and Don C. Benjamin, eds. *Old Testament Parallels: Laws and Stories from the Ancient Near East.* 1991. Reprint, New York: Paulist Press, 1997.

Matthews, Victor H., Bernard M. Levinson, and Tikva Frymer-Kensky, eds. *Gender and Law in the Hebrew Bible and the Ancient Near East.* JSOTSup no. 262. 1998. London: T & T Clark, 2004.

May, Larry. *Sharing Responsibility.* Chicago: University of Chicago Press, 1992.

Mayes, A. D. H. *Deuteronomy.* Grand Rapids, Mich.: Eerdmans, 1979.

McBride, S. Dean, Jr. "The Polity of the Covenant People: The Book of Deuteronomy." *Interpretation* 41 (1987): 229–44.

McCarthy, Dennis J. *Treaty and Covenant: A Study in Form in the Ancient Oriental Documents and in the Old Testament.* Rome: Biblical Institute Press, 1978.

McConville, J. G. *Deuteronomy.* Apollos Old Testament Commentary no. 5. Leicester, England: Apollos, 2002.

———. "Deuteronomy's Unification of Passover and Maṣṣōt: A Response to Bernard M. Levinson." *JBL* 119 (2000): 47–58.

McKenzie, John L. *A Theology of the Old Testament.* Garden City, N.Y.: Doubleday, 1974.

McKeon, Michael. *The Origins of the English Novel, 1600–1740.* Baltimore: Johns Hopkins University Press, 1987.

Mealand, D. L. "Community of Goods and Utopian Allusions in Acts ii–iv." *Journal of Theological Studies* 28 (1977): 96–99.

Mendelsohn, I. "Samuel's Denunciation of Kingship in the Light of Akkadian Documents from Ugarit." *Bulletin of the American Schools of Oriental Research* 143 (1956): 17–22.

Mendenhall, George E. *The Tenth Generation: The Origins of the Biblical Tradition.* Baltimore: Johns Hopkins University Press, 1973.

Mendenhall, George E., and Gary A. Herion. "Covenant." In *ABD* 1:1179–1202.

Meyers, Carol. *Discovering Eve: Ancient Israelite Women in Context.* New York: Oxford University Press, 1988.

———. *Exodus.* Cambridge: Cambridge University Press, 2005.

Milgrom, Jacob. *Cult and Conscience: The Asham and the Priestly Doctrine of Repentance.* Leiden: Brill, 1976.

———. "Priestly Terminology and the Political and Social Structure of Pre-Monarchic Israel." *Jewish Quarterly Review* 79 (1978): 65–81.

———. "Of Hems and Tassels." *Biblical Archeological Review* 9 (1983): 61–65.

———. "The Ideological and Historical Importance of the Office of the Judge in Deuteronomy." In *Isac Leo Seeligmann Volume: Essays on the Bible and the Ancient World*, ed. Alexander Rofé and Yair Zakovitch, 3 vols., 3:129–39. Jerusalem: E. Rubinstein, 1983.

———. *Numbers.* Philadelphia: Jewish Publication Society, 1989.

Millard, Alan R. "An Assessment of the Evidence for Writing in Ancient Israel." In *Biblical Archaeology Today: Proceedings of the International Congress on Biblical Archaeology, Jerusalem, April 1984*, ed. Janet Amitai, 301–12. Jerusalem: Israel Academy of Sciences and Humanity, 1985.

———. "The Infancy of the Alphabet." *World Archaeology* 17 (1986): 390–98.

Miller, Robert D., II. *Chieftains of the Highland Clans: A History of Israel in the Twelfth and Eleventh Centuries* B.C. Grand Rapids, Mich.: Eerdmans, 2005.

Moran, William L. "The Ancient Near Eastern Background of the Love of God in Deuteronomy." *CBQ* 25 (1963): 77–87.

———. "The Gilgamesh Epic: A Masterpiece from Ancient Mesopotamia." In *CANE*, 4:2327–36.

Muffs, Y. *Love and Joy: Law, Language, and Religion in Ancient Israel.* New York: Jewish Theological Society of America, 1992.

Naveh, Joseph. *An Early History of the Alphabet.* Jerusalem: Magnes Press, 1982.

Nelson, Richard D. *Raising Up a Faithful Priest: Community and Priesthood in Biblical Theology.* Louisville, Ky.: Westminster/John Knox Press, 1993.

———. *Deuteronomy: A Commentary.* Louisville, Ky.: Westminster John Knox Press, 2002.

Neufeld, E. E. "The Prohibitions against Loans at Interest in Ancient Hebrew Laws." *HUCA* 26 (1955): 355–412.

Nicholson, Ernest W. *God and His People: Covenant Theology in the Old Testament.* Oxford: Clarendon Press, 1986.

Nicholson, Graeme. *Plato's Phaedrus: The Philosophy of Love.* West Lafayette, Ind.: Purdue University Press, 1999.

Niditch, Susan. *Folklore and the Hebrew Bible.* Minneapolis: Fortress Press, 1993.

———. *Oral World and Written Word: Ancient Israelite Literature.* London: SPCK, 1996.

———. *Ancient Israelite Religion.* New York: Oxford University Press, 1997.

Nissinen, Marrti, ed. *Prophecy in its Ancient Near Eastern Context: Mesopotamian, Biblical, and Arabian Perspectives.* Atlanta: Society of Biblical Literature, 2000.

Noth, Martin. *The Laws in the Pentateuch and Other Studies.* Trans. D. Ap-Thomas. Philadelphia: Fortress Press, 1966.

Novak, David. *Covenantal Rights: A Study in Jewish Political Theory.* Princeton: Princeton University Press, 2000.

O'Connor, David. "The Social and Economic Organization of Ancient Egyptian Temples." In *CANE* 1:319–29.

Olyan, Saul. "Honor, Shame and Covenant Relations in Ancient Israel and Its Environment." *JBL* 115 (1996): 201–18.

Oppenheim, A. Leo. Review of Sidney Smith, *The Statue of Idri-mi. JNES* 14 (1955): 199–200.

———. "The City of Assur in 714 BC." *JNES* 19 (1960): 133–47.

———. *Ancient Mesopotamia: Portrait of a Dead Civilization.* Chicago: University of Chicago Press, 1964.

Otto, Eckart. "Soziale Restitution und Vertragsrecht: *Mīšaru(m), (an)durāru(m),* kirenzi *parā tarnumar, šemitta* und *derôr* in Mesopotamia, Syrien, in der Hebräischen Bibel und die Frage des Rechtstransfers im Alten Orient." *RA* 92 (1998): 125–60.

Oz-Salzberger, Fanya. "The Jewish Roots of Western Freedom." *Azure* 13 (2002): 88–132.

Pangle, Thomas L. *Montesquieu's Philosophy of Liberalism.* Chicago: University of Chicago Press, 1973.

Pardee, Dennis. *Ritual and Cult at Ugarit.* Atlanta: Society of Biblical Literature, 2002.

Parker, Simon B. *The Pre-Biblical Narrative Tradition: Essays on the Ugaritic Poems Keret and Aqhat.* Atlanta: Scholars Press, 1989.

———. *Stories in Scripture and Inscription: Comparative Studies on Narrative in Northwest Semitic Inscriptions and the Hebrew Bible.* New York: Oxford University Press, 1997.

Paul, Shalom M. *Studies in the Book of the Covenant in Light of Biblical and Cuneiform Law.* 1970. Eugene, Ore.: Wipf & Stock, 2006.

Petit, Philip. *Republicanism: A Theory of Freedom and Government.* Oxford: Oxford University Press, 1997.

Pitt–Rivers, Julian. "Honor." In *International Encyclopedia of the Social Sciences,* 19 vols., 6:503–10. New York: Macmillan, 1968–91.

Pojman, Louis P., and Robert Westmoreland, eds. *Equality: Selected Readings.* New York: Oxford University Press, 1997.

Poland, Lynn. "Defending Biblical Poetics." *Journal of Religion* 68 (1988): 426–34.

Posner, Richard A. "Theory of Primitive Society with Special Reference to Law." *Journal of Law and Economics* 23 (1980): 1–53.

Preuss, Ulrich K. "Two Challenges to European Citizenship." *Political Studies* 44:3 (1996): 535–42.

Propp, William H. C. *Exodus 1–18.* AB no. 2. New York: Doubleday, 1998.

Rabinowitz, Isaac. *A Witness Forever: Ancient Israel's Perception of Literature and the Resultant Hebrew Bible.* Bethesda, Md.: CDL Press, 1993.

Rank, Otto. *The Myth of the Birth of the Hero.* Trans. Gregory C. Richter. New York: Brunner, 1952.

Redford, Donald B. *Akhenaten: The Heretic King.* Princeton: Princeton University Press, 1984.

———. "The Literary Motif of the Exposed Child." *Numen* 14 (1967): 202–28.

———. "Scribe and Speaker." In *Writings and Speech in Israelite and Ancient Near Eastern Prophecy,* ed. Ehud Ben Zvi and Michael H. Floyd, 145–218. SBL Symposium Series no. 10. Atlanta: Society of Biblical Literature, 2000.

Redman, Charles, R. *The Rise of Civilizations: From Early Farmers to Urban Society in the Ancient Near East.* San Francisco: Freeman, 1978.

Rendsburg, Gary A. "Notes on Genesis xxxv." *VT* 34 (1984): 361–66.

Rendtorff, Rolf, "Directions in Pentateuchal Studies." *Currents in Research: Biblical Studies* 5 (1997): 43–65.

———. *The Covenant Formula: An Exegetical and Theological Investigation.* Trans. Margaret Kohl. Edinburgh: T & T Clark, 1998.

Reviv, H. *The Elders in Ancient Israel: A Study of a Biblical Institution.* Jerusalem: Magnes, 1989.

Richardson, Heather Cox. *The Greatest Nation of the Earth: Republican Economic Policies during the Civil War.* Cambridge, Mass: Harvard University Press, 1997.

Richetti, John, ed. *The Cambridge Companion to the Eighteenth-Century Novel.* Cambridge: Cambridge University Press, 1996.

Ricoeur, Paul. *Figuring the Sacred: Religion, Narrative, and Imagination.* Minneapolis: Fortress Press, 1995.

Riesenberg, Peter. *Citizenship in the Western Tradition: Plato to Rousseau.* Chapel Hill: University of North Carolina Press, 1992.

Robertson, John F. "The Social and Economic Organization of Ancient Mesopotamian Temples." In *CANE,* 1:444–46.

Rodd, Cyril S. *Glimpses of a Strange Land: Studies in Old Testament Ethics.* Edinburgh: T & T Clark, 2001.

Rofé, Alexander. "The Law about the Organization of Justice in Deuteronomy (16:18–20; 17:8–13)." *Bet Miqra* 21 (1976): 199–210 (in Hebrew).

Sacks, Jonathan. *The Dignity of Difference: How to Avoid the Clash of Civilizations.* London: Continuum, 2003.

————. *Radical Then, Radical Now.* London: Continuum, 2003.

————. *To Heal a Fractured World: The Ethics of Responsibility.* New York: Schocken Books, 2005.

Sanders, Seth L. "What was the Alphabet For? The Rise of Written Vernacular and the Making of Israelite National Literature." *Maarav* 11 (2004): 25–56.

Sasson, Jack M., et al. *Civilizations of the Ancient Near East.* 4 vols. Peabody: Hendrickson, 1995.

Schaeffer, Claude F. A. *Le Palais Royal d'Ugarit.* 5 vols. Paris: Impr. Nationale, 1955.

Schaper, Joachim. "Exilic and Post-Exilic Prophecy and the Orality/Literacy Problem." *VT* 55: 3 (2005): 324–42.

————. "The 'Publication' of Legal Texts in Ancient Judah." In *The Pentateuch as Torah: New Models for Understanding Its Promulgation and Acceptance,* ed. Gary N. Knoppers and Bernard M. Levinson, 225–36. Winona Lake, Ind.: Eisenbrauns, 2007.

Schloen, J. David. *The House of the Father as Fact and Symbol: Patrimonialism in Ugarit and the Ancient Near East.* Winona Lake, Ind.: Eisenbrauns, 2001.

Schniedewind, William. *How the Bible Became a Book.* Cambridge: Cambridge University Press, 2004.

Seigel, Jerrold. Foreword to Pierre Manent, *An Intellectual History of Liberalism,* Trans. Rebecca Balinski, vii–xiv. Princeton: Princeton University Press, 1995.

Shils, Edward. *Center and Periphery: Essays in Macrosociology.* Chicago: University of Chicago Press, 1975.

Shklar, Judith N. *Montesquieu.* Oxford: Oxford University Press, 1987.

Silver, Morris. *Prophets and Markets.* New York: Barnes and Noble, 1983.

Singer, Itamar. "The Treaties between Hatti and Amurru." In *COS* 2:93–106.

Sivan, Gabriel. *The Bible and Civilization.* Jerusalem: Keter, 1973.

Ska, Jean-Louis. "Biblical Law and the Origins of Democracy." In *The Ten Commandments: The Reciprocity of Faithfulness,* ed. William P. Brown, 146–58. Louisville, Ky.: Westminster John Knox, 2004.

Smelser, Neil J. "Toward a Theory of Modernization." In *Tribal and Peasant Economies: Readings in Economic Anthropology,* ed. George Dalton, 29–50. Garden City, N.Y.: Natural History Press, 1967.

Smith, Mark S. *The Origins of Biblical Monotheism: Israel's Polytheistic Background and the Ugaritic Texts*. Oxford: Oxford University Press, 2001.

Smith, Matthew Westcott. "Republicanism." In *International Encyclopedia of Government and Politics*, ed. Frank N. Magill, 2:1172–75. London: Fitzroy Dearborn, 1996.

Snell, Daniel C. *Life in the Ancient Near East: 3100–332 B.C.E.* New Haven, Conn.: Yale University Press, 1997.

Sohn, Seock-Tae. "I Will Be Your God and You Will Be My People": The Origin and Background of the Covenant Formula." In *Ki Baruch Hu: Ancient Near Eastern, Biblical and Judaic Studies in Honor of Baruch A. Levine*, ed. R. Chazan et al., 355–72. Winona Lake, Ind.: Eisenbrauns, 1999.

Sonnet, Jean-Pierre. *The Book within the Book: Writing in Deuteronomy*. Leiden: Brill, 1997.

Speiser, E. A. "The Biblical Idea of History in Its Common Near Eastern Setting." *Israel Exploration Journal* 7 (1957): 201–16.

Sperling, David S. "An Arslan Tash Incantation: Interpretations and Implications." *HUCA* 53 (1982): 1–10.

Steinberg, Naomi. "The Deuteronomic Law Code and the Politics of State Centralization." In *The Bible and the Politics of Exegesis*, ed. David Jobling et al., 161–70. Cleveland: Pilgrim Press, 1991.

Sternberg, Meir. *Hebrews between Cultures: Group Portraits and National Literature*. Bloomington: Indiana University Press, 1998.

———. *The Poetics of Biblical Narrative: Ideological Literature and the Drama of Reading*. Bloomington: Indiana University Press, 1985.

Stol, Marten. *Birth in Babylonia and the Bible: Its Mediterranean Setting*. Groningen: Styx, 2000.

Street, Brian. *Literacy in Theory and Practice*. Cambridge: Cambridge University Press, 1984.

Sweeney, Marvin A. "The Critique of Solomon in the Josianic Edition of the Deuteronomistic History." *JBL* 114 (1995): 609–22.

Tadmor, Hayim. "Treaty and Oath in the Ancient Near East: A Historian's Approach." In *Humanizing America's Iconic Book: Society of Biblical Literature Centennial Addresses 1980*, ed. Gene M. Tucker and Douglas A. Knight, 142–52. Chico, Calif.: Scholars Press, 1980.

Talmon, Shemaryahu. "Kingship and the Ideology of the State." In *World History of the Jewish People*, ed. Ben-Zion Netanyahu, 8 vols., 4:3–26. Tel Aviv: Massadah, 1979.

Talmon, Shemaryahu, ed. *Shemot*. Tel-Aviv: Davidzon Etti, 1993 (in Hebrew).

Te Velde, H. "Scribes and Literacy in Ancient Egypt." In *Scripta Signa Vocis: Studies about Scripts, Scriptures and Languages in the Near East presented to J. H. Hospers*, ed. H. L. J. Vanstiphout et al., 253–64. Groningen: Forsten, 1986.

———. "Theology, Priests, and Worship in Ancient Egypt." In *CANE* 3:1731–49.

Thackeray, H. S. J. *Josephus*. 9 vols. London: Heinema, 1926.

Thomas, Rosalind. *Literacy and Orality in Ancient Greece*. Cambridge: Cambridge University Press, 1992.

Tigay, Jeffery. "*šābûa*." In *Biblical Encyclopedia*, 8 vols., 7:468–79. Jerusalem: Bialik Institute, 1950–88 (in Hebrew).

———. "On Evaluating Claims of Literary Borrowing." In *The Tablet and the Scroll: Near Eastern Studies in Honor of William W. Hallo*, ed. M. E. Cohen, D. C. Snell, and D. B. Weisberg, 250–55. Bethesda, Md.: CDL Press, 1993.

———. *Deuteronomy*. Philadelphia: Jewish Publication Society, 1996.

Tsevat, M. "The Basic Meaning of the Biblical Sabbath." *ZAW* 84 (1972): 447–59.

Uffenheimer, Benjamin. "Myth and Reality in Ancient Israel." In *The Origins and Diversity of Axial Age Civilizations*, ed. S. N. Eisenstadt, 135–68. Albany: State University of New York Press, 1986.

Van der Toorn, Karel. *Family Religion in Babylonia, Syria and Israel: Continuity and Change in the Forms of Religious Life*. Studies in the History and Culture of the Ancient Near East, no. 7. Leiden: Brill, 1996.

Van Dijk, Jacobus. "Myth and Mythmaking in the Ancient Near East." In *CANE* 3:1697–1709.

VanGemeren, Willem A., ed. *New International Dictionary of Old Testament Theology and Exegesis*. 5 vols. Grand Rapids: Zondervan, 1997.

Van Seters, John. "The Historiography of the Ancient Near East." In *CANE*, 4:2433–44.

von Rad, Gerhard. *God at Work in Israel*. Trans. John H. Marks. Nashville, Tenn.: Abingdon, 1980.

von Waldow, H. Eberhard. "Social Responsibility and Social Structure in Early Israel." *CBQ* 32 (1970): 182–204.

Walsh, Richard G. *Mapping Myths of Biblical Interpretation*. Sheffield, England: Sheffield Academic Press, 2001.

Walzer, Michael, et al., eds. *The Jewish Political Tradition*. 2 vols. New Haven, Conn.: Yale University Press, 2000–2003.

Warner, Sean. "The Alphabet: An Innovation and Its Diffusion." *VT* 30 (1980): 81–90.

Watt, Ian. *The Rise of the Novel*. Berkeley: University of California Press, 1967.

Watts, James W. *Reading Law: The Rhetorical Shape of the Pentateuch*. Biblical Seminar no. 59. Sheffield, England: Sheffield Academic Press, 1999.

Weeks, Noel. *Admonition and Curse: The Ancient Near Eastern Treaty/Covenant Form as a Problem in Intercultural Relationships*. Edinburgh: T & T Clark, 2004.

Weinfeld, Moshe. *Deuteronomy and the Deuteronomic School*. Oxford: Clarendon Press, 1972.

———. "Tithing in the Bible: Its Monarchic and Cultic Background." *Be'er Sheva* 1 (1973): 122–31 (in Hebrew).

———. "Judge and Officer in Ancient Israel and the Ancient Near East." *Israel Oriental Society* 7 (1977): 65–88.

———. " 'Temple Scroll' or 'King's Law.' " *Shnaton* 3 (1978–79): 214–37 (in Hebrew).

———. *Deuteronomy 1–11*. AB no. 5. New York: Doubleday, 1991.

———. *Social Justice in Ancient Israel and in the Ancient Near East*. Jerusalem: Magnes Press, 1995.

Westbrook, Raymond. "Jubilee Laws." *Israel Law Review* 6 (1971): 209–26.

———. "Biblical and Cuneiform Law Codes." *Revue Biblique* 92 (1985): 247–64.

———. "Social Justice in the Ancient Near East." In *Social Justice in the Ancient World*, eds. K. D. Irani and M. Silver, 149–64. Westport, Conn: Greenwood, 1995.

Westenholz, Joan Goodnick. "Thoughts on Esoteric Knowledge and Secret Lore." In *Intellectual Life of the Ancient Near East*, ed. Jirí Prosecky, 451–62. Comple Rendu, Recontre Assyriologique Internationale 43. Prague: Oriental Institute, 1998.

Whitt, William D. "The Story of the Semitic Alphabet." In *CANE*, 4:2379–97.

Winter, Irene. "Royal Rhetoric and the Development of Historical Narrative in Neo-Assyrian Reliefs." *Studies in Visual Communication* 7 (1981): 2–38.

Yoffee, Norman. "The Economy of Ancient Western Asia." In *CANE*, 3:1387–99.

Young, Ian M. "Israelite Literacy: Interpreting the Evidence." *VT* 48 (1998): 239–53, 408–22.

Zevit, Ziony. *The Religions of Ancient Israel: A Synthesis of Parallel Approaches.* London: Continuum, 2001.

Zewi, Tamar. "The Particles הנה and והנה in Biblical Hebrew." *Hebrew Studies* 37 (1996): 21–37.

# Index of Scriptural References

## ISAIAH (cont.,)

30:8     127
32:1     195 n.90
35:2     187 n.100
43:4     186 n.89
50:1     210 n.44
54:5–8     187 n.95
57:3–10     187 n.95
61:10–11     187 n.95
62:4–5     187 n.95

## JEREMIAH

2:2     187 n.95
2:20     187 n.95
3:1–5     187 n.95
3:6–25     187 n.95
8:8     211 n.51
13:27     187 n.95
23:10     187 n.95
29:1–23     209 n.23
30:2     127, 209 n.23
32:10–12     210 n.44
32:6–14     127, 131,
          200 n.41
33:21     119
34:8–16     206 n.113
36:2–3     209 n.23
36:10     118
37:13     166
38:2     166

## EZEKIEL

16:4–14     44–45, 187 n.95
18:5–9     203 n.78
43:11     211 n.52
44:24     193 n.54
44:31     46
45:17     201 n.52

## HOSEA

2:4–10     187 n.95
13:10     195 n.90

## AMOS

2:6     203 n.84
2:6–8     207 n.125
4:1     207 n.125

7:13     201 n.52
8:4–6     207 n.125

## MICAH

5:9     191 n.24
6:1–2     37

## NAHUM

1:2     184 n.61

## HABAKKUK

2:2     119

## PSALMS

2:7     27, 63
8:5–6     22, 187 n.100
15:5     203 n.78
21:6     187 n.100
72:1–4     191 n.32,
          193 n.69
91:15     186 n. 89
135:4     184 n.67
147:15     119

## PROVERBS

7:3     118
22:7     97
25:6     187 n.100
28:8     203 n.78

## JOB

24:3     97

## RUTH

1:1–2     220 n.88
4:3–6     91

## LAMENTATIONS

5:12     187 n.100

## ESTHER

3:7     219 n.79

## NEHEMIAH

5:1–3     87, 206 n.113
7:72–8:18     115
8:7–8     211 n.48

## I CHRONICLES

29:3     184 n.67

## 2 CHRONICLES

17:7–9     197 n.12,
          209 n.23
19:8–11     117
26:16–20     191 n.26
31:3–6     201 n.52

## NEW TESTAMENT
## ACTS

2:44–45     222 n.21
4:32–35     222 n.21

## ROMANS

13:1–2     173

## I CORINTHIANS

7:20     173
12:13     173

## GALATIANS

3:28     173

## I PETER

2:13–15     173

# Subject Index